20.00

D1635923

SWING IT!

SWING IT!

THE

Andrews Sisters

STORY

John Sforza

THE UNIVERSITY PRESS OF KENTUCKY

Publication of this volume was made possible in part by a grant from the National Endowment for the Humanities.

Editorial and Sales Offices: The University Press of Kentucky
663 South Limestone Street, Lexington, Kentucky 40508–4008

04 03 02 01 00 5 4 3 2 1

Frontispiece: LaVerne, Patty, and Maxene volunteer their services at the famous Hollywood Canteen in 1944. Author's Collection.

Library of Congress Cataloging-in-Publication Data

Sforza, John, 1965-
    Swing it! : the Andrews Sisters story / John Sforza.
        p.   cm.
    Filmography: p.
    Includes bibliographical references (p.   ) and index.
    ISBN 0-8131-2136-1 (cloth : alk. paper)
    1. Andrews Sisters. 2. Singers—United States—Biography.
I. Title.
ML421.A47S46   1999
782.42164'092'2—dc21   99-10970

To my parents,
Marie and Mickey,
for their love and support.

"We were such a part of everybody's life
in the Second World War.
We represented something overseas
and at home—a sort of security."

—Patty Andrews

Contents

Acknowledgments   xi

Introduction   1

1   We'll Hit the Big Time   16

2   "That's Us! That's Us!"   23

3   They Made the Company Jump   50

4   Three of a Kind   65

5   Voices of an Era   71

6   We've Got a Job to Do   82

7   Riding High   94

8   Success Abroad   112

9   A Love Song Is Born   122

10   Disharmony   136

11   The Last Mile Home   146

12   The Love We Used to Know   156

Appendix A: Top-Thirty Hits (Compiled from *Billboard*)   175

Appendix B: Top-Ten Hits (Compiled from *Variety*)   181

Appendix C: Most Played Jukebox Records of World War II   183

Appendix D: Gold Records   185

Appendix E: On the Air   189

Appendix F: The Small Screen   195

Notes   197

Filmography   207

Discography   217

Bibliography   267

Index   269

Song Index   279

Photos follow pages 100 and 164

Acknowledgments

A percentage of the author's profits from the sales of this book will be donated to the American Cancer Society in memory of LaVerne Andrews (1911–1967).

Special thanks to Andrews Sisters fans Everett R. Searcy, for his helpful correspondences regarding dates and places, and Ray Hagen, for his kindness in supplying photographs from his private collection. Thanks also to Diane Gray, and to Robert Boyer for his timely assistance in helping to tie up loose ends.

*They had so much energy. The Andrews Sisters
had more energy than any other singing group.*
—*Saul Chaplin*

Introduction

The 1940s were extremely energetic years. The mere mention of this decade conjures up such nostalgic images as zoot suits, bobby-soxers, jukeboxes, and big bands; Uncle Sam posters, draft notices, ration stamps, and victory gardens; Nash motor cars, drugstore egg creams, and dish night at the local movie house.

It was a decade that most of today's younger generation could not relate to or comprehend, through no fault of their own. Times were different—times were simpler. Imagine an era before the Baby Boom, the Cold War, Woodstock, and the sexual revolution. Saturday nights were for dating, Sundays were for worship and relaxation. Television was nearly unknown to millions of Americans who gathered around a small box or, income permitting, a large console called radio, the biggest communications and entertainment medium of the day.

A turn of the radio dial could offer a vast array of entertaining shows: Fred Allen's *Texaco Star Theater, The Bob Hope Show,* the frightening squeal of the *Inner Sanctum* door, Bing Crosby's *Philco Radio Time,* the defiant Charlie McCarthy trading quips with Edgar Bergen during *The Chase and Sanborn Hour,* the dramatic *Lux Radio Theater,* the sound of a cluttered closet exploding on *The Fibber McGee and Molly Show, The Shadow* (Who knows what evil lurks in the hearts of men?), *The Martin and Lewis Show,* Lucille Ball

1

innocently scheming in *My Favorite Husband,* an off-key violin solo on *The Jack Benny Show,* a movie star granting a GI's written-in request on *Command Performance,* Frankie lilting during *Songs by Sinatra, The Bickersons* bickering, *The Gulf Screen Guild Theater, Amos and Andy, Suspense,* the "Hi-Ho-Silver"-ing of *The Lone Ranger.* The television of its day, radio allowed the imagination of its listeners to escape to faraway mythical places.

The two most outstanding components of the 1940s were unrelated by definition, yet they blended so perfectly in the minds of all Americans that one actually seemed to balance the other and subsequently stabilize the nation. The first was of course the second World War—a harrowing, tumultuous conflict that saw the sacrifice of millions of people worldwide before the victory of the Allied Forces sent America's economy on a production boom that stretched well into the next decade. The other outstanding component of the war-torn decade was its music. Big band, swing, boogie-woogie, eight-to-the-bar, and be-bop sent America's youth reeling to the jitterbug and the lindy in dance halls and nightclubs throughout the nation. The country's older generation appreciated ballads and similar fare by the same versatile musical artists. It was perhaps the last time in American popular music history that three generations purchased and played records by the same musicians.

Like many Hollywood films of the era, the music of the 1940s provided an escape for the American public. The songs were happy, gay themes set to lively arrangements, perhaps subconsciously designed to take the country's collective mind off of the dark realities brewing overseas. Songs like "The Trolley Song," "Scrub Me Mama with a Boogie Beat," "His Rocking Horse Ran Away," and "Cow Cow Boogie" were far removed from the newsworthy happenings of the day.

Simultaneously, much of the music of the decade tastefully reminded the nation that it was involved in a full-scale fight. There was a job to be done, and many pleasures and luxuries that were previously taken for granted by many people were to be sacrificed for ultimate victory. America sang along to such patriotic and even ironic tunes as "This Is the Army, Mr. Jones," "There'll Be a Hot Time in the Town of Berlin (When the Yanks Go Marching In)," "He's 1–A in the Army (And He's A-1 in My Heart)," and "The Vict'ry Polka." The music of the war years gave Americans hope that the massive struggle called World War II would not devour them. If there were songs to sing—songs about love, devotion, sacrifice, patriotism, victory, and a day when freedom would ring once again—then there was something right in the world, something to send chills up one's spine when Kate Smith belted out Irving Berlin's new composition, "God Bless America."

Because the music of the era has been so lovingly remembered by today's older generation, and because it has been so painstakingly restored and mass-produced by musical technicians and record companies for younger generations, the original artists who performed the music have become legendary icons. Bing Crosby, Judy Garland, Frank Sinatra, Kate Smith, Al Jolson, Ella Fitzgerald, Dinah Shore, Dick Haymes, Helen Forrest, Mel Torme, Betty Hutton, and Johnny Mercer were some of the biggest performers of the era.

Bandleaders were abundant and became music industry superstars, including Glenn Miller, Benny Goodman, Kay Kyser, Artie Shaw, Vaughn Monroe, Harry James, Sammy Kaye, and the Dorsey brothers—Tommy and Jimmy. Canaries—girl singers featured with the big bands—were on a meteoric rise during the 1940s, among them Doris Day, Peggy Lee, Rosemary Clooney, Lena Horne, Margaret Whiting, Ella Mae Morse, Jo Stafford, and Helen O'Connell, all of whom eventually embarked on successful solo careers, as the big band era came to a close a decade later.

Vocal groups had their share in the musical spotlight of the day. In most cases they solidified the family concept, including the Mills Brothers, the King Sisters, the Ink Spots, the Dinning Sisters, the Merry Macs, the Fontane Sisters, the Song Spinners, the DeMarco Sisters, the Modernaires, and the Pied Pipers. Most of these groups enjoyed years of success.

Another vocal group remains, and it is this group that personified the musical sound of the 1940s and defined the sound of the female vocal group in American popular music. They were the Andrews Sisters: Patty, Maxene, and LaVerne. Patty was a lively, boisterous, fun-loving blonde who sported an open-mouthed, mile-wide smile, an appealing sense of good-natured merriment, and a comical ability to mug for the camera—or to mug just for the fun of it. She led the trio with her exciting and self-confident vocal tone. Maxene was a pretty, ready-for-action brunette with petite features, sparkling eyes, an overbite, a slight gap between her front teeth, and a hearty, infectious laugh. She could out-talk both of her sisters with a no-nonsense manner. Her ever-changing harmony vocal, most often wielded in soprano, initially gave the impression of four blended voices rather than three. Completing the trio with a resonant contralto harmony vocal was LaVerne, a tall, self-deprecating, slightly reserved redhead with large expressive eyes, a sometimes shy smile, and a tremendous appetite. She was the worrier of the group, was well-spoken, though not as verbal as either of her sisters, and was most often the last one out of the dressing room, to the annoyance of her siblings. LaVerne's quick wit and subtle comic delivery often made her an audience favorite.

Matching shoulder-padded gowns, suits, and military uniforms outfitted these three entertainers, topped with pompadour hairstyles, and completed by open-toed high heels. They were three girl-next-door, real-life sisters who, if rumor and their mother be trusted, did not get along very well. They had the fastest, loudest harmony this side of the equator, all accentuated by wild yet almost perfectly syncopated choreography and a comedic flair that surfaced readily during personal appearances.

Critics have used such words as quintessential, ubiquitous, and ineffable when reviewing this vocal group, whose perfect unity of musical phrasing often left the listener unaware that this singing entity was in fact three separate voices. The trio's popularity was so immense during the 1940s that they were known worldwide by their first names alone. Their complete dominance on record charts and jukebox lists compiled by *Billboard* and *Variety* magazines, combined with their long list of hits and phenomenal record sales, made them as much a part of their era—historically and socially—as the legendary Beatles would later become a part of the 1960s. Known as Maxene, Patty, and LaVerne, they were the Andrews Sisters—a singing trio that dazzled the entertainment industry with their enormous success and enviable endurance.

After serving a six-year apprenticeship in vaudeville in the

1930s (numerous road tours with Ted Mack and other bands), the trio made recording their foremost priority. This they did well and in abundance, resulting in approximately one hundred million records sold from just over six hundred recorded songs spanning a studio-recording career of three decades. They remained the best-selling vocal group of all time until they were surpassed by the Beatles in the 1970s. The sisters claimed over one hundred songs on top-thirty *Billboard* charts during their heyday, with forty-six of those recordings reaching top-ten status (that's more than Elvis or the Beatles). At a time when a million sales certified a gold record, the trio earned nine of them. They were the toast of the recording industry of the 1940s with an astounding eighty best-selling Decca singles, many of which sold upward of 350,000 copies each.

There were unforgettable mega hits, including "Bei Mir Bist Du Schon (Means that You're Grand)," "Beer Barrel Polka (Roll Out the Barrel)," "Beat Me Daddy, Eight to the Bar," "I'll Be with You in Apple Blossom Time," "Boogie Woogie Bugle Boy," "Don't Sit under the Apple Tree (With Anyone Else but Me)," "Pistol Packin' Mama," "Jingle Bells," "Rum and Coca Cola," "Don't Fence Me In," "Ac-cent-tchu-ate the Positive," "South America, Take It Away," "Christmas Island," "Winter Wonderland," "Near You," "I Can Dream, Can't I?," and "I Wanna Be Loved."

Hollywood beckoned the trio in 1940. The merger resulted in three box office bonanzas one year later with Abbott and Costello (*Buck Privates, In the Navy,* and *Hold That Ghost*), two all-star wartime extravaganzas (*Follow the Boys* and *Hollywood Canteen*), a "Road" picture with Crosby, Hope, and Lamour (*Road to Rio*), two soundtrack assignments for full-length Walt Disney features (*Make Mine Music* and *Melody Time*), and nine other money-making, poorly produced, and critically panned films for Universal Pictures.

The sisters also found a great deal of success on radio. They hosted their own shows (*The Andrews Sisters Show* for ABC and *The Nash-Kelvinator Musical Showroom* for CBS) and were regular per-formers—appearing three times a week—on the popular CBS se-ries *Club 15* from 1947 to 1951. Cabaret engagements provided record-breaking runs for the trio in renowned nightclubs, theaters, and hotels throughout the world. Countless guest appearances on television shows throughout the 1950s and 1960s introduced the trio and their music to a new, younger generation. Even Broadway made use of the Andrews talent with a nostalgic show called *Over Here!*, starring Maxene and Patty Andrews at New York City's Shubert Theater in 1974.

The Andrews Sisters are listed in the *Penguin Encyclopedia of Popular Music* as "still the biggest girl group ever." Records by this legendary trio are still being released, mostly on compact disc, some sixty years after their original releases, and the sisters have served as inspiration for such successful artists as Mel Torme, the Lennon Sisters, the Pointer Sisters, Manhattan Transfer, Barry Manilow, and Bette Midler. Guitarist Les Paul was greatly influenced by the trio, having accompanied them on many road tours to open the shows. Paul's wife, Mary Ford, accompanied her husband on the tours, so it was no surprise when, several years later, Ford began recording her voice three times over her husband's guitar licks, resulting in many hit records on the Capitol label during the 1950s. The sisters also counted Elvis Presley among their fans. A photograph of Elvis's TV room at Graceland (published in the 1993 book *Graceland: The Living Legacy of Elvis Presley*) shows the 1962 Dot album *The Andrews Sisters' Greatest Hits* face up on the record cabinet housing his personal collection.

Although the sisters' immense popularity and numerous entertainment accomplishments often dwarf those of other groups, Maxene, Patty, and LaVerne were not the first sister act to achieve nationwide recognition. Throughout the history of American popular music, many "girl groups" have enhanced the scene with various types of memorable singing styles.

The Boswell Sisters were the pioneers of girl groups. Before achieving the distinction of being the first female vocal group to gain national popularity, the Boswells (Connee, Martha, and Vet) were originally a duo until Vet became old enough to join the group. Hailing from New Orleans, the sisters became popular radio personalities in the late 1920s. Their jazzy Brunswick recordings, most of which were filled with scat arrangements and frequent tempo changes, exemplified their innovative style of vocalizing. Among the sisters' hits were "Crazy People," "Everybody Loves My Baby,"

"Shout, Sister, Shout," "Heebie Jeebies," "Shuffle Off to Buffalo," and "Forty-Second Street." The trio became regular favorites on Bing Crosby's popular radio series sponsored by Camel cigarettes in the 1930s, and they were featured in several motion pictures, including Paramount's *The Big Broadcast*. The Boswells disbanded in 1935 when both Martha and Vet married and retired from show business. Connee, who suffered from polio and was confined to a wheelchair, continued as a successful soloist.

The slightly less popular Pickens Sisters (Patti, Jane, and Helen) were born and raised in Georgia, and were favorites of the NBC radio network during the 1930s. They seemed to display more of a precise and operatic style of harmonizing than did the Boswells. The Pickenses appeared in Hollywood's *Sitting Pretty* in 1934 and on Broadway in *Thumbs Up* one year later. Their 1935 separation was similar to that of the Boswells—two sisters married and retired while Jane continued as a soloist.

The Barry Sisters (Claire and Merna) enjoyed success in the late 1930s with their Yiddish harmonizing. The girls were most popular among their own ethnic group, and they remained so for twenty years, with triumphs on records, radio, television, and in cabaret.

The late 1930s also witnessed the formation of the Dinning Sisters (Ginger, Lou, and Jean), well-known for their regular radio appearances on NBC's *National Barn Dance,* a show that highlighted country-western music. The trio's sweet, high-pitched harmonies debuted on disc form on Capitol Records in 1945 (they were the first artists to debut on records in book album form). The girls' recording of "Buttons and Bows" in 1948 became a million-seller and a top-ten *Billboard* hit. The trio worked for Universal Pictures in one film, *Strictly in the Groove,* and for Walt Disney (voices only) in *Fun and Fancy Free* and *Melody Time.* They also appeared in films for Paramount and Columbia studios during the 1940s.

The four King Sisters (Luise, Alyce, Donna, and Yvonne) were featured as part of the big band sound of Alvino Rey's orchestra during the early 1940s. The close and mildly swinging harmonies of the King Sisters were an intrinsic part of Rey's unit. The girls appeared in several films, and their popularity continued during the

1950s and 1960s with frequent family television specials during the Christmas holiday seasons. Two other sisters, Maxine and Marilyn, were also part of the group, mainly as substitutes at different times. Among the group's best-selling hits were "Mairzy Doats," "San Fernando Valley," "The Hut Sut Song (A Swedish Serenade)" and "Chiquita Banana," the latter of which the famous banana company adopted as their theme song and still uses to this day.

Somewhat similar in sound to the four King Sisters were the five DeMarco Sisters (Arlene, Marie, Jeanne, Ann, and Gloria). The DeMarcos were featured weekly on Fred Allen's radio show during the mid-1940s, as they harmonized popular tunes of the day. Their recording career continued into the 1950s.

The Fontane Sisters (Margie, Bea, and Geri) lent their lilting blend mostly to ballads in the late 1940s, before achieving greater success in the next decade with such early rock-n-roll hits as "Hearts of Stone" and "Seventeen" for Dot Records. The girls originally billed themselves as The Three Sisters when they made an appearance in the 1944 Abbott and Costello film *In Society*. They later joined Perry Como on radio, television, and in RCA record releases, generating such hits as "A Dreamer's Holiday," "Hoop-Dee-Doo," "I Cross My Fingers," and "A, You're Adorable (The Alphabet Song)."

Along with the 1950s came the intertwined, homespun harmonies of the McGuire Sisters (Christine, Phyllis, and Dorothy), who gained national recognition on Kate Smith's NBC radio show in 1952, and later as program regulars on Arthur Godfrey's popular television series. The sisters achieved a trio of million-selling Coral hits ("Goodnight, Sweetheart, Goodnight," "Sincerely," and "Sugartime") and they were captioned as America's best-selling vocal group when they graced the March 1958 issue of *Life* magazine. The girls were also featured in extravagant television advertisements for the Coca-Cola Company during the 1950s. The trio officially retired in 1968, although Phyllis continued successfully as a soloist. The McGuires reunited in 1984 for a successful comeback, singing superbly and looking eternally youthful. Their current cabaret act features a fine mix of old and new material, and they have been enjoying standing-room-only gigs in New York, Atlantic City, and Las Vegas. Phyllis is said to be working on a book concerning the trio's lengthy career, as well as her headline-making relationship with now deceased mafia head Sam Giancana.

From 1955 to 1968, the lovely Lennon Sisters grew up in front of millions of Americans who tuned in weekly to see them on Lawrence Welk's long-running television series. As a result of their accomplished singing abilities (learned from their father), their irresistible charms, and their poised professionalism, Dianne, Peggy, Kathy, and Janet were quickly dubbed "America's Sweethearts." The Lennons, undoubtedly the most successful act ever associated with the Welk organization, were a trio for several years after the temporary retirement of Dianne, who opted for the life of mother and homemaker. She returned to the act in the mid-1960s, restoring the quartet's beautiful choir-like blend. Following a disagreement with Welk, who, in the girls' collective opinion, was not allowing them to mature professionally or financially, the sisters left the show to star in a short-lived television variety series with veteran comedian Jimmy Durante. During the run of this series, the sisters suffered a great loss when their beloved father was killed by a mentally disturbed fan. Currently, aside from performing regularly at the Welk Theater in Branson, Missouri, the Lennons have published their collective memoirs. Their now out-of-print Dot singles and albums feature some of their best-remembered recordings, including "Tonight, You Belong to Me," "White Silver Sands," "Scarlet Ribbons," "Greensleeves," and Schubert's "Ave Maria."

The pop-rock sound of the 1960s was promoted by scores of girl groups, including Martha and the Vandellas, the Chiffons, the Shirelles, the Marvelettes, the Murmaids, the Ronettes, the Shangri-Las, the Cookies, the Toys, and the Dixie Cups. More famous than all of these, however, were the Supremes (Diana Ross, Mary Wilson, and Florence Ballard), who popularized the Motown sound of the decade. The Supremes created the unique sound of two back-up singers and one lead, rather than employing strict three-part harmony. They had many hits, including "Stop! In the Name of Love," "Back in My Arms Again," "Love Child," "Baby Love" and "I Hear a Symphony." Ballard left the group in 1967 and was replaced. Ross embarked on her own solo career two years later. She, too, was replaced and the group became known as Mary Wilson and the Supremes. Replacements included, the Supremes charted nineteen top-ten *Billboard* hits before disbanding in the 1970s.

The Pointer Sisters had several chart toppers during the 1970s and 1980s in the musical categories of soul, pop, disco, and even country-western (the Grammy-winning "Fairytale"). The Pointers were originally a quartet until the departure of sister Bonnie. As a trio, Anita, June, and Ruth have achieved platinum record sales with hits such as "I'm So Excited" and "Jump (For My Love)."

The country-western field has also seen its share of successful female vocal groups. The Carter Sisters (Anita, June, and Helen) were successful through the 1940s, 1950s, and 1960s, harmonizing now legendary hillbilly tunes with their mother, Maybelle, who was one of three members of the original Carter Family, pioneers of country-western music and the first vocal group to achieve a million-selling record ("Wildwood Flower," 1928). Maybelle and her daughters performed frequently at the Grand Ole Opry in Nashville, Tennessee, often singing their own compositions ("The Kneeling Drunkard's Plea" and "Wall to Wall Love"), as well as playing their own instruments, including the autoharp. June went on to further success with husband Johnny Cash.

Barbara Mandrell united with her two sisters, Louise and Irlene, for a successful two-season television series for NBC in the early 1980s. The show was canceled at the sisters' request when the workload began to affect Barbara's health. Mother-daughter team Naomi and Wynonna Judd exploded onto the country-western scene soon after with such hits as "Rockin' with the Rhythm of the Rain" and "Grandpa, Tell Me 'bout the Good Old Days." The Judds recorded over their own original tracks, updating traditional country-western singing with slick harmonies. One critic observed the contemporary edge and noted, "The Judds owe as much to the Andrews Sisters as they do to the Carter Family." Naomi retired recently, citing health problems, and Wynonna is now a solo act. The Forester Sisters, the McCarters, the Sweethearts of the Rodeo, and Trio (comprised of Dolly Parton, Emmylou Harris, and Linda Ronstadt) have also enjoyed varying degrees of success.

Many more sister acts have left their mark in show business, from vaudeville's early days to the present. Some of the standouts have included the Dollys, the Duncans, the Gumms or Garlands (featuring a pre-teen Judy Garland and her two older sisters), the Cherrys, the Nortons (the resident girl trio of Vaughn Monroe's band), the Clarks, the Moylans, the Frazees, the Bells, the Clawson Triplets, and the very successful but non-related Chordettes.

What exactly was it that the Andrews Sisters possessed that enabled them to outshine their competitors? While there are many possible answers to this question, the best explanation of their sustained success could very well have been their versatility. The trio had major hits with nearly all types of music, and they handled different rhythms with ease. They sang swing, boogie-woogie, eight-to-the-bar, country-western, folk, calypso, ragtime, blues, ballads, inspirational, gospel, seasonal favorites, and a host of songs derived from or based upon Yiddish, Italian, Irish, French, Czechoslovakian, Russian, Swedish, Spanish, Brazilian, and Mexican melodies. Patty recalled, "We did them all. We tackled anything and everything they put before us and tried to come up with a new and fresh interpretation of the songs. Waltzes became 4/4 beats, fox trots became boogie-woogie, traditional songs became swinging rhythms and it was a ball doing it. We took the submitted song and turned it upside down and inside out until it came out the way we hoped."

The sisters' versatility shone through in all aspects of their performing. They accompanied a varied group of legendary entertainers—on records, radio, and television, in films, and in stage shows—including Bing Crosby and brother Bob, Frank Sinatra, Al Jolson, Perry Como, Nat King Cole, Dick Haymes, Rudy Vallee, Julius LaRosa, Judy Garland, Morton Downey, Carmen Miranda, Danny Kaye, Dan Dailey, Andy Williams, Dean Martin, and Diana Ross and the Supremes. The trio demonstrated a flair for comedy, sharing laughs in skits with such comic greats as Bob Hope, Milton Berle, Jimmy Durante, Groucho Marx, Abbott and Costello, the Ritz Brothers, Louis Nye, Shemp Howard, Eddie Cantor, Ray Bolger, George "Gabby" Hayes, W.C. Fields, Sophie Tucker, Marjorie Main, Frank Morgan, Cass Daley, Judy Canova, Martin and Lewis, Garry Moore, Lum and Abner, and Johnny Carson. The sisters were a crucial part of the big band era, although they are inexplicably overlooked in most books on the subject. They worked with nearly every famous conductor of the day, including the Dorseys (Jimmy and Tommy), Glenn Miller, Benny Goodman (Patty's favorite), Joe Venuti, Bunny Berigan, Les Brown, Xavier Cugat, Fred Waring, Gene Krupa, Guy Lombardo, Axel Stordahl, Nelson Riddle, Jerry Gray, Tony Pastor, Alfred Newman, Paul Whiteman, Desi Arnaz, Artie Shaw, Woody Herman, Ted Lewis, Mitchell Ayres, Carmen Cavallaro, Buddy Rich, and Les Paul.

The sisters became the musical voice of their era and actually vocalized the big band sound with their 1939 recording of "Begin the Beguine," a million-seller for Artie Shaw's band, and they continued this success when they vocalized several Glenn Miller instrumentals, including "Pennsylvania 6–5000," "Tuxedo Junction," "Kalamazoo," "Chattanooga Choo Choo," and later, "In the Mood." The girls took this process a step further when they started to sing boogie-woogie, as reviewer Leonard Maltin has observed:

> In 1940, the Andrews Sisters brought something new to the listening public—the first of many landmark recordings. "Beat Me Daddy, Eight to the Bar" was a reflection of the growing popularity in jazz circles of boogie-woogie music. But no one had yet turned this piano phenomenon (popularized by such great keyboard artists as Albert Ammons, Pete Johnson, and Meade Lux Lewis) into a vehicle for a popular song, or even thought about adding lyrics to the rolling rhythm of boogie. "Beat Me Daddy" was such a hit that it launched a tidal wave of boogie songs, many of which the girls recorded.

The current swing, boogie, and jump-and-jive craze can be traced all the way back to all of these artists and these history-making recording sessions.

Country-western music followers have also been fans of the Andrews Sisters since their successful collaborations with Burl Ives, Ernest Tubb, and Red Foley for Decca Records from the mid-1940s through the early 1950s. Many music historians forget just how well the trio handled country material. Their renditions of the folk "Down in the Valley," the hillbilly "Nobody's Darlin' but Mine," the comical sagebrush "I Didn't Know the Gun Was Loaded," the western-swing "I'm Bitin' My Fingernails and Thinking of You," the country-boogie "Where Is Your Wandering Mother Tonight?" and the country-pop "Don't Fence Me In" demonstrated their ability to successfully adapt to music styles quite different from their swing specialties, as well as indicating the savvy of their management to capitalize on popular musical trends.

During World War II, the sisters found themselves naturally drawn into entertainment duty and, as with many other personalities of the day, they devoted their star-power to assisting the home front effort, simultaneously inspiring America's fighting forces and its allies. Maxene recalled of those war years,

> If there was a dark side to those trying years, there was a bright side, too—a sense of national unity, real togetherness, a feeling so strong, so exhilarating and so unifying that it did more than help the country to survive. It helped us to win the war. The Andrews Sisters were right in the thick of all this, for the same reasons that millions of other entertainers were—because we *wanted* to be. We wanted to visit every USO club and military base and GI hospital we could find, both in the states and overseas. If we were on tour doing four and five shows a day, seven days a week, fifty weeks each year in cities all across the United States, we still found time to visit the servicemen and -women. And when Patty, LaVerne and I went overseas for the USO, we often added four or five impromptu shows to our schedule every day, for any two or three soldiers who might ask us.

Indeed, there was an innate desire instilled in all three sisters to please their audiences, to be happy and to inspire happiness through their music. This aspect of their music was all the more evident when war zones were the cause of much of the country's uneasiness and apprehension. Writer William Ruhlmann observes,

If, after half a century, we still cannot think of the
Andrews Sisters without remembering World War II, it
may be because they continue to embody the positive
national spirit called forth during that time. Perhaps
especially in these less certain days, we admire their
clarity, their enthusiasm, their sense of humor. In the
diversity of their style, they demonstrated the power
of American popular music to assimilate the nation's
many cultural strands without losing individuality.
Just as a common enemy forced Americans to think of
themselves as a unified whole, their pop music brought
them together. It served to relieve them for a moment
and renew them for the continuing struggle. Those
who think of this as frivolous music miss the point: in
those days, having a good time was as much subject
to rationing as gasoline, and there was always the
chance that your luck could suddenly run out. All the
more reason, then, to raise your voice and sing along
with the Andrews Sisters, roll out the barrel, we'll
have a barrel of fun!

Despite the many triumphs throughout their career, the sisters'
personal harmony was never quite as smooth as their professional
harmony, although it is likely that this has been exaggerated over
the years. The trio, after all, performed professionally on a constant
basis (with the exception of two and half years) from 1931 to 1966,
and had their compatibility been as strained as was so often rumored, it seems unlikely the group would have survived that long.
Yet the girls have become almost as well known for their feuding
as for their singing. Olga, their mother, once told a reporter that she
encouraged her daughters to sing to cease their constant arguing.
Like any sisters, the girls fought and would eventually reconcile, but
because of their popular status, their clashes became perfect entries
for worldwide gossip columns.

Although many of their spats stemmed from professional disagreements such as song arrangements, wardrobes, and hairstyles,
their squabbles sometimes crossed that line and caused personal

rifts. Constant companionship took its toll, and in the mid-1950s personality conflicts resulted in an uncomfortable two-and-a-half-year separation. When all was forgiven and the sisters reunited, they once again successfully entertained audiences throughout the world and recorded frequently until eldest sister LaVerne's untimely death in 1967. Seven years later, Maxene and Patty reunited profession-ally and starred on the New York stage in the Broadway musical *Over Here!* After a very successful nine-month run, the show came to an abrupt end amid frantic confusion. The show's producers blamed the sisters, who were rumored to be squabbling. Maxene blamed the producers, telling reporters that she and Patty had never gotten along better, while Patty blamed Maxene over salary issues. The sisters went separate ways, and it seems they remained distant until Maxene's sudden death in 1995.

Perhaps the true reason why both Maxene and Patty were unwilling to put their differences behind them will never be public knowledge, as Patty has usually joked about the split in interviews over the past twenty-five years. Oddly enough, whenever Maxene was questioned regarding the rift, she always claimed that she was unaware of the reason it occurred and that she was eager for a reunion, personally or professionally. Perhaps the cause of their falling out was more intense than their many fans cared to realize— fans who could not picture one sister without the others.

Whatever the case, the Andrews Sisters nevertheless became the most successful and enduring female vocal group in the history of show business, making good use of their abundant talents throughout years of dedicated work. No matter what the girls did, few artists of their time could do it any better. Maxene, Patty, and LaVerne possessed a certain musical magic that holds its appeal even today.

1

We'll Hit the Big Time

The year was 1931. America was suffering from a grave economic depression. The stock market crash of 1929 was all too recent; bread lines still formed at soup kitchens throughout most of the nation. Times ahead looked bleak and uncompromising. Despite all this, three young girls in Minneapolis were hoping and yearning to break into show business.

In April of 1931, while on Easter vacation from school, Maxene, Patty, and LaVerne Andrews were participating in a talent contest at the local Orpheum Theater. The show was sponsored by the Clausen School of Dance, where LaVerne's piano accompaniment services earned free dancing lessons for herself and her sisters. A successful touring band directed by Larry Rich provided music for the talent show. Rich and his orchestra had been traveling the RKO vaudeville circuit, and the bandleader was in search of new talent to accompany him on the road. The three Andrews girls performed "On the Sunny Side of the Street" with LaVerne on piano. The trio's competition included a young, unknown ventril- oquist named Edgar Bergen, who went on to fame with wooden sidekick Charlie McCarthy, and who would later father actress Candice

Bergen. The three sisters captured first prize in the contest in a unanimous vote from the judges. Larry Rich acted as master of ceremonies; he was so impressed with the girls that he told them that they would soon hear from him. High hopes teeming, the girls returned to school.

The sisters spent the summer months that year at Lake Minnetonka in Mound, Minnesota, with their two uncles, Pete and Ed (brothers of their mother), who operated a general store. While the trio enjoyed their stay in the country, Larry Rich contacted their parents, Peter and Olga Andrews, and asked their consent to let the girls travel with him as part of his entertainment unit. Olga came from a musical family and had always encouraged her daughters to sing, but their father was not so easily sold on the idea.

The girls were understandably thrilled on hearing of Rich's offer; however, Peter thought his girls were much too young to leave school and travel the country (Patty, the youngest, was only thirteen at the time). LaVerne and Maxene would not even consider going without Patty, who was the lead singer of the group, so they asked their mother to try to change their father's mind. Olga tried, and Peter gave in reluctantly. The girls joined the Rich troupe in Atlanta, Georgia. They then boarded a bus for Birmingham, Alabama, to begin performing.

All three sisters were born in Minneapolis, but each one at a different address, due to the family's frequent relocations. LaVerne Sophie was born July 6, 1911, while her father, Peter Andreos, was employed as an ice cream maker (Peter had changed his last name from Andreos to Andrews upon his arrival in America from his homeland of Greece). LaVerne bore a strong resemblance to her father. The trio's mother, Norwegian-born Olga Sollie, gave birth to a second daughter, Angelyn, two years after LaVerne's arrival, but the infant died of pneumonia at eight months. This tragedy was a tremendous blow to the family-oriented couple, but they were nonetheless eager to have more children. Maxene Angelyn was born January 3, 1916, the same year that Peter purchased a pool hall. Maxene inherited her mother's soft and pretty features. Patricia Marie followed on February 16, 1918. Patty inherited physical fea-

tures from both of her parents and eventually bore a stronger resemblance to Maxene than to LaVerne.

The Andrews family moved from Minneapolis to Mound in
1920, but they returned to Minneapolis four years later when Peter
opened a restaurant. Two years elapsed before Peter sold the eatery
and began operating the Andrews Fruit Company. He later formed
a partnership with friend James Karalis and opened another pool
hall, which remained in existence until the mid 1930s. While their
parents' time was occupied with business affairs, the three sisters
became engrossed in music.

It began one afternoon when LaVerne brought both of her
sisters to the family piano and gave each of them a musical note to
sing (Patty was only seven at the time). The girls sang "Dinah" in
three-part harmony in an attempt to imitate their idols, the popular
Boswell Sisters. Patty handled the easiest part—the lead. Maxene
sang second-part harmony, a soprano to Patty's lead, while LaVerne
handled the third-part contralto or bass. LaVerne and Maxene then
began weaving harmonies around any lead that Patty would sing.
The more they sang, the closer and more polished the harmonious
blend became. Maxene recalled, "Musically, it was like something
had opened up inside of my head and afterwards, whenever I heard
a song, I heard it in harmony. It's interesting—I even find myself
listening to the kitchen radio and I catch myself whistling my harmony part to the songs, never the melody."

The girls began singing whenever they had the chance. They
would race home from school during the weekdays to hear the
Boswell Sisters sing on Bing Crosby's radio show. They were mesmerized by the Boswells, who were the first female vocal group to
achieve nationwide success. Patty once told an interviewer that she
and her sisters copied the Boswell style so deftly that they even
adopted the trio's New Orleans drawl. The Boswells were innovative singers during the jazz age, and their collaborations with
Bunny Berigan, Joe Venuti, and the Dorsey brothers, coupled with
their complicated scat arrangements, gained them a great deal of
respect among the musical giants of their day. The trio not only
had major influence on the Andrews Sisters, but also on the singing styles of artists like the Mills Brothers, Ella Fitzgerald, and Mel

Torme. The Boswells laid the groundwork for all ensuing female vocal groups. The Andrews Sisters, in the years following the success of the Boswells, would greatly enhance the dimension of the female vocal group, perfecting singing styles that had never before been attempted by a girl group—styles still widely mimicked to this day.

When Larry Rich hired the Andrews girls to tour with him, the sisters had already been singing together for several years. The girls had been performing for schoolmates at parties, as well as singing at local political meetings, masonic temples, and veterans' hospitals. While touring with Mr. Rich, the sisters would now have to hone their talents. Unfortunately, fame did not come quickly, and fortune seemed nowhere in sight. The girls' eyebrows were tweezed upon their arrival in Birmingham, followed by heavy applications of makeup, in an attempt to make the girls appear older. They even donned bellboy uniforms as their stage costumes to mask Patty's underage figure. A tutor accompanied the girls to ensure that they received adequate schooling, but they seemed to slip out of sight whenever it was time for a lesson. The tutor may have spent more time searching for the girls than she did instructing them.

Traveling with Larry Rich had one great advantage—the girls were now receiving payment for their singing services; however, they were a little disappointed with their actual salary. They received only one dollar per day, and that had to then be divided in three! Compared to today's astronomical entertainment salaries, these low wages seem mind-boggling, even in the days of the Great Depression. The professional guidance of Rich, however, greatly compensated for the monetary loss, and performing before large audiences was educational for the trio. They toured with Rich and his band until the late summer months of 1932. Maxene attributes the trio's primary success to Rich, who took the girls under his wing and furnished all of their meals, clothing, and hotel fees. Maxene recalled those days of traveling with Rich's fifty-five-member troupe: "[He taught us] . . . how to walk on the stage and when to get off the stage. [He told us] . . . 'You have to empathize with your audience.' We said to him, 'What does that mean?' and he said, 'You've got to bring them into you.' What he was saying was, you have to try and get something back from them, and we would always practice it, and it seemed like it came very natural to us."

After leaving Rich's tour, the girls were joined by their mother in New York City. There they met actor Rufus Davis, who befriended the girls, loaned them some money, and even found them temporary work. The sisters then toured with Joe Howard's vaudeville unit for several months before joining Ted Mack's popular band, but were less than thrilled when Mack left them stranded in Denver not long after. Peter then came to New York from Minneapolis to join his wife and daughters. The girls' parents would now accompany them on all of their road trips, as Peter became very protective of his daughters and insisted on traveling as a family.

Peter's big touring car, a 1929 Buick and later a 1931 Packard, provided the transportation. Peter handled the driving while the girls rehearsed in the back seat. Travel by car took much longer in those days, as Maxene once recalled,

> People drove slower and there weren't any divided highways. If you got stuck behind a truck going up a mountain, there wasn't a thing you could do except grin and bear it. We didn't have tape decks or four speaker stereo systems to entertain us during the long automobile trips, and while only a few cars had radios, that was one luxury we enjoyed. We listened to a lot of music in that car, and thanks to the two most popular radio comedians, Jack Benny and Fred Allen, we got plenty of laughs to relieve our boredom.

The Andrews family was now living in a Chicago hotel. The girls were temporarily unemployed, but as usual, they rehearsed diligently. Daily they retreated to a hot, uncomfortable, windowless storage room in the hotel and practiced their arrangements using the old upright piano in the room. They did not arrive early enough on some days, in which instances the room was already being used by another rehearsing trio—the Gumm Sisters (Virginia, Sue, and Frances Ethel). The Gumms were living with their mother, Ethel, in the same hotel and also were unemployed at the time. Maxene, Patty, and LaVerne soon acquired work with Georgie Jessel at the World's Fair. They recommended the Gumm Sisters as their replacements when their stint ended. Jessel hired the Gumms and took special interest in the youngest sister, Frances Ethel, who would soon change her name to Judy Garland.

A booking in Texas soon afterward afforded the Andrews Sisters the opportunity to appear regularly at the Riverside Club in Fort Worth in November 1935, and they were broadcast on the radio from the club four times a week, which added to their exposure. They then toured the Midwest with Maury Sherman's orchestra. During this time the trio began working with Leon Belasco's orchestra. Belasco had first heard them when they were appearing at the Royal Frolics in Chicago. The sisters soon became featured vocalists with Belasco's band. Concerning an engagement at the Century Room of Dallas's Adolphus Hotel, a critic wrote, "An evening with Leon Belasco's band offers an ingratiating variety of music. There are the Andrews Sisters, a peppy and thoroughly capable trio in the Boswell tradition. Patty goes it solo now and then, as well she can." Prior to the Dallas gig, the girls recorded three studio sides with Belasco, and these became the trio's first commercial record releases. Patty once joked that only family, friends, and the girls themselves bought these early discs, released on the Brunswick label.

The band soon began performing at the New Yorker Hotel in Manhattan. The girls had become good friends with band trumpeter Vic Schoen, whom Belasco had hired to work with the trio, as well as to rewrite arrangements that had recently been lost in a hotel fire while the band was playing in Kansas City. Schoen quickly developed a rapport—both professional and personal—with the sisters, especially with Patty, and he soon began writing orchestral arrangements that greatly complemented the trio's somewhat unusual brand of harmony. The foursome would become permanent coworkers when Belasco's band dissolved in July 1937. Belasco said that he disbanded due to health problems; he went on to become a bit player and character actor in films and television shows over the next three decades. The trio parted from

Belasco on friendly terms, grateful to him for allowing them to take all of their arrangements with them.

The girls then returned to Minnesota with their parents, staying with uncles Pete and Ed in Mound. The trip back home was intended to be brief; little did the girls know that their father had other ideas.

Less than a year ago, Patty, LaVerne and Maxene Andrews were obscure vocalists in an overcrowded entertainment world—but today—as if by magic, the name Andrews Sisters is a household word throughout the nation.
—Decca Records, 1938

2

"That's Us! That's Us!"

Home again in Minnesota, Peter was sure that his daughters would be eager to return to a normal lifestyle. His intention was to enroll all three girls in business school. Peter was determined to see them settle into secretarial positions, feeling that such occupations were more respectable than entertaining. He thought they would welcome the opportunity, especially after more than six years of living on the road.

To the contrary, the girls had fallen in love with show business, not minding the long hours of rehearsals, late night shows, missed meals, and cheap hotels. They pleaded with their father to allow them three more months of pursuing their dreams. Peter agreed to the arrangement, and the family returned to New York City's Tin Pan Alley, a booming Manhattan music publishing mecca at the time. Rehearsals resumed immediately as the girls visited scores of music publishers. One of these gentlemen, Bernie Pollack of Mills Music, gave the girls a piano and allowed them to rehearse all day in his office in the Brill building, but there were many others who told Olga, "Mrs. Andrews, take your girls home—they sing too loud and move too much!"

The girls did not despair, nor did they change their style. Perhaps they sensed that the public would welcome a new sister act, since both the Boswells and the Pickenses had recently disbanded. This doubtless fueled their determination to succeed. Daily, Maxene, Patty, and LaVerne would go to Hector's cafeteria at Fiftieth Street and Broadway for lunch, splitting one sandwich and one cup of coffee between them, purchased with the fifteen cents that their mother had given them. Throughout these early years, the girls took solace in the fact that they had each other when times were hard. They truly enjoyed one another's company, though each had her individual likes and dislikes.

The girls soon found work at New York's Hotel Edison, thanks to Vic Schoen, who was working there with Billy Swanson's band. When Schoen heard that the girls were in town, he set up an audition for them. Although Swanson was unimpressed with the girls when they auditioned, the hotel's owner, Maria Cramer, was quite pleased. She insisted that Swanson hire the girls to sing on a radio show called *Saturday Night Swing Club,* which aired from the hotel every Saturday night. Needless to say, the girls were excited—perhaps this would be their big break—but their optimism proved short-lived.

Saturday night arrived and the trio sang one chorus of "Sleepy Time Down South." Immediately following the broadcast, Swanson fired the girls, taking full advantage of the fact that Maria Cramer had returned to South America to nurse her ailing husband. All hope was not lost, however. A man by the name of David Kapp had heard the trio's broadcast on a taxi cab radio. Contrary to popular belief, this was not the first time that Kapp had heard the girls—he first heard them singing "Christopher Columbus" a year earlier in Kansas City, with Belasco's band. Kapp's brother, Jack, was president of Decca Records, a newly established company that employed such successful artists as Bing Crosby, Al Jolson, Connee Boswell, the Mills Brothers, and newcomer Judy Garland. David was the director of artists and repertoire at Decca. He was so taken with the trio's Edison broadcast that he asked friend and business associate Lou Levy, a vaudeville actor-dancer turned music publisher, to find the trio and arrange an audition. Levy located the trio at the Edison the night after their broadcast. Maxene remembered,

The Edison had a nice soda fountain off the lobby, and the next night we went in there for a soda. We were leaving New York. We'd had one shot. You might say it was the low point of our career. Then this fellow walks in and says his name is Lou Levy. He was this much above being a zoot-suiter. He had pointed toe shoes, with the wide snap brim hat, and the pockets in the back of his jacket. We were terrified of zoot-suiters. But he told us that Dave Kapp had been at a Tommy Dorsey opening at the Hotel Commodore, and over a radio in a taxi on the way home he heard us singing on the broadcast from the Edison, and he wanted to sign us to Decca.

The Andrews Sisters entered Decca studios in Manhattan the following Monday morning, accompanied by Peter and Olga. After a brief audition, Mr. and Mrs. Andrews signed the contract, as the girls were too young to make it legal, and their daughters went to work. Patty remembers the audition for Jack Kapp, "We only had one song we sang for him, and it was very funny because it was 'Night and Day,' and instead of singing the melody, we sang our take-off chorus, our second chorus, thinking that would make us different from anybody else. But it was because of that he signed us up to make our first record."

According to *Newsweek* magazine, Lou Levy was so taken with the trio that he loaned them five hundred dollars and appointed himself their manager. Maxene recalled, however, that Levy was at first reluctant to manage the girls, since he was already managing songwriter Sammy Cahn. It seems that the Kapp brothers persuaded Levy to take on the sisters as additional clients. Levy himself then began to choose most of the sisters' recording material. Along with Cahn, Levy formed the Leeds Music Corporation around this time, which became extremely successful and profitable, and produced much of the sisters' sheet music pieces over the next decade.

Not long after the Decca audition, the trio recorded "Why Talk about Love?" and "Just a Simple Melody." Their second session for Decca was soon to follow. The song "Nice Work If You Can Get It," written by George and Ira Gershwin, was assigned to the girls as the record's A side, but the trio did not yet have a song to fill the record's remaining side. The sisters stumbled upon an obscure Yiddish tune entitled "Bei Mir Bist Du Schon" in their search for a B side filler. Just how the girls discovered the tune is open to debate.

Maxene often said in interviews that Levy presented the song to her and her sisters, claiming that it was an old Yiddish lullaby that his mother sang to him when he was a child. Sammy Cahn, who, along with Saul Chaplin, would write an English translation to the Yiddish lyrics, claimed in his autobiography, *I Should Care,* that he gave the sheet music copy of the Yiddish tune to the Andrews Sisters when Patty noticed a copy of it on his piano during a visit to his New York apartment. Cahn recalled how he stumbled upon the tune,

> In the old days, Saul Kaplan-Chaplin, Lou Levy and I would periodically saunter up to the Apollo Theater in Harlem. On the stage one night are two black guys. Johnny and George, I believe, was the name of the act. They sing a song called "Bei Mir Bist Du Schon" in the original Yiddish. Don't ask me how or why they're doing this, but there they are . . . and these guys are standing there doing this Yiddish song in front of this almost ninety-nine percent black audience. And about the theater: I don't know if you've ever been up to the Apollo, but I can promise you that, when the beat gets going there, it's the same as in a cartoon. The building expands and contracts. I can't explain it, but it's a frightening thing. The whole theater literally starts to undulate and you feel that this place is going to cave in—it can't handle the excitement. I turned to Lou and Saul and I said: 'Can you imagine what this song would do to an audience that understood the words?' We laughed at each other.

When Cahn saw bandleader Tommy Dorsey shortly thereafter, he tried to convince the maestro to use the song during his upcoming gig at New York's Paramount Theater. Dorsey dismissed the idea, telling Cahn he was crazy. Cahn then found a sheet music copy of the tune and put it on the piano in the office-apartment that he shared with Levy. Cahn recalled,

> Lou Levy had been hanging around Jack Kapp of Decca Records and his brother, Dave Kapp, and one day, Levy brought the Andrews Sisters up to our apartment. On the piano was this copy of a song in Yiddish. Patty, she was the talker, said, "What is this, a Greek song?" Because they were Greek. "No," I said, "though it might as well be." "How does it go?" I played it for them, and they started to sing right along and rock with it. "Gee," said Patty, "could we have it?"

This entire scenario never occurred, according to Maxene. It does seem a bit odd, no matter how musically inclined the sisters were, that they would immediately start singing along to the Yiddish lyrics of a song that they had never even heard before; however, it is probable that Cahn did give the song to the girls, or more likely to Levy, after interest in it was expressed.

"Bei Mir" was composed several years earlier, in 1932, by Sholom Secunda, who wrote the melody, and Jacob Jacobs, who penned the Yiddish lyrics. The song was featured in a Yiddish musical, *I Would If I Could*, and the composers sold it to the show's producers for a mere thirty dollars. After learning the Yiddish song phonetically from Levy, the sisters worked out an arrangement with Vic Schoen, their musical arranger and conductor, and the group soon recorded the song for Decca. Immediately following the recording session, the girls were approached by Jack Kapp, who had heard them singing over the intercom system. While he was pleased with the melody, Kapp informed the girls that the song could not be released in its current Yiddish form, fearing that the disc would be labeled an ethnic record and would therefore have limited appeal to the public.

Levy asked Cahn and Chaplin to write an English version of

the song; they did, though somewhat reluctantly. The songwriting team felt that the song should be recorded by Ella Fitzgerald, an up-and-coming vocalist, rather than by an unknown girl trio. Nevertheless, Cahn soon obliged; in his autobiography he maintains that he wrote the English words without the assistance of Chaplin. The trio then re-recorded the song, now titled "Bei Mir Bist Du Schon (Means that You're Grand)." Literally translated, the title means "by me, you are beautiful." Some of the musicians backing the girls during the session were Vic Schoen and Bobby Hackett on trumpets, Dave Barbour on guitar, and Stan King on drums. Levy, Cahn, and Chaplin were also at the session.

Within a matter of days after its release, the record that resulted from the trio's history-making session became a smash hit, ousting "The Music Goes 'Round and 'Round" from its number-one chart position. "Bei Mir" went on to hold *Billboard*'s number-one slot for the next five weeks. Confused record buyers hounded music store clerks, asking for that new French hit, "My Mere Bits of Shame." There was such a clamor for the record, as well as for sheet music copies of the song, that one woman was knocked down by frantic customers at a Manhattan record store. She broke her leg in the melee and then proceeded to sue the store's owner, who apologized and paid her one hundred dollars in damages.

The sisters themselves discovered that their song was a hit on a cold morning in January. While living in Manhattan's Whitby apartments, the girls were awakened by their father who, in a frenzy, ordered them to get out of bed and get dressed, his heavy Greek accent seeming thicker than ever to the three bleary-eyed girls. Still half asleep, the sisters followed Peter outside into the winter weather, scurrying after him until they reached a record shop near the corner of Forty-fifth Street and Broadway. There in the middle of the crowded city, traffic had stopped, while a crowd of people gathered around a speaker that was blaring the strains of a new song, "Bei Mir Bist Du Schon." When the record finished playing, the bystanders all shouted out, "Play it again!" And it was played again and again. Maxene remembers leaning against the side of a building and crying, while Patty darted through the crowd, excitedly repeating to strangers, "That's us! That's us!" Under grey and frigid skies that early morning, the three young girls from Minnesota realized, probably for the first time, just what the world might hold in store for them.

After its post-Christmas release in 1937, "Bei Mir" sold over 350,000 copies in only one month, establishing the Andrews Sisters as successful recording artists. Disc sales soon amounted to one million copies, making the Andrews Sisters the first female vocal group to achieve a gold record. Co-lyricist Saul Chaplin recalled,

> Nobody expected it. It had an odd history. The record came out on a Tuesday before New Year's Eve, and it was just plodding along. Suddenly, all of New Year's Eve weekend, it was played about fifteen times on "The Milkman's Matinee," the WNEW all-night record show (in NYC), and that one weekend did it. I remember it very clearly. On Friday before New Year's Eve, it sold like seven thousand copies and the following Monday, it sold seventy-five thousand. All weekend you could not turn it off. It was on every single disc-jockey program at least four or five times during the night.

Total sales of "Bei Mir" would reach fourteen million by 1950 and the song would gross more than three million dollars by 1960. "Bei Mir" was such a sensation that the Kapp brothers upped the sisters' salary to five hundred dollars a week (they had previously been getting fifty dollars per session). Vic Schoen soon formed his own orchestra, which backed the girls on most of their recording successes. Over the next fifteen years, the Andrews Sisters would be the one and only female group to be included in America's top-ten list of best-loved pop music vocalists.

"Bei Mir Bist Du Schon" took the girls from vaudeville obscurity and rocketed them to stardom. The song, which also became the country's best-selling sheet music, offered an entirely new sound to the record-buying public—a vocalized swing sound that was just as danceable as any of the big band instrumentals. It was the Andrews Sisters' cohesive harmony and perfectly timed vocal syncopations that set them apart from their predecessors, the Boswell and Pickens sisters. Patty once said that although the trio adopted such a heavy southern drawl in "Bei Mir" to sound more like the Boswells, they actually ended up sounding more "like shrimp trawlers."

Throughout the remaining 1930s, the Andrews girls perfected their feel for the swing idiom. Utilizing their powerhouse harmonies, the girls became the voice of the big band era. Music historian Tony Palmer notes that "Patty, Maxene and LaVerne were rambunctious, highly stylized performers who adapted the qualities of swing instrumentation to the capabilities of the human voice." The intention of the trio was to vocally emulate the sound produced by three harmonizing trumpets. Maxene recalled, "You get with an orchestra, and you listen to three great trumpets playing. When vaudeville went kaput, we started to get jobs with little bands, and we'd sit there on the bandstand and listen to the musicians play, so we knew that this is the way you wanted to blend." Patty agreed, saying, "I was listening to Benny Goodman and to all the bands. I was into the feel, so that would go into my own music ability. I was into swing. I loved the brass section." William Ruhlmann similarly observed, "'Boogie Woogie Bugle Boy' is a perfect example of the way in which the Andrews Sisters adapted their vocal lines to the sound of a horn chart." Other examples of this can be heard in their scats preceding Patty's solo in "Oh, Johnny! Oh, Johnny! Oh!," as well as during similar scat arrangements in "Daddy" and "The Carioca."

The trio's sound was completely its own, although it was based on the singing style of the Boswell Sisters. Many of the Andrews Sisters' early recordings have noticeable Boswell influence, but the Andrews style was far different from the Boswell style—it was a more modern and conventional style that would guarantee the Andrews Sisters years of success in various musical genres. It would also add a timeless dimension to much of their recorded work.

"Bei Mir Bist Du Schon" received an award as the "Most Popular Song of 1938" from the American Society of Composers, Authors and Publishers. It was also featured in Warner Brothers' *Love, Honor, and Behave* with Priscilla Lane, and it was recorded in cover versions by the orchestras of Guy Lombardo, Tommy Dorsey, and Jimmie Lunceford, as well as by Ella Fitzgerald, which Sammy Cahn must have appreciated. Judy Garland also recorded the song for MGM's *Love Finds Andy Hardy*. Garland's version, different from the trio's in that she sang the first half of the song in cantorial fashion before swinging the remainder, was unfortunately omitted from the film before its release; but the soundtrack recording was saved and is available today on a compact disc compilation of Judy's film soundtracks. When Benny Goodman and his orchestra performed their version of the song during Goodman's now-legendary 1938 concert at Carnegie Hall, the audience was driven into a hand-clapping, foot-stomping frenzy. A United Press syndicated story at the time reported, "At one point, the audience—which included scores and scores of standees—almost took over the performance from Benny Goodman and his swinging orchestra. During the playing of Sholom Secunda's 'Bei Mir Bist Du Schon,' the audience burst into rhythmic shouts and handclaps, which momentarily produced more decibels than the instruments on the stage. The orchestra met the challenge, however, with a tremendous fanfare that made the clappers give up."

"Bei Mir" was immediately translated into many different languages. Ironically it even became a favorite selection of the Nazis in Germany; however, the song was banned in that country when the Third Reich discovered that the song's composer and lyricist were Jews. Concentration camp inmates loved the song and sang it with each other for comfort during the war years. Sholom Secunda's daughter, Victoria, in her biography of her father, *Bei Mir Bist Du Schon: The Life of Sholom Secunda,* notes, "the song was, in the current argot of the record business, a 'monster hit.' Business was so good at the Gaiety Music Shop on Broadway that people crowded in front of the store's clerk, gave him fifty cents, and he handed them a rolled up copy of the sheet music to 'Bei Mir' all without exchanging a word."

The sisters soon asked Cahn and Chaplin to write another set of English lyrics to yet another Yiddish tune, "Yossele, Yossele," as a follow-up to "Bei Mir." The team assisted and the girls recorded "Joseph! Joseph!" Though not the runaway hit that "Bei Mir" proved to be, the song did become a best-selling record. Desiring further visibility, the girls began making frequent appearances at Jewish women's clubs, singing Yiddish versions of their two hits, which probably helped fuel the misconception that the Andrews Sisters were of Jewish descent. These appearances served to increase their growing popularity.

The trio's recording of "Bei Mir," as well as their recordings of other melodies from Spain, Italy, Russia, and Czechoslovakia during the next two years, brought about a tremendous change in the recording industry of the 1930s. Whereas songs influenced by different ethnic styles had previously been frowned upon by music publishers and record company executives alike, the Andrews Sisters' recordings created more opportunity for cultural songs to make hit records. Victor Greene writes about the Andrews Sisters and their contributions to this medium in his book *A Passion for Polka*:

> While one cannot designate any one thematic type for the thousands of cuts that produced sales totaling tens of millions of records throughout their incredible career, one can say that in this early period at least, and occasionally later, they were the leading popular vocalists to draw their works heavily from the ethnic reservoir. It is difficult to say if this policy of exploiting ethnic music was a fully conscious one, but certainly Lou Levy, who was closest to them at this time and became their agent, provided a good rationale: the newer musical genres, he believed, which the major music publishers had previously avoided, provided great commercial potential.

Suddenly, the Andrews Sisters were in high demand. They were signed by Wrigley's to participate in its "Double Everything" chewing gum commercial spot, which ran for thirteen weeks over a CBS coast-to-coast hookup. They were then featured as regulars on radio's *Just Entertainment*, the Chicago-based program hosted by Jack Fulton for NBC. They appeared every weeknight on the series and flew to New York on weekends for recording purposes. Sholom Secunda made a guest appearance on one installment of the radio series and was interviewed before conducting the orchestra while the sisters sang his new composition, "Dream of Me." Sadly, as a result of public domain confusion and misrepresentation of the song by music publishers, Secunda was never awarded his fair share of royalties for "Bei Mir Bist Du Schon." He thus found it ironic that he received more money from Wrigley's—the radio show's sponsor—to be photographed with the Andrews Sisters, than he had received for writing the popular song.

The sisters were now being sought after for guest appearances on the top network radio shows of the day. One of those appearances was on *The Paul Whiteman Show,* during which they sang a wild, no-holds-barred rendition of the well-known spiritual "The Lonesome Road," featuring an uncharacteristic and brief solo by LaVerne. Paul Whiteman had actually auditioned the girls during their vaudeville years and had turned them down, categorizing their sound as trivial. When the trio's growing popularity guaranteed a larger radio audience, however, Whiteman made haste to welcome them. Fred Waring, another famous conductor at that time, had also turned the trio away not once, but three times during the 1930s, when the trio auditioned for his famous group of Pennsylvanians. The sisters worked with Waring only one time in New York during World War II. Maxene recalled,

> When Fred Waring introduced us at the Stage Door Canteen, he said, "You know, some of you might think I'm pretty smart because of the success the Pennsylvanians have had. But I'm pretty dumb. I had three girls audition for our group three years in a row, and each time I told them no. Twice I even told them to go home. If I had hired them, I could have had the Andrews Sisters for seventy-five dollars a week!" He was telling the truth. He told us our voices were too husky. Each of those rejections was a blow to us. Every time he turned us down after we auditioned, Fred's decision told me that maybe we weren't that good, that maybe we weren't going to make it all the way to the top. But when Fred said what he did at the

Stage Door Canteen that night, he was telling us that we had made it all the way to the top after all.

The trio's Decca sessions were now becoming more numerous, as were their hit records, including "Ti-Pi-Tin," based on a Spanish melody, and "Oh, Ma-Ma! (The Butcher Boy)," taken from Italy's "Luna Mezzo Mare." It is interesting to note now, some sixty years later, how the music of the Andrews Sisters does not sound nearly as dated as the music of some of the other artists of the same period. Although "Oh, Ma-Ma!" was a hit for the sisters, it was an even bigger hit for Rudy Vallee. Comparing the versions today, however, Vallee's rendition sounds like something taken directly out of a Looney Tunes short. He greatly overstates the novelty of the song. The sisters' version handles the parody on a more sophisticated level. The instrumentation in the trio's take of the song sounds as though it could have been recorded years after Vallee's, though both were recorded in 1939. Another hit that same year, "Oh, Johnny! Oh, Johnny! Oh!" similarly demonstrates the advanced musical sound of the Andrews Sisters. The song was a huge hit for novelty singer "Wee" Bonnie Baker, who sang it coyly within the rather confining arrangement of Orrin Tucker's band. However, in their version of the song, the sisters let loose with perfectly harmonized syncopations and scats, backed by Vic Schoen's blaring trumpet arrangements and driving beat.

Another of the trio's early hits, a vocalization of Fats Waller's "Hold Tight-Hold Tight (Want Some Sea Food, Mama?)," was recorded with Jimmy Dorsey's orchestra. Patty once said that Dorsey's power-packed band suited the trio's harmonies to perfection. The song became a huge hit upon its release, as well as a jukebox favorite at a time when you could play your favorite selection for just a nickel. Its success continued, despite an unfavorable review from famed columnist Walter Winchell, who wrote that a phrase in the song ("voo-diddy-aka-saky")—a supposedly nonsensical term that the sisters picked up from comic Larry Kent and inserted throughout the number—had a vulgar meaning. Winchell also suggested that the lyrics were risqué and that parents should not allow their children to listen to the record. Although the trio was probably unaware of the song's masked innuendo, or at least claimed to be over the years, Winchell may have been better informed than the girls. Writer David Lennick notes that it was "a song with connotations they didn't grasp at the time."

The commotion surrounding "Hold Tight" only seemed to generate more interest in the record, as Maxene remembered: "Winchell came out implying that it was a dirty song, so it was banned from the airwaves, which increased the sales of the records because people wanted to know what was terrible in the song."

The Andrews Sisters were certainly not the first artists to record a song that was thought to be indecent by a minority of the population. The issue of what belonged in a song had been brewing for years prior to the sisters' success. The Boswell Sisters' recording of "Minnie the Moocher's Wedding Day" in 1932, a song that portrayed the cocaine industry in New York City's Chinatown in the early 1930s, is one such example. Even Cole Porter's composition "Love for Sale" was criticized as obscene many years ago. Another example of this debate is the Andrews Sisters' 1938 recording of "When a Prince of a Fellow Meets a Cinderella (A Modern Fairytale)." Some of the song's more evocative lyrics were "Does he slip her a slipper? No sir! / Not if he can slip her a kiss," "Does she leave him at midnight? No, sir! / Not if she can linger till dawn," and "Does she cuddle up closer? Yes, sir! / Baby, how's about it with you?" Although these lyrics, written by James Van Heusen and M. Kurtz, might not raise an eyebrow from today's pop music fans, they were considered suggestive sixty years ago. The lyrics and others like them, however, were not thought to be as dangerous to society as the sisters themselves were. The trio was threatening to the older audiences of the late 1930s, who were accustomed to the mellower sounds of artists like Russ Columbo and Guy Lombardo. The Andrews Sisters burst on the popular music scene with their sometimes hectic, almost frantic vocalizing. The sisters were not afraid to take old sentimental standards and turn them upside down and inside out. They introduced new sounds, vocal forms of swing, boogie-woogie, and eight-to-the-bar, that had massive appeal to teenagers and young adults. Mature audiences did not fully accept the sisters until they released soft ballads like "Mean to Me," "I Love You Much Too

Much," "I'll Be with You in Apple Blossom Time," and "Down in the Valley." Like Elvis years later, the trio shook a solid musical foundation with their nontraditional vocalizing. Reporter Alice Craig Greene pointed out in 1946 that "the dynamic Andrews brand of song was entirely different from the soft, crooning harmonies in vogue. When the sisters Andrews emitted their hearty, slightly nasal blasts in a startling new tempo, audiences were apt to retreat in apprehension. People suffering from the effects of a long, drawn-out hangover wanted to be lulled, not stimulated."

When the trio recorded "Begin the Beguine" with Bob Crosby's Bobcats, it was the first time that they vocalized a big band instrumental, as Artie Shaw's orchestra had already achieved a million-seller with its own recording of the Cole Porter standard. The sisters reversed the typical big band arrangement with this recording. Nearly all band hits at that time would showcase the orchestra, with a brief vocal interlude from a featured singer just about halfway through the arrangement. The sisters made their vocals the focus of the recording, as the band took a back seat to the melody. "Begin the Beguine" became a huge hit for the trio and was featured constantly in their repertoire over the next fifteen years.

The sisters opened an engagement at New York's famed Paramount Theater on Forty-fourth Street with Jimmy Dorsey and his orchestra. They were so successful during this first run at the theater that they were held over for a second week and the management immediately signed them for a future engagement at twice their original salary. During all of their appearances at the Paramount during the 1930s and 1940s, the girls were a sensation, topping previous house averages and causing lines around the block—before Frank Sinatra made that a regular occurrence. After their shows, the girls would exit the theater via a stage door and make a mad dash—usually led by Patty—to their car in order to avoid the crush of fans. According to Newsweek, the sisters had more return engagements at the Paramount, thirteen in all, than any other singing attraction. Patty remembered those appearances well: "You did four or five shows a day starting probably around ten o'clock. You had other acts on the bill and an orchestra, a big band, and so you closed the show, and you did maybe twenty minutes at the most.

The whole show could run an hour because they had a picture to put on . . . about four or five songs, something like that. We were very fortunate, because we had so many hits, so we'd be singing all our hits."

The girls then premiered on the CBS radio series *Honolulu Bound* with Phil Baker (also known as *The Phil Baker Show*). They appeared on it every Saturday night for the next nine months, singing many of their hit songs as well as commercial jingles for Dole pineapple products, the show's sponsor. During the course of the shows, Decca president Jack Kapp heard and liked a catchy polka melody that he presented to the girls, telling them that he was eager to have them record the Czechoslovakian tune. The melody, written in 1934 by Jaromir Vejvoda, was called "Modranska Polka." English lyrics were then written by Lew Brown and Vladimir Timm, who transformed the number into "Beer Barrel Polka (Roll Out the Barrel)." Soon after, the polka was recorded as an instrumental for Victor Records in Europe by Will Glahe, a German musette accordion bandleader.

After examining a sheet music copy of the song, the girls came to the conclusion that they were not interested in the piece and neatly filed it under a stack of other sheet music, where they hoped it would soon be forgotten. One day, however, Kapp asked Maxene, "Whatever became of that polka that I wanted you girls to record?" Maxene replied, "Well, we honestly didn't feel that it was right for us, so we decided not to use it." "I see," responded Kapp, summoning his presidential authority, "then I imagine that you girls aren't very fond of recording." Maxene read between the lines and informed her sisters of Kapp's comments. They quickly worked out an arrangement with Vic Schoen and recorded the song along with a jive number called "Well, All Right! (Tonight's the Night)." The two songs were released as a Decca single, which immediately sold upwards of eight hundred thousand copies and soon turned into a gold record for the girls. The song was played constantly on the radio and, thanks to its party atmosphere lyric, became a favorite selection in jukeboxes at bars and restaurants, as well as at weddings and other gatherings. It became one of the trio's most popular hits.

Despite its tremendous success, the Andrews Sisters never

developed a liking for the song, and Vic Schoen despised the melody. He once said he "hated it and arranged it as badly as I could, but it turned out to be their biggest hit." Recorded covers of the song by other artists soon followed, including versions by Bill Gale, Sammy Kaye, and Lawrence Welk.

Writer Victor Greene comments on the effect of the trio's two monster hits of the late 1930s:

> "Bei Mir" and "Beer Barrel Polka" were significant as crossover ethnic pieces that became a part of our national popular culture, but they also helped to establish by 1940 an entirely new popular music category on the national charts, providing mainstream recognition at the national level for bands performing crossover music. The popular music industry, which had already incorporated the western or country-western categories by the end of the depression, now embraced a new kind of popular music termed "international." The reference itself may have been new, but it actually referred to a musical genre that had been emerging from crossover ensembles since the start of the depression.

The sisters opened a second engagement at New York's Paramount with Glen Gray's orchestra and then returned there for a run with Gene Krupa and his band. *Variety* carried the following assessment: "With Krupa, the Andrews Sisters are socko! The femme trio has catapulted to stardom in short order, chiefly via their Decca discs. They almost had to do the entire booking before begging off and only eased out by a rhythmic scat piece of business paced by Patty. The girls are becomingly costumed in red-blue contrast and are palpably a draw here, judging by the entrance salvo." Regarded as "the Bible of show business," *Variety* hailed the sisters during each of their Paramount gigs over the next decade.

The sisters were headlining successful engagements throughout the entire United States, including appearances at Philadelphia's Fox Theater, Pittsburgh's Stanley Theater, Baltimore's Hippodrome, and Atlantic City's Steel Pier. Maxene once recalled the difficulty of varying their program according to regional tastes:

> A song that was well-received in one town might not go over in another. When "Bei Mir" came out, it took about a year to convince the people in California that it was a big hit, yet through all that time, it was a smash in the East. It took a long time for that song to get around the country, and I don't think it was ever popular in the Midwest; but if you sang a polka in the Midwest—like the hits we had with "Beer Barrel Polka" and "Pennsylvania Polka"—you were a smash. It was frustrating for us because we were always faced with the need to change our act, our songs, on short notice after finding out that a certain song that had gone over so well in our last city all of a sudden was bombing with our new audiences. It was only after the great migration to our cities in the years that followed World War II that the musical tastes of Americans became something closer to universal.

These changes in repertoire and accompanying arrangements happened less frequently for the trio as their popularity increased and their touring shows became more precisely planned and lavish.

The popularity of "Beer Barrel Polka," as well as many of the trio's recordings, extended worldwide. When the Andrews Sisters toured Italy for the USO in 1945, they awoke the first morning of their stay in Rome to a crowd of fifty Italians singing "Roll Out the Barrel" in their native tongue under the trio's hotel window.

The trio graced the cover of *Billboard* magazine, the world's foremost entertainment weekly, for the first time in their career in June 1939. The girls' popularity rose to such heights over the next decade that they appeared on six more *Billboard* covers, more than any other vocal group in the magazine's history of pictorial covers.

Bing Crosby was Decca's biggest star during the 1930s, as well as a good friend to both Kapp brothers. Jack Kapp was particularly fond of pairing artists on his label. He had already paired the sisters with drummer Ray McKinley for a swinging vocal rendition of "Billy Boy" with Jimmy Dorsey's orchestra, and he thought that the sisters would also blend well with Crosby. It has been rumored over the years that Crosby was less than thrilled when Kapp suggested the collaboration. Crosby had worked frequently with the Boswell Sisters and, according to Maxene, he thought the Andrews Sisters' singing style was not the ideal sound for a girl trio. Patty disagrees, saying that the sisters' rhythmic drive was precisely what attracted Crosby, having himself performed in the trio called the Delta Rhythm Boys, which sang jazz arrangements years earlier with Paul Whiteman's orchestra. The sisters themselves were a little apprehensive about recording with Crosby. Maxene explained, "When we came to Decca, it never dawned on us that Mr. Kapp would call us and say, 'How would you like to make a record with Bing Crosby?' Now, that was unheard of for us because not only were we so excited, we were so nervous!"

Patty was so nervous during that first session with Crosby that she was unable to look directly into his eyes. She recalled, "I was so nervous I didn't think I'd be able to sing. He was on one side of the mike and we were on the other, facing him. But I knew that if I looked at him I would not be able to open my mouth." According to music historian Joseph Laredo, "Crosby was not unaware of the intimidating effect he often had on female duet partners, and in the case of one particular skittish radio co-star, he'd gone as far as gently taking her hand in a paternal gesture of reassurance. By averting her eyes to the ground during that first session, Patty stumbled across an interesting Crosby idiosyncrasy: 'He had a thing with his foot,' [she said]. 'He would move it right-to-left, right-to-left and so on—just like a metronome.'"

Maxene recalled the following regarding the many recording sessions with Crosby: "Bing loved to kid around with my sister, Pat, because he didn't read music, and we would come in on the record dates with just a sheet of lyrics, but with the routine of the record, and he and Pat would go to the piano. And Vic Schoen only played piano with two fingers—and so, they'd go to the piano and Bing would say, 'Okay, Pat, what am I singing?' So Pat and Vic would run down the whole routine for him, and it would be once or twice and

he was prepared." Vic Schoen also remembered Crosby's professionalism and easiness in the studio, although he was usually unaware
of what they were recording that day:

> He was open, and many, many times when he came in
> he was surprised by the way things shaped up because
> he hadn't foreseen it that way. When he's off by him-
> self, he has a guy play for him—'cause he couldn't
> play—and the guy plays it as he thinks it should be
> played, unaware that it could be played in a different
> tempo or with a different treatment. Sometimes I took
> things and gave them Latin treatments, whereas in the
> original that wasn't indicated, or, one way or another,
> it became changed, but he went along with it because
> it apparently was better than the thought that he had
> originally. We never had any problem with Crosby. I
> never did. And I took some risks. I took a lot of risks
> in the way I wrote for them. But he loved it, so I went
> on doing it. I never had any indication to stop doing
> it or to change it.

Tensions during that 1939 session were eased when singer-
comedienne Carmen Miranda stopped by the studio to visit and
pose for pictures. Miranda would become a motion picture star at
Twentieth Century-Fox studios as well as a featured vocalist at
Decca. She was wowing audiences at the time with her rendition of
"South American Way" in the Broadway musical "Streets of Paris,"
which also featured the up-and-coming comedy team of Abbott and
Costello. Miranda, in six-inch platform heels and exotic fruit-laden
headpieces, caused such a stir with her introduction of "South
American Way" (which the Andrews Sisters recorded for Decca that
same year) that critics dubbed her "The Brazilian Bombshell."
Miranda and Abbott and Costello would later join the sisters for
successes on records and film.

Crosby and the sisters recorded "Ciribiribin (They're So in
Love)" and "Yodelin' Jive" (which became a top-ten hit) with Joe
Venuti, the great jazz violinist. The songs were superbly done, es-

pecially "Ciribiribin," in which the trio's rapid scatting nicely balanced Crosby's crooning. Jack Lawrence, who had written the English lyrics to Italy's "Ciribiribin" and who was present at that session, recalls, "Harry James had started using this old Italian song (composed by A. Pestalozza) as his theme, featuring his golden trumpet sound. I had a ball writing this lyric, giving it a Romeo-Juliet balcony setting. Among the many record covers the song had, the one I truly felt captured the fun of the lyric was the first teaming of the Andrews Sisters with Bing Crosby. Listening to them, it's obvious they're enjoying their performance."

The disc became the Andrews Sisters' eighth best-selling Decca record in less than two years, selling over five hundred thousand copies. According to Maxene, Crosby told the girls that anything they wanted to record with him in the future would be fine. It was the massive record sales of Bing Crosby and the Andrews Sisters, separately and jointly, that would primarily make Decca Records the profitable and respected company that it was soon to become, boasting as its slogan, "the fastest-selling records in the world."

Several biographers in years past have suggested that there were two sides to Bing Crosby—a sort of Jekyll-and-Hyde personality. Both Patty and Maxene have stated that there were several occasions when the trio would not approach Crosby in the studio until it was time to record, feeling that he did not want to be bothered. Patty said that she was able to determine his state of mind the minute he walked into the studio by observing the position of the hat he was wearing. Maxene made a similar observation: "The first thing you learned about Bing was that he was the epitome of the perfect singing companion. The second thing you learned was that though he was a great, great gentleman, he could be just a little moody. If that hat was planted firmly on his head, don't kid around. If that hat was real jaunty—why, then you could kid him. A little." Maxene once referred to Crosby as "a loner," and she said that he sometimes left the recording studio after a joint session without even saying goodbye. Not long before he died, Bing responded to the sisters' perceptions of him by saying that if he seemed indifferent in any way, it was simply because he may have been unfamiliar with the material that was to be recorded (he left both the selection and the arrangement of material to the trio and Vic Schoen), and that his concentration level must have been more intense than the girls realized. Schoen once reflected,

> Bing could be very intimidating, and his exterior was sometimes cool, if not cold. If he liked what was going on in the studio he gave it everything he had, although he didn't appear to be making an effort to do so. He had a remarkable ability to create and improvise in front of a microphone. He expressed his acceptance by doing the things required of him. If he didn't like something, he simply didn't do it. I can recall a rehearsal I was overseeing once with Bing and a female vocalist who he felt wasn't singing up to his high standards. He just put on his hat and left the studio without saying a word to anyone. It was a very awkward situation.

Whatever the case, most of the trio's sessions with Crosby were fun, especially if someone—usually Crosby—fluffed the lyrics; both acts were always eager to record together. Listening to "Ciribiribin," as well as later recordings like "Pistol Packin' Mama," "I'll Si-Si Ya in Bahia," "Black Ball Ferry Line," "Apalachicola, FLA," and "A Hundred and Sixty Acres," it is evident that all four performers truly admired each other and enjoyed what they were doing. The girls mustered all of their collective strength not to laugh at many points throughout the recordings, as Crosby would improvise and toss in an unwritten lyric here or there. He said of the trio, "I like singing with them. It's fun." Patty described their singing union as "a happy marriage. We loved singing with Bing, just so much fun. Bing was happy when he was singing with us. Doesn't he sound happy?"

After the trio's successful teaming with Crosby, Kapp realized the sisters' full potential. He raised their collective weekly salary from 500 to 650 dollars a week, and he designed a new contract that awarded the trio five percent of royalties for all records sold—retroactive. The only other recording artist at that time given such prestigious treatment as a royalty clause in their contract was Crosby himself, who had been recording for over a decade, unlike the sisters, who had yet to complete three years at Decca. Royalties were soon to become a mainstay in the recording industry of the 1940s, to the delight of all musical artists.

The Andrews Sisters joined the CBS show *The Moonlight Serenade* with Glenn Miller and his orchestra just after Christmas, 1939. The network executives and the sponsors (Chesterfield cigarettes) were not sure that Miller alone could attract a large enough radio audience, so the sisters were signed as a temporary added attraction to guarantee higher ratings. As a result of the pairing, the show was a huge success, airing three nights a week. The trio sang current Decca hits, including "Say Si Si" and the lively party number "Let's Have Another One," as well as hot arrangements of current top tunes, such as "I've Got No Strings" from Walt Disney's *Pinocchio* and "The Donkey Serenade" (based on "Chanson," a 1920 piano piece by Rudolf Friml). Patty said it was during this time that the trio started receiving staggering amounts of fan mail, as well as many call-in requests to the show.

Contrary to popular belief, the Chesterfield shows were not the first time that the sisters had worked with Miller. Six months earlier, the trio had toured with the maestro and his orchestra, playing one-night stands in Massachusetts, Vermont, Philadelphia, and Washington, D.C.

Associates of Glenn Miller have said in interviews that the bandleader was not particularly fond of the trio's vocal style, and as a result of his feelings, many associated with the show thought that conflicts might arise between Miller and the trio; but the trombonist actually got along well with the girls. Maxene remembered Miller and the thirty-eight broadcasts in which she and her sisters appeared: "The listener response was sensational, and Glenn was signed for another year, while we went back to the personal appearance tour we were already under contract for and which we actually preferred. But during those weeks we came to know Glenn as a thorough professional, a quiet man who went to extremes to make sure his band performed to its maximum potential and that every member of it conducted himself in a one-hundred-percent professional manner." Maxene continued with an example of Miller's high expectations, "It was our arranger, Vic Schoen. As Vic was entering the studio one day, he pulled out a pack of Lucky Strikes and lit up a cigarette. Glenn was walking in right behind him. He caught up with Vic and said, in firm and unmistakable tones, 'If you have to smoke, don't you ever let me catch you smoking anything but a Chesterfield as long as you're associated with this show.'"

Maxene reminisced about Miller's assumed death a little over four years later:

> Glenn Miller disappeared on a flight across the English Channel. Our colleague on the Chesterfield shows had been headed for Paris to begin preparations for a Christmas show for the troops there. We quickly sent our sympathy, and it was heartfelt, to his wife, Helen. But there just didn't seem to be anything else we could do. We felt helpless and so sad. Glenn was our friend, a man we genuinely liked and admired, and now he was gone, another wartime casualty. It was an enormous loss to all of us, and to the music of America. His disappearance on December 15, 1944, has never been explained. Neither his body nor his plane has ever been found. He was headed across the channel ahead of his orchestra to supervise arrangements personally for their Christmas show. That was Glenn's demand for perfection reflecting itself again. Another, less demanding conductor might not have gone there ahead of his band, and Glenn might still be with us today. But that wasn't the Glenn Miller way. He wanted to get there early and make sure everything was precisely the way he wanted it to be.

Associates of Miller were relieved when they saw how well he got along with the Andrews Sisters, but conflicts soon arose among the sisters themselves. During several weeks throughout their thirteen-week Chesterfield gig, the girls were singing together but not speaking to each other. Larry Bruff, a communications and public relations assistant hired for the series, recalled, "After a few weeks, the girls weren't even talking to each other—they'd gotten into a fight or something—and so we were having a helluva time trying to figure out what they wanted to sing." Actually, the girls' falling-out was so severe that only Patty reported to CBS studios for one broadcast in January 1940, which caused the already staggering amount of fan mail to increase ten-fold, demanding the return of Maxene and LaVerne.

The sisters seldom allowed their personal conflicts to interfere with public performances, but the girls became rather famous for their squabbling, due to more than enough publicity on the subject. Maxene once said that the disagreements and fights between herself and her sisters in rehearsal halls and such must have seemed loud and furious, but she stressed that the clashes were kept strictly on a professional level. She claimed that personal difficulties did not become a problem until much later in the trio's career. Many arguments would stem from discussions on how a song should end, where Patty's solo should be placed, or which scat arrangement would best complement the melody. All the sisters had creative, though at times differing, ideas and each of them demanded to be heard. When Merv Griffin asked about the trio's mid-1950s separation, Patty joked, "The Andrews Sisters really had only one big fight. It started in 1937 and it's still going!" She added in that same 1985 interview, "We argue and fight just like any other sisters."

There was actually a reason for the girls' hostility toward each other during the broadcasts with Miller, belying Maxene's claim that personal problems were absent early on. During the latter part of 1939 and carrying over into the next year, both Patty and Maxene had well-publicized disagreements with their parents—mainly Peter—concerning the men they were dating. Patty was dating conductor Vic Schoen, while Maxene had gotten involved with manager Lou Levy. Peter thought the girls should not mix business affairs with love interests. He voiced his disapproval of his daughters' suitors on more than one occasion, and even made personal threats against Levy and Schoen.

The situation worsened when a severe argument concerning Levy and Schoen occurred between Patty and Maxene and the rest of the family—LaVerne and her parents—while they were living at the Piccadilly Hotel in New York City, causing both Patty and Maxene to leave the hotel the night of January 28, 1940, and not return. LaVerne sided with her parents on the issue, contributing to Patty's solo appearance on the CBS show two nights later. It seems ironic that Patty introduced a new ballad on that broadcast, "I Love You Much Too Much," in an arrangement obviously tailored to the trio's harmony skills. Maxene related the following to William Ruhlmann in January 1995 in an extensive cover story for *Goldmine* magazine:

> I was the rebellious one. I said to my father, "You're not gonna pick out the man for me to marry." And so consequently my dad and I didn't see eye to eye on many things. But LaVerne adored them, and of course, they adored her. She was very close to my mother and father. It was just one of those things. If any problems came up, she never took Patty's or my part, she always sided in with Mom and Papa. I think the story itself was blown so much out of what it really was. The whole thing was, my dad slapped me. He'd never slapped me before, but when he slapped me for no good reason, I think that I had just made up my mind that I wasn't gonna take it anymore. That started the whole ruckus.

Ruhlmann also interviewed Lou Levy, Maxene's former husband, for the same article. When discussing that incident, it seems he sparked some fiery emotions that obviously had not been extinguished in the passing of fifty-five years. Levy said,

> You mean the whole big story when I was going to marry Maxene and he chased me with a gun? It's goddamned true, but they made it sound like a press story. It's true. It is true. The girls will deny it, but I'm not denying it. Sure he did, so what? I was marrying his daughter. I was a Jew. Who the hell gives a . . . A

Jew song made them, a Jewish record company made
them, a Jewish picture company made them. What the
hell has Jews got to do with it? Jewish songwriters, a
Jewish manager. I was born a Jew, I don't work at it.
I'm telling the truth. You got a microphone? I'll tell it
to the world. Sure, I was born a Jew. I guess I'll die a
Jew. My family were Jews. I haven't worked at it.

Unfortunately, this somewhat ranting tone is the same that
Levy took when approached for an interview for this project. When
contacted by telephone at his New York City offices, he refused the
interview request, saying, "What else is there to say about the
Andrews Sisters that hasn't already been said?" Considering that an
Andrews Sisters biography was heretofore non-existent, this seemed
an odd remark to make about the best-selling female vocal group
of all time, especially from someone who worked and lived so closely
with them.

Although Levy is known to have a knack for embellishing
stories—as did Maxene in regard to people, places, and dates, in
several interviews she granted during the 1980s and 1990s—there
was some truth in his recollections to Ruhlmann. Peter's threats to
Levy and Schoen were actually reported to the police, who searched
the family's hotel suite and found an unregistered revolver in Peter's
room. Peter was arrested on a Sullivan Law charge (which prohib-
ited the carrying of an unlicensed firearm) and spent the night in
jail. Olga bailed him out the following day with five hundred dollars, and the couple smiled for photographers and reporters at the
time of his release. Maxene tried to visit her father in jail, recalling,
"I went over to see my dad because I was shocked he was arrested.
Of course, I was hysterical seeing him behind bars, but the desk
sergeant was the guy who got me—this guy, in great profanity, is
reading me out, telling me that if I was his kid, he'd beat the you-
know-what out of me. I just ran from the police station because I
just figured, there'd never been any kind of scandal in our family,
and I didn't want to prolong it, I didn't want to add to it."

Vic Schoen told the *New York Daily News* at the time of Peter's
arrest that Mr. Andrews was being too protective of his daughters:

"You know how parents are. They think their daughters are still just kids. They felt that the girls shouldn't mix business with love affairs. I suppose they've forgotten that they had to run away from their parents to get married when they were young." Although none of the sisters spoke to reporters during the ordeal, Patty reportedly told friends that any talk of marriage was untrue, at least at that stage of their career. She soon stopped seeing Schoen outside of their working relationship. Maxene, however, continued to secretly date Levy.

Personal problems aside, the Chesterfield shows on CBS were so well received that the sisters opened an engagement with the Miller orchestra at the Paramount Theater. The stage shows were similar in format to the radio shows. It is interesting to note that the sisters and Miller's band initially appeared at the Paramount without Glenn Miller, as Miller was hospitalized with grippe and a severe sinus infection the day before the opening. He returned to his baton the second week of the engagement. His substitutes during that week included Gene Krupa, Tommy Dorsey, Dick Stabile, and Charlie Barnet. As the trio belted out "Ciribiribin," "Say Si Si," and other Decca hits, *Variety* reported, "The Andrews Sisters' unusual handling and nifty harmonizing of even these comparative oldies gives them an entirely fresh touch."

*Four years ago, the Andrews girls were just another
song trio, as far as the trade was concerned. Today,
their recording sales have passed the 7.5 million mark,
their theater grosses run from $5–$10,000 over
the house averages, they have appeared on the biggest
of the commercial radio shows and have chalked up
three Universal picture hits,* Buck Privates,
In the Navy *and* Hold That Ghost.
—Billboard, *1941*

3

They Made the Company Jump

Emerging from the late 1930s as the top trio in the nation, the
Andrews Sisters were wowing the record-buying public with song
arrangements that jumped to their loud, robust harmonies. Rather
than crooning, the girls used their strong vocal cords to full advantage, making their blend completely their own and much more
cohesive than any other vocal group.

The girls themselves were a bit astonished by their growing
popularity, as Maxene recalled:

When we opened at the Casa Manana in Culver City,
California on June 7, the audience included one of the
biggest name orchestra leaders of the previous twenty
years, Paul Whiteman, who was filming his new
movie, *Strike Up the Band*. He caught our eleven

o'clock show that night. On the same evening, we sang in front of Bing Crosby's orchestra leader, John Scott Trotter, Phil Harris and Dennis Day from *The Jack Benny Show,* character actor Andy Devine, and one of the popular comedy acts, the Ritz Brothers. For the Andrews Sisters, it was a night to remember.

Unfortunately, there has recently been a handful of books on the popular music history of the 1930s and 1940s that downplay the popularity and achievements of the Andrews Sisters, accusing them of doing little more than copying the style of their predecessors, the Boswell Sisters. The Andrews Sisters did indeed copy the Boswell style (both Patty and Maxene have admitted to this), and evidence of such emulation can be heard in such early Andrews Sisters hits as "Says My Heart" and "Where Have We Met Before?"; but with their very first record release, "Jammin'," as well as with what immediately followed ("Bei Mir" and so on), their vocal style, perfect timing, harmonious blend, and musical phrasing all showed that they were more than mere imitators. In subsequent recordings, it was obvious that the trio was headed away from the dominant jazz style of the period and leaning more toward the growing swing idiom. It is inevitable for a vocal group to be compared to a similar group that came before them, but the Andrews Sisters used the Boswell influence to create their own musical specialties. Had the Boswells not disbanded in the 1930s, it is unlikely that they would have successfully adapted to the variety of musical styles in which the Andrews Sisters would excel. The sisters were able to successfully record almost any type of music, including swing ("Hold Tight-Hold Tight"), boogie-woogie ("Boogie Woogie Bugle Boy"), eight-to-the-bar ("Beat Me Daddy, Eight to the Bar"), jazz ("I'm in a Jam"), ragtime ("Alexander's Ragtime Band"), calypso ("Rum and Coca Cola"), classical ("Lovely Night"), folk ("The Blue Tail Fly"), country-western ("Don't Rob Another Man's Castle"), gospel ("In the Garden"), dixieland ("South Rampart Street Parade"), blues ("Lonesome Mama"), ballads ("I Wanna Be Loved"), inspirational ("Whispering Hope"), seasonal ("Jingle Bells"), and various ethnic-flavored melodies. The trio had the ability to switch from the raucous "I

Didn't Know the Gun Was Loaded" to the melodic "I Can Dream, Can't I?" (both recorded in 1949) with ease. This was due mainly to the versatility of their polished, professional and—good or bad, depending on which critic you read—commercial sound. The Andrews Sisters successfully sailed many previously uncharted musical waters.

Throughout the Thanksgiving Day weekend of 1940, the sisters appeared at the Roxy Theater in Atlanta, Georgia, of which a critic wrote,

> The Andrews Sisters opened an engagement with Bunny Berigan and his orchestra at the Roxy yesterday. The trio was so well received that they had to resort to a novelty, a fantasy of songs that they have made famous, in order to leave the stage. They slipped into the wings before the spellbound audience realized that they were gone. Patty's mannerisms are a special attraction. She also converses with the audience, paying special attention to the people in the loge, which she called "the shelf." The Andrews Sisters bring down the house with a number of tunes that accompanied them in their rise to fame.

As a result of their numerous hit records and their increasing popularity nationwide, Hollywood realized that the Andrews Sisters might prove to be lucrative property in motion pictures. The girls were soon called to Tinseltown to negotiate a contract with Universal Pictures. The girls accepted the offer and signed a five-year contract with the studio, something they would later regret. The executives at Universal were eager to cast the sisters opposite the three Ritz Brothers, who were already an established comedy act in such films as *You Can't Have Everything* and *The Three Musketeers*. The Andrews Sisters and the Ritz Brothers were first paired for a musical comedy called *Argentine Nights* (1940).

Working on film was a new experience for the sisters. They took their work very seriously, so they did not appreciate the many practical jokes and shenanigans which Al, Harry, and Jimmy Ritz were fond of executing on the set. Nonetheless, both groups made an effort to get along during filming. The film was completed in a short time. Unfortunately, it was a terrible film debut for the sisters and received unfavorable reviews. It even caused a riot in one Argentine theater due to the way Argentine people were portrayed in the film. As a result of all the turmoil, the Andrews Sisters were released from their contract.

The negative publicity continued. The famed *Harvard Lampoon* voted the trio's debut "the most frightening of the year." Although all three sisters agreed with this statement (they once told a reporter that their appearance in the film sent them "screaming from the projection room"), they later joked, "We don't hold any grudges against those nice Harvard boys. We'd like to sing at a Harvard prom. We'd scare 'em to death!" The sisters were aghast at how unattractive the studio's makeup artists and hairstylists had made them appear on screen. According to Patty, one of the makeup men who worked on the girls for this film had also worked on the famous monsters in Universal's earlier horror flicks, including *Frankenstein* and *Dracula*. When the girls attended the New York premiere of the film at the Fordham Theater in the Bronx, they were horrified at their own images on the movie screen. Patty recalled, "We looked so ugly on screen that we walked back to Manhattan from the Bronx, and Maxene was in tears all the way."

The girls appeared far too made up in the movie, especially around the eyes, and the camera close-ups, especially during "Rhumboogie" (their first number in the film), were not at all flattering. Comparing the trio's physical appearance in Universal's *Argentine Nights* to their appearance in Paramount's *Road to Rio* seven years later, one would scarcely be able to tell that both films featured the same girls. The trio's appearance in *Argentine Nights* gave critics all the ammunition that they needed to harp on the sisters' features, a practice that continued for many years. LaVerne was particularly self-conscious about her looks. When the trio first started performing, LaVerne stood on Patty's right and Maxene on Patty's left; however, LaVerne and Maxene switched places when LaVerne discovered that her left profile photographed best. LaVerne tried various make-up techniques designed to enhance her features, including lipstick applications used by Bette Davis and Lucille Ball, in order to make her lips look fuller.

If *Argentine Nights* served one purpose, it introduced the Andrews Sisters to the motion picture, and from that point on vocal groups in movies would never be the same. Until the trio, most groups in films simply stood gathered around a microphone and harmonized, but from the first downbeats of "Rhumboogie," the Andrews Sisters pounced onto the screen, arms flailing and hips swinging. The girls' wild movements and fancy footwork accentuated their rapid harmonies, and they launched the vocal group into movement in all Hollywood musicals to follow.

The trio's disappointment with their film debut was somewhat compensated by their steady increase in hit records, including "Rhumboogie," "Ferryboat Serenade (La Piccinina)," and rocking versions of two memorable boogie hits—"Beat Me Daddy, Eight to the Bar" and "Scrub Me Mama with a Boogie Beat," based on the Irish folk song "The Irish Washerwoman." The sisters also had hits that year with a risky coupling of two lovely ballads, "Mean to Me" and "Sweet Molly Malone." *Billboard* wrote,

> A definitely unusual platter comes from the Andrews trio this week, with the girls pulling a surprise on their legions of admirers by delivering a pair of sweet, slow ballads, in sharp contrast to their usual output of sock rhythm stuff. To anybody who knows the splendid vocal ability of this threesome, it will come as no surprise that the momentary about-face is carried off with all the excellence and quality that have made them the country's number-one singing trio. The blend they achieve on "Mean to Me" is as good as anything they have ever done in a swingy vein.

The sisters hold the distinction of charting more *Billboard* hits than any other vocal group in music history, including the Beatles. An astounding 113 of the trio's Decca recordings from 1938 to 1951 appeared in the magazine's top-thirty listings, with forty-six of those same songs holding top-ten positions (eight more than Elvis

Presley). Eight of the trio's recordings reached the number-one position. The Mills Brothers came closest to the trio with sixty-five top-thirty hits from 1931 to 1968.

Several months following the release of *Argentine Nights,* Universal decided to renew the trio's contract and cast them opposite another comedy team, Abbott and Costello. Bud Abbott and Lou Costello's first film release, *One Night in the Tropics,* had not fared much better than *Argentine Nights* in theaters, but the studio executives thought that pairing the acts might work. They were taking a chance, and not only did the gamble pay off, but it surpassed all expectations. *Buck Privates,* a comedy about army life, was filmed on Universal's back lot within twenty-four days. Hollywood legend estimates the cost of production for the film at under two hundred thousand dollars. Shortly after its release, it grossed over 4.7 million dollars, an astronomical amount of money during the early 1940s, and a tremendous profit for the studio as well. *Buck Privates,* as well as the two Abbott and Costello films with the sisters that quickly followed, saved Universal from desperate financial difficulties and near bankruptcy. According to Maxene, the film remained the studio's biggest money maker until the 1975 release of *Jaws.*

Buck Privates, which up till that time grossed second only to *Gone with the Wind,* was a monumental success. It guaranteed Abbott and Costello and the Andrews Sisters long-term employment with the studio. This worked out better for Abbott and Costello in the end, who received a much higher grade of material to work with than did the sisters.

The film received excellent reviews. A critic wrote the following in the *New York Times:* "With Abbott and Costello dropping gags once a minute and the Andrews Sisters crooning patriotic boogie-woogie airs, well, it's going to be a merry war, folks." *Buck Privates* is probably the sisters' best remembered film, with the trio singing four songs. The first, "You're a Lucky Fellow, Mr. Smith," featured the trio singing to a group of departing servicemen on a makeshift set of New York's Grand Central Station; the song is also performed as a reprise at the end of the film. The second song, "I'll Be with You in Apple Blossom Time," became so popular that the trio adopted it as their theme song. The tune was originally written in 1920, but it had not been successfully identified with any particular artist until the trio recorded it. Recording the song for both Decca Records and Universal Pictures, however, was not easy.

The studio executives at Universal did not want the song featured in the comedy. They thought the lyrics, which tell of a soldier promising his love as well as a wedding to his bride-to-be upon his return, were too sentimental to suit the fast-paced antics of the film. When their opinion was swayed with the help of the film's director, Arthur Lubin, the executives relented but refused to pay the customary publishing fee of two hundred dollars. The song's publisher received his fee directly from the Andrews Sisters, and the song was used in the film. The studio also refused to compromise on costumes or scenery, and so the number was filmed with the girls dressed in khaki military garb, seated on a wooden fence and surrounded by blossoming crepe-paper apple trees.

While the trio was in the midst of their Decca recording session of the song, they were interrupted by Jack Kapp, who told them, "Don't record that song. The last thing America needs is a female Ink Spots!" He was probably making reference to the song's arrangement, most notably the question-and-answer segment during Patty's solo. The girls panicked, especially Maxene and LaVerne, who loved the song. Lou Levy persuaded Kapp to at least allow the girls to finish the recording. Kapp agreed, but informed Levy that he had no intentions of releasing the record. After a bit of convincing from Levy and the sisters, Kapp changed his mind and released the disc, which soon became a best-selling record. The girls were appearing in Chicago when they first heard the record played on the radio, and they were distressed. Both Patty and Maxene had colds when the song was recorded ("Scrub Me Mama with a Boogie Beat" was recorded at the same session), and they both felt that their vocalizing was slightly off-key and out of tune with the harp throughout much of the recording, especially the beginning. Maxene was so upset that she begged Kapp to let them re-record the tune, but he would not hear of it. He told Maxene that he feared the girls would be unable to recapture the soft, sentimental mood that was so evident in the original take.

The trio's third and fourth songs in the film were released back to back on another Decca single, which became another fast best-seller due mainly to the A side—the trio's classic recording of the Oscar-nominated "Boogie Woogie Bugle Boy." It was a classic jump tune that will forever be associated with the Andrews Sisters, thanks in part to Patty's wild and energetic solo, as well as to a knockout band arrangement by Vic Schoen. Listening closely, one can detect that the trumpet introduction is actually a fast version of "Taps," an innovative move on Schoen's part; it is surprising that at this time in American history, such usage was not regarded as inappropriate or distasteful. The B side of the record was another boogie-woogie number, "Bounce Me Brother with a Solid Four." The trio's vocal precision and harmonious blend in "Boogie Woogie Bugle Boy"—for both the movie soundtrack and Decca Records—were outstanding. It was vocal perfection for the sisters, and that sound became the definitive voice of the 1940s. Perhaps no other song or performance brings World War II to mind so quickly and unmistakably. Remarkably, some of the executives at Universal were skeptical as to just how well the public would accept vocalized forms of boogie-woogie. Obviously, they neglected to consider the trio's previous boogie-woogie hits, which were selling millions of copies. Upon hearing the film soundtrack recording of "Boogie Woogie Bugle Boy," the executives changed their minds; the studio's publicity department was instructed to tout the girls as "Those song-sational singers of boogie-woogie music, the Andrews Sisters."

The trio, in their films and in personal appearances, always executed dance routines as they sang, which added to their appeal. Universal Pictures, in their famous uncooperative fashion, would not permit the sisters to learn the dance routines on company time, and so every night during the filming of *Buck Privates*, the girls would meet with choreographer Nick Castle to learn and practice their steps. Castle worked with the girls during each of their three films with Abbott and Costello, and his staging displayed the sisters to their best advantage.

As a result of the monetary gains pouring in from *Buck Privates*, Universal was eager to start production of a second project for Abbott and Costello and the Andrews Sisters. Filming was immediately scheduled for *In the Navy*, a sequel to *Buck Privates*.

The studio executives, however, did not want to lose momentum while filming proceeded, so they decided to first release a film that Abbott and Costello had been rushed through immediately following the production of *Buck Privates*. *Hold That Ghost* was to be released as the duo's second film of 1941. The plot revolved around a supposedly haunted mansion, willed to the boys by a dying gangster. There were no musical numbers in the mystery-comedy. When it was released to selected preview audiences, Universal had comment cards distributed to obtain audience feedback. Each time, the cards all contained variations of one question: "Where are the Andrews Sisters?" Patty remembered, "We made two films with the boys, *Buck Privates* and *In the Navy*. But for the third film, *Hold That Ghost*, the producers got a lot of resentment that we were originally excluded. Then they called us in from New York, and they stuck us in at the end." A rush was ordered on the production of *In the Navy* while musical sequences were added to *Hold That Ghost*.

In the Navy, like its predecessor, was a perfect vehicle for the antics of Abbott and Costello, and it initially out-grossed *Buck Privates*. When *In the Navy* premiered at Loew's Criterion in Manhattan, over forty-nine thousand people saw the film during the first week of its release. Theater management kept the doors open until five o'clock in the morning to accommodate the huge crowds. In the film, the sisters sing five songs, the best being "Gimme Some Skin, My Friend," part of a nightclub scene. It was the best staged and most entertaining number that the sisters would ever commit to film during their five years at Universal. Another song, "The Oceana Roll," was to be filmed with the trio as a follow-up to "Boogie Woogie Bugle Boy," but the song was deleted from the original production plans. "Hula Ba Luau," the trio's Hawaiian opus in the film, was lavishly filmed on the largest set the studio had ever constructed. The soundstage was built as a replica of the grounds at the Royal Palms Hotel in Honolulu, and the sisters were backed by sixty Hawaiian musicians and singers as well as forty dancers. The sisters also participate in a comic scene with Costello, wherein he dreams he is the captain of a battleship, entertaining the girls in his private quarters. Patty tells him, "You must enjoy your quarters," to which he responds, "Oh, money means nothing to me!" Costello and the trio are then tossed about the cabin as the ship takes a frantic course under Costello's command.

Hold That Ghost was released shortly after *In the Navy*. In it the trio sings "Sleepy Serenade" and "Aurora," the latter nicely filmed with a chorus of men in tuxedos and top hats. "Aurora" also became a Decca hit. The sisters promoted the film with Abbott and Costello at the time of its release, making personal appearances at the Steel Pier in Atlantic City, New Jersey, where the two acts had initially met three years prior. The sisters greatly enjoyed working with the duo, making fast friends with Costello. Maxene related, "Bud, we didn't get to know that well. Bud wasn't too socially inclined." She also said, in a separate interview, that she never knew anyone who wanted or really enjoyed movie stardom more than Lou Costello.

The trio's friendship with the rotund comedian continued over the next few years. Maxene admired Costello for his defense of the underdog, especially when he dealt with the difficult studio executives. She recalled,

> Universal was a terrible studio at that time. The executives running the studio would do anything they could to keep you from making demands. Lou caught on to this early. If there was something he wanted, he knew he'd have to fight for it—and he did. God bless him for that. He didn't do it to be difficult or hotheaded, and he didn't fight only for himself—he fought for everybody involved in the Abbott and Costello film. Lou never fought over anything in front of people either. If he had a beef with the studio, he brought in Eddie Sherman and they'd go to the front office together. That's where he made his demands.

One of Costello's favorite pastimes during a break in filming was organizing a poker game in his dressing room. Milton Krasner, one of the cameramen on *Buck Privates*, remembered, "I used to watch them play poker between takes. The stakes were often very high. If they were really into a game and didn't want to stop, they'd pay the assistant director not to call them back on the set until they'd finished the hand." Patty concurred, as she told Abbott and Costello biographers Stephen Cox and John Lofflin, "Bud and Lou always gambled. They had a place on the set just to gamble. They just played cards all the time." Maxene also recalled the matches, "The boys would play with their friends, Mike Poston and Alex Gottlieb. They had wild games. My eyes were open so wide at the amount of money on that table. It was nothing to play thirty, forty and even fifty thousand dollars a hand. These poker games went on practically every day we worked."

The trio was now living in California in a split-level home. LaVerne lived upstairs with her parents while Patty and Maxene shared the ground floor. Although all three sisters were close, Patty and Maxene often paired off without LaVerne when not performing or appearing as a trio. Five years separated LaVerne from Maxene, while Patty was only two years younger than Maxene. LaVerne was also much more of a homebody than either of her sisters, content to stay home and read or keep their parents company while her sisters went out shopping or to nightclubs. The entire Andrews family was often invited to Lou Costello's home for barbecues. Costello was the perfect host to the trio, and he admired the fact that the sisters' parents lived and traveled with them. Peter, Olga, and the girls were quite fond of Costello and his wife Ann. Maxene has referred to Costello as a great family man who was jovial and fun to be with; she recalled, "We were quite close to Ann and the kids. We'd go over to their home on many weekends. None of us could afford a swimming pool, so we'd use theirs. Oh, and the good food they would put out for us! When you get around Italian families, honey, mostly they're full of love, they're very tactile, and they love to feed you." Patty said Costello's wife Ann was "just a lovebug."

When Costello was bedridden with rheumatic fever in 1943, the girls visited him on weekends. Together they would watch films in his home theater, which had been specially constructed by the studio executives. Universal had a vested interest in their most popular comedian and wanted to make his months of recuperation as comfortable as possible, as well as to get him back on the lot as soon as possible. Maxene recalled her feelings upon seeing Costello, usually so energetic and full of life, being wheeled from room to room in a movable bed: "Here's a man with all of this ambition and energy and desire, and who's at the threshold of probably his greatest success in movies, flat on his back for about a year. One time, while I sat and just observed him, I thought, what a tragedy! We were watching some movie in the little theater in his house. And here was this little funny man laid up like this. I really had tremendous affection for that man."

Immediately after Costello recovered from his long illness, tragedy struck. His infant son had somehow climbed out of his playpen in the backyard one afternoon and drowned in the family swimming pool. Costello was beside himself with grief. Lou Jr. was more precious to the comedian than any degree of fame or Hollywood trappings, as his friends knew. Maxene said that Costello's illness, coupled with the loss of his only son, greatly affected his personality.

> We began to stop calling because we thought we might be bothering Lou. He didn't seem to be as fun-loving and as warm. I think it was just a conglomeration of things that contributed to his change in behavior. He seemed to anger easily, but he was certainly nothing like the character he was portrayed to be in the [TV] movie of the week, *Bud and Lou*. He was very generous in loaning us films from his library, but it got to the point where I'd drive over to his home and the place would be overrun with strangers—people everywhere. I'd wait until someone brought me the film and then I'd leave. Lou was not as attentive as he had been before. Maybe having the crowds of people around helped him forget the pain he felt—or maybe it was just that we had all gone our separate ways. But there was a difference in his attitude."

Regarding Costello's personality, Patty also remembered, "Lou had a dominating type of personality. And Bud was the second banana, as far as Lou was concerned. They were not like their on-screen personas at all."

Maxene became Mrs. Lou Levy on July 28, 1941. The couple had continued dating even after Peter voiced his disapproval a year earlier. Maxene and Levy secretly eloped to Elkton, Maryland, for a quick ceremony. The only other person who knew of the marriage was Patty, in whom the couple confided; but LaVerne, the trio's parents, and even the press remained clueless for nearly two years. The honeymoon to Mexico was put on hold until May of 1943, when the couple announced their union. They began living together shortly thereafter.

Between their hectic filming schedules with Abbott and Costello, the trio made time for appearances in Omaha, Chicago, Pittsburgh, and Cleveland, as well as at the Paramount in New York, with Ina Ray Hutton and her all-girl orchestra and with Johnny Long and his band. During the first week of their appearances with Long, the sisters drew an impressive sixty-six thousand dollars. During the second day of that engagement, Patty was forced to solo through two shows when doctors forbade Maxene and LaVerne from performing, due to heavy colds, high fevers, and grippe. The following day, five shows were cut to four, enabling all three sisters to work while a nurse was stationed backstage. Maxene remembered the effect sickness could have on the act, "One of our constant fears was illness. Our tours were often long and fatigue often set in. We wanted to say yes to every request, but we always had to remain aware of our health. We couldn't afford to get rundown and then catch a cold or the flu. If one of the three of us got sick, it would be disaster. People didn't want to see two of the Andrews Sisters. They wanted to see all three."

It was around late 1941 that Maxene, Patty, and LaVerne discovered that a pair of dancing sisters, whose last name also happened to be Andrews, was billing themselves as "The Andrews Sisters." This was particularly confusing when the name of the act appeared in print and on theater marquees. The singing sisters took the dancing sisters to court, and a judge ruled that since Maxene, Patty, and LaVerne were already established star personalities, the dancing team would have to change the name of their act to avoid any public misconceptions.

Hit records by the trio continued to accumulate, including a great arrangement of Sammy Kaye's hit "Daddy," featuring some clever lead and back-up parts during Patty's solo; a parody of Al Jolson's once sacred classic, "Sonny Boy," during which Patty spoke, assuming the voice of a child; a cover of Glenn Miller's "Chattanooga Choo Choo"; and "The Shrine of Saint Cecilia," a lovely wartime ballad set in a bombed-out village.

America became deeply embroiled in the World War II at the end of 1941. The Draft Bill had just been passed in the middle of the previous year, no doubt fueling the enormous success of *Buck Privates*. The girls felt the war on a personal level, as Maxene explained: "One of the effects of the war was that the school systems in Greece were suffering from a lack of educational materials. Because of our Greek heritage, the three of us began sending school supplies to Papa's native land to help the children continue their educations. Mama's side was affected, too. She had relations in Norway who were living under Nazi occupation. As the days and weeks unfolded, it was soon clear that 1941 would be a year crowded with major events for all of us." Major events included the bombing of Pearl Harbor, as Maxene remembered,

This is a uniquely American story, one that started for the Andrews Sisters on a cold December Sunday in Cincinnati, Ohio, when I noticed something different when LaVerne, Patty, and I arrived at the Shubert Theater. The sidewalk was empty. From a vantage point of fifty years, it's clear to see that the absence of a line in front of the theater that day was symbolic. We went inside and started down the center aisle toward the stage. The theater was dark. As we walked farther down the aisle, we could see that the doorman and the stagehands were gathered in a small cluster on the stage, huddled around a small table model radio. There was only a bare light bulb illuminating that one small spot on center stage. When we came within hearing distance, a radio announcer told LaVerne, Patty, and me what the workers on the stage already knew: Pearl Harbor, a place we'd never heard of, had been attacked. Suddenly, the empty sidewalk outside the theater symbolized a stark reality: the world was different now and would be for the rest of our lives.

Lou Levy was now billing the group as "The Andrews Sisters— the trio that makes records and breaks records." Within four years, the girls had sold over eight million records, and personal appearances were very rewarding. During one twelve-month period, the trio headlined at fourteen theaters; at each house they broke previous attendance records and topped the house average by as much as twenty thousand dollars. The trio, with even greater success awaiting them, was rising to heights of popularity unattained by any other female vocal group in show business history.

I wanted to be an Andrews sister. My wish was that they could become a quartet and I'd be the fourth singer.
—June Allyson, 1993

4

Three of a Kind

With the arrival of 1942, the Andrews Sisters found themselves well-established recording artists, successful radio and movie personalities, and the most profitable stage attraction throughout the entire nation. Perhaps the most comical acknowledgment of the trio's popularity is in the Samuel Goldwyn film *They Got Me Covered*. The picture's star, Bob Hope, unknowingly drugged by villainess Lenore Aubert, begins to see the actress's image in triplicate. Impudently, he exclaims, "Wait a minute. I know who you are. You're the Andrews Sisters!"

The sisters were now Universal's biggest singing attraction after operatic star Deanna Durbin, and the studio cast the trio with Harry James and his orchestra in a film called *Private Buckaroo*. Although the film did well at the box office, it was deservedly panned by critics, who recognized an unimaginative script, the stale comic antics of Joe E. Lewis and Stooge Shemp Howard (this duo was a far cry from the talents of Abbott and Costello), and the ham acting of Dick Foran. Strangely, this film is shown more often today on television than any other Andrews Sisters film, and it is also available on video. The film's only saving grace—although the critics found fault with this as well—was its musical score, which included the trio's "Three Little Sisters" and "Don't Sit under the Apple Tree (With Anyone Else but Me)," the latter of which became an Andrews

Sisters standard, popularized shortly before the film's release by the Glenn Miller orchestra. It became one of the biggest hits of World War II.

The sisters transcended musical gender boundaries in "Don't Sit under the Apple Tree," just as they had with their 1940 recording of "I'll Be with You in Apple Blossom Time," another male narrative sung by a female trio. Some biographers of Frank Sinatra have credited Old Blue Eyes with making this leap first with his recording of "Saturday Night Is the Loneliest Night of the Week" in 1945, five years later. Sinatra's song laments the loneliness of a girl whose soldier boy went off to fight the war. The lyrics are written from a female point of view, yet the public accepted the musical story from a male vocalist. The Andrews Sisters similarly presented male lyrics in a female voice in "Don't Sit under the Apple Tree" (1942) and "The Blond Sailor" (1945).

Two more Andrews Sisters films were produced in 1942. The first, *What's Cookin'?*, featured the trio with Woody Herman's orchestra and a group of young studio contract players, including Gloria Jean, Donald O'Connor, and Peggy Ryan, in a plot concerning the plights of a bunch of starstruck kids hoping to hit the big time. *Give Out, Sisters,* a nicely tailored vehicle for the trio (which deserves to be available on video, as well as several more of the trio's films) featured the trio as nightclub entertainers trying to further the career of a young dancer, and the film produced the smash hit "Pennsylvania Polka." The song could not fail, considering much of the nation's love affair with polkas. The trio's lively delivery of the tune included some fun scatting by Patty and the great catch phrase that the girls sang at the top of their lungs, "Everybody has a mania to do the polka from Pennsylvania." Maxene once claimed, "Polkas fit our style of singing perfectly because of our upbeat, almost aggressive way of belting out our repertoire."

The trio was turning out more hit material on Decca Records, including "When Johnny Comes Marching Home," a swing adaption of the Civil War standard; "Mister Five by Five," based on portly Jimmy Rushing, a blues belter with Count Basie's orchestra; a knockout rendition of "Massachusetts"; and "Here Comes the Navy," a patriotic ditty adapted to the melody and arrangement of "Beer

Barrel Polka." One of the trio's biggest hits of the year was an amusing rendition of Johnny Mercer's "Strip Polka," which the censors concluded was too racy for inclusion on radio's *Your Hit Parade* series. The trio's version climbed to number-six on *Billboard*'s top-ten charts, and the magazine said the following of its debut: "While there have been many earlier entries, and many more will be coming along later, the Andrews twist to the tune is in a class by itself. Nothing offensive about the lyrics, though it is doubtful whether the network radio executives will let it pass by because of its theme. Moreover, the Andrews gals wisely shun any innuendos or resort to double entendre inflections to spice the side. They make it stand up by itself, and big enough, with their stellar rhythm singing."

Due to a musicians' strike beginning in August 1942, the sisters recorded only one song, the lovely ballad "There Are Such Things," over the following one-year period. The song was popularized by Frank Sinatra, assisted by the Pied Pipers with Jo Stafford, and backed by Tommy Dorsey's orchestra. The sisters often included it in their concert format, but the Decca recording was never released. When the recording ban was lifted, the sisters and Bing Crosby were in the studio nine days later, their first collaboration since 1939. The girls arrived at the Los Angeles studios following a day of filming at Universal, still in full make-up, while Crosby arrived straight from the golf course—pipe in mouth, hat on head, ready to record. This nighttime session was unusual for Crosby, who preferred early morning sessions, feeling that his voice was at its fullest in the morning (this to the dismay of LaVerne, who liked to sleep in).

The group completed the session in ninety minutes, and a million-selling record was born. Several photographers were on hand to record the event as Crosby and the trio rehearsed and kidded each other, as well as Vic Schoen and Jack Kapp. After several takes, final masters of "Pistol Packin' Mama" and "The Vict'ry Polka" were completed, resulting in the first of four million-selling collaborations between Crosby and the trio. The quartet's version of Al Dexter's "Pistol Packin' Mama" held positions on *Billboard*'s top-ten charts for nine weeks, climbing as high as number two. Sheet music copies of the song, featuring a photo of Crosby and the girls taken during the session, also sold over a million copies. Maxene recalled that session,

> The first record after the strike was with Bing, backed by Vic Schoen's band. It was called "Pistol Packin' Mama." The song didn't have anything to do with the war. It came from a story about a woman who owned a honky-tonk joint and whose husband operated a whiskey still in the mountains of Kentucky. A songwriter, Al Dexter, met the woman on his travels and learned that she carried a pistol for protection from both the moonshiners and the revenuers. She told Dexter that at night she'd go looking for her husband in the hills, hollering his name into the dark. "Lay that pistol down, Ma, or I ain't comin'," she said he'd call back. The woman asked Dexter to write a song about it. He did, but that's not the end of the story. He wasn't convinced that the song had much potential, so he recorded it as the "B" side—the "flip" side—of a record with another one of his songs called "Rosalita," on the "A" side. "Pistol Packin' Mama" sold over a million copies for us."

Crosby and the sisters proved to be a surefire combination still, after not having recorded together in four years.

There was a definite camaraderie between both acts; Vic Schoen once discussed the way in which Patty and Crosby worked together during many of their carefree solo spots: "I used to write parts for them, even though they couldn't read it, but they could read the words, of course, and those things that one would call improvisations were actually written for her and the same with Crosby, except he would take what I wrote and enlarge on it most of the time. The magic thing that happens there is that he took what I wrote for him and added himself to it. Sometimes it wasn't even what I had written for him, but what I had written gave him another idea." One of those improvisations can be heard in "Pistol

Packin' Mama" as Crosby quips in baritone, "Lay that thing down before it goes off and hurts somebody." Listening closely, one can hear the trio coming out of a laugh when they follow shortly thereafter with the chorus. Crosby succeeded in actually cracking up the girls in the group's recording of "A Hundred and Sixty Acres." Everyone decided to leave the laugh in the recording instead of doing another take.

Two days following the "Pistol Packin' Mama" session, Crosby joined the trio for another Decca encounter that produced "Santa Claus Is Coming to Town" and "Jingle Bells" (originally titled "The One Horse Open Sleigh" when it was written in the 1850s, but now given swing treatment in an arrangement by Vic Schoen and Patty). The record sold one million copies upon its release. Sales of the disc in its original and re-released forms now total over ten million. When Crosby threw the now famous line "Oh, we'll have a lot of fun!" into his duet segment with Patty during the song's first take, Patty started laughing and lost her place. She was prepared for the quip in the final released take.

Several other male vocalists over the years have collaborated with sister acts in hopes of matching the success of Bing Crosby and the Andrews Sisters. Throughout the 1940s, bandleader Vaughn Monroe teamed with his resident girl trio, the Norton Sisters, for several hit recordings, including "There! I've Said It Again" as well as a cover of the Andrews Sisters' hit "Rum and Coca Cola." During the late 1940s and the early 1950s, Perry Como joined the Fontane Sisters during their pre-rock-n-roll years for several best-selling records, including "A, You're Adorable (The Alphabet Song)" and "A Dreamer's Holiday." Como also sang with the Dinning Sisters on radio during the 1940s. These collaborations of artists in the 1940s and 1950s could not compare to the astounding success of Crosby and the Andrews Sisters, who placed twenty-three of their forty-seven recordings together in the top-thirty charts (excluding three duets by Patty and Crosby).

The Andrews Sisters starred in three Hollywood musicals for Universal in 1943. The first, *How's About It?*, featured the girls as a trio of elevator operators in a music publishing building, hoping to be discovered. The second, *Always a Bridesmaid,* cast the girls as nightclub hostesses. The third, *Swingtime Johnny*, found them working in a munitions factory, joining thousands of women across the country who were doing their part to help win the war. The film offered one or two entertaining segments, one being the trio's vocalization of "Boogie Woogie Choo Choo." Just prior to the finale of *Swingtime Johnny*, a scene featured the trio as mother (Maxene), daughter (Patty), and granddaughter (LaVerne—dressed in an oversized baby bonnet and seated in a huge high chair). This segment, as well as "Six Jerks in a Jeep" from *Private Buckaroo*, best illustrates how the executives at Universal Pictures misused the talents of the Andrews Sisters. The scene from *Swingtime Johnny* was a feeble attempt to copy "The Sidewalks of New York" segment from MGM's Judy Garland-Mickey Rooney hit *Strike Up the Band*. Universal, however, did not have the immense sets, talented supporting players, or witty screenplay writers to make the trio's segment as funny and entertaining as the Garland-Rooney flick four years earlier. The scene exemplifies the girls' frustration with Universal, and their resulting eagerness to be done with the contract.

The trio headlined at the Paramount with Mitchell Ayres and his orchestra during the summer months of 1943, drawing nearly a half million dollars during a six-week engagement. The trio then became series regulars on CBS's *The Roma Wines Show,* starring actress Mary Astor (*The Maltese Falcon, Meet Me in St. Louis*). The show was aired every Thursday night, and the girls were featured regulars for eight weeks, singing hits such as "Pistol Packin' Mama" and "Bei Mir Bist Du Schon." The trio's last record release of the year was "Shoo Shoo Baby," which made *Billboard*'s top-ten list for sixteen consecutive weeks, backed by a sweet and sophisticated arrangement of the folk classic "Down in the Valley." The disc sold over five hundred thousand copies, adding to the trio's phenomenal record sales, which now totaled over twelve million.

*The Andrews Sisters have managed to pick up
a potent style of delivery that wows the listeners
—sends every tune they warble sliding right into
the groove. What makes these three jukebox royalty is
fundamentally their own. They have a zest, a kind of
earthy gusto that gets under the skin of John Doe or
GI Joe, makes him relax and feel good. The girls
like to sing, like the people they're singing to,
and that genuineness gets across.*
—Disc, August 1946

5

Voices of an Era

The mid 1940s proved to be the Andrews Sisters' most popular and lucrative years. The girls were earning twenty thousand dollars a week from concert appearances, not to mention payments and royalties from recordings, radio appearances, and film commitments, and they spent their hard-earned thousands with enthusiasm.

The trio had a costly one-acre, well-landscaped suburban estate built for their parents and themselves in the Brentwood section of Hollywood. Maxene and Lou Levy opted for their own home in the Hollywood hills, not far from the Brentwood estate. The Levys also purchased a ranch on Cold Water Canyon in the San Fernando Valley. Patty, LaVerne, Peter, and Olga found themselves neighbors of such Hollywood stars as Gary Cooper, Tyrone Power, Deanna Durbin, Nelson Eddy, and Cesar Romero. The girls would often bump into their famous neighbors on the street while walking their dogs at night.

The sisters collected dogs. Maxene opened a kennel in California in the mid-1940s that housed as many as seventy-five boxers, Dobermans, and cocker spaniels. She even entered some of the dogs in shows. Maxene was an all-around animal lover, keeping two hundred chickens, two calves, and four cows on the ranch. She remembered, "The farm animals were a wartime necessity. There was a shortage of dairy products, so Lou and I decided to produce our own milk, cream, and butter. Through an interview with the *Minneapolis Star Journal,* I told our friends and neighbors back home, 'Now our parents get three quarts of cream a week, the dogs get skimmed milk, we have a barnyard, and everybody's happy.'"

One of the trio's favorite pooches was a prized Doberman they called Danny Boy. Maxene also favored a tiny black cocker spaniel named Tyrone, after her sisters' neighbor Tyrone Power. She remembered how the dog seemed to understand what people said to him. She recalled one night during the war in particular, when the trio was playing at the Hippodrome Theater in Baltimore, Maryland:

> During our shows, Tyrone would sit obediently and
> patiently offstage, waiting in the wings for me to come
> off. Except for that night in Baltimore. Tyrone got
> tired of waiting, or of our act, and walked onto the
> stage. After we finished our number and before we
> went into our next one, the three of us just stood
> there looking at him—and he sat there, head cocked
> and tail wagging, looking at us. Finally, Patty put her
> hands on her hips and said to Tyrone for the first time
> in his life, "Now what would you do if Der Fuehrer
> walked in here right now?" That little thing got right
> up from where he was sitting, in the middle of the
> stage, walked to the front, straight to the floor micro-
> phone, lifted his leg and wet the base of the mike. The
> applause was deafening.

Of course, a favorite pastime for the sisters was listening to music. Maxene's interests were with classical music, and her home housed an extensive collection of classical records. Patty was a devoted swing and jazz fan and loved to catch Nat King Cole in concert whenever she could. LaVerne enjoyed listening to and singing any and all types of music, though her heart really belonged to Crosby and Sinatra.

There were no servants at the Brentwood estate. Patty and LaVerne handled the housekeeping, while their parents tended to the cooking, which was no small feat. All three sisters had tremendous appetites. LaVerne once admitted to a reporter that she ate as many as six full meals a day and ate candy by the pound. Patty and LaVerne both decorated their bedrooms lavishly. Patty's room was filled with large, embroidered satin spreads, china lamps, glass tables, ceramic elephants, and a porcelain doll collection. LaVerne's room was even more elaborate. The dressing tables held more than one hundred perfume bottles of various shapes and sizes, as well as a collection of miniature glass animals—mostly cats. Also in LaVerne's room was a one-of-a-kind Hollywood possession—a perfectly round bed, measuring seven feet in diameter, that had marble steps leading up to the mattress. The bed was specially built against a wall of mirrors and cost fifteen hundred dollars to construct.

Unlike her sisters, who sometimes frequented Hollywood's popular nightspots, LaVerne was a homebody. She also possessed a huge wardrobe, and was repeatedly voted one of the ten best-dressed women in Hollywood during the 1940s. She was rather partial to fur, owning eight fur coats (which the three would sometimes wear to film premieres) and one mink stole. Several of the trio's cousins, who had followed the girls to Hollywood, were their closest friends, and they inherited much of the trio's wardrobe. The trio also loved jewelry (LaVerne's arms were usually covered with bracelets), especially diamonds, which they used as part of their professional wardrobe. The girls would also joke that the diamonds were "hockable," in case of an emergency. Another of LaVerne's hobbies was ice hockey. A devoted fan, she presented the winning team of the 1946 season with their championship cup.

Decca Records released eight new singles by the trio in 1944. Six of the discs became bestsellers, one went gold, and the other reached platinum status. Every one of the trio's releases that year became a hit, climbing the charts, dominating jukeboxes, and providing huge sums in royalties (the trio received the standard two cents on each disc sold, subtracted from the record's thirty-five-cent purchase price). Among the bestsellers were "Tico Tico," a vocalization of the frantic Brazilian melody; "Corns for My Country," a swing novelty that lamented the disadvantages of dancing with servicemen at the Hollywood Canteen; "Sing a Tropical Song," in which the girls adopted an effective Jamaican accent, promoting a calypso craze to sweep the music industry long before Harry Belafonte sang his "Banana Boat Song"; and two hits with Bing Crosby: "Is You Is or Is You Ain't (Ma' Baby?)," which sold over a half million copies during the first ten days of its release, and "Accent-tchu-ate the Positive," both of which became top-ten hits. Backing "Is You Is" was a swinging and patriotic "There'll Be a Hot Time in the Town of Berlin (When the Yanks Go Marching In)," which Frank Sinatra introduced on his CBS radio show. Crosby and the trio's Decca recording of the song shot to number one on the *Billboard* charts and held the position for six weeks.

The trio's gold record of the year resulted from another teaming with Crosby. When Crosby arrived at the studio, he was unfamiliar with "Don't Fence Me In," the trio's choice for the A side of the disc. Patty taught the trio's arrangement of the Cole Porter composition to him in thirty minutes, and it was recorded in two takes (during the first take, Crosby lost his place following Patty's solo and embarked on his own musical journey, causing the sisters to break up in laughter). "The Three Caballeros," from the Walt Disney film of the same name, was recorded as the B side. The record sold over one million copies, the quartet's third gold platter in less than twelve months.

Although "Don't Fence Me In" was written by Porter in 1933 as a satirical view of the West (even during its immense popularity, Porter would jokingly refer to the song as "that old thing"), Crosby and the girls recorded it in a simple, straightforward manner with a sophisticated Vic Schoen arrangement. Other artists, including Roy Rogers, gave the melody a definite western bounce. The song became another number-one *Billboard* hit for the group, and it remained in the top-ten for seventeen weeks. The quartet's version of the song, now considered to be a Cole Porter standard, is probably the best-remembered and most recognized tune of the Crosby-Andrews association. Cole Porter biographer Charles Schwartz writes, "'Don't Fence Me In' had almost instant appeal. At a time when Adolf Hitler and Nazi Germany were threatening the existence of the free world, the song had a reassuring ring to it, epitomizing as it did all that was American, pure, and rural."

The sisters found themselves in New York City in the fall recording two songs for Decca—"I'm in a Jam (With Baby)" and "One Meat Ball." Only thirty minutes remained of the session when the girls decided to record a calypso number called "Rum and Coca Cola." Patty recalls that last-minute decision: "We had a recording date, and the song was brought to us the night before the recording date. We hardly really knew it, and when we went in we had some extra time and we just threw it in, and that was the miracle of it. It was actually a faked arrangement. There was no written background, so we just kind of faked it." The song had clever lyrics, written by veteran comedian Morey Amsterdam, who would find his greatest fame on television playing writer Buddy Sorrell on *The Dick Van Dyke Show* years later. The girls astutely used the same accent that had worked so well for them in their hit "Sing a Tropical Song."

"Rum and Coca Cola" was recorded in less than ten minutes and sold a whopping seven million copies. Demand for the disc was so great that Decca had to borrow shellac (in short supply during the war) from other record companies in order to press the number of records needed for public demand. The trio's recording captured *Billboard*'s number-one spot for seven weeks and prompted other calypso-flavored hits such as "Stone Cold Dead in the Market" and "Come with Me, My Honey." Patty has often referred to "Rum and Coca Cola" as her favorite Andrews Sisters recording. Although it turned out to be one of the trio's biggest hits (it became the third best-selling record of the decade, following Crosby's "White Christmas" and Patti Page's "Tennessee Waltz"), it also proved to be one of the most troublesome.

A lawsuit claimed that the tune's melody was a copy of an old calypso ditty written years earlier in Trinidad. Shortly thereafter, a court ruling declared that the number was indeed based on the 1906 "L'Année Passée," written by Lionel Belasco and Massie Patterson.

The original publisher of the song, Maurice Baron, agreed to a financial settlement, waiving the right to any future royalties. Furthermore, network radio shied away from the song because it mentioned an alcoholic beverage. Patty recalled, "It was restricted because of the word rum. You couldn't advertise liquor on the air." Sales of the disc were even banned in some cities throughout the country because of the lyrics, which suggested that American servicemen were celebrating their leaves soliciting nighttime services from the women of Trinidad. The song's lyrics were a bit suggestive for the time and did not sit well with many flag-waving patriots. The song nevertheless survived all the opposition and remains one of the best-remembered songs of World War II.

Maxene explained the sisters' take on the song: "The rhythm was what attracted the Andrews Sisters to 'Rum and Coca Cola.' We never thought of the lyric. The lyric was there, it was cute, but we didn't think of what it meant; but at that time, nobody else would think of it either, because we weren't as morally open as we are today and so, a lot of stuff—really—no excuses—just went over our heads." The following story from *Billboard* magazine, concerning a Phoenix, Arizona, eatery, demonstrates the popularity of the song, as well as the Andrews Sisters, at the time of the record's release: "Because the waitresses and other employees got 'tired of hearing it played for eight straight hours,' the leading jukebox tune—'Rum and Coca Cola' with the Andrews Sisters—has been taken off the record list at Bacon's Grille here. Employees said they liked to hear the tune once in a while, but declared that 'all the time is too much.' Now getting top play at the twenty-four-hour grille are 'Don't Fence Me In' with Bing Crosby and the Andrews Sisters and 'Ac-cent-tchu-ate the Positive' with Bing Crosby and the Andrews Sisters."

Remarkably, the trio held three positions on *Billboard's* top-ten charts for seven consecutive weeks during this period, with "Rum and Coca Cola" (#1), "Don't Fence Me In" (#2), and "Ac-cent-tchu-ate the Positive" (#4). The girls were the only vocal group of the 1940s to hold three simultaneous positions on the top-ten charts for new releases. Bing Crosby and the Andrews Sisters, separately and jointly, dominated the recording industry of the 1940s. The trio followed their recording success with a month-long engagement at the Paramount in New York with Mitchell Ayres' band. The sisters drew in more than ninety-four thousand dollars during the first week of shows, singing "Lullaby of Broadway," "Is You Is or Is You Ain't (Ma' Baby?)," "Corns for My Country," "Down in the Valley," and a medley of hits. Screaming fans heard encores of "There'll Be a Hot Time in the Town of Berlin (When the Yanks Go Marching In)," an appropriate crowd-pleaser with its patriotic lyrics, swinging rhythms, and thunderous orchestral arrangement.

Three films soon surfaced. *Follow the Boys* was a surprisingly well-scripted and entertaining first-rate production from Universal. It featured an all-star cast, including George Raft, Marlene Dietrich, Orson Welles, Dinah Shore, and Sophie Tucker, doing their best for the war effort. The trio was featured singing a medley of hits and a brief rendition of "Shoo Shoo Baby" toward the end of the film. The girls were next loaned out to Warner Brothers by Universal to appear in *Hollywood Canteen,* another all-star production featuring Bette Davis, John Garfield, Joan Crawford, and Joan Leslie to entertain the boys, as well as the home front. The girls could be heard singing the title song as the opening credits rolled, and they appeared singing "Corns for My Country" and "Don't Fence Me In." "Don't Fence Me In" was also sung by Roy Rogers and the Sons of the Pioneers in the same film. The girls took a comical spin while singing "Corns for My Country," as Patty clowned a bit and even did her Katharine Hepburn impersonation. The girls performed some light dance steps during the number, but the small area of the platform stage on which they were singing limited further performance. Although working for the elite Warner Brothers studio, which operated on a grander scale than Universal, the sisters still did not appear as pretty on screen as they were in person, and their costumes in *Hollywood Canteen* were not very complimentary, although as they danced, one could get an eyeful of Maxene's legs through the generous slit in her skirt. It was a reflection of the trio's immense popularity at this time, as well as how respected they had become in the entertainment world of the 1940s, to be sought after and included in such extravagant Hollywood productions with the major stars of the period. The trio was even asked to sing the theme song of the star-studded film, "Hollywood Canteen." The girls were soon and unfortunately back at Universal for another mediocre project, *Moonlight and Cactus,* in which the trio sang a total of six songs, including the amusing novelty "Send Me a Man, Amen!"

The trio's record sales had reached mind-boggling proportions. By the end of 1944, they had sold over thirty million Decca singles, making them the best-selling female vocal group in show business history. This was achieved at a time when the record-buying public was only a fraction of what it is today, and when phonographs were considered a bit of a luxury, unlike the household necessities stereos have since become. Nash automobiles and Kelvinator home appliances sponsored the trio in *The Andrews Sisters Show,* which debuted on New Year's Eve, 1944, on the Blue network (soon to become ABC). The pilot aired a week earlier and featured Frank Sinatra as the first guest star, as well as "Wild" Bill Elliott.

The plot of the series revolved around a dude ranch that the girls had inherited from their uncle. It co-starred ranch hand George "Gabby" Hayes, best remembered for his appearances in many westerns with John Wayne and Roy Rogers. Gabby would trade insults with a different guest star each week, Bing Crosby being the first to suffer his wrath during the New Year's Eve broadcast. Also on hand weekly were Foy Willing and the Riders of the Purple Sage, a country-western group in the tradition of the Sons of the Pioneers. Dewey "Alamo" Markham joined the cast as Alamo, the cook, as the weeks progressed, and Marvin Miller announced. Vic Schoen and his orchestra supplied the musical backing. Many guest stars paid visits during the show's run, among them Eddie Cantor, Groucho Marx, Bob Hope, Rudy Vallee, Peter Lorre and Sydney Greenstreet, Marjorie Main, Lum and Abner, Carmen Miranda, and Abbott and Costello.

In addition to the pilot, Frank Sinatra appeared in a more memorable episode on March 4, 1945. In it he arrived to help the trio round up some ruthless cattle rustlers, and his slight build provoked some humorous teasing from Gabby:

Maxene: "Hi-ya, Frankie, What'd'ya say?"
Frank: "I'm wild and woolly and full of fleas and I ain't been curried below the knees."

Gabby: "Yeah? You're pale and weak as I've ever seen. You
  got lots o' color, but who likes green?"
Patty: "Quiet down, Gabby. Frankie, this is our ranch
  foreman, Gabby Hayes."
Gabby: "Hi-ya, Frankie!"
Frankie: "Hi-ya, cranky!"
Patty: "Frankie, you know Maxene, of course, and this is
  our other sister, LaVerne. She's one of your most ardent
  fans. Say, LaVerne, say something to Frankie."
LaVerne: "Tell me, are you really Bing Crosby's son?"
Maxene: "LaVerne! How can you say that after you voted
  Frankie the best actor, the best dancer, the best come-
  dian, the best orchestra leader of the year?!"
Frank: "What about my singin', ma'am?"
LaVerne: "Oh! Do you sing, too?"
Frank: "I just didn't know I was this far out west, but let
  me at these rustlers. Do you see this sheriff's badge on
  my chest?"
Gabby: "Where is it?"
Frank: "My badge?"
Gabby: "No, your chest."

LaVerne assumed the part of the dizzy, somewhat off-the-wall
sister in the series, a part she played to the hilt. Her deadpan delivery in the most dim-witted of tones easily made her the audience
favorite. LaVerne was also a good sport when the dialogue included
unflattering remarks about her looks, which it often did. When Bob
Hope visited, LaVerne drew a tremendous laugh from the studio
audience when she mused, "I like Bob Hope. He asked me to go to
Alaska with him on an expedition." "Why, isn't that just thrilling!"
remarked Maxene. "Yes!" LaVerne replied, then asked inquisitively,
"Uh, what's a lead dog?"
  One of the series' best song finales was a beautiful rendition
of the cowboy classic "Empty Saddles," featuring the trio with
Sinatra and the Riders of the Purple Sage. The girls blended well
with Sinatra, taking on a much different musical quality than they
did with Crosby. It is unfortunate that label jumping, so common

in today's music industry, was not practiced much, if at all, during the 1940s. Although there was enough of a variety of artists on the Decca label to repeatedly team the sisters with over the years, a collaboration between the Andrews Sisters and Frank Sinatra would have undoubtedly resulted in several hit records, if based on nothing else but the great audience response when Sinatra sang with them on radio and television. A joint appearance at New York's Paramount would also have been extremely well received, considering how popular both acts were at the theater during repeated separate engagements there, this being the period before Sinatra progressed into the saloon singer and icon of popular music that he was to become in the 1950s. He collaborated with various artists during the mid-1940s, including the trio, Dinah Shore, and Judy Garland—all of whom he frequently performed with on radio. He did record one Columbia duet with Shore, "My Romance," and the almost surreal tone of the blended vocal demonstrates his skill at collaboration.

When a celebrity appeared on *The Andrews Sisters Show,* also known as *The Eight-to-the-Bar Ranch,* the girls would in turn make an appearance on that star's radio series. They enjoyed trading appearances, and they especially liked working with Groucho Marx. They loved telling reporters of the time when Groucho discovered that he was traveling on the same train as the sisters. Upon hearing the news, he quipped, "I thought they made all their trips by broom!" The girls never let themselves to be taken too seriously; their good-naturedness was refreshing in an industry focused on glamour.

The Andrews Sisters Show was a huge success. It was heard in New York every Sunday afternoon on WJZ radio, and was transmitted to overseas troops via the Armed Forces Radio Service (AFRS). The trio sang many of their hits on the show, as well as other popular tunes of the day, and Patty's solos were substantial crowd-pleasers, judging by audience reaction. The girls enjoyed doing the show each week, but LaVerne was often nervous about fluffing her lines. Every Saturday night, LaVerne relaxed by taking a long hot bath and getting to bed by 8:30 to calm her nerves so she would be alert for Sunday's broadcast.

One memorable show happened on April 12, 1945. Just as America's foes were beginning to lose their battle momentum, President Franklin D. Roosevelt died at 3:35 p.m. in Warm Springs, Georgia, of a massive cerebral hemorrhage, while posing for a portrait. The girls were just about to go on the air with guests Abbott and Costello when they received the sad news. The show's writers quickly penned a moving eulogy for FDR and oddly asked Gabby Hayes, perhaps Roosevelt's most outspoken critic, to deliver the address over the airwaves. Hayes obliged and acted with great emotion and sorrow. This infuriated Maxene, as she felt that Gabby should have refused the assignment due to his political views and personal feelings.

The Andrews Sisters Show was broadcast from Hollywood, and it remained on the air until it went on a two-month hiatus in June of 1945. The girls had a more important commitment to fulfill.

*I remember how well behaved the GIs were while
we were on stage. The boys would come up onto the stage
after we were finished and say things like, "Do you mind
if I kiss you on the cheek?" Or they'd give us a big hug.
But they never, never would leave their seats while we were
performing. After the hell they fought in and survived,
they were still respectful and polite.*
—Maxene Andrews, 1993

6

We've Got a Job to Do

Maxene once claimed that she and her sisters really did no more than any other entertainers of the day as far as personal and professional service toward the effort for victory during World War II. This was a bit of an understatement. The girls got involved as early as 1940, when they appeared as part of an all-star lineup for a Red Cross radio benefit. Maxene recalled,

> LaVerne, Patty, and I sang as part of a two-hour radio show, which was broadcast simultaneously over every Los Angeles station, plus NBC and CBS, from nine to eleven on a Saturday night. The mayor, Fletcher Bowron, proclaimed the day Radio Red Cross Day. Dorothy Lamour, Olivia de Havilland, Patricia Morrison, and others worked as volunteers in selling tickets on the air in advance of the show, hoping to

top our goal of $25,000. The lineup was a Hollywood's Who's-Who: Shirley Temple, Gene Autry, Orson Welles, Charles Laughton, Don Ameche, Kenny Baker, Lum and Abner, Jimmy Cagney, and Edward G. Robinson.

The trio's wartime dedication to America was truly inspiring, mainly because of the girls' heartfelt patriotism for the nation that had awarded them their astounding success. The girls' feelings were encouraged by the patriotism of their parents. Maxene said,

It was a tense and tragic time, but it was an exhilarating time, too—with all of us pulling toward the victory that Americans believed would come one day in the uncertain future. The Andrews Sisters felt the same way. Our parents, in their early fifties, were super patriots that supported the war and FDR with enthusiasm. That rubbed off on LaVerne, Patty, and me, and we were able to project our Americanism to our audiences. The response to our own enthusiasm became so great that the Air Corps crews began naming their fighter planes and bombers after our song titles. All type of planes—C-47s, B-52s, B-17s— had some of our titles painted on their noses, especially "Pistol Packin' Mama" and "Shoo Shoo Baby."

The girls felt that personal efforts on their collective part were in order, and so in many cities during their touring in the early forties they would ask three servicemen to dine with them as their guests for the evening. If business meetings or social commitments prevented the opportunity, the girls often left the cost of three dinners with restaurant management, along with instruction that the first three enlisted men to walk through the door be served as guests of the Andrews Sisters. When the girls performed at army camps and naval bases in California, they often gave as many as six shows a day, and between the shows they would visit nearby USO centers and munitions factories so as not to ignore the women who were aiding the war effort from the home front. Only sixteen months after the bombing of Pearl Harbor, Irving Wallace wrote, "The Andrews Sisters have appeared—in all kinds of weather—before more Army camps, more Navy and Marine and Air Force gatherings than any other trio of singers in the country. They like their pay for these appearances best—an accolade of worship from the boys who don't mean maybe when they call them 'the three jive-bombers.'"

The sisters also volunteered their free time to entertain enlisted men by singing for them and dancing with them, as well as serving food, signing autographs, and just chatting. They could be found at the famous Hollywood Canteen in California, as well as at the Stage Door Canteen in New York City—retreats for servicemen on leave or waiting to be shipped overseas. Stars would report to one of these two locations after a day of recording, filming, or performing to mingle with members of the fighting forces. At the Hollywood Canteen, it was not unusual to find Dinah Shore on stage, Marlene Dietrich greeting visitors at the door, Barbara Stanwyck dishing out soup and sandwiches, or Deanna Durbin making small talk with a far-from-home GI. Servicemen were starstruck. One enlisted man stationed in California in 1944 remembered, "One night, I went with a couple of my buddies to the Hollywood Canteen. It was pretty late, close to midnight. I forget which band was playing on stage—Tommy Dorsey, maybe, but I do remember everybody dancing. All of a sudden, in walked the Andrews Sisters. They got on stage and started singing with the orchestra. Well, everybody on the dance floor stood there mesmerized. All the dancing stopped and all eyes were focused on them. They did a few songs and the place went crazy. They were great."

During the war, the sisters also entertained wounded soldiers in hospitals throughout the country. This was not the easiest volunteer work, yet many female stars—most notably Frances Langford, as well as Judy Garland and others—put their uneasiness aside for the men who sacrificed greatly for their country. During one visit to Oak Knoll Hospital in Oakland, California, the Andrews Sisters asked nurses if they could visit the paraplegic ward. The nurses discouraged the girls, explaining that their emotions might get the better of them and certainly a loss of emotional control would not be of any service to the boys. The girls stood firm, politely explaining that they were there to entertain all the patients, for this was their way of giving something back to the heroic fellows. (Maxene once said, "Every time we visited the GIs, it did as much for our morale as it did for theirs. Their enthusiasm over our performance was matched by the respect they showed us, both here and when we went overseas for the USO.")

After the trio convinced the nurses that they could handle the situation in Oakland, they entered the paraplegic ward. As the nurses had warned, the sisters were a bit shocked upon seeing men missing arms and legs. Initially, the trio had to look slightly over the boys' heads, but once they started talking and singing to their audience, they found the patients responsive and appreciative. The trio then began touring such wards on a regular basis. Maxene told radio talk-show host Joe Franklin that the Andrews Sisters were the first female entertainers allowed to tour such hospital wards.

During another hospital visit, one that Maxene referred to as a sentimental journey, the trio performed at the Snelling Veterans Hospital during a trip back home to Minneapolis. Some of the patients, veterans from World War I and the Spanish-American War, remembered all the way back to 1920, when a four-year-old Maxene Andrews sang for them during a visit to the hospital with her father. This prompted her to think years later that she may have been one of only a handful of entertainers who sang for veterans from the Spanish-American War through Desert Storm. There were many such poignant scenes involving servicemen. Maxene recalled the following scene:

> We went down to the docks during an appearance in Seattle and sang for the boys as their ship pulled away into the Pacific, headed for combat. At the request of military officials supervising the departure, we sang, "Don't Sit under the Apple Tree." The scene is still vivid in my memory. We stood down on the pier, looking up at all those young men leaning over the ship's rails, waving and yelling and screaming. Any time that scene was reenacted, and it was happening

countless times every day in groups large and small all over the country in 1942, one thought nagged at you: How many of the young men shipping out wouldn't come back? I can still see the mothers and sweethearts standing on that dock and singing along with us as the ship sailed away to war.

Literally thousands of performers—famous as well as unknown—joined the Hollywood effort to entertain the troops. Maxene related the following bittersweet story:

A popular singer named Ann Moray was walking through the wards of a field hospital near Anzio as a member of a USO troupe. She was cheering up the wounded victims of that battle, one of the most ferocious engagements of the entire war. She had no musicians to accompany her, so she sang to the troops by herself—"Ave Maria," "I Love You Truly," and other selections that she knew were traditional favorites, even among combat-hardened men. One of the bed-ridden veterans motioned for her to come over to his side. "Will you sing a song for me," the GI asked. "I'm going to die. Will you sing 'Abide with Me' at my funeral?" Ann went out of her way to assure him that she would have to wait many years to honor his request, but he insisted that he was going to die. He asked her again. "Promise. Please." Ann said softly, "I promise." That night the young soldier died. Two days later, Ann Moray stood in the rain next to his freshly dug grave on the beachhead at Anzio and sang:

"Abide With Me, fast falls the eventide
The darkness deepens. Lord, with me abide
When other helpers fail and comforts flee
Help of the helpless—oh, with me abide."

Throughout the war, the trio appeared frequently on many

shows for the Armed Forces Radio Service, which transmitted the programs overseas via short-wave. These shows were tailored specifically to servicemen, and included *Mail Call, GI Journal,* and the most popular series of the time, *Command Performance, U.S.A.* *Command Performance* would gather as many as a dozen top-name celebrities for a single episode, and answer every request written in by servicemen abroad, including such varied wants as Lana Turner frying a porterhouse steak, Errol Flynn showering on mike (requested by a group of soldiers who had been stuck for some length of time in a steamy jungle), and Judy Garland singing "Over the Rainbow." Dinah Shore made the most appearances during the series' run, returning thirty-five times. One memorable show of the series featured the Andrews Sisters, Bing Crosby, Dinah Shore, Bob Hope, Judy Garland, Frank Sinatra, and Jimmy Durante, spoofing the *Dick Tracy* comic strip characters. Another show featured the trio with Crosby and Garland, lampooning *Your Hit Parade* (their version was titled "Your All-Time Flop Parade"). Still another show—an embarrassing one for Maxene—featured the girls with Crosby and Hope. They sang "Rum and Coca Cola," then joined Crosby toward the end of the show for "Don't Fence Me In." As the girls were leaving the stage, Maxene slipped and fell. Patty, in an effort to keep Maxene from falling, grabbed the hem of her sister's skirt and unwittingly pulled the skirt off. Crosby assisted the girls off stage before returning to the mike to comment to Hope, "Everybody takes falls on this show with you on." Hope answered slyly, "Oh, you're a quick hand brother! Thank you Patty, LaVerne, and Maxene. You did a great job. Nice exit."

Another form of entertainment for the troops were V-Discs (Victory Discs). The sisters recorded a series of V-Discs during the war, volunteering their recording services to the War Department's Special Services Division. These twelve-inch records were not released for commercial sale, but were instead shipped overseas to American and other Allied troops. Most of the girls' V-Disc recordings featured new versions of their biggest Decca hits. Other artists who participated in the program were Frank Sinatra, Bing Crosby, Judy Garland, Dick Haymes, Helen Forrest, and the Mills Brothers, as well as nearly all of the big bands.

The sisters, like many other Hollywood stars, participated in war bond rallies and drives, including a 1942 all-star excursion that took them cross-country with Bing Crosby, Bob Hope, Dorothy Lamour, Abbott and Costello, and the Marx Brothers. The train would stop in different towns throughout the trip, and the group would entertain the huge crowds that had gathered for the event. Afterward the stars would mingle with the people and sell war bonds before they boarded the train once again to continue on to another city. This routine was executed often by single stars (most notably Carole Lombard, who lost her life in a plane crash during one such trip), as well as by groups of Hollywood's finest, and the journeys helped raise millions of dollars for the United States government. Following the war, the sisters often volunteered their services in radio showcases for the United State Treasury Department, the American Red Cross, and the American Cancer Society.

At the end of June 1945, the Andrews Sisters embarked on an eight-week overseas tour for the USO, to entertain tens of thousands of fighting servicemen, a trip they had been hoping to make since the war began. Maxene remembered the departure:

> Not long after the great news about V-E Day, we got other great news: The USO wanted us to go overseas. We were going to be soldiers in greasepaint at last. We received a phone call to get to New York as fast as possible. When we asked exactly where we were being sent, the USO told us not to ask. We were met in New York, taken to a hotel and then told to go to Saks Fifth Avenue and pick up our USO uniforms. After that, we were asked to report to an address on New York's West Side to audition. Patty had a quick response to that. She told the USO representative, "The Andrews Sisters don't audition for *anybody!*" and that was that. The subject never came up again. We were driven immediately to Fort Dix, New Jersey. There, in the middle of the night, we were routed out of bed and driven under cover of darkness to LaGuardia Airport, where we boarded an Air Corps plane with its windows covered.

Unbeknownst to the sisters at the time, they were on their way to Italy and Africa. The USO was highly secretive regarding the girls' itinerary, for governmental security reasons. The trio's mother was opposed to their overseas trip for this very reason. Olga was not allowed to accompany her daughters to the point of departure, nor would she know their whereabouts during the course of the trip. Aside from the shroud of secrecy, there were many rules and regulations given to the girls concerning what to do and what not to do while in the company of servicemen. Maxene recalled,

> [We were told] the most important baggage is your stage wardrobe. A GI doesn't want to see you in slacks, and he's not interested in your uniform. He wants to see you like the girls back home on an important Saturday night date. Remember that, and take your best clothes with you.

The girls were told not to take any cameras with them. Maxene defiantly broke this rule, and each time the sisters flew to different destinations during the USO tour, she squeezed into the cockpit and snapped away. The girls were also told not to complain during their tour, not to make any political or patriotic speeches, and not to refer to the fighting forces as "boys," as a great deal of training effort had made men of these boys.

Finally, the girls were told to "keep it clean." An editorial was reprinted in their USO booklet, taken from the GI newspaper, *Stars and Stripes*. It noted, "Call it sentimental, but when the doughboy thinks of girls from home, he thinks of his mom, his sister, his best girl. He's seen enough of the other girls. Girls from home have to be nice."

The trio's first show in Italy was at Caserta, where they performed in the same opera house in which the legendary tenor Enrico Caruso made his debut. While the girls were based in Caserta, they slept in deserted nurses' quarters—just the three of them among rows and rows of cots. LaVerne, already homesick, chose the cot in between her sisters to feel snugger. There was a large bathroom with many toilets, which the girls used to the soldiers' advantage. The

USO supplied performers with a weekly allotment of nine bottles of beer, which totaled to twenty-seven bottles for the trio. They gave the beers to the soldiers daily as they sat out on the steps of the building which housed the nurses' quarters (no men were allowed inside) and chatted with the GIs. Refrigeration problems were solved by the sisters, who stored the bottles in the toilets in the large bathroom.

The trio entertained some exceptionally large audiences during their trip. One day, at a racetrack built by Mussolini in southern Italy, the girls performed for seventy thousand soldiers, doing five shows for groups of fourteen thousand cheering men. The girls also had some unpleasant experiences during their tour. Maxene recalled one such encounter as the girls strolled down a street in Rome on a hot summer afternoon:

> As required . . . we were in our USO uniforms, the winter ones we were issued, with our jackets over our shoulders, our neckties loose, and our collars unbuttoned. . . . Our walk had lasted only a few minutes when a young officer . . . stopped us and started snapping questions. I've always believed he stopped us because we were women. . . . He blocked the sidewalk so we couldn't walk around him, and barked at us, "Put those jackets on . . . Where are your insignia? . . . Pin them on . . . And button up your collar . . . And tighten your tie!" Then he stepped around us and resumed his walk, apparently all barked out.

The trio was also witness to a scene of blatant racism, as were several other stars during their USO tours, including Kathryn Grayson. The briefing materials that they received instructed the sisters not to worry about entertaining the officers and to keep out of the Officers' Club. The girls found themselves on the same bill with a band of black musicians; they arrived as the band was still playing. Maxene peeked out from the curtain at this outdoor concert and saw soldiers everywhere, as far as the eye could see. She also noticed that the front three rows were empty. When Maxene questioned a second lieutenant about the vacant chairs, she was told that they were being reserved for the officers. Maxene then asked where the members of the band would be sitting. "Oh, they'll find something out there," came the reply. "That was obviously impossible," recalled Maxene, "even all the trees were taken." The sisters refused to sing until the second lieutenant changed his mind. He balked, and so the girls kept him and the whole crowd waiting for nearly thirty minutes. After a discussion with his superiors, the lieutenant finally relented; as the band members took their seats in the first three rows, the sisters started their show.

During their tour, the trio sang for servicemen from the backs of trucks and in hangars, makeshift tents, and open fields—wherever a crowd gathered, large or small. They would often add as many as five unscheduled shows for any two or three GIs who might happen to ask. The girls summed up their reactions in a press interview at a camp show, saying, "The expressions on a GI's face are wonderful. Here, it's 'try and please me.'" The girls were surprised to be flown from one destination to the next by a nineteen-year-old pilot. He would entertain the girls by coming as close as possible to the treetops without actually touching them. Most often, the girls sat in the fuselage, clutching their parachutes. The trio's most requested song from the GIs was "Rum and Coca Cola," which the soldiers called "the national anthem of the GI camps." The trio entertained more than 180,000 soldiers during their USO tour.

Although the Andrews Sisters were seasoned show business performers at the time of their overseas tour, they realized that the GI audience was different from any other—totally accepting, easily pleased, and grateful for any reminder of home. It was a valuable experience for other entertainers as well. Singer Margaret Whiting recalled, "I really learned my craft during the war. I was a kid and I was learning. It was the training that I got in front of those audiences, working with stars like the Andrews Sisters, Judy Garland, Red Skelton, and all the big names." Bob Hope recognized the unique adulation from the country's men in uniform and became determined early on during the war to give something back to them. Over a period of fifty years, Hope gave back through selfless dedication, sacrifice, and self-peril.

Judy Garland particularly enjoyed her work for the USO. She wrote the following for a *Hollywood Reporter* article in 1942:

> Touring the camps was reminiscent of my old vaude-
> ville days. Many of the performers were people who
> had played on the same bill with my sisters and me.
> . . . Meal times were fun. . . . We ate in the mess hall
> with all the boys, and a steady diet of steak and
> potatoes, fried chicken, and pie wrought havoc on the
> brand new figure I had worked so hard to acquire. . . .
> The immense thrill and gratification of doing what
> little I could to entertain came first . . . the friendships
> made with the boys and the knowledge that we can
> never do enough for the soldiers who have left their
> homes and families to fight our battles."

Many memorable incidents occurred during the Andrews Sisters' tour. Perhaps the strangest was when they were asked to sign their names on the side of a plane that was preparing to carry out a bombing mission over Europe. The girls were also asked by several soldiers to transport thousands of dollars won from craps and poker games back to the states to mothers, wives, and girlfriends. One soldier offered Maxene half of the winnings if she'd oblige. The girls refused these requests as politely as they could. Another notable event happened in Naples, Italy. Patty explained,

> We were sent to a Port of Embarkation to entertain
> five thousand boys in a hangar who were miserably
> unhappy. They thought they were being shipped back
> home and they'd suddenly heard that, instead, they
> were being shipped to the Pacific. Before we went on,
> the commanding officer said, "Patty, I've got some
> good news to tell the fellows. Just take this piece of
> paper out there and read it." I looked at the paper—
> V-J Day had just been announced! "Fellows," I said,
> "you don't have to go to Japan, the war is over!" You
> could have heard a pin drop. There was no reaction;

they thought it was part of the show. But my sisters, who were on stage, began to cry. Then a fellow who was up on a rafter started to scream. He was caught by the guys underneath him and then all hell broke loose! It was like the three of us had stopped the war!

When the trio returned to the States in August 1945, *The Andrews Sisters Show* resumed and aired weekly. Vocalist Curt Massey was added during the ensuing five weeks. The show was so successful that during the trio's two-month engagement at New York's Paramount that fall the format of their stage shows was identical to that of the radio series. The Paramount stage was decked out in country-western style, as were the sisters, wearing the cowgirl outfits they donned each week for their radio show. The Riders of the Purple Sage backed the trio at the Paramount, joining Patty for "Nobody's Darlin' but Mine," while Vic Schoen's orchestra supplied the instrumentals. During one week of the engagement, the sisters drew 115,000 dollars from 150,000 patrons.

Maxene remembered a short side trip that the girls made during most of their New York appearances throughout the war. "We always went over to Times Square between shows and did other shows over there. Most of the performers on Broadway did the same thing. There was a big stage right there in the middle of the square, and thousands of people would line up to buy war bonds and listen to us sing while they waited. Then we'd hurry back before we were due in the theater again."

The trio's wartime dedication to victory truly endeared them to the tens of thousands of servicemen and women that they entertained. Their tireless efforts to this cause also endeared them to the homefront population, who recognized and appreciated the group's sacrifices. The girls' services also greatly added to their exposure, and their astounding success had now made them the most popular and profitable attraction in the entertainment industry.

The pictures were hits at the box office, but they were nightmares to the girls. Poor makeup, poor costumes, poor lines. Camera angles went by the board. They accentuated the negative of the Andrews' physiognomies, and practically eliminated all traces of the positive. People meeting them in person were surprised to find them many more times attractive than they were on screen.
—Swank, 1946

7

Riding High

Her Lucky Night was the trio's last feature for Universal Pictures. Shortly before the girls were to begin filming, they made a visit to family and friends in Minneapolis. During their four-day retreat, LaVerne organized a baseball game with some cousins and friends while the trio was staying with uncles Pete and Ed at Lake Minnetonka. She soon regretted her enthusiasm when one of her pitches came sailing back and smacked her in the eye. The trio stalled the studio for a few weeks as LaVerne nursed her shiner.

The girls were eager to fulfill their contract with Universal Pictures. They had grown weary of unflattering camera shots and mindless scripts that allowed them to do little more than speak in unison. They were disappointed with nearly all of their projects. Since the Abbott and Costello films, the studio had repeatedly assigned them to quickly produced B movie escapist fare, and they were now anxious to concentrate on recording and concert tours. The girls also wanted to shake but not totally abandon their reputation as boogie-woogie and novelty singers in order to attempt more serious music.

Although all of the trio's films for Universal were successes at the box office, the girls found the motion picture industry rather binding and unrewarding. The sisters often had to wait in the wings for hours, just to perform a brief acting scene or musical number. The energetic sisters found the process bothersome and time-consuming. Maxene once recalled meeting the Modernaires, Glenn Miller's vocal group, at a boxing match in the early 1940s. (Maxene and Lou Levy attended fights frequently.) The Modernaires told Maxene that they were in Hollywood waiting to shoot a sequence in a Miller musical that was currently filming. The sisters embarked on a concert tour soon after. When they returned several weeks later, Maxene encountered the Modernaires once again and asked them, "What are you kids still doing out here?" "We haven't shot our number yet," came the reply.

The negative reviews that many of their films received were also a great disappointment to the sisters. The critics acknowledged the studio's mishandling of the trio's talents, but instead of pinpointing Universal, the critics continually blamed the sisters. Many of the critics' reviews, especially those printed in the *New York Times,* seemed to consider the quality of the critiqued work, which was really out of the sisters' control. Some were questionable. Reviewing *Buck Privates,* one *Times* critic wrote, "The Andrews Sisters do hectic things with a tune, they're good! But, please even when it's good, we don't like agony singing." The reviewer may have been referring to Patty's ferocious growl during her solo in "Boogie Woogie Bugle Boy," yet the song was nominated for an Academy Award for Best Song in a Motion Picture, and it became one of the trio's greatest hits, as well as their most identifiable song. A *Times* review of *Give Out, Sisters* stated, "The Andrews Sisters haven't come up against such weak tunes in a long while," yet "Pennsylvania Polka" became a huge hit. A *Times* review of *Private Buckaroo* claimed, "The Andrews Sisters' harmony, to this effect, remains one of a nail being scratched against a slate blackboard." Granted, the song "Six Jerks in a Jeep" was a poor endeavor and probably should have been cut (someone at Decca had the good sense to reject it after the trio recorded it for the label), but the trio's remaining numbers in the film, especially, "Three Little Sisters" and "Don't Sit under the Apple Tree (With Anyone Else but Me)," were perfectly harmonized and became smash hit records.

Perhaps the movie critics would not have been so disappointed with the girls had they signed with a different studio. It is interesting to imagine what an Andrews Sisters movie might have been like if filmed by MGM or Twentieth Century-Fox. Fox once offered to buy the trio's motion picture contract from Universal. The sisters' films were netting too much of a profit to let them slip away, however, so Universal refused the offer. MGM offered the girls seventy-five hundred dollars for a soundtrack recording session, but they were bound to Universal. At a different studio, the girls might have had a better chance, given well-developed scripts, Technicolor settings, and lavish production numbers. The girls might also have had the opportunity to display their comedic flair, which surfaced best during live performances. *Disc* magazine observed, "Both personal appearances and radio programs have demonstrated the sisters' flair for comedy, particularly in the case of blonde Patty, who clowns for the sheer fun of it, whether or not there's anyone around to see her. On road tours, Maxene, Patty, and LaVerne are always sellouts, display a natural gift for costume, stage effect, timing, and all the other tricks of skillful showmanship. Though they've made numerous pictures, and fans have flocked to see them, something of their unusual gay exuberance is lost on the screen."

Universal did not build a musical around the Andrews Sisters as MGM did with Judy Garland or as Fox did with Betty Grable, even though the sisters— along with Deanna Durbin—were Universal's hottest musical properties. A prime example of how poorly the executives at Universal filmed the trio—and there are many examples that can be cited—is the trio's "Down in the Valley" from *Moonlight and Cactus*. In the scene, footage of a sobbing man whose girlfriend just ended their relationship is repeatedly interspersed with footage of the trio singing. The song therefore stood little chance of coming off well, inviting negative reviews. The studio soundtracks, however, recorded the trio's harmonies to their best advantage. The studio employed more sophisticated recording techniques than did Decca Records, which is why the trio's adhesive blend is much fuller and more pronounced in their films than it is on their records, especially their early 1940s recordings for Decca. The trio's soundtrack recordings of "Boogie Woogie Bugle Boy," "Aurora," "East of the Rockies," and "Il Bacio" (with the operatic Gloria Jean) nicely showcased their vocal abilities.

A final critical jab that deserves rebuttal is the needless focus the critics placed on the sisters' physical appearance. One critic even went so far as to compare the sisters' photogenic abilities to that of Abraham Lincoln. The girls themselves were relatively unperturbed by the fact that they were not glamour queens. The trio's mother assured them early on that their talents and personalities were more important than their looks. Celebrity interviewer, columnist, and author James Bacon, interviewing the trio in 1952, summed things up accurately by writing, "The girls are no Elizabeth Taylors, but they are far from frightening. All three have large, dark brown eyes with heavy black lashes, nice figures, and pretty legs." Maxene said that her mother was always helpful to the girls when they had insecurity problems. Olga was extremely proud of her daughters, perhaps especially so because it was she who had encouraged them to sing at young ages. Olga also had a wonderful sense of humor, which each of her three daughters inherited. During one of their road tours, the girls and their mother stopped at a small-town diner to eat. Olga dropped a nickel in the jukebox and played an Andrews Sisters' hit. When the waitress came to take the order, Olga said, "Listen to those Andrews Sisters. Aren't they just terrible?" "Awful," replied the waitress. "That's the worst singing I've ever heard!" The girls roared with laughter.

The girls continued to turn out hit records in 1945, including the lyrical wartime ballad "The Blond Sailor," a German tune they brought back to the States and popularized after their USO trip; "Along the Navajo Trail," a top-ten hit with Bing Crosby; "Put That Ring on My Finger"; "Money Is the Root of All Evil (Take It Away, Take It Away, Take It Away)," recorded with Guy Lombardo's orchestra; the amusing novelty "Her Bathing Suit Never Got Wet"; and the spiritual, "Patience and Fortitude," which featured a male chorus backing some great scat work by Patty. During that year alone, records by the Andrews Sisters sold over five million copies.

The royalties were split four ways between the three sisters and manager Levy, and the foursome formed a legal partnership to control the earnings. The partnership was actually the result of the formation of a corporation, with the four principals each receiving 25 percent of the earnings. This also allowed the sisters to sell the company and claim the money as capital gains, taxed only at 25 percent, and to avoid confiscatory tax rates on high personal income.

Levy stressed that the concept was in every way legal: "We were partners, we split everything four ways. We paid all the expenses. Whatever was left, we split four ways, twenty-five percent each. We never had any arguments that way. It was legitimate. We all admitted that it was expensive. The company paid it. Nothing wrong with that. Uncle Sam was paying it, legitimate. We didn't evade the taxes. It was to avoid the taxes we made it a partnership. It all worked out for everybody."

The Nash-Kelvinator Musical Showroom, starring the Andrews Sisters, soon premiered on CBS radio in October 1945. Once again the trio was teamed with Curt Massey, a baritone in the Crosby tradition. The Ambassadors, a vocal group who borrowed much more from Broadway than they did from the Mills Brothers or the Ink Spots, and Vic Schoen and his orchestra were also weekly regulars. The show was produced very lavishly (with the possible exception of the inane chitchat used as filler between songs), with top name guest stars and fanfare musical finales. The Showroom was first broadcast from New York City, then later from Hollywood. The trio received the impressive sum of ten thousand dollars per broadcast.

The show featured a well-received segment called "The Green Room," in which a celebrity would appear, doing whatever it was that he or she did best. Among the famous visitors stepping up to the microphone were Abbott and Costello, performing their classic "Who's on First" baseball comedy routine; Irish tenor Morton Downey crooning "Carolina Moon"; Judy Garland singing her signature "Over the Rainbow"; Broadway sensation Ethel Merman belting out "I Got Rhythm"; and Hoagy Carmichael providing piano accompaniment for the cast as they sang his composition "Stardust." Also appearing as guests were Sophie Tucker, Jane

Powell, Xavier Cugat, Rudy Vallee, and the Mills Brothers. The finale of each *Showroom* broadcast offered rich Vic Schoen arrangements of "Night and Day," "It's a Grand Night for Singing," and "Symphony," performed by the sisters with Curt Massey and the Ambassadors. The trio was also featured singing knockout renditions of popular songs of the day, and Patty and Massey delivered a weekly duet. Massey's seemingly effortless harmony vocals, contrasting Patty's lead, found the baritone at his vocal best.

One hour before the trio completed their last *Showroom* broadcast from New York on November 14, 1945, they appeared on CBS's *Songs by Sinatra*. Patty teamed with Sinatra for "A Kiss Goodnight," later followed by the trio's swinging "Begin the Beguine." All four participated in a comedy skit concerning the rugged schedule of shows at the Paramount (very familiar to both acts). This segment, which had the bobby-soxers in the studio audience screaming wildly, was the closest Sinatra and the sisters came to a joint appearance at the famed theater. Sinatra closed the show singing a reprise of "Empty Saddles" with the trio, originally from the sisters' *Eight-to-the-Bar Ranch* series.

The trio's Decca hits continued to dominate jukeboxes throughout the country, hence their nickname "the queens of the jukebox machines." The sisters had become a household name. Never before had a female vocal group so dominated the popular music scene, and never since. One of their first hits of 1946 was "South America, Take It Away" (with Bing Crosby), a song first introduced by Betty Garrett in the Broadway musical *Call Me Mister*. The disc sold over one million copies, making it the sisters' sixth gold record. It climbed as high as number two on the *Billboard* charts and remained in the top ten for sixteen weeks. The trio followed this success with another top-ten hit, "Rumors Are Flying," accompanied by Les Paul's brilliant guitar stylings.

The Les Paul Trio began opening shows for the sisters on theater tours in the mid 1940s, before Paul earned even greater recognition with his wife Mary Ford in the 1950s. Lou Levy recalled, "Watching his fingers work was like watching a locomotive go. People hadn't seen anything like that before. He was one of a kind, perfect for the girls." Maxene also remembered Paul fondly: "Les is a genius, pure and simple. He used to sit in his dressing room between shows on our tour and make guitars. When he bought his own home outside New York, he built several recording studios, doing all the electrical and acoustical work himself, without ever studying electrical engineering. It was all in his head."

Vic Schoen, who became fast friends with Paul, also remembered Paul's passion for combining music and electronics—in particular, a headless aluminum guitar that Paul created: "It was like something from Mars, very wide across, with tuning pegs that protruded from the top of the wings. Les was always trying to build some damned electronic contraption. Some of it worked, some of it didn't. But you could always count on him to come up with something no one else had thought of." Paul himself recalled the aluminum invention and some of the trouble it caused him on stage: "When the hot spotlights hit it, it started doing all kinds of crazy things. At first, I didn't know what was happening. I thought, 'Holy God, what's wrong with my ear?' So I'd tune it again and get it right. Then the guy pulls the spotlight off the Andrews Sisters and onto me, and I start sinking into another key again. I said, 'There goes my invention.'"

The sisters were impressed by Paul's musical ability, and he admired the sisters personally and professionally. The girls were especially taken with the way his playing seemed to complement their sound. Maxene recalled,

> It was a cinch to go out and sing after Les' act. We could just walk out and lay on top of what he'd already started. And it was wonderful having him perform with us. He'd tune into the passages we were singing and lightly play the melody, sometimes in harmony. He made it much easier for us to enjoy what we were doing because he really propelled us along. We'd sing these fancy licks and he'd keep up with us note for note in exactly the same rhythm. He was totally attuned to what we were doing, almost contributing a fourth voice. But he never once took the attention away from what we were doing. He did everything he could to make us sound better.

The Andrews Sisters: Maxene (left), Patty (center), and LaVerne (right) pose for the first time in their oft-worn military uniforms in a publicity shot for *Buck Privates* (Universal, 1941), the first of three films that year with Bud Abbott and Lou Costello and the film in which the trio introduced the Oscar-nominated "Boogie Woogie Bugle Boy." (Unless otherwise noted, all illustrations are from the author's collection.)

Maxene, Patty, and LaVerne, circa 1920 (*opposite top*)(courtesy of Diane Gray), 1946 (*opposite bottom*), and 1951 (*above*).

Left, Patty, LaVerne, and Maxene in the mid-1930s. (Courtesy of Ray Hagen.)

Below, LaVerne, Patty, songwriter Jimmy McHugh (seated), and Maxene during a 1939 NBC radio remote broadcast.

Above, The sisters and bandleader Glenn Miller during a rehearsal for the Chesterfield-sponsored radio show *The Moonlight Serenade* in January 1940. (Courtesy of Ray Hagen.) *Below,* Sharing a laugh over the comics, 1940.

Above, LaVerne, Patty, and Maxene clown around on Universal's back lot in their "Rhumboogie" costumes from *Argentine Nights* (Universal, 1940). *Below*, Patty, Lou Costello, LaVerne, Bud Abbott, and Maxene in *Buck Privates* (Universal, 1941).

Above, Lou Costello convinces the girls that he's a captain in *In the Navy* (Universal, 1941), the sisters' second film with Abbott and Costello.

Right, the trio pose for a publicity shot for *In the Navy.* (Courtesy of Diane Gray.)

Above, Maxene, Patty, Gloria Jean, and LaVerne share a backstage laugh during the filming of *What's Cookin'?* (Universal, 1942).

Left, the sisters pose with bandleader Ted Lewis in a publicity still from *Hold That Ghost* (Universal, 1941), the trio's third and final film appearance with Abbott and Costello.

Above, The trio with "Stooge" Shemp Howard in *Private Buckaroo* (Universal, 1942). *Below*, LaVerne, Patty, and Maxene in *Give Out, Sisters* (Universal, 1942), with Decca partner Dan Dailey leading the orchestra.

LaVerne, Patty, and Maxene end a year-long musicians' strike by recording "Pistol Packin' Mama" with Bing Crosby on September 27, 1943. (Courtesy of Everett R. Searcy.)

Clowning with Shemp Howard in *How's about It?* (Universal, 1943).

Above, "Thanks for the Buggy Ride" from *Always a Bridesmaid* (Universal, 1943). *Below*, The sisters and two members of Mitchell Ayres's orchestra in *Swingtime Johnny* (Universal, 1943).

Above, LaVerne, Patty, and Maxene entertain the troops in a scene from *Follow the Boys* (Universal, 1944). Entertainment footage used in the film, including the sisters' appearance, was taken both from studio production and actual on-location segments. *Below*, Patty wasn't really playing the guitar when the trio sang "Don't Fence Me In" in *Hollywood Canteen* (Warner Bros., 1944).

Above, LaVerne, Maxene, and Patty pose for a studio portrait in 1944. *Below*, Maxene photographs her sisters and her parents, Peter and Olga, in front of the Brentwood estate in 1944.

"The Hand-Clapping Song" from *Moonlight and Cactus* (Universal, 1944) with Elyse Knox and Tom Seidel.

Patty in her bedroom with her porcelain doll collection, 1944.

Maxene also remembered Paul for the perfect gentleman that he was to the trio, as compared to other top musicians of the day who resented the sisters for their commercial success and lack of technical musical knowledge. She recalled less-than-perfect working arrangements with Artie Shaw's band, "If Artie's guys didn't like a certain passage we were singing, they'd play it out of tune or miss it entirely. They hated us because we were the stars and they had to be background music for us." Biographer Mary Alice Shaughnessy noted Paul's admiration for the trio, "Les' attitude toward the Andrews Sisters was far more respectful. He admired nothing more than commercial success, and these brash young sisters happily enjoyed an abundance of fame. Just a few years earlier, they had been struggling to make forty-five dollars a week on radio. Now, the effervescent 'Rum and Coca Cola' girls were earning a million a year on stage, screen, and records. Les welcomed the opportunity to study them in full flight."

Throughout the 1940s, the trio's record sales seemed infinite. According to *Disc* magazine in the summer of 1946, only Bing Crosby, the biggest and most respected name in the entertainment industry of the day, was selling more records than the Andrews Sisters. More hits followed. The trio performed a driving version of "The House of Blue Lights" with Eddie Heywood's orchestra, which became a bestseller and was popularized again years later by several other artists. Another gold disc resulted in the girls' collaboration with Guy Lombardo and his Royal Canadians on a pair of songs: "Christmas Island" and "Winter Wonderland," both of which are still heard on the radio and jukeboxes every Christmas season.

The trio's concert appearances at this time were numerous and very profitable. Aside from appearances at Atlantic City's Steel Pier and the Chicago Theater in Illinois, the girls starred at Cincinnati's Albee Theater, Detroit's Downtown Theater, and Philadelphia's Earle Theater, as well as headlining engagements in Providence and Boston. The sisters then opened a 1946 Christmas engagement at New York's Paramount with Tony Pastor's orchestra, the Les Paul Trio, and a couple of novelty acts, including a dance team. Said *Billboard,* "It packs speed, gets laughs in the right spots, and is strong enough to sustain itself for the full hour it runs."

The Levys soon adopted a baby girl and named her Aleda Ann. They had been waiting to start a family for some time, but Maxene had reservations abut the idea considering the trio's hectic schedule. The Levys decided to employ a couple, guardians of a sort, who would stay with the infant while the sisters traveled. The following year, the Levy family would grow to four as Maxene and Lou adopted a boy, whom Maxene named Peter, after her father.

The sisters were now starting to encounter new competition in their musical field, most notably the Fontane Sisters and the more popular, at least at this time, Dinning Sisters. During an engagement in Chicago, the Dinnings (Ginger, Lou, and Jean) attended one of the Andrews Sisters' shows at the Chicago Theater. The Dinnings went backstage after the show to meet the Andrews trio, and as they approached the girls' dressing room, the Dinnings were delighted to hear that Maxene, Patty, and LaVerne were playing their Capitol recording of "Brazil." Each group discovered that they were mutual fans. Lou Dinning once compared herself and her sisters to the Andrews Sisters, saying, "Let's face it, the Andrews Sisters were way ahead of us. We tried our darndest to be as commercial as they were, but weren't flashy enough. We were all kind of shy. We came from a farm in Oklahoma. We never took dancing lessons or anything."

The Andrews girls next lent their blend to the soundtrack of the Walt Disney film *Make Mine Music* (1946), which featured entertaining skits accompanied by animated songs performed by an all-star cast. Although the sequences were smartly executed, the film did not capture the surreal blend of music and animation that Disney had captured in 1940's *Fantasia,* which offered a classical score by Beethoven, Tchaikovsky, and Schubert. Despite some clever segments the film did poorly at the box office. The trio sang "Johnny Fedora and Alice Blue Bonnet," the story of two hats who fall in love in the window of a department store. Although critics termed the segment silly, it was merely ahead of its time, its "silliness" not fully appreciated at the time. The segment is still shown today, often spliced between regular programming on cable television's Disney Channel. The sisters enjoyed working with Disney, whom Maxene once referred to as a perfect gentleman.

Shortly before the trio's Paramount opening with Pastor, the sisters were once again the featured story on the cover of *Billboard* magazine, with a caption that read "Andrews Sisters: #1 for Nine Years." After years of dedication and hard work, the Andrews Sisters had become the most celebrated vocal group in show business history.

There are many reasons why the sisters enjoyed such phenomenal worldwide fame. First and foremost, the girls were exceptional singers. Patty provided a strong, solid lead, while her sisters supplied the slickest harmony in the business. Each sister was equally vital to the group's sound. The girls' rich harmonic output and unerring precision in phrasing—largely a result of daily four-hour rehearsals—were outstanding. Reporter Mary Morris observed an Andrews Sisters rehearsal in 1945 and wrote, "I found the girls hunched around an upright piano, singing. They made faces, beat their feet while their bodies jumped and swayed. Even the arranger's derriere wiggled madly on the piano seat. The whole room jumped, and I sat on the desk, chin in hand, catching the wail in their voices, the contagious rhythm and excitement." The girls' timing was flawless, and unless they were harmonizing, one would assume that only one girl was singing. Their voices blended together perfectly in pitch and rhythm, as is evident in their renditions of "Three O'Clock in the Morning" and "Now, Now, Now Is the Time," backing Russ Morgan on the latter in double time during the second chorus. The overall sound was incredibly unique. Patty recalled, "We never interchanged parts. LaVerne always sang the low harmony. Maxene sang the upper harmony and I always sang the lead, or melody, as well as the solos. The reason for this was simple. By having only one lead voice, our sound was always consistent and identifiable. I believe this to be the reason my voice is still so easily recognizable today."

The girls were also innovative vocal arrangers. The trio knew what to do with a song to give it their own distinctive touch. The girls were not afraid to take an established song and make it their own. Take for example their rocking rendition of "Three O'Clock in the Morning," which had been popularized years earlier as a waltz. In this regard, the Andrews Sisters were far ahead of their time musically, refusing to abide by the standards of the day. The trio's unusual and ingenious arranging, assisted by Vic Schoen, is also exemplified in their recordings of "From the Land of the Sky Blue Water," "Pagan Love Song," and "South American Way." Although all of the orchestrations in the recordings were swinging and sensational, they took a back seat to the fabulous harmonies. Patty explained, "We used to do arrangements; we didn't just sing a song. We built it up, and did our re-de-dees and ra-da-das and all of that. If you listen to the records, you will hear that we sing, and then pa-pa-pa from the brass. There was nobody playing under us, no sustaining notes under us."

LaVerne was the only sister who could read music, which she learned to do as a young girl with aspirations of becoming a concert pianist (although, since their sister's death, Patty and Maxene repeatedly made a point of telling interviewers that none of the three could read music). LaVerne's contralto (or bass) supplied the group with a harmonious foundation for the melody. It was LaVerne who would interpret difficult musical passages to Maxene early on if her sister had problems finding her part.

Maxene, who handled the Andrews checkbook and most other business affairs, was undoubtedly the prettiest of the three. She was the soprano of the group, but she also supplied the middle harmony. Basically, Patty sang the lead or melody while Maxene and LaVerne sang in higher and lower harmony octaves, respectively; however, when Patty would sing an exceptionally high note, Maxene would sing notes that fell between Patty's lead and LaVerne's bass, thus providing a middle harmony (although Maxene could actually sing much higher than she did on records). It was probably Maxene's ever-switching harmony vocals (abundant in such songs as "South American Way," "Alexander's Ragtime Band," "Say Si Si," and "East of the Rockies"), coupled with her innovative use of counter-melodies, that gave the trio their distinctive blend. Maxene also flavored songs by inventing trick wordage, most evident in the trio's finale of their 1940 hit "The Woodpecker Song."

Patty was the most outgoing and fun-loving sister, as well as the clowner of the group. She once told a reporter, "I'm ignorant and that's why I'm happy!" Patty also had a knack for amusing her sisters and easing tensions, as Maxene recalled: "Patty was the fun one of the group, the clown who kept us laughing during those endless periods of backstage boredom between shows when we were doing five and six shows a day. Patty was wonderful. She helped not only LaVerne and me but the rest of the acts in our show and the members of our orchestra keep our sanity. I don't know who helped her, but she sure helped us." Patty could make her sisters, especially Maxene, laugh readily. During World War II, when everyday items such as meat, sugar, coffee, and gasoline were rationed, nylons were also in short supply, as they were needed for military clothing and parachutes. Maxene remembered, "You couldn't buy them anywhere. Many women began using leg makeup and some drew a penciled line down the back of each leg to look like the seam in the stocking. The Andrews Sisters couldn't get nylons any more often than anyone else, so we appeared on stage with that makeup on our legs. But we refused to draw the seam down the back, convincing ourselves we looked as if we were wearing seamless hose. Patty probably would have drawn seams if LaVerne and I had let her, and she might have made them intentionally crooked."

Patty's vocal talents were amazing. She was able to supply whatever the song called for, be it the powerful range of Judy Garland, the bawdiness of Betty Hutton, or the tenderness of Doris Day. It was Patty's area of expertise to invent novelty segments in many of the trio's recordings, including the spoken word in their parody of Al Jolson's "Sonny Boy." Patty's wild solo in "Boogie Woogie Bugle Boy" was her own invention. Singer Mel Torme regarded Patty as one of his favorite singers, saying:

The Andrews Sisters were one of the most successful trios in the business. They had more hit records to their credit than you could count, and one of the main reasons for their popularity was Patty Andrews. She stood in the middle of her sisters, planted her feet apart, and belted out solos as well as singing the lead parts with zest and confidence. Patty exuded an eyes-closed, smile-on-her-face persona that was irresistible. The kind of singing she did cannot be taught; it can't be studied in books, it can't be written down. Long experience as a singer and wide-open ears were her only teachers, and she learned her lessons well. She had a gamin type of personality, a piquant face and expressive eyes. All in all, one of the great acts, with fine three-part harmony, clever staging, and above all, the singing voice of Patty Andrews.

The second reason for the trio's endurance was their versatility. Aside from singing all types of popular music of their day, they demonstrated a flair for comedy, evident in some of their film appearances, but much more obvious in their stage and radio shows. James Bacon wrote in 1952, "The girls are natural comediennes. They recently played three weeks at the Coconut Grove. That engagement probably did more than any other to dispel the notion that they were just three girls in front of a microphone." Celebrity biographer and music historian George T. Simon once wrote of the act, "Their showmanship easily transcended their lack of musicianship, and they developed into engaging entertainers and produced an easily identifiable sound." The trio's great desire to please their audiences was evident, as was their commitment to their trade. They once drove in pouring rain from Erie, Pennsylvania, to Buffalo, New York, to catch a train to Chicago, where they were scheduled to appear. Upon their arrival in Buffalo, they discovered that they had missed the last train to Chicago, so they chartered a private plane to get them there in time for the first show. The girls were unfazed when theater management in Chicago told them that they could have missed the first show rather than going to all that trouble.

The sisters' dedication to and love of their craft was perhaps best demonstrated by their tolerance of traveling conditions, especially during the war. For train travel, performers needed government priority papers testifying that the trip was essential for the war effort. Flying was even more complicated, so most often the girls toured by automobile, with their father pulling chauffeur duty. Some all-night drives were required to get the girls to their next destination in a timely fashion, so often the sisters huddled together and slept in the back seat. More than once during train trips, the girls sat on their suitcases in the aisle—certainly not what one would expect for a trio of singing superstars.

The third reason the trio became so well known was the massive worldwide exposure they had throughout the 1940s and 1950s—more than any other pre-Beatles vocal group. The sisters were constantly performing live, and were perhaps the busiest entertainers of their day, working forty-nine to fifty weeks out of the year. During their brief vacation periods, they usually returned to Minnesota to visit family and friends. Maxene once observed, "We were young, blessed with boundless energy and incredibly naive. It was a murderous schedule, but it was standard in the industry." Their manager, Lou Levy, was a driving force behind the trio's celebrity and success; he was often referred to as "the fourth Andrews sister." Levy provided the girls with most of their hit material, having an uncanny sense for picking songs that fit the girls' singing specialties to perfection, as well as songs that had good potential of becoming smash hits. Maxene attributed the following to Levy: "Lou remained the guiding genius behind these successes. He couldn't read music any better than we could—meaning he couldn't read it at all—but he had a unique talent, an instinct, for what was good and would be commercially successful. He especially had a gift for knowing exactly what would be a perfect fit for the Andrews Sisters' style of music."

Levy was one of the most respected publishers of the 1940s, and his Leeds Music Corporation grew enormously over the years. Levy's Duchess Music Corporation also was profitable, and he sold these interests to MCA for more than four million dollars as part of an arrangement that allowed Levy to act as a director of MCA and operating head of MCA-Leeds Music. Levy's publishing interests were not limited to pop music, as music historian Russell Sanjek notes:

> Levy owned nearly two dozen other catalogues,
> including one formerly belonging to Clarence Will-
> iams, a pioneering black A&R producer of race music;
> and the Wabash and Mayo catalogues, into which
> much early rhythm-and-blues music of the 1930s and

1940s . . . was placed. With a keen eye for the international market, Levy picked up the American rights to many songs that became American hits, as well as two of the Beatles' earliest successes, "I Want to Hold Your Hand" and "P.S. I Love You."

Vic Schoen was another member of the original core team of professionals that propelled the girls to stardom. As their musical arranger and conductor, he was as capable as Glenn Miller or Tommy Dorsey. He became very well respected in the music industry. Although he worked mainly with the sisters, his work was not limited to them; he often accompanied other established recording artists on records, including Bing Crosby, Dick Haymes, Ella Fitzgerald, Danny Kaye, Hoagy Carmichael, Dinah Shore, Patti Page and the Weavers, and the Weavers' female lead Ronnie Gilbert. With Schoen's assistance on vocal arrangements and instrumentals, the Andrews Sisters produced a sound that blew the roof off the recording studio, especially in such songs as "Three O'Clock in the Morning," "I Had a Hat (When I Came In)," and "I Didn't Know the Gun Was Loaded."

There are current music critics who downplay the sisters' contributions to American popular music, despite the girls' incredible success and lengthy career. Some argue that the music scene of the 1940s and 1950s was much less competitive. It is true that the trio did not have to compete with many groups from other countries, as is the case with many of today's artists; but the Andrews Sisters' competition here in America during their heyday should not be discounted. Extremely popular during the trio's peak time were such legends as Jolson, Crosby, Sinatra, Cole, Como, Haymes, and Garland. Competing vocal groups alone—the Mills Brothers, Ink Spots, King Sisters, Dinning Sisters, Norton Sisters, Fontane Sisters, Merry Macs, Pied Pipers, Modernaires, Song Spinners, Four Hits and a Miss—could have easily knocked the trio from their perch. Aside from Garland, dozens of female vocalists who were featured with big bands blossomed into successful soloists and became fierce competition for the trio as all vied for coveted top-ten slots on the *Billboard* charts. The careers of all of these great entertainers lasted entire lifetimes, surviving constant changes in the music industry. The Andrews Sisters had the talent and drive to succeed, and they earned their rewards in the era now referred to as "the golden age of vocalists."

The music industry of the 1940s was perhaps even more competitive than today's in at least one aspect. Years ago, as many as ten artists or more could have recorded the same material within days or weeks of each other, and the subsequent releases might reach the record stores and the airwaves simultaneously. It was not uncommon to see the same song on the best-selling record charts performed by several different artists—vocalists, harmony groups, big bands, and solo instrumentalists. Artists not only had to compete with similar acts, as is still the case, but they also had to arrange and interpret their material in hopes that it would rise above one or more covered versions of the same song. Perhaps this competition regarding similar material was a reason why the sisters and many other artists of their era toured so diligently and with great frequency, so as to give as much exposure as possible to their own arrangements. Because of their popularity, touring was financially rewarding for the sisters during the late forties and early fifties.

The sisters continued to soar with several successful personal appearances throughout the country. Concerning a Las Vegas engagement at the Flamingo in March of 1947, *Billboard* wrote, "Even the croupiers stopped crouping to catch their act!" The girls enjoyed working in Vegas. According to Maxene, she and her sisters were the first act to perform at the Flamingo, owned by infamous mafia gangster "Bugsy" Siegel. Although the girls had little involvement with Siegel himself, Maxene once recalled, "He was one handsome son-of-a-gun, only you never called him Bugsy. You said, 'Good morning, Benny,' bright as you could, and kept moving." The trio also played at the Riviera several times during the 1940s, where they received a top salary of fifteen thousand dollars a week. The girls performed in Las Vegas regularly during the late 1950s and 1960s. Maxene remembered a woman stopping the girls just before they were to go on stage during one of their Vegas shows, asking them if they would recite the lyrics of "Bei Mir Bist Du Schon," as it was her favorite song. Maxene obliged and quickly rattled off the lyrics. The girls were announced just as Maxene had finished, and they were opening the show with "Bei Mir." But as they stepped up to the microphone, Maxene drew a blank and could not remember any of the lyrics she had just recited. Maxene would often fluff the lyrics of a song; she explained, "I don't know where they come from, but the strangest words just flow out of my mouth." She said it was helpful in such situations to be facing Patty, as she could watch Patty forming her next word and usually find her place quickly.

After focusing for two years on recording and touring, the sisters were once again before the cameras in late 1947, but this time for a more upscale studio—Paramount. The girls appeared as them-selves in the fifth installment of the "Road" pictures, *Road to Rio,* starring Bing Crosby, Bob Hope, and Dorothy Lamour. The plot concerned a pair of entertainers who, fleeing from a carnival show that they accidentally burned to the ground, stow away on a cruise ship bound for Rio de Janeiro. They encounter Miss Lamour on board, who is being hypnotized by her evil aunt, unbeknownst to all three. After the boys' cover is blown, they agree to work with the ship's orchestra to pay for their passage. The Andrews Sisters join Crosby for "You Don't Have to Know the Language," one of many fine tunes written for the film by two of Crosby's favorite songwriters, Johnny Burke and James Van Heusen.

The girls appeared perfectly coifed and outfitted in sequined dresses. Their makeup was well done, and they had never before appeared so attractive on screen. This appearance marked the only time that the girls worked with Crosby in a movie, although they are often erroneously credited with having appeared in *Road to Utopia.* Watching Crosby and the sisters in *Road to Rio,* it is easy to see how much they enjoyed working with each other. Crosby is playful with all three sisters at different times during the perfor-mance, even trying to make LaVerne laugh just before the song's last line. One flaw occurs at the very end of the number when, after completing their final turn, Patty miscalculates her last step and collides with LaVerne as she swings out her hip. LaVerne keeps her composure, despite the substantial bump. The film out-grossed every other theatrical release of 1948, including MGM's *Easter Parade* with Judy Garland and Fred Astaire. A publicity shot of the trio with Crosby from the film graced the cover of *Billboard* in March. The trio befriended Dorothy Lamour during the film's production, and the four ladies then embarked on a personal appearance tour with Crosby and Hope to promote the film.

The sisters guest-hosted the popular *Your Hit Parade* radio series for four weeks in 1947. Their last appearance featured them singing a swing version of the Freddy Martin hit "Managua, Nicaragua." Personal appearances continued at Chicago's Oriental Theater and San Francisco's Golden Gate Theater. The girls had now reached their tenth anniversary as successful recording artists, and their current best-selling Decca hits proved that they were still riding high. These included a popular top-ten cover version of pianist Francis Craig's melodic "Near You," which comedian Milton Berle adopted as his theme song; the tender ballad "How Lucky You Are"; "Toolie Oolie Doolie (The Yodel Polka)," a Swiss melody that remained in the top-ten for eleven weeks; "The Blue Tail Fly" with Burl Ives—a dip into the growing folk music market, two years before the Weavers burst upon the scene with "Goodnight, Irene"; and three hits with Bing: "You Don't Have to Know the Language," "Tallahassee," and "A Hundred and Sixty Acres." "Civilization (Bongo, Bongo, Bongo)" was a huge hit that year, a result of the girls' collaboration with comic legend Danny Kaye. The song was taken from the musical *Angel in the Wings,* and its top-ten success encouraged the sisters to team with Kaye for other Decca releases. "Civilization" climbed to *Billboard*'s number-three position, outshining other recordings of the song by Louis Prima, Ray McKinley, Jack Smith, and Woody Herman.

The sisters liked Danny Kaye and enjoyed working with him. When his wife, Sylvia Fine, was present, however, things were more difficult, as she coached him through his performance in a time-consuming manner. Maxene remembered one session with Kaye that took six hours just to record one side, as Mrs. Kaye supervised from the control room. Generally Kaye and the sisters had fun recording their material, as is evident in "The Big Brass Band from Brazil," "Amelia Cordelia McHugh," "It's a Quiet Town (In Crossbone County)," and Patty and Kaye's duet "Orange Colored Sky."

8

Success Abroad

A nightly radio show called *Club 15* premiered on the CBS network
in mid-1947. The show was hosted by bandleader Bob Crosby
(Bing's brother) and sponsored by Campbell Soup Company. Featured with Crosby were Margaret Whiting and the Pied Pipers, while
baritone Del Sharbutt handled the announcing chores. After the
show's first season, Margaret Whiting and the Pied Pipers were
replaced by Jo Stafford and the Modernaires. Songstress Evelyn
Knight then replaced Stafford. Dick Haymes replaced Crosby two
years later and remained host until Crosby's return the following
year. The Andrews Sisters joined the cast three months after the
show's debut. It was their first regular radio series since their *Showroom* broadcasts for CBS. The high rate in personnel turnover during
the run of the series was partially due to the stars' contractual
commitments apart from the radio show, as well as the sponsors'
concerns to keep the format fresh. The Andrews Sisters were considered to be the main attraction of the show and remained as regulars, appearing Monday, Wednesday, and Friday evenings for nearly
four years. *Club 15* became the trio's longest radio stint.

The girls sang their hits on the show, as well as hundreds of popular songs of the day. They also performed some specialty tunes, including such amusing fare as "The Headless Horseman," with Dick Haymes, and "Hang on the Bell, Nellie!" with Bob Crosby and Del Sharbutt. During the show's frequent "All-American Rainbow" segment, the girls sang a five-minute ditty called "I Hear America Singing," a rousing patriotic production in which they were assisted by Crosby and Sharbutt. The sisters sang their own arrangements of "The Tennessee Waltz" and "Music by the Angels," both of which featured rare solo spots by LaVerne rather than Patty. They also sang the popular Campbell Soup slogan ("Mmm, mmm, good!") and participated in commercials for Campbell and Franco-American products throughout the shows.

Although they had no personal problems working with Crosby and Haymes—both on records and on radio—the girls were not accustomed to Haymes' style of song arranging. He insisted on dividing segments of the song equally between himself and the sisters. According to Maxene, the trio was more concerned with the quality of the finished product rather than who sang how many lines, so they usually let the crooner have his way. One session proved troublesome, however, when the trio and Haymes joined Bing Crosby in March of 1947. Maxene recalled,

> The only artist we had problems with was Dick Haymes. I guess maybe they figured we were a strange act to work with because we didn't read music. So, when we would come into the recording session, we would have the secretary type out all of the lyrics and type out the direction of how it would go. And nobody ever disagreed. Crosby said, "Anything the girls want to do." Dick counted lines, so he ruined a wonderful recording session that we could have had with "There's No Business like Show Business" because he made everybody change things in it.

Maxene's claim here is rather questionable. The released final cut of "There's No Business Like Show Business" is a nicely balanced group effort. Actually, the sisters, Patty's solo spots included, sing as many as five more lines than both Crosby and Haymes, so it seems that Haymes may have altered the arrangement to the sisters' advantage. Perhaps the girls themselves were not perceived by other stars to be very cooperative. Leon Belasco, the orchestra leader whose band backed the trio during road tours in the mid-1930s, once confided to an interviewer that the girls were a bit lazy in learning new song arrangements and that they were not eager to adapt to changes in already existing arrangements.

The sisters took a brief leave of absence from *Club 15* in 1948, when Patty hit her mouth as she was getting into a car. Her lip required seven stitches, and when the trio returned to the show, the writers had Patty joking about the incident with Bob Crosby:

Bob: "Well, Patty, we sure are glad to have you back in *Club 15*. It must make you awfully mad to get hit in the mouth with the top of a convertible."

Patty: "Oh, not me, Bob. I got a bang out of it."

Bob: "You mean you could laugh about getting a cut lip?"

Patty: "Robert, it had me in stitches!"

Bob: "How many stitches did you have?"

Patty: "Seven."

Bob: "Gee, seven stitches in your lip. It sounds like a lot."

Patty: "You said a mouthful!"

Maxene: "You know something, Bob? You Crosbys are lucky you didn't form a trio. When one Andrews can't sing, we all stop working."

Bob: "Well, it's different with us Crosbys. When one Crosby can't sing, the rest of us have to start working!"

Shortly before the trio joined radio's *Club 15*, a song promoter and movie agent named Marty Melcher, who had worked with the sisters at times, formed a talent agency with Dick Dorso and Al Levy (no relation to Lou). The Andrews Sisters became clients of Melcher's Century Artists, and Patty soon began dating Melcher. The relationship blossomed quickly and it was not long before he proposed. They were married October 19, 1947, beside the pool at Maxene's ranch, and they soon purchased their own home. The couple made an attractive appearance, both tall and slender with broad smiles and lively personalities.

Another musicians' strike went into effect January 1, 1948, and a recording ban was ordered for all instrumentalists. Unlike the 1942–1943 strike, this one had been anticipated. Many artists, including the sisters, accordingly scheduled numerous recording sessions with their record companies prior to the strike so that their disc output would not slow during the ban. Some artists, including Frank Sinatra ("Nature Boy"), Ella Fitzgerald with the Song Spinners ("My Happiness"), Dick Haymes, and Sarah Vaughan recorded a cappella. The ban lasted a few days short of one year. In that time, the sisters got around the strike by employing a harmonica ensemble called the Harmonica Gentlemen (harmonicas were not considered to be musical instruments at that time, and so harmonica players were not part of the union). Shortly following the onset of the strike, while all instrumentalists were more or less locked out of the studios, the trio recorded "Heartbreaker" and "(Everytime They Play the) Sabre Dance" with the Harmonica Gentlemen. Both groups joined Danny Kaye three months later for "The Woody Woodpecker Song" and "Put 'Em in a Box, Tie 'Em with a Ribbon (And Throw 'Em in the Deep Blue Sea)." When released by Decca, both records became *Billboard* hits, but as a result of these releases and their success, harmonicas were quickly ruled musical instruments and banned for the duration of the strike. Nonetheless, the girls managed to record four sides at a time when most other studio artists were forced into inactivity.

Although the trio's recorded performance of "Sabre Dance" (based on Aram Khachaturian's "Gayne Ballet Suite") is impressive, largely as a result of the trio's impeccable vocal timing, it is unfortunate that they recorded the song without the benefit of a full orchestra backing them. Live versions of the trio performing the number with a complete orchestra are far superior to the Decca version. "Sabre Dance" is a good example of multiple recordings of the same song in the 1940s recording industry. Aside from the trio's Decca version, the song was also recorded by Woody Herman's orchestra on the Columbia label, Victor Young's orchestra on Decca, Freddy Martin's orchestra on RCA Victor, Ray Bloch's orchestra on

Signature, Macklin Marrow's orchestra on MGM, pianist Oscar Levant on Columbia, the Angie Bond Trio on Dick, and the Harmonickings on Jubilee. Listeners enjoyed various interpretations of many pop hits of the day, while artists competed to release their material as quickly as possible, so as to be the first on the charts.

The sisters were featured in a second full-length, animated feature for Walt Disney, *Melody Time* (1948). The trio sang the narrative for a sketch called "Little Toot," the familiar story concerning the mishaps of a mischievous tugboat. This was the last film in which the sisters worked as a trio, although *Road to Rio* had already marked their last appearance on screen. The sisters continued to make guest appearances on radio shows for the Armed Forces Radio Service, including *Command Performance* and *Remember*, working with Gordon MacRae and Arthur Treacher. Maxene recalled working with Treacher during the war, when he appeared on and off with the sisters during their USO tour: "He seemed very stuffy, somewhat like some of his roles. He obviously didn't enjoy being around the GIs. At various stages on our tour, people would ask us where he was and we'd say we didn't know—but we did. We knew he was at the British Officers' Club. Arthur even got somebody to fly him back to England for a little private R&R during the middle of our tour."

The trio was no longer appearing at the Paramount in New York City due to scheduling conflicts with theater management. They soon began performing at the Roxy Theater. *Variety* wrote the following of their first Roxy show during the summer of 1948:

> It is by now an old story that the Andrews Sisters
> have emerged from a straight singing trio to a prime
> entertainment unit. They've kept pace with changing
> modes with a constant refurbishing of material, and
> Patty is just reaching her apex as a comedienne. The
> latter is a great focal point for the trio and she paces
> the girls to top mittings. While the majority of tunes
> delivered are those culled from their long list of hits,
> they've given most of them new bits of business to
> sustain interest. The early part of their turn is devoted

mainly to the oldies, done with the same relish that made them hits on Decca's lists. In addition, they've concocted a bright spoof on the wives of the top cowboy filmsters, including a sequence wherein they don horse outfits and the equines appear to be doing the chirping. Another top song is "Hawaii," which they build up into one of their biggest numbers. The girls do extremely well for themselves at this house and Vic Schoen's batoning during their stand gives them solid musical backing.

In the midst of their successful Roxy engagement, the girls received word that their mother was very ill, so they immediately flew back to Brentwood to be at her bedside. Olga passed away on July 3, 1948, just three days prior to LaVerne's thirty-seventh birthday. The death of their mother was a great loss to the girls and to Peter, with whom they stayed for one month before returning to their performing schedule. Maxene has said that her father was greatly affected and saddened by her mother's death. It was actually one of only two times that Peter cried in front of the girls (the first was when President Roosevelt died a few years earlier). Their month-long stay in California with Peter helped him cope with his loss, but eventually the sisters had contractual commitments to fulfill.

The girls opened their first engagement abroad at the London Palladium in August 1948, following a successful engagement there by Danny Kaye. During their four-week stint, hundreds of fans who were unable to obtain tickets to the sold-out shows stood in the streets to cheer them as they came and went from the famed theater. The critics raved. *Variety* wrote, "The girls are obliged to stay over their allotted time because of the demand for encores." David Lewin of the *Daily Express* declared, "The audience gave the Andrews Sisters the Danny Kaye roar!" The *Daily Herald* stated, "The fans were aroused to a frenzy," while the *London Times* added, "The Andrews Sisters gaily demonstrate their euphonious expertise in a witty performance—the Palladium becomes one big party." The shows ran a little over sixty minutes each, not including encores.

During one show, Patty spotted Irving Berlin in the audience and called him on stage to join the girls for "Alexander's Ragtime Band." Another show was attended by Princess Margaret, Queen Elizabeth's sister.

The sisters sailed to England in style on the famous Queen Elizabeth cruising ship, and they had been instructed to sail with adequate food supplies, as much of Europe was still suffering from the aftermath of World War II. As a result, the trio took along canned foods, including soups (Campbell, of course), tuna, frankfurters, and vegetables. One evening while the trio was staying in Manchester, they invited some guests to their hotel suite for a bite to eat. They sent a dozen cans of frankfurters and vegetables to the kitchen for the hotel chef to prepare and send back. A waiter returned much later with a huge dome-covered tray. When Maxene lifted the lid, she found merely eight hot dogs atop a mound of boiled potatoes. The girls never questioned anyone as to what happened to the remainder of the meal, as Maxene reasoned that whoever helped themselves to the food must have needed it.

Decca released two songs that the trio recorded while in London for their Palladium engagement. Side A delivered "You Call Everybody Darling," a popular country-western ballad adapted to a classic swing arrangement, which included some bouncy back-up vocals from Maxene and LaVerne during Patty's brief solo spot (a precursor to the vocal style that Diana Ross and the Supremes would popularize years later). The disc was backed by "Underneath the Arches," which featured the girls in close-knit harmony. Both songs became top-ten hits. More hits followed, including a frantic samba rendition of "Cuanto la Gusta," the girls' first pairing on records with Carmen Miranda. Another successful release was the amusing novelty hit "The Money Song," backed by the Italian ballad "Bella Bella Marie." Their records continued to receive a great deal of play on radio and jukeboxes, as they would for several more years.

LaVerne became the last sister of the three to wed, marrying Lou Rogers on November 12, 1948. Rogers was a trumpet player with Vic Schoen's orchestra, supplying the tropical-sounding trumpet solo during "Rum and Coca Cola." The ceremony took place in

Maxene's home. Rogers moved in with LaVerne and Peter, and all three shared the Brentwood estate.

The sisters suffered another personal loss eight months after their mother's death. When Jack Kapp died suddenly on March 25, 1949, of a cerebral hemorrhage at the age of forty-seven, his passing greatly affected the Decca roster of talent. Music historian Joseph Laredo notes, "Many feel that the premature passing of Jack Kapp took much of the joy out of recording at Decca for the label's established artists. The Andrews Sisters in particular keenly felt his loss, and were content to let their Decca contract lapse at the end of 1953."

The sisters greatly admired Jack Kapp—a good and true friend to them over a dozen years. He was actively involved in their recording career, and he offered much advice and praise. Patty remembers especially "what a bear he was with us about enunciation." Kapp made sure that every word of every recording was clearly and distinctly pronounced. He had an intercom system installed in the recording studios to deliver sound from the actual recording sessions into his office, which enabled him to be in two different places at the same time. Jack was also passionate about the melody of a song, not wanting the performer to stray too far with improvisations. He felt that songwriters had a particular sense of how their compositions should sound and that sticking to the melody would come as close as possible to what the songwriter initially intended. That may have been the reason Kapp did not release the trio's 1946 recording of "Three O'Clock in the Morning," a traditional waltz that the trio converted to a swinging big band arrangement, until 1950. Kapp had a life-size portrait of Pocahontas hanging in both his New York and Los Angeles studios. The famous Native American was pictured standing on the shore, looking out over the water, her arms outstretched in search of Captain Smith. The cartoon bubble on the poster had her asking, "Where's the melody?"

Jack was a friendly, creative, and respected businessman who, along with his brother Dave, had a keen sense for talent. Even though Jack was the president of the company, he was readily available to everyone from Crosby and the sisters to any one of his mailroom employees with an open door policy. He created one of the most successful and profitable record labels in popular music history. Milton Rackmil, the company's vice-president, stepped in as the head of Decca after Jack's death. Rackmil's background, however, was strictly financial. Maxene remembered Rackmil as "a bookkeeper. I think that when Milton took Jack's place, the heart went out of the company. It was just like a glass bowl dropped and went into pieces, because everything just flew in every direction. You knew that the days of Decca were over." Dave Kapp soon clashed with Rackmil, and he soon left Decca to join RCA. The sisters, who had become accustomed to the recording studio as a home away from home, had found an extended family in the Kapp brothers. Within three years, without the guidance of their mentors, the sisters' recording career at Decca floundered.

Decca released five new singles by the Andrews Sisters during the first few months of 1949; all five discs, including "More Beer!" and "Let a Smile Be Your Umbrella," became bestsellers. The girls had previously experimented with country-western styled numbers with success ("Pistol Packin' Mama," "Down in the Valley," "Don't Fence Me In"), but these arrangements had been pop-styled to fit the sisters' brand of vocalizing. Now the girls attempted a true hillbilly sound with Ernest Tubb. They recorded "Don't Rob Another Man's Castle" (a huge hit for country-western singer Eddy Arnold) and a western-swing ditty, "I'm Bitin' My Fingernails and Thinking of You." The disc sold over five hundred thousand copies and proved the sisters again successful in a musical crossover, which is common today but was rarely practiced in the 1940s. The success of the quartet prompted other pop vocalists to collaborate with country-western stars, producing hits such as "Slipping Around" (Margaret Whiting and Jimmy Wakely) and a few hits by Kay Starr and Tennessee Ernie Ford ("I'll Never Be Free" and "Oceans of Tears").

Tubb was enthusiastic about recording with the sisters, as were other artists who worked with them. The trio had become one of the most respected names in the entertainment business, and for any artist, recording with the Andrews Sisters would most likely result in a hit record release. Tubb brought the "Fingernails" tune to his session with the girls, hoping they would like it. They did, and Tubb's vocals on this track suited the trio much better than it did on the backing forlorn ballad. Tubb was tall and lanky. He towered over the sisters, who had to stand on a box on one side of the mike so that the voices would balance. Although the sisters enjoyed working with the "Texas Troubadour," they were not exactly accustomed to his singing style. Maxene recalled, "He sang different than anybody I've ever heard. He sang the melody of the song, but the timing was different. It wasn't like we were used to—you sing eight bars, and then you sing eight bars, and then you sing eight bars. Not with him. He just sang eight bars, ten bars, eleven bars, and then stopped, whatever it was. So, we'd just start to follow him—and then got paid on 750,000 records sold that never came above the Mason-Dixon Line!"

Patty joined *Club 15* costar Bob Crosby that same year for a comical Decca rendition of "The Pussy Cat Song (Nyow! Nyot Nyow!)," which became a number-twelve hit. This success prompted Patty to seek out other Decca artists for future duets, including Bing Crosby, Danny Kaye, Dick Haymes, Alfred Apaka, and Jimmy Durante.

Considering the overwhelming success the trio had enjoyed over the past thirteen years, it probably did not occur to them that even more triumphs awaited them as the 1940s drew to a close. It also may not have occurred to the girls that more personal tragedies would befall them in the near future, including the death of their father and divorces for Patty and Maxene. These events would no doubt contribute to dissension in the group and ultimately lead to a temporary separation, but not before the sisters reached the pinnacle of their performing success. Laudative cabaret engagements and recording hits would serve to bond the trio over the next two years.

9

A Love Song Is Born

The Andrews Sisters were planning to record a lovely ballad entitled "I Can Dream, Can't I?" in the summer of 1949. The song had been written in 1937 by Sammy Fain and Irving Kahal. Dave Kapp suggested the tune to the trio; it had always been his favorite song, and he was eager to be involved in their arrangement of it. The girls asked Gordon Jenkins to back them on the recording. Jenkins, with his lush string section and accompanying chorus, was a master at evoking a distinctively melancholy quality in his music that no other arranger could capture. He did his most outstanding work with several different artists throughout the 1950s, including the Andrews Sisters, Dick Haymes, Frank Sinatra, Peggy Lee, Ella Fitzgerald, Judy Garland, and the Weavers.

Dave Kapp decided that Patty would solo through the first verse, while Maxene and LaVerne joined her for the remainder. "I Can Dream, Can't I?" would be different than most of the girls' previous recordings, which showcased them as a harmony group. Kapp's brother, Jack, had previously been against extended solos showcasing Patty. He reasoned that such productions might signal the end of records by the Andrews Sisters and the beginning of solo discs by Patty Andrews; he had the foresight to realize that such a happening might encourage the trio to disband. But when the girls recorded "I Can Dream, Can't I?," Jack was not there to protest the proceedings.

The girls recorded "I Can Dream, Can't I?" in New York, and the finished product was one of the most professional, artful, and haunting ballads ever recorded. The arrangement of the tune by Gordon Jenkins, his wistful string section, his background chorus, the girls' vocal execution of the disconsolate lyric, and Patty's polished, sophisticated vocal prowess all meshed to produce a sound markedly different than anything the sisters had achieved before. The recording's distinctive, high-brow quality gained the sisters the respect of fans and critics alike who had not taken them very seriously in previous years.

Backing the ballad was a lovely rendition of "The Wedding of Lili Marlene." The lush harmonies lent beautifully to the flowing melody, with the chorus swelling dramatically during Patty's solo. Jenkins had accomplished an effect with the Andrews Sisters that he had not captured with previous artists, including Dick Haymes. The disc immediately sold over one million copies and it was later judged "the best-selling record of 1949." It rose above such notable competition as Frankie Laine's "The Cry of the Wild Goose," Doris Day's "Again," Kay Starr's "Bonaparte's Retreat," and the smash hit "Baby, It's Cold Outside," recorded as a duet by Margaret Whiting and Johnny Mercer as well as by Dinah Shore and Buddy Clark.

"I Can Dream, Can't I?" shot to number-one on the *Billboard* charts and remained in the top ten for twenty consecutive weeks. It also fulfilled Jack Kapp's predictions, as rumors soon began to surface that Patty might be leaving the group. When William Ruhlmann interviewed Patty and her second husband, Walter Weschler, in 1995, the subject came up and seemed to hit a nerve, as the couple became rather defensive: "I don't want to get into that. It never happened that way," Patty said. "That never happened" added Weschler, "She stood out on her own. So, right away, everybody said, 'You're gonna go out on your own.' That's bull——. Absolute baloney. Besides which, in those days, you didn't suddenly make a hit song and go out. You couldn't do that." Patty continued, "So much stuff came out, lies like that, that it irritates me."

Ruhlmann concluded, "But even if Patty herself resisted the idea, as with any prominent performer in a group who begins to get separate recognition, there were industry and business pressures that could in turn lead to unintended dissension within the group."

Another big hit during the summer was Jo Stafford and Gordon MacRae's million-selling rendition of "Whispering Hope" on the Capitol label. They collaborated in June to record the lilting inspirational ballad, written in 1868 by Alice Hawthorne, and their duet version became a number-four hit. The Andrews Sisters' Decca recording of "Whispering Hope" had been done nearly two years earlier in a secretive session, as Jack Kapp expected the number to do very well for the girls and did not want another artist beating them to the charts. For some unknown reason, however, the recording was shelved and remained unreleased until shortly after the Stafford-MacRae version. While the trio's rendition sold well, it did not become the runaway smash that was anticipated. Perhaps their version came too late. Had it not been detained, their Decca single might have given the Capitol release some stiff competition. Levy's Leeds Music made certain that the trio's arrangement did not appear to be a copy of the Stafford-MacRae take by captioning the sheet music copy of the song, "Arranged and Recorded by the Andrews Sisters." The sisters harmonized softly and beautifully on "Whispering Hope" before Patty broke into her solo while LaVerne and Maxene echoed the same lyrics in double time. The flip side of the disc was a vocalization of "Lovely Night," the "Barcarolle" from *The Tales of Hoffman*.

Another outstanding release by the trio that year was their rhythmic rendition of "Malagueña," the Latin-American ballad about a beautiful gypsy girl. The song was re-popularized in an all-Spanish rendition by Connie Francis in 1960. "Malagueña" is an Andrews Sisters masterpiece; the girls pace their harmony in perfect unison with Vic Schoen's sweeping orchestrations. It was the flip side of the platter, however, that made the disc a hit—an amusing novelty called "Hohokus, N.J." The sisters performed at a block party in Hohokus to promote the song. Patty was amused when, twenty-five years later, a man approached her and asked if she remembered him. She had to honestly say no, to which he replied,

"I was the motorcycle cop that led your limousine to the block party in Hohokus!" More hits followed, among them "The Blossoms on the Bough"; "The Wedding Samba" with Carmen Miranda; two hits with Bing Crosby: "Have I Told You Lately that I Love You?" and "Quicksilver," both recorded with heavy country-western influences; and a coupling with Russ Morgan and his orchestra that resulted in "Charley, My Boy" and a rousing marching rendition of "She Wore a Yellow Ribbon," from the John Wayne film of the same name. The girls recorded two more movie themes that year with actor-singer Dan Dailey, from two MGM blockbusters: "Take Me Out to the Ballgame" and "In the Good Old Summertime."

Professionally, things were progressing excellently for the girls. Personally, however, they were going through some difficult times. Maxene and Lou Levy had been experiencing marital problems—they separated in September 1948 and divorced March 11, 1949. Working together caused some of the strain in the marriage, although Levy continued to act as the trio's manager following the divorce. During the summer months of 1949, Patty's marriage to Marty Melcher was also in turmoil—and much more publicized than her sister's problems.

During his marriage to Patty, Melcher was associated with the Century Artists talent agency, whose clients included the trio, Gordon MacRae, and Doris Day. MacRae and his wife, Sheila, were good friends of the Melchers, enjoying many Sunday afternoons at Marty and Patty's house playing volleyball in the backyard. Day had made her screen debut a year earlier in *Romance on the High Seas,* and though she had been steadily racking up hit records since the mid 1940s during her tenure with Les Brown's big band, she had not yet achieved stardom. Her film debut dramatically changed that, as Hollywood quickly began fashioning her many talents into one of its biggest entertainment attractions. She would fulfill all expectations placed upon her over the next two decades, as she became a star personality throughout the world. Melcher befriended Day and spent a good deal of time with her, accompanying her on many publicity promotions. It was not long before rumors started to fly concerning the twosome.

Melcher confided in Doris, claiming that his marriage to Patty was failing. The couple soon separated, and Melcher moved out of the house into his own apartment. Doris Day recalled,

> At the time, a lot of people jumped to the conclusion that his leaving Patty was motivated by an affair he was having with me. Not so. There was absolutely nothing between us when Marty left Patty. But I heard that Patty was very angry for a while. . . . After his separation, Marty and I did start to see each other regularly. Marty had no children with Patty, and the more he was around the house, the more he became involved with Terry, my son, who responded to him wholeheartedly. . . . Marty, on the other hand, seemed to find in Terry the child he wanted but never had with Patty. I felt bad about Patty. I liked her very much and I know she still loved Marty, but I also know that no third person ever breaks up a marriage. A person does not leave a good man for someone else. But I heard that Patty suspected that Marty and I were having an affair and that was why he moved out. I never saw her after that until years later, so there was no chance to discuss it with her. Anyway, what is there to discuss? No amount of denial by "the other woman" can ever allay the angry suspicions of a wife. But I did feel very bad about Patty.

Day attested to Melcher's obsessive need to amass money, which may have contributed to his separation from Patty. Day said, "It has been said by some people who knew Marty rather well that he was attracted to Patty Andrews because of her money, and that he quickly left her for me when he became aware of the size of my potential earnings." One of the people Doris was speaking of was no doubt Dick Dorso, Melcher's partner in Century Artists, who recalled, "What you've got to realize to understand Marty was that he worshipped money. It was his god, and it was all that he was really focused on. To accumulate money was Marty's drive, from the moment he hit Hollywood until the day he died."

Warner Brothers musical executive Sam Weiss also remarked on Melcher's greed. He recalled the following concerning Patty's separation from Marty:

Patty was just as nice a gal as you'd ever want to meet, great gal, everybody loved her, but Marty stepped all over her, got everything he could out of her, and when he had a chance to better himself with a new client, Marty couldn't get rid of Patty fast enough. I knew Doris very well from my band connections, long before she came to Hollywood. So it was inevitable that I wound up being a close friend of hers, and that meant seeing a lot of Marty once he moved in on Doris. There were some rough times about that. I got a call from Doris' mother one night. "Sam," she said, "I'm scared to death. I'm alone in the house and Patty Andrews is at the door yelling that she wants to get in to get at Marty. She's mad as hell." "Hold on, Alma," I said, "don't open the door, I'll be there right away." "She's going to kill somebody," Alma said, "she's yelling terrible things." I parked about a block away from the house and snuck around through the backyard to have a look. Patty was on the porch with someone and she had a baseball bat in her hand. She was spitting fire. There was no doubt, from the way she was swinging that club, that she meant to use it. I snuck away and phoned Alma from the corner drugstore. "Where's Doris?" I asked. "She went with Marty Melcher for some publicity thing." Patty left after an hour or so, and it was true that Marty and Doris were on a legitimate publicity mission, but the fact was that the only thing Marty loved was money. He loved Patty's money until Doris' money came along and then, because there was more of it, he loved Doris' money more.

Bandleader Les Brown was no more impressed with Melcher

than most others who knew him. Brown summarized Melcher as a pushy, grating, crass, money-hungry man who lived off of Patty until he found a more lucrative prospect in Doris. Patty received a divorce from Melcher on March 31, 1950, and she asked for no alimony or community property. One year after the divorce, Melcher married and began to manage Doris Day. He deceitfully mishandled her finances over many years and left her flat broke, as well as five hundred thousand dollars in debt, at the time of his death in the late 1960s. Bob Hope, a friend of the trio's as well as Doris Day, saw in Melcher what many others did, once saying, "I always had a feeling, when Melcher was around, that he wasn't looking out for Doris as much as he was looking out for himself." Needless to say, Patty was well rid of Melcher.

Peter Andrews died of a heart attack in the midst of these problems. This was a tremendous blow to the trio, who lost their father during painful divorce proceedings, just a little over a year after their mother's sudden passing. The girls were away from home when their father died, en route to Washington, D.C., with Dick Haymes and the Modernaires, to attend a party for the employees of Campbell Soup Company. When the girls arrived in New York to switch planes, airport security took them into a private room and told them of their father's death. They immediately boarded the first flight back to Los Angeles. The trio's parents divided the Brentwood estate among their three daughters in wills. After Peter's death, LaVerne and her husband remained in the house, which was full of Andrews Sisters records, scrapbooks, awards, and other memorabilia.

The girls' parents seemed to be the integral glue that held the family together. The sisters greatly respected their parents, perhaps even to the extent that they made the ultimate effort to respect each other as well, and put their personal differences aside or even worse, stifled them completely. Peter and Olga were the main part of a core system that the sisters could fall back on—the other principals being Levy, Schoen, and the Kapp brothers. Once the trio's parents and Jack Kapp were gone and problems then arose between the girls and Levy and Schoen, the secure world that the sisters had known for so long began to unravel. The sisters were now forced to cope with these changes, which at this point at least had not yet affected their professional career.

Decca capitalized on the success of radio's *Club 15* in 1949, releasing an album of songs featuring the sisters, Dick Haymes, Evelyn Knight and the Modernaires, with Jerry Gray's orchestra. Among the eight songs on the album was the trio's recording of "He Rides the Range (For Republic)," a novelty that spoofed the western movies made by Republic Pictures. The song is a prime example of the girls' cohesive blend, flawless timing, and incredibly explosive style, especially during the finale. It is hard to believe that the sisters produced such a powerful sound gathered around only one microphone (three other mikes were placed throughout the orchestra—in the reeds, the brass, and the rhythm sections), without elaborate modern boards and other sophisticated equipment. It is also significant to recall that all albums then were recorded live in the sense that all of the principals—vocalists and musicians—were in the studio performing together simultaneously. The absence of prerecorded tracks and overdubbing ensured an energetic atmosphere that can be heard throughout most of the tracks. Patty recalled the process, referring to sessions with Bing Crosby, "Today, everybody has a microphone; we had one microphone, he was on one side and we were on the other side, all sharing the mike. I think that's where the feel was, you see; if you're separated, you're not going to get that feel. We got the feel from each other."

The sisters returned to New York's Roxy during the summer to headline a three-week engagement, about which *Variety* said, "The Andrews Sisters are a show in themselves. Completely poised, they mug, kid around and use all sorts of things to flavor their tune pitching and the net result is a socko session." During the Roxy appearance, the girls performed mostly novelty tunes, including "Go West, Young Man"; "Feudin' and Fightin'"; "Hohokus, N.J."; the cowboy classic "Riders in the Sky," during which the trio was backed by the Roxy chorus; and their big satirical finale, a medley of "Sonny Boy" and "Mammy." An audience favorite was their rendition of "Be-Bop Spoken Here" (which Patty recorded with Crosby on Decca), during which the girls drew howls wearing huge bop hats and oversized sunglasses.

The trio scored another top-ten hit with Gordon Jenkins. "I Wanna Be Loved" was an outstanding sequel to "I Can Dream, Can't I?" It became the number-one song in the country, remaining on the top-ten charts for fourteen weeks. *Billboard* wrote, "This is a magnificent record! Amidst a rich mood setting by Jenkins, Patty Andrews sings her heart out on this wonderful oldie. Should be one of the big slicings of the year." The record sold just under a million copies. Jenkins saved the hook of the song until the very end of the recording, at which point the girls hold the final note while the strings and chorus swell. It is hard to find a copy of the original Decca disc that is not worn gray at the end of the A side. A follow-up to this release was another project with Jenkins—a tender reading of "There Will Never Be Another You," popularized during World War II, backed by "Can't We Talk It Over?" The disc became a bestseller. The sisters had now become as well known for their ballads as they were already known for their swing and boogie-woogie hits.

The trio enjoyed their seventh and final cover story for *Billboard* magazine in June of 1950, when the entertainment weekly covered the girls' latest Decca session with Al Jolson, which produced "Way Down Yonder in New Orleans" and "The Old Piano Roll Blues." Maxene remembered what a cut-up Jolson could be in the studio: "Jolie was always on stage—center stage—and if he could get some laughs by clowning around right up until the recording light went on in the studio, he'd go for them." Other hits this year included "A Penny a Kiss—A Penny a Hug" and "A Bushel and a Peck," which helped the trio to be voted number-one in a list of the country's top singing groups compiled by *Billboard* in the magazine's fall disc jockey supplement.

The Andrews Sisters became the talk of the town when they held a remarkably successful engagement in the posh Venetian Room at the Fairmont Hotel in San Francisco. Reviewing the vast variety of material now comprising the trio's stage act, the critics showered the girls with praise. Herb Caen of the *San Francisco Examiner* wrote, "About the Andrews Sisters—brother, they're great!" Ivan Paul observed in the same newspaper, "The girls put on a terrific show." Jack Rosenbaum of the *San Francisco News* declared, "Easy to see why they're tops in American popular music," while the *Chronicle's* Robert McCary assessed, "The Andrews Sisters are more popular than dollar bills!" Radio reviewers also raved. Pat McGuirk, on his KCBS show *This Is San Francisco,* said, "A show the likes of which this village hasn't seen in years and years," while the host of *The Ann Holden Hour* commented, "The act has a fresh, new, young impact bubbling with originality and spontaneity. They are not only the nation's top singing trio, but tops as comediennes and all-around entertainers."

Benjamin H. Swig, president of the Fairmont, wrote a letter to Lou Levy after the trio's hotel engagement, saying, "It gives me great pleasure to report that from the opening night, they have done the greatest business of any attraction ever presented in the history of the Fairmont Hotel. The girls have packed the room for two shows a night, even on what are ordinarily our weakest nights."

Another very successful engagement was the Andrews Sisters' return to New York's Roxy in the summer of 1951, with Dean Martin and Jerry Lewis opening the show. Martin took ill for several days and was replaced by Patty, who performed the five shows a day with Lewis, as well as the five shows a day with her sisters. Years later, during a 1965 guest spot with Jerry Lewis on *The Tonight Show,* hosted by Johnny Carson, the trio recalled that engagement with Martin and Lewis, although the duo had separated bitterly a decade earlier and remained distant. The following is some of the dialogue from that humorous exchange:

> Johnny: "What were you girls doing here the other day when I ran into you in the hall?"
> LaVerne: "Dean Martin."
> Patty: "The Dean Martin Show."
> Johnny: "Oh! Oh! Oh!"
> Maxene: "Is that a dirty word?"
> LaVerne: "No!"
> Jerry: "No, it's not a dirty word!"
> Patty: "It's not a dirty word. In fact, you want to know something—many years ago, Dean and Jerry and the three of us—"

Jerry: "It can be Jerry and Dean now. When we were together it was Dean and Jerry. Now you can say Jerry and Dean."

Patty: "But I haven't been on your show yet."

Jerry: "I blew it!"

Patty: "So, anyway, the boys and the three of us girls were working the Roxy Theater together—"

LaVerne: "We were girls then!"

Patty: "I've got news for you, this act may break up! Anyway, we worked together, and Dean got sick for about three days and I did the act with Jerry. It was very high class—he spit in my face five times a day for five shows, and did very classy stuff. It really helped my career!"

Jerry: "It straightened Dean and I out, too!"

Patty: "I have only one regret, though. If I stuck with him, I might have been Dean Martin, right?"

Jerry: "And I'd be on your show, 'cause I can't get on his."

Maxene underwent hysterectomy surgery in California during the second week of the trio's Roxy engagement, so Patty and LaVerne performed without her. The theater management reported that ticket sales did not decrease during Maxene's absence.

The sisters were soon off to Europe to open another engagement at the London Palladium, and then do some touring in Glasgow and Blackpool. Their tour included one stop at the Hippodrome Theater, about which the *Birmingham Post* wrote, "To announce the Andrews Sisters as queens of rhythm does them considerably less than justice, in that it fails to take account of the brightest gift that this trio from America has to offer; that, most demonstrably, is their sense and enaction of comedy." Concerning an appearance at Scotland's Empire Theater, the *Glasgow Evening News* had the following to say: "The merry Andrews Sisters cram sixteen songs and snatches of past hits into their slick, timed-to-perfection act, wiggle their hips to the rhythm of a twenty-piece band in this potpourri of top-grade harmony and top-grade humor." A clever spot in that show occurred after Patty sang Nat King Cole's "Too Young," her latest *Billboard* hit, and Maxene and LaVerne retaliated with a specialty number, "Why Do They Give the Solos to Patty When There's So Much of Us Going to Waste?" The *Scottish Daily Mail* also praised the trio's act: "The Andrews Sisters have rhythm, harmony, humor and above all, enchanting personalities. Only the National Anthem stopped the audience from cheering and whistling. They are better on the stage than on the screen and they themselves enjoy the show!"

While visiting Paris with LaVerne during the 1951 European tour, Patty announced her engagement to Walter Weschler, the trio's pianist. Weschler had joined Vic Schoen's orchestra in 1944. The couple married on Christmas Day of 1951 during a civil ceremony at the Brentwood estate. Maxene was the maid of honor and LaVerne's husband, Lou, served as best man. Patty and Weschler combined their honeymoon with the trio's upcoming performance schedule in Las Vegas. It seems that Patty found true happiness in this union.

The trio performed at Philadelphia's Latin Quarter in the fall, just before appearing on *The Frank Sinatra Show* on CBS-TV. They opened the CBS program with a comical "Peony Bush," during which the girls performed some light dance steps as Patty looked out to the audience and exclaimed, "You didn't know we could dance, did you? Well, we can't!" The trio enjoyed working with Sinatra on radio and television, but according to Maxene, the crooner seemed indifferent to the girls at times. Maxene recalled one meeting in particular, when she was visiting Tokyo. She was lifted off her feet from behind while getting into a limousine, whirled around, and given a big kiss—it was Sinatra with a friendly greeting; however, when the girls would meet Sinatra at social functions and such, he would sometimes ignore them. Maxene once referred to him as "a peculiar man." Maxene also recalled when Sinatra entertained the troops during an overseas USO tour with Phil Silvers, saying, "I guess they just had a wing-ding, whatever it was. Sinatra demanded his own plane. But Bing said, 'Don't demand anything. Just go over there and sing your hearts out.' So, we did."

In 1951, Patty Andrews recorded nine Decca solos without Maxene and LaVerne, the most outstanding of these being her rendition of "It Never Entered My Mind" with Gordon Jenkins' orchestra and chorus. Also notable was her dramatic styling of two more songs with Jenkins—"If You Go" and "That's How a Love Song Is Born," both beautiful, lilting ballads. She also recorded the tender "How Many Times (Can I Fall in Love?)" with Victor Young and his Singing Strings, assisted by Tommy Dorsey on trombone. Another love tune with Jenkins, "I'm in Love Again," charted on *Billboard*. These soft love ballads were musical vehicles much better suited to a solo vocalist than a harmony trio, hence Patty's selection. Maxene and LaVerne were not threatened by these solo outings by Patty, and Maxene has stated in interviews that she especially encouraged Patty in the endeavors. The three sisters recorded "Old Don Juan" in April with bandleader Desi Arnaz and, at the end of that month, the girls went to Nashville, Tennessee, to record a series of songs with country-western singer Red Foley, hoping to repeat the success they previously had with Ernest Tubb. Among the songs recorded with Foley during the two-day Decca sessions were "Satins and Lace," "I Want to Be with You Always," "Where Is Your Wandering Mother Tonight?," and "Bury Me beneath the Willow," as well as two country-gospel favorites, "It Is No Secret (What God Can Do)" and "He Bought My Soul at Calvary." Both gospel songs received a good deal of play on the country-western radio stations throughout the country.

Near Easter, Decca released a ten-inch album of gospel songs by the sisters with Victor Young's orchestra. While the project would doubtless have been better if recorded with Gordon Jenkins' orchestra, the girls lent a true sincerity to each of the eight songs with their intertwined harmonies. LaVerne's contralto was more pronounced in these songs than on any other of the trio's Decca recordings, especially in "In the Garden" and "Softly and Tenderly." Shortly after this release, the girls recorded what may be their all-time greatest work, "The Three Bells (The Jimmy Brown Song)," with Jenkins and his group. Jenkins began the inspirational ballad simply with three echoing bell chimes, followed immediately by Patty's first verse. Her seasoned vocal skills greatly enhanced the melody, and when her sisters joined in on each of the three choruses, the harmonious results were extremely effective. Jenkins' choral group sang the third verse a cappella.

The song told the story of Jimmy Brown, a simple village dweller whose birth, marriage, and death were signified by the ringing chapel bells in his little valley town. The song was adapted from the French melody, "Les Trois Cloches," composed in 1945 by Jean Villard. It was first given recognition in a haunting 1946 recording by French songstress Edith Piaf, backed by Les Compagnons de Chanson (a vocal group comprised of nine young Frenchmen). The French a cappella version ran just over four minutes. In 1948 Bert Reisfeld translated the song into English as "The Three Bells." The most popular version of the song in America was recorded by a country-western group in 1959. The Browns' (Jim Ed and his sisters, Maxine and Bonnie) beautiful RCA record sold over one million copies and became the nation's number-one hit on *Billboard's* pop and country top-ten charts. The Browns shortened each of the song's three verses to keep its playing time under three minutes (the original composition was eleven minutes) so as not to limit its airplay.

The Andrews Sisters' version of the ballad was the first recorded English version, as well as their longest recording for Decca (running three minutes and thirty-four seconds). Although the trio's version should have been well received (both the quality of the material and the performance indicated such), the Decca release did not prove successful. Even the reviewers at *Billboard* recognized both the record's appeal and potential, writing, "The Andrews Sisters do their most effective job in ages with a superb assist from Jenkins' forces. Could be a big record." Unfortunately, most popular music fans are unaware that "The Three Bells" is even part of the trio's recorded body of work. Another song, "When the Angelus Is Ringing," composed by Joe Young and Bert Grant in 1945, and loosely based on the melody of Villard's "Les Trois Cloches," was recorded by several popular artists that year, including Frank Sinatra, Margaret Whiting, Vaughn Monroe with the Moon Maids, and Tommy Dorsey and his orchestra.

The sisters now found themselves at a height of popularity previously unattained by any other act (with the exception of Bing Crosby) in show business history. Their music had earned a permanent place in American culture.

10

Disharmony

Vic Schoen, the man who had been identified with the Andrews Sisters for over a decade, and whose orchestra had accompanied the girls in over ninety percent of their recordings, parted from the trio in late 1951. He went on to work with several other artists, producing major hits, including Patti Page's "Old Cape Cod" and the Weavers' "On Top of Old Smoky." But never again was the maestro to become so well associated with another singer as he and his band had become with the sisters. Schoen eventually married and divorced Kay Starr, then wed Marion Hutton of Glenn Miller fame (Betty Hutton's sister).

Although Schoen's decision to leave the girls was not forced, it was nevertheless traumatic, especially for the trio, who sorely missed him and his remarkable skill at arranging music. The girls had lost their parents and Jack Kapp, Maxene had divorced Lou Levy, Dave Kapp had left Decca for RCA, and now, Vic Schoen was leaving. The team behind the trio's enormous success had slowly disappeared. Schoen recalled the split to interviewer William Ruhlmann:

> It was very slow deterioration because it held together somehow. It wasn't very comfortable, and by 1951 it

136

had all gone to hell, everything. That's when I left them. It was the house of hostility, and there was a reason for it, as I understand now, but at the time I couldn't see a reason. Somehow, what had worked for so long, nearly seventeen years—they began to think that those old ways were no longer working. That is, Lou Levy had sort of become an enemy, and there's no logic to any of it. But Patty married our piano player, Walter Weschler, and he had ambitions, I guess, to be their everything, manager and creator from that point on. It was so bad. It was uncomfortable. It seemed that this thing should break up, but we didn't know how to do it. They could never fire me for some reason or another, and I could never say, "I quit." But it happened.

These tensions among the individuals involved compounded the problems, although the incident causing the final split seems trivial. While the sisters were performing with Schoen in Scotland, Kay Starr attended one of the shows. She stood in the wings during the sisters' performance and briefly stuck her head out from behind the stage curtain. She was immediately recognized by the audience, and the adulation that followed interrupted the trio's act. The sisters were furious, and since Kay had flown from the States to see Schoen, Vic found himself on the receiving end of the trio's anger. The episode also resulted in a rift between Vic and Kay. Shortly thereafter, Schoen was approached by NBC-TV to become musical director of *The Dinah Shore Show*. He weighed the offer against the tense situation that his relations with the sisters had become and decided that it was time to part ways.

This was the period when things started falling apart for the Andrews Sisters. They had signed with MCA, a booking agency in 1952, and hired Bo Roos as their business manager. Soon, Lou Levy filed suit at Superior Court in Los Angeles requesting that the sisters be removed as directors of the Eight-to-the-Bar Ranch Corporation, claiming that they had failed to assign their yearly earnings to the corporation. Levy also noted that the IRS was claiming the corporation owed over one hundred thousand dollars in back taxes. It was becoming an ugly public fight. Meanwhile, on a more positive note, the sisters performed for the king and queen of Greece, their father's birthplace, and they appeared later that year at the McKinley Auditorium in Honolulu, Hawaii. Five months later, Decca released an album of Hawaiian songs featuring the trio with Alfred Apaka, backed by Danny Stewart and his Islanders. The liner notes on the back of the album boasted, "There is nothing—and we mean nothing—that the Andrews Sisters cannot do! They are at home in any type of popular song, in every beat and seemingly, in every language."

The trio began recording with a number of different orchestras after Schoen's departure, including those led by George Cates, Skip Martin, Sy Oliver, and Russ Morgan. The trio's recordings were numerous as ever. They included a masterful cover of Al Martino's "Here in My Heart" with Dick Haymes, in his best vocal performance with the trio, and Nelson Riddle's orchestra. The quartet's intense rendering of the ballad featured Patty singing at the very top of her vocal register. Other releases in 1952 were "Adios," a vocalization of the Glenn Miller hit years earlier; "Carmen's Boogie," a swinging boogie-woogie version of the "Habanera" from the opera *Carmen*; and a couple of collaborations with Bing Crosby, including "I'll Si-Si Ya in Bahia," "South Rampart Street Parade," and "Cool Water"—a slow, straightforward reading of the cowboy classic. The latter two marked the last time the Andrews Sisters collaborated with Crosby on record. Their years of recording together had produced more smash hits than any other combination of acts in the history of popular music. They went out with a bang: concerning "South Rampart Street Parade" (music by Bob Crosby, whose band adopted the melody as their theme song; lyrics by comedian Steve Allen), *Billboard* wrote, "The Groaner and the Andrews Sisters come through with a sock rendition of the Dixieland oldie." Steve Allen once said that hearing the song performed by Crosby and the trio was "the biggest thrill of my songwriting career," and writer Joseph Laredo called the performance "a joyride for the ears."

Patty's solo records continued, including "I'll Walk Alone" and a very plaintive rendition of "You Blew Me a Kiss." The incredible success of "I Can Dream, Can't I?" as well as "I Wanna Be Loved" suggested that similar future solos would prove to be hits for Patty, but most of her solo recordings never even found their way into the top-thirty charts. Although many factors contributed to the slow demise of the trio, perhaps the public felt that—despite Patty's impressive solo performances—there was something missing, namely Maxene and LaVerne. When Patty sang alone, there was no balance of harmony, which the trio's fans not only looked forward to, but also had come to expect. Even if the harmonious interlude was brief, as it was in "I Can Dream, Can't I?" and "I Wanna Be Loved," it was there, and it sustained the listeners' interest throughout. Patty's voice alone sounded foreign to many fans of the Andrews Sisters, just as the harmony would have perhaps seemed misplaced had Patty been a popular soloist for years, and then started singing with a group.

Aside from this, a sweeping change in the music industry loomed on the horizon, with the rhythms of rock-n-roll soon to explode onto the scene, changing the tastes of a majority of the young record-buying public. Also, a new and younger wave of popular music vocalists were starting to gain recognition. Talented performers on the rise included Tony Bennett, Eddie Fisher, Rosemary Clooney, Teresa Brewer, Patti Page, and Pat Boone. The sisters had been performing together successfully for nearly fifteen years, achieving phenomenal fame and setting records still unsurpassed. With so many accomplishments behind them, retirement did not seem an unlikely possibility.

The girls were also having problems personally. Patty was tiring of being one-third of a group. Throughout the years, many critics focused on Patty's talents as a singer, dancer, and comedienne, labeling her the main attraction of the group—which she was to a certain extent. Without Patty, there certainly would have been no Andrews Sisters, but could Patty alone sustain the interest that the public had in the trio? Wally Weschler was now managing the girls, following Lou Levy's departure. Perhaps Weschler had his wife's best interests as a soloist in mind rather than what might have benefitted the group as a whole, or what might have propelled the act to a new plateau. Regardless, Weschler possessed neither Levy's impressive experience nor Levy's innate ability to know what direction the sisters should go to meet with success.

Patty felt that since she was the lead singer of the group and probably the most recognizable (therefore the most popular of the three), she deserved a higher salary. Maxene and LaVerne considered this an unfair request. The girls had always divided their salary equally in three parts. Each sister then contributed a portion of her earnings to provide for their parents, and a managerial share that went to Levy. It is more than likely that Maxene and LaVerne were personally hurt by Patty's request for more money, as each sister worked as hard as the other to achieve the success they were enjoying. When Patty discovered that her desires had met with opposition, she decided to separate from the group and become a solo act. Maxene said that Patty's decision to leave was not what bothered her and LaVerne the most—it was rather the manner in which their sister departed that did not sit well with the two older siblings. Both sisters read about Patty's separation in the newspapers. Maxene said that Patty never confronted them with a formal announcement regarding her decision to leave—she just went public.

Although Maxene and LaVerne disagreed with Patty regarding division of salary, both thought that Patty was more than capable of going it alone, and they both said in interviews that they would not have stood in her way. Shortly before Christmas of 1953, Patty Andrews departed from her sisters on less than amicable terms. It seems that her attitude leading up to the separation took most of the fun out of being an Andrews sister for both Maxene and LaVerne, and perhaps for Patty as well. One of the most evident characteristics of the group had always been that the girls enjoyed themselves—that they all loved what they were doing. Tensions diminished that gaiety. Maxene said that perhaps Weschler was the driving force behind Patty's request for more money; it is interesting to note that Patty's views regarding such issues as salary and billing noticeably changed after her marriage to Weschler. Although Patty was a contributing factor to the trio's separation, however, she was not the only factor.

Perhaps the girls had just been part of each other's lives for much too long. At that time, they had been performing publicly for over thirty years. Vic Schoen was once quoted as saying, "I never could understand their phenomenal success. And I don't think they did either. Certainly, they didn't handle it too well. They had led a very sheltered life and they always wanted to break loose. And when they did, after their parents died, it seemed to me that they were so filled with guilt that they began taking it out on each other. They were always squabbling." The sisters never really included themselves in the party-going throng of other Hollywood celebrities. Maxene recalled, "We were never really social with any of the artists. We worked with them, we loved them and respected them, but socially we never got together. I guess it was just the closeness of the sisters, that we went back to Mama and Papa and we had each other."

Maxene also remembered how naive she and her sisters were, especially during the early years, saying,

> The Andrews Sisters, in spite of their success, were like three little country girls. When we would walk on the stage, or when we would go to the recording studio, we were the Andrews Sisters. And when that job was done, we went home—we were just the kids. And we were still, for a long time, under the ruling hand of my father and my mother. And when you lived with them, you did as they said. And God love 'em, they weren't the kind of people that sat down and—though I always felt that my mother was a liberated woman—they never sat down with the three of us and had a family discussion. It was my father's word or it was my mother's word—and that was the end of it. So, when we came into New York and we hit this tremendous success, everything we did after that, we did by rote, I guess. Because I don't think we were ever really conscious of how successful we were. I really believe that.

Tensions can mount over many things when siblings are concerned. The Andrews Sisters were constant companions, working together during the day, living together at night. The girls rehearsed together, dressed together, ate, primped, partied, slept, performed, and vacationed together. Perhaps this constant togetherness finally took its toll; after all, each sister had her own tastes and own distinct set of friends. Patty once said that the sisters spent many years getting in each other's way and living each other's lives. Maxene elaborated:

> We never, ever thought of singing together as anything hard because it was such a joy; but, about the three of us, we were as different as day and night. The only thing we ever had really in common—outside of the love of our parents—was the love of our work. We didn't like each other's boyfriends, we didn't like each other's tastes in clothes, and so there was always little sparks there. Now, with my sisters, who never vocally expressed themselves that much, I must have been a big pain in the neck to them, because I was the one who always said, "Come on, we gotta rehearse, come on, we gotta do this, we gotta do that"—and I left no time for saying, "Hey, why don't we take a few weeks off? Why don't we go on vacation? Do something."
> But, it was like getting on that treadmill of success, and once you were on it, it's like being on the merry-go-round, and it just doesn't stop.

Maxene has always said that after her parents' deaths, and following hers and Patty's divorces, the Andrews Sisters' world became very insecure. The girls did not know how to cope with insecurities, and things began to fall apart. Personal fights and interference by husbands only added to the tensions, making a separation more likely as time progressed. "Our husbands wanted to take different roads and our emotions pulled apart," said Maxene.

No longer part of the Andrews Sisters, Patty embarked on a solo career, with her husband acting as her manager and pianist. Lou Levy always thought that Patty would be successful without her sisters. He once said, "Patty was a great, great tap dancer. Patty could have been a great dancer. Patty could have been one of the greatest comediennes in the musical theater. I always thought I would go on with her and without the girls, 'cause I felt she had all the ingredients to make up a star. She could dance, she could take a joke, give a joke, fall on her face. She was a great, great piece of talent. Where she got lost—someday, I'll tell the true story. Until then, I'll just tell you she was a fantastic performer."

Patty opened at the Last Frontier in Las Vegas with her new solo act in the summer of 1954. LaVerne was in the audience on opening night, but she did not go backstage after the performance. Patty also held engagements at Philadelphia's Latin Quarter, Mapes Skyroom in Reno, and Ciro's in Hollywood, performing a critically acclaimed act that featured non-Andrews Sisters material. Her show included a novelty number based on the exploits of the famous Sadie Thompson—"The Rains Came Down," written by husband Weschler, and a quick-change tramp routine ("Lady Clown") as a finale. Patty briefly continued recording duets for Decca with Bing Crosby—"Dissertation on the State of Bliss (Love and Learn)," and Jimmy Durante—"It's Bigger than the Both of Us." Patty then signed a contract with Capitol Records, joining a roster that included Sinatra, Martin, Cole, Garland, Jo Stafford, and Kay Starr. As a soloist, Patty experimented on six single releases with a variety of material, including such early rock-n-roll material as "Music Drives Me Crazy" and "Broken." "Broken" was penned by Mike Stoller and Jerry Leiber, the songwriting team who began supplying Elvis Presley with most of his hit material two years later. These two numbers were Patty's best performances in the rock-n-roll style. Some of her solos, including "Boog-a-da-Woog," would have suited the trio much better than Patty alone. "Too Old to Rock and Roll" and "Without Love" found Patty in her prime, while "A Friendship Ring" was vocally much too dramatic. A standout release was a Mitch Miller-style singalong version of "I Never Will Marry," in which she recorded herself three times. The harmony vocals in it sounded eerily similar to the trio (this dispels the notion that Patty sang the lead part in the trio because she had no ear for harmony, which Maxene was fond of saying in different interviews over the years). Patty's most popular solo recording for Capitol was her rendition of the famous inspirational ballad "Suddenly, There's a Valley," which proved to be a *Billboard* hit for her, although versions by Jo Stafford and the Mills Brothers sold much better. Although most of her solos were nicely executed, Patty's success as a solo act still did not come close to the astounding success she earned as part of the Andrews Sisters.

After the sisters' falling out, Maxene opened at the Blue Angel in New York City with her own nightclub act. Reviews were pleasant, but not as glowing as Patty's initial press clippings. Maxene lost interest immediately. She then studied drama for several months. Shortly thereafter, Maxene and LaVerne joined forces to form a new act. They tried to negotiate with successful British singer Dorothy Squires, hoping to have her join the act as Patty's replacement. When this did not materialize, the sisters held auditions for a lead singer, but they could not make a decision on anyone they thought would be suitable, so they decided to continue as a duo.

In November 1954, Maxene and LaVerne appeared on Red Skelton's television show on CBS. As part of a comedy skit, Skelton donned a blonde wig and sang with the girls. Patty saw the show and was not at all amused. She contacted her lawyers, who in turn sent letters to Maxene, LaVerne, and Skelton, stating that Patty was not pleased with the misrepresentation, and that the segment was not to be repeated at any future time with the same or different principals. Several days after the Skelton show, the three sisters met in Superior Court in Long Beach, California, as Patty sued LaVerne for a larger share of personal properties, including $10,000 worth of home furnishings that Olga had bequeathed to her daughters in her will. Patty alleged that LaVerne, the administratrix of the will, failed to comply with a court decree of distribution under Olga's will, which awarded LaVerne a half interest in the properties, and Maxene and Patty a fourth interest each. LaVerne countersued Patty, claiming that her younger sister was already in excess possession of properties. The judge denied Patty's petition for a contempt of court citation against LaVerne. During the court proceedings, Patty and LaVerne did not acknowledge each other. Maxene released a statement at the time saying that she sided with LaVerne on the legal disputes.

Despite Patty's opposition, Maxene and LaVerne tested audience reaction to the Andrews Sisters (without Patty) during a ten-day tour of Australia. Audiences were pleased and critics gave flattering reviews. The success of the duo did not ease the mounting tensions in the trio's court case, however. Maxene seemed to be feeling the brunt of the stress more than her sisters, as she was hospitalized a few days before Christmas after swallowing eighteen sleeping pills. Some of her neighbors told police that Maxene had been despondent over the recent family problems, which prompted the authorities to report the incident as a suicide attempt. LaVerne denied this to reporters, saying that it was just an unfortunate accident. Maxene was released from the hospital in time to spend the holidays with her children.

It's wonderful to think of ourselves as partners again,
and to know that when we get together socially,
it's because we honestly want to.
—Patty Andrews, 1959

11

The Last Mile Home

After a year of recording solo, Patty was experiencing only moderate success on Capitol Records. Although her singles proved that she did not need her sisters to successfully carry a tune, something vital seemed to be missing, at least in the minds of Andrews Sisters fans. Patty's ballads displayed impressive vocal workmanship, and some of her novelty tunes perfectly suited her style of musical funmaking, but the public—especially the record-buying public—was much more partial to the trio. Fans never expected the sisters to disband, for they had practically become an American institution. The public was eager for a reunion.

The sisters themselves soon decided that they wanted to sing together again, so they reunited—personally and professionally— once again dividing their salary in three equal shares. Capturing the 1956 reunion for history's sake, a photograph of the trio taken in Maxene's kitchen featured the sisters literally "burying the hatchet" in a large cake. The picture appeared in newspapers throughout the country. The reunited trio appeared in a television special on Patty's thirty-eighth birthday, to the delight of their fans. LaVerne once told an interviewer, "It just wasn't wanting to sing together again, but the public never really wanted the Andrews Sisters to break up. We received 2,000 letters a week after we appeared together on an anniversary special." The special was called "Shower of Stars," and to appear on the show, Patty flew from Las Vegas and Maxene from New York to join LaVerne in Hollywood. Red Skelton introduced the trio (it seems that no hard feelings were harbored from the comedy skit two years earlier), and the sisters sang a medley of their greatest hits, including "Bei Mir Bist Du Schon" and "Beer Barrel Polka."

A prominent figure in reuniting the trio was famous Hollywood producer Dore Schary. While the sisters were still not speaking, Schary approached them with the idea of producing a film biography of their career. He assigned writer David Susskind to work with the trio. Though the film biography never materialized, LaVerne later said, "A strange thing happened during those discussions with David Susskind. We discovered that we were actually enjoying each other's company. By then, each of us had settled in our private lives—so returning to our career seemed a logical move." Shortly after their reunion, the sisters were interviewed by a reporter at the famous Brown Derby. During the talk, in walked the McGuire Sisters, who were in Los Angeles for a two-day visit. Christine, Phyllis, and Dorothy spotted the Andrews Sisters and a mutual admiration society was formed. The McGuires joined in the discussion of the film biography of the Andrews trio when a bystander suggested that the McGuires should play their famous predecessors on screen. Looking the girls over, LaVerne remarked, "Nope, we can't use 'em— they're too pretty!" Phyllis McGuire remembered meeting the Andrews Sisters for the first time in the early 1950s in New York City: "We had advice from Patty, Maxene and LaVerne when we first came to New York, and they told us what to do and what not to do, and we followed that advice, so therefore, they really helped us along our way."

Reunited, the trio returned to old stomping grounds—the Flamingo in Vegas, opening the show with the appropriately selected "Born to Be with You," the current Chordettes hit. *Variety* wrote, "There's no reason why they should not resume their role among sure-fire regulars on the golddust circuit." The sisters' first priority as a trio was recording. New releases by the Andrews Sisters, now on the Capitol label, soon appeared in record stores once again, and the girls were singing better than ever. Renditions of "Crazy Arms" and "Stars, Stars, Stars" reunited them with previous collaborators Vic Schoen and Gordon Jenkins, respectively. Other standout recordings included "Give Me Back My Heart," "By His Word," and "Torero." The trio even attempted some light rock-n-roll fare, "One Mistake" and "Invitation to a Dance." These songs, enhanced by the dramatic effect of stereo and the use of overdubs by the trio—creating six voices rather than three—resulted in a brand new sound for the sisters. A recording of the Don Robertson composition "Alone Again" was executed well, but inexplicably never released. Concerning the sessions that were released, *Billboard* noted, "Fine piping from the veteran chicks should find favor with both teens and adults." It is unfortunate that this change in style was not pursued in future recordings; but none of the new material charted. The public seemed to prefer hearing the trio singing their old hits rather than their more current sound.

Perhaps part of the reason why the trio could not successfully develop this new style was that, although they handled the material convincingly, there was too much of an age gap between the now forty-something sisters and the teen record-buying public to form a bonding relationship. Also, the younger Fontane and McGuire Sisters were currently satisfying the demand for a harmony-infused rock-n-roll sound among the younger generation. Interestingly, when Andrews Sisters recordings like "One Mistake" are compared to McGuire Sisters hits like "Sincerely," it is the Andrews' numbers that adhered more to the core rock-n-roll sound, with heavy backbeats, electric guitars, and louder vocal registers. Their lack of success in the rock-n-roll arena may have also had to do with timing, as the top-forty charts were favoring newer group talent like the Sisters DeJohn, DeCastro, and Laurie. Other single artists, like Chuck Berry, Bill Haley, and Elvis Presley, were beginning to win the majority of the teen vote as far as record sales were concerned, resulting in some of the fiercest and most diverse competition the Andrews Sisters had ever seen.

Also contributing to the trio's lackluster recording comeback may have been the lack of guidance they received at Capitol. Maxene elaborated on the trio's working relationship with Voyle Gilmore, their producer at the time: "We had all the respect in the world for Voyle, but he lacked leadership with us. I think most every artist at that period of time needed some leadership as to the kind of music they were doing—is this the right song?—listening for a piece of music for us. We couldn't do all of that. Somebody had to be on the lookout for the Andrews Sisters, and we were not getting that at Capitol. There was no direction. And we were used to a lot of direction. At Capitol, we were just floundering."

The label then put the sisters to work on album releases in addition to the singles. The first release paired them with Vic Schoen and his orchestra, and featured sixteen re-recordings of their old Decca hits. Capitol knew that fans of the sisters would gobble this album up. The company also knew that it would be able to release such recordings in the future under the guise of a greatest hits collection, and make no mention of the fact that the recordings were not the Decca originals. Two other albums followed. "Fresh and Fancy Free" teamed the trio with Billy May and his orchestra; it featured sparkling arrangements of songs that the sisters had never before recorded, including "The Song Is You," "My Romance," "Let There Be Love," and "Younger than Springtime." The next release, "The Dancing '20s"—also with May—featured the trio singing songs such as "Barney Google" and "Show Me the Way to Go Home." An air of vitality and an overall carefree mood permeated the latter album. Stereo techniques enhanced the trio's blend, accentuating each voice distinctly in a more mature tone.

Once again, the trio was headlining throughout the world. They visited many popular television shows of the day, including those hosted by Perry Como, Julius LaRosa, Jimmie Rodgers, Ray Bolger, and Andy Williams. They appeared on *Masquerade Party* disguised as the Marx Brothers, and as mystery guests on *What's My Line*. The trio was hoping to star in their own weekly television series in late 1959—a sitcom that would feature them as a trio of sisters operating a bill collection agency. They even volunteered their own savings to commence production. Their plans were cut short, however, when they were sued by the Federal Government for over two hundred thousand dollars owed in back taxes, which they had neglected to pay from 1949 to 1953. Adding to this misfortune, the sisters suffered a personal setback when LaVerne lost her home (the Brentwood estate that the girls had constructed for their parents) in the massive Bel Air fires in November of 1961. A three-year drought in this area, just north of Hollywood, allowed the fire to feed on dried brush while two thousand firemen battled to control the four-day inferno. Neighbors of LaVerne also left temporarily homeless included Burt Lancaster, Zsa Zsa Gabor, and Joan Fontaine. All of the trio's memorabilia—records, sheet music, scrapbooks, awards—were lost in the blaze. LaVerne and husband Lou Rogers paid for the reconstruction of the home and continued to live there.

The trio soon appeared at the Talk of the Town nightclub on Piccadilly Circus in London. Although the trio's road tour schedules were still a bit hectic, they did not compare to the nonstop race they had run a decade earlier. Patty observed, "At the Talk of the Town, we did one show a night and had Sundays off. It's the only way to do show business!" The sisters were now much more relaxed with each other, and they were once again thoroughly enjoying what they were doing. After the girls left Capitol in 1959, they recorded two songs for Kapp Records, owned and operated by their old friend Dave Kapp from Decca. They also recorded two songs for Decca two years later in 1961. They then went to work for Dot Records, a company that employed many popular artists, including Pat Boone, Lawrence Welk, the Lennon Sisters, the Fontane Sisters, the Mills Brothers, Jimmie Rodgers, Tony Martin, Louis Prima and Keely Smith, Gale Storm, and Billy Vaughn. The company boasted that it had "the greatest talent on record!" The sisters then produced a series of stereo albums at Dot Records.

The Greatest Hits of the Andrews Sisters (volumes one and two) featured yet more re-recordings of Decca hits. Some, including "Ti-Pi-Tin" and "Pistol Packin' Mama" were far different from the Decca originals, but just as enjoyable, if not more so. Two of the songs from the volume two release had never even been recorded by the sisters, let alone being two of their greatest hits ("Three Little Fishies" and "You Are My Sunshine"); but the tunes were currently featured in the trio's nightclub act and the executives at Dot urged the group to include them on the album. Another album, "Great Golden Hits," included a Walter Weschler composition called "The Irish Twist," which was actually a revamping of "Scrub Me Mama with a Boogie Beat." The trio's 1940 hit might have been misconstrued as racist during the civil rights movement of the 1960s. The updated version also provided the sisters with an opportunity to cash in on the newest dance craze and "twist" when they performed the number during their stage shows.

The Andrews Sisters Present featured the trio singing twelve popular songs of 1962 and 1963 and included many musical categories from pop ("I Left My Heart in San Francisco") and rock-n-roll ("Mr. Bass Man") to country ("Still"), folk ("Puff! The Magic Dragon") and ethnic material ("Watermelon Man" and "Sukiyaki"). The majority of the tunes were well done, but Weschler's contribution on this release ("The Doodle Song") was pure filler and nothing more. *Great Country Hits* followed, including good yet untraditional arrangements of "The Tennessee Waltz" and "Wabash Cannonball"; but saxophones and pianos too often replaced fiddles and steel guitars on the rest of the selections. *The Andrews Sisters Go Hawaiian* and *Favorite Hymns* came next, but both albums conveyed the impression that not much planning or production was being devoted to the releases. The Hawaiian selections were actually rather pleasing, including a tender arrangement of "The Hawaiian Wedding Song" and the comical "Hawaii." The album of hymns, however, was hastily produced. It was arranged by Weschler, and some of the selections sounded more like carnival music than sacred fare. Nor were the sisters in very good voice, especially in their rerecording of their lovely Decca rendering of "Whispering Hope." The project lacked detailed planning and execution. Maxene recalled, "I wish I could say they were wonderful, but this is getting into the thing of 'what to do with the Andrews Sisters.'" *The Andrews Sisters—Great Performers* was the last release—and a marked improvement, being one of the most original and entertaining projects that the trio had undertaken during their four years at Dot. Pleasing selections, including "Is It Really Over?," "Satin Doll," "I Forgot More than You'll Ever Know about Him" (which Patty recorded solo for Decca a dozen years earlier), and motion picture theme songs from *Come September* and *A Man and a Woman*, comprised the album, released in 1967. The trio's harmony had by now acquired a much different sound than it had during their Decca and even their Capitol days, due to the passing of years as well as to the crystal clear output of Dot's stereo albums. Although the sound was a bit coarser, it was unmistakably the Andrews Sisters and, according to fan Johnny Carson, it was "still the best blend in the business."

Personal appearances continued to be rewarding for the trio, including frequent and well-received nightclub engagements at the Chi Chi Starlite Room in Palm Springs, the Blue Room of the Hotel Roosevelt in New Orleans, the International on Broadway and 51st Street in New York City, the seven-hundred-seat Nugget in Sparks, Nevada, and the Cave in Vancouver, Canada. Television guests stints were just as frequent. During 1965, the trio made three appearances on *The Tonight Show,* hosted by Johnny Carson. The sisters performed an opening medley of "Got a Lot of Livin' to Do," "My Favorite Things," and "I Left My Heart in San Francisco" on the first show. Patty then tied an oversized baby bonnet on Carson's head as he served as foil for the trio's comical rendering of "Sonny Boy." The sisters also sang a polka medley, during which Patty cut loose with a "stripper" routine. When they returned to their seats on the couch, Carson quipped, "You're the only singing group I know that may be closed down!" The sisters often pushed the limits with risque bits of business, in the years prior to the sexual revolution; such song lyrics or performance gimmicks peppered their girl-next-door image. Take, for instance, Patty's attempts to begin a striptease during the trio's "Strip Polka" in Universal's *Follow the Boys.* Just as she begins to disrobe in front of thousands of servicemen, her sisters fly to her side, scolding and dressing her. It gave the wholesomeness of the act a naughty edge while not going as far as being embarrassing in any way. An anonymous writer observed the following in the mid 1970s:

> The Andrews were fully as professional as their con-
> temporary incarnations like the Pointer Sisters and
> Bette Midler. They had an unerring knack for provid-
> ing patter with precision, breathtaking syncopations
> leavened with topical comedy. They represented the

girls next door jazzed up to an irresistible pitch of alluring excitement that never became too intense to be fun. And during an era not yet sufficiently consciousness-heightened to be defensive about sex roles, the Andrews may have symbolized some kind of an ideal: they were hep enough to be pin-up girls, but as a family there was something solid about them that any young lady could identify with and admire.

The trio sang a ten-minute medley entitled "One More River" during their second appearance on *The Tonight Show,* on March 12, 1965. It included snippets of such Decca hits as "Near You," "Down in the Valley," and "The Blue Tail Fly." Due to its length, the executives at NBC gave the sisters some flack about performing the medley, which they featured in their nightclub act as part of the "hootenanny" craze that was at that time sweeping the nation. Carson himself made a point of not attending the afternoon rehearsal—after witnessing and thoroughly enjoying Patty's striptease performance a month earlier. He wanted to be surprised by the trio's performance that night. The sisters did sing their medley after they opened the show with a swinging "Bei Mir Bist Du Schon," still recognized and appreciated by 1965 audiences. After their medley, the audience went wild, repeatedly cheering "more!" Carson had to squelch the applause by assuring the audience that the sisters would sing again. It seems that no hard feelings lingered among the sisters from their mid-1950s separation, as Patty indicated: "Actually, I'll tell you something, Johnny, that was the best thing that ever happened to the Andrews Sisters, breaking up for those two years, because we were so involved in working all the time that we didn't have a chance to really respect each other in our own private lives, and when we were able to get away and to see the picture a little clearer—you know, now we go out and we enjoy our work much more and we have a lot more fun and, uh—we split the money three ways!" Carson joked, "There seems to be a rather hostile attitude here," and Patty mused, "I just thought I'd let you know what we were fightin' about!"

The trio next appeared on *The Dean Martin Show* and were

asked to return for two more appearances. They opened the second show singing a rousing, hand-clapping medley of "What Now My Love?" and "That's How Young I Feel" before joining Martin for a medley of hits, including "Memories Are Made of This" and "Rum and Coca Cola." Singing a medley of tunes from their "Dancing '20s" album, the girls next appeared on *The Sammy Davis, Jr. Show*. On it the sisters joined co-guest stars Diana Ross and the Supremes for a medley in which the sisters sang hits of the Supremes ("Stop! In the Name of Love," "Baby Love," and "Where Did Our Love Go?"), while the Supremes sang hits of the Andrews Sisters ("Bei Mir Bist Du Schon," "Apple Blossom Time," and "Beer Barrel Polka"), before both groups sang Davis's famous "Birth of the Blues."

As the sisters were enjoying these successes, LaVerne became unexpectedly ill. Her condition was diagnosed in October 1966; she had cancer. LaVerne's condition grew worse; she suffered through much of 1967 as the cancer spread. When she became too ill to continue performing, Patty and Maxene were forced to select a replacement. While they hoped that their sister would make a recovery, they still had to fulfill previously booked commitments. Joyce DeYoung joined the act. She was considerably younger than LaVerne, but her imitation of LaVerne's contralto harmony seemed very much on target. Patty and Maxene opened an engagement with Joyce at Harvey's in Lake Tahoe. LaVerne sent her sisters flowers on opening night, and she telephoned the group on Sunday night to wish them luck. The next morning, May 8, 1967, LaVerne Andrews passed away from cancer complicated by pneumonia at the age of fifty-five. She died at the Brentwood estate with her husband, Lou, at her bedside. She was cremated two days later.

Since LaVerne's death, rumors have surfaced that she drank heavily during the last year of her life to ease her pain. These rumors were perhaps fueled by the fact that her husband was working as a liquor salesman at the time of her death. Maxene was quoted in the *National Enquirer* as saying that LaVerne began drinking heavily during her illness, but the sensationalist nature of the tabloid calls into question the accuracy of the quote. Carroll Carroll, one of the script writers for radio's *Club 15* series on which the trio starred for nearly four years, remembered LaVerne fondly in his

biographical composition *None of Your Business, or My Life With
. . .* (written with J. Walter Thompson). Carroll recalled one time
in particular when, in the midst of a morning rehearsal, LaVerne
excused herself from the proceedings and became sick to her stom-
ach. When she returned minutes later, she vowed never again to
touch liquor—"nothing but champagne!" she insisted.

Maxene and Patty decided that they did not want to go on
performing without LaVerne, who had formed the Andrews Sisters
when Patty was only seven years old. Although only five years
separated LaVerne from Maxene, LaVerne had a somewhat moth-
erly relationship with her younger sisters, being closer to her parents than were her siblings. LaVerne was forever ladylike and could
even be a bit prudish at times. During some recorded Decca studio
patter between Crosby and the sisters before they began singing
"There's a Fella Waitin' in Poughkeepsie," Crosby sang several different verses of his own X-rated lyrics to the melody—Patty and
Maxene laughed, LaVerne did not. The eldest sister was at her
happiest when she was singing, loving all types of music. She had
an intrinsic sense of harmony, and when Maxene sometimes had
trouble finding her own harmony part, LaVerne would interpret the
passages to her sister. LaVerne's witty and self-deprecating sense of
humor endeared her to many, who considered her to be the most
reserved and sweetest of the three. Although she often worried about
her appearance and her performance, she never showed any signs
of uneasiness on stage, always appearing completely poised. She
loved to dance, and she moved the most naturally of the three in
front of the cameras and the audiences. Maxene remembered:
"LaVerne was the swinger of the group on stage. She was a great
dancer, was very fashion conscious, and she had a beautiful figure.
She had a great sense of humor, and she loved people."

LaVerne's abrupt passing ended a bonding legacy for the sisters, and things would never again be quite the same.

12

The Love We Used to Know

While Patty and Maxene were appearing at Lake Tahoe at the time of their sister's death, Paradise College offered Maxene the position of Dean of Women. Such a request came out of the blue, as Maxene's formal education came to an end when she was just fifteen years old. She once said that, at the time of the offer, she had never even seen the inside of a college, and could not imagine working in one. She had been considering a non-show business outlet, however, since she did not find it very rewarding to sing without both of her sisters. She announced that she would accept the position in August 1968, leaving Patty to continue as a soloist. She taught speech and drama at the school, in addition to working in encounter groups with drug abusers and troubled teens. She soon became vice president of the college, with a total of five departments under her supervision.

While Maxene taught, Patty was performing. Aside from appearing on several talk shows and making a cameo appearance in the film *Phynx* in 1970, she made a guest appearance on Lucille Ball's popular television series *Here's Lucy*. Patty portrayed herself on the show, asking Lucy's hiring agency to supply two girls—a brunette and a redhead—to portray her sisters in a performance she was planning for an Andrews Sisters fan club reunion. Lucy volunteered her own services as LaVerne, and daughter Lucie to fill Maxene's role. They performed a medley of the trio's hits with Desi Arnaz Jr. stepping in as Bing Crosby.

Patty starred in a Los Angeles musical theater production in 1971 entitled *Victory Canteen,* set during World War II. The show was well received, and the show's score was even recorded during a live performance and released on twelve-inch albums that were released for promotional use only. (Today these discs sell upwards of two hundred dollars each.) The rights to the play, which had a musical score by Richard and Robert Sherman, were soon purchased by Kenneth Waissman and Maxine Fox, who planned to transport the show to the Broadway stages of New York City. The producers were eager to reunite Patty and Maxene for the new musical, which was touted as the most lavish and expensive Broadway production to date. Although Patty was eager to revise her role, Maxene was skeptical at first. Retirement, however, did not appeal to her and, looking forward to singing with Patty once again, she agreed.

The entire show was rewritten by Will Holt, who tailored the production to the talents of the sisters. Broadway was the only show business medium that the Andrews Sisters had not yet attempted. During the early 1940s, there had been some talk of the trio starring in a musical production of "Cinderella." Patty would have played the lead while Maxene and LaVerne would have played the mean step-sisters, but the project never materialized. Patty and Maxene opened in *Over Here!* on March 6, 1974, at the Shubert Theater in New York City, directly opposite the former Paramount, where the sisters had enjoyed many successful runs thirty years earlier.

Over Here! was a success. Clive Barnes of the *New York Times* wrote, "Broadway finally has a blockbuster—you'll have a barrel of fun!" Author George T. Simon noted: "Casting the two remaining sisters in a show set during World War II when the girls had achieved such immense popularity turned out to be a masterful stroke. It also afforded both Patty and Maxene, who had appeared in several grade B movies, the opportunity to really display their skills as comediennes for the first time and to spread a final luster on two of the most successful of all popular singing careers."

Patty and Maxene played a singing duo called the DePaul Sisters, entertaining troops for the USO. The DePauls began thinking that a trio sounded much better than a duo, and so they began their search for a third girl. They found their missing voice in Mitzi, played by Janie Sell, whose imitation of LaVerne's third-part harmony was just about as close to the real thing as any Andrews Sisters fan could expect. Sell won a Tony for her performance. Also featured in the cast were a group of young performers with soaring careers ahead of them, including Marilu Henner, Treat Williams, Ann Reinking, Sal Mineo, and a twenty-year-old John Travolta. Uniformed once again in military garb and backed by a big band, the sisters sang the title number, as well as "Wartime Wedding" and the finale, "No Goodbyes." They were joined by Janie Sell for some lively three-part harmonizing in "We Got It!" and "The Big Beat." Maxene had a solo, "Charlie's Place," while Patty had two—"The Good Time Girl," with lyrics that would have been more than banned had they been sung three decades earlier, and "Where Did the Good Times Go?" Patty's powerful rendering of this nostalgic ballad was one of the show's highlights, as she stood alone at stage right, leaning against a wardrobe trunk.

The show belonged strictly to the sisters, which was emphasized at the very beginning of the production. As the orchestra swelled to the strains of the overture, picture images of the Andrews Sisters, posed at different stages throughout the 1940s, were spotlighted onto the stage curtain from the balconies above. The play was contained in two acts, and it was followed by Act 3, in which Patty and Maxene returned to the stage to sing a medley of their Decca hits. This act was the crowd-pleaser; "Bei Mir Bist Du Schon," was a particular favorite. Maxene recalled, "The minute Patty would start to sing the first few notes of the verse, the people would go crazy." And true to her comic fashion, Patty would shower herself and Maxene with a fine mist of saliva as she put extra verve into the brief verse that she sang in the original Yiddish.

Patty and Maxene were still using dance routines in their numbers, though both sisters were nearly sixty years old. Patty explained, "The Andrews Sisters always got their blend without standing still and putting their heads around a mike. We were the first harmony group to ever move and we started a whole new style. We felt the rhythm, the music, and we always danced. Until the Andrews Sisters, harmony groups simply stuck their three or four heads around a mike and went for a blend." Maxene remembered the stingy executives at Universal during the trio's heyday, who were uncooperative when it came to anything that might better the act, including production values, wardrobe, and even choreography. She said, "Patty created most of our dance steps, 'cause they were so damn cheap they wouldn't get a choreographer." The sisters performed eight shows a week of *Over Here!*, including Wednesday and Saturday matinees. Maxene said at the time, "This is a breeze, only eight shows a week. One Labor Day at the Steel Pier in Atlantic City, we did eleven shows with fifteen-minute intermissions!"

The soundtrack of *Over Here!* was released on Columbia Records. The following review by Roy Hemming soon appeared in *Stereo Review* magazine: "Patty and Maxene Andrews sing with their usual irrepressible buoyancy and warmth, though their voices are considerably huskier than they used to be—a condition probably not helped by today's engineering fidelity, in contrast to recording standards of their previous heyday. And when they launch into the show's final song, 'No Goodbyes,' you can't help hoping that they mean every word of it, that they'll go right on singing and entertaining in their inimitable way for a long time to come."

A nostalgia craze had been brewing even before the sisters' show arrived at the Shubert Theater. Bette Midler had recorded "Boogie Woogie Bugle Boy" in 1972, and the rock version of the trio's song once again became a top-ten hit. Midler followed this success with more Andrews Sisters recordings, including "In the Mood" and "Lullaby of Broadway." Patty remembered, "Bette's record was a big plus for us and for the show. When I first heard the introduction on the radio, I thought it was our old record. When Bette opened at the Amphitheater in Los Angeles, Maxene and I went backstage to see her. Her first words were, 'What else did you record?'" During another of Midler's concerts, Maxene went on stage and presented her with an honorary bugle.

Over Here! added to the nostalgia revival, and once again the Andrews Sisters were in the spotlight. References, mostly in a comical vein, were being made to the trio on many popular television shows of the day, including *All in the Family, The Odd Couple, The Mary Tyler Moore Show,* and *The Carol Burnett Show.* The success of the Broadway show prompted MCA, Capitol, Dot, and their subsidiaries to release Andrews Sisters album compilations. Many imports from Great Britain also became available, including a three-volume set of albums featuring most of the trio's hits with Bing Crosby. Two of the re-released collections (*The Best of the Andrews Sisters,* a double selection from MCA, and *Boogie Woogie Bugle Girls* from Paramount) even charted on *Billboard.*

Over Here! received excellent reviews. Jack Kroll wrote in *Newsweek,* "The Andrews Sisters remain muses emeritus of our innocence, and in their fifties, they have returned in this show to tell it like it was. Used with taste and tact, the girls (lib or no lib, that's the word) are beautiful as they stomp around, those mid-American faces wreathed in radiant smiles, cracking wise and harmonizing astonishingly like the old Decca singles." The show was so well received that it was scheduled for a national tour beginning in January of 1975. Then chaos set in.

Newspaper gossip columns were hinting at backstage differences between the sisters. Maxene denied these reports, insisting that she and Patty had never gotten along better. Soon after, stories began circulating concerning problems between the sisters and the producers. On January 4 it was announced that the road tour was canceled, and the play closed amidst threats, confusion, and possible lawsuits. Both sisters blamed the producers, saying that Equity rules were being ignored and that the producers were too young and inexperienced to handle such a production (Maxene was much more publicly vocal about the latter claim). The producers, in turn, blamed the sisters. Waissman and Fox said that the Andrews Sisters were to blame for the cancellation. They said both sisters were demanding more money, though Maxene denied this.

The producers also claimed that they had received a note from Maxene's doctors, stating that Maxene would only be able to perform on the road if she received a raise. Maxene was indeed having medical problems with her legs and with high blood pressure, hence the doctor's note, which requested that the producers pay her medical bills while on tour. It seems that money was an issue between the producers and the sisters as well as between the sisters themselves, and this was more than likely a contributing factor to the demise of the national tour. Patty's husband, Walter Weschler, had negotiated her contract, and he demanded that Patty receive one thousand dollars a week more than Maxene, as well as a higher percentage of the show's profits. The division of salary that separated the sisters twenty years earlier was once again surfacing.

Maxene was very outspoken at the time of the tour's cancellation, especially concerning the producers. She told the following to *Daily News* columnist Rex Reed:

> I learned that they had gone over to see Patty and her husband to play one sister against the other. . . . They have a two-year contract with us. Even if we had been difficult and asked for more money, as they claim, why didn't they just take us into Equity arbitration and force us to go on the road? . . .
>
> . . . They allude to "a massive feud." I don't know what they're talking about, because they are so rude that I haven't even seen them in two months. All negotiations had been conducted by lawyers. . . .
>
> On December 9, we met with the lawyers and the deal was solidified. Everything was fine until Monday, December 16, when they delivered a letter backstage demanding that we retract all doctors' claims, agree to do all publicity, make the third act at the end of the show where we do our old hit songs a definite part of each performance, and sign our consent before the curtain time, or the tour would be canceled. . . . We had one hour to decide. It was seven o'clock at night, we couldn't reach our lawyers, and naturally we didn't sign, so they made an announcement over the loudspeakers that the cast must

> meet in costume after the show and the Andrews Sisters were not invited.
>
> I went to the meeting anyway and Ken Waissman said, "Get out, you're not wanted here." The cast was stunned, so I got up and said fine, but first I want to talk to the cast. I explained that we loved them all and were very sorry that the show was not going on the road, but it had nothing to do with us. The entire case applauded and I left.

Reed also pointed out in his January 5, 1975, *Daily News* article that the controversial third act that the producers insisted on was never part of the sisters' contract. The sisters did not want to guarantee the performance on a regular basis in the event that one of them should become sick. One understudy was supposed to serve for both sisters, and according to Maxene, the understudy could not even sing. Maxene also noted that the producers were not following Equity rules that stated there be an understudy for each and every character, and that during one performance, the stage manager, who was white, played the part of a black train porter. The show that seemed to be a golden opportunity to reunite the Andrews Sisters was now just a memory that had lasted a mere nine months.

Even worse, the cancellation was about to drive a permanent personal wedge between the sisters. Although Maxene put a great deal of blame on the producers, she acknowledged that part of the problem was that she and Patty had been represented separately. "This is the first time we have ever worked under an unequal salary," she said. "The biggest mistake is that we were both represented separately, not as an act, and it cannot go on this way. Maybe the time has come to go our separate ways. But it was wrong for Waissman and Fox to pit one sister against the other. They created the problem by negotiating separately at the beginning and we never got together to iron it out. So now there is friction," she told Reed.

Over Here! cast member Marilu Henner, who went on to greater fame in such television hits as *Taxi* and *Evening Shade*, intimated in a 1994 autobiography that the sisters themselves were responsible for the show's demise. She wrote, "At Christmas, the bottom dropped out. Two weeks before I was supposed to go on the road, the producers pulled the plug. The Andrews Sisters had apparently failed to work out some of their sibling rivalries, so that was it." Henner also recalled rather chaotic early performances of the play, which caused John Travolta to have second thoughts about continuing on Broadway:

> Johnny's big show stopping number at the end was an outrageously complex segment that required three treadmills, the orchestra rising on its hydraulic lift, and lots of precise commotion on stage and frantic costume changes off stage. Johnny was especially excited that night because we had heard that Bette Midler was in attendance. With very little rehearsing, though, the climax was wired for disaster. It should have worked. Johnny starts tapping on the table and singing "I'm Dream-Drumming." He wants to be a Gene Krupa. At this moment, his little tune turns into an extravaganza with a complete set change. The orchestra gets treadmilled across the stage, playing sequined instruments, and the Andrews Sisters come over the top level, also sequined. Within seconds, it broke down into frenzied chaos. Folding chairs and music stands toppled; people missed their marks and collided; Johnny started improvising, trying not to look totally lost and embarrassed. The audience loved the show. But Johnny was devastated and vanished afterward. At two in the morning, he called from the airport. Despondent and humiliated, he said he was leaving the show and flying that night to L.A. I talked him out of it. It wasn't hard—there were no flights out and he had no money.

After the show's cancellation, Maxene was abruptly informed by Patty's lawyers that she was not to speak to her sister, not to call her on the telephone, nor attempt any means of communication— all this according to Maxene. She also said that Patty offered no explanation for her actions, and she added that Wally Weschler might have had a part in the misunderstanding. Maxene did not mask her dislike of Patty's husband at this stage in the sisters' career, saying that she was insulted that Weschler requested part of LaVerne's estate royalties after her death. Maxene insisted for years after the show's cancellation that she was completely unaware as to the cause of her falling out with Patty. She once guessed that perhaps Patty had read some false publicity that so infuriated her that she decided to break all ties to her sister. That explanation would seem odd, since both sisters knew by then what publicity—positive and negative—could accomplish.

Immediately following the play's end, Maxene got together a nightclub act, which was very unsuccessful, while Patty made television appearances, including a regular stint as a judge on *The Gong Show*. Maxene then toured the country in a musical production of *Call Me Madam* and later in *Pippin*. Maxene made a successful comeback in 1979, with a refurbishing of her nightclub revue. She first appeared at Studio One in Los Angeles, then opened a two-week engagement at New York's Reno Sweeney. *Variety* wrote the following about the Reno Sweeney show: "Andrews is a pro. She knows how to involve the crowd with song as well as with spoken word, as she has a distinguished musical background. The session is both pleasant and rousing. It's easy to get sentimental about her era and the singers who populated it. But more important was the skill which these entertainers acquired. Their careers lasted entire lifetimes, surviving constant changes in style and custom." Rex Reed called Maxene's comeback "one of the brightest attractions of the entire nightclub season," although she herself said that she preferred to think of herself as a new act.

Maxene next appeared in New York at the Copacabana and the Bottom Line. The highlight of the act occurred when the house lights dimmed and pictures of the Andrews Sisters, tracing their lives from their early childhood days in Minneapolis to the present, flashed onto a screen while Maxene sang a wistful rendition of "Where Did the Good Times Go?" One observer noted, "She seems to be singing as if she were wishing that her sisters were still singing with her."

Top to bottom, LaVerne, Maxene, and Patty in 1944.

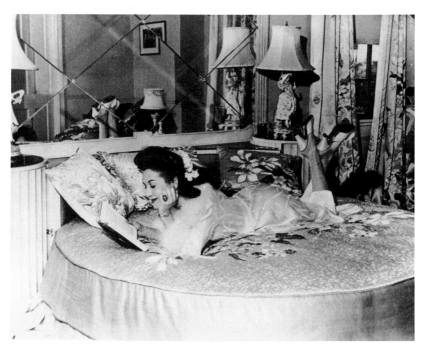

Above, LaVerne relaxes in her bedroom on her famous round bed, 1944. *Below*, LaVerne, Patty, and Maxene lounging in Patty's bedroom in 1944.

Nightclubbing with Frank Sinatra in 1945. (Courtesy of Ray Hagen.)

LaVerne, Maxene, and Patty autograph dollar bills for servicemen during their 1945 USO tour of Italy and Africa. (Courtesy of Diane Gray.)

Opposite top, The sisters during an overseas USO performance. (Courtesy of Diane Gray.) *Opposite bottom*, LaVerne, Patty, and Maxene in *Her Lucky Night* (Universal, 1945).

LaVerne, Patty, and Maxene rehearse for their *Musical Showroom* series on CBS radio in late 1945.

Above, The Decca recording session for "The Freedom Train" (their only Decca session captured on film) finds the sisters with Bing Crosby (center) and Irving Berlin on May 29, 1947. (Courtesy of Ray Hagen.) *Below*, The Andrews Sisters during a Decca recording session, circa 1947.

Opposite, Maxene, LaVerne, and Patty pose for a portrait during the production of *Road to Rio* (Paramount, 1948), in which they star opposite Bing Crosby, *above.*

Above, The Andrews Sisters with Dan Dailey during a 1949 Decca recording session. *Below*, Maxene with her adopted children, Aleda Ann and Peter, circa 1949.

Top to bottom, LaVerne, Patty, and Maxene in 1952.

Maxene with LaVerne and Red Skelton during an appearance on the comic's 1954 CBS television show. (Courtesy of Ray Hagen.)

The Andrews Sisters bury the hatchet in 1956 following a two-year separation.

Above, by 1960 "Bei Mir" had grossed over $3 million.

Left, Maxene, Patty, and LaVerne during a Capitol recording session in 1957.

The sisters appear on *The Joey Bishop Show* in 1966.

Above, left to right, Joyce DeYoung (LaVerne's replacement), Maxene, Patty, Dean Martin, and Lena Horne sing "The Idle Rich" on Martin's television show in 1967. *Below*, Maxene's daughter, Aleda Ann, visits her mother and Patty backstage in 1974 at the Shubert Theater during *Over Here!*

Patty brought her own nightclub act to New York's Les Mouches in March of 1980. Strangely enough, Patty's reviews did not measure up to those of her sister's. *Variety* wrote,

> In her current cabaret act, one of the two surviving Andrews Sisters displays too much Andrews and too little Patty. Andrews tends to make the entire act seem like one long medley. From the glimpse one gets of her vocal potential, the act is depriving the audience of a great deal, as the singer has a marvelously expressive bluesy quality. Her sense of phrasing is also not to be underestimated, as her great skill at handling both words and music shows how aware she is of how a line should go, as well as how to deliver it just so. Andrews has no problem in charming an audience as she moves around the stage as the seasoned pro she is.

Five years had now passed since the sisters had parted ways, and they still were not speaking to one another in 1980. Maxene had made futile attempts at reconciliation, often pleading with Patty publicly in radio and television interviews to contact her and work things out; however, in two separate *New York Daily News* interviews, both sisters made it clear that a reunion was nowhere in sight. When Patty's act debuted at Les Mouches, she granted an interview to reporters. She bluntly blamed Maxene for the closing of the Broadway show, and she also said that Maxene was jealous of her and that she would no longer tolerate her sister's greed. This seemed an odd accusation, as it was Patty, with her husband, who demanded a higher salary as well as a higher profit percentage of the show during its run. It was only a matter of days before Maxene, performing in Florida, retaliated with her own interview, saying that jealousy was never an issue on her part and that Patty had lied. She also once again blamed Patty's husband, saying that Weschler never really liked her and LaVerne, and that he often listened in on telephone extensions whenever she or LaVerne called Patty. It was evident that the sisters would remain at odds.

Patty began performing in several different nostalgic revues, including *Swinging Singing Ladies* with Lainie Kazan, Eartha Kitt, and Della Reese; then in *Great Ladies of the Silver Screen* with Mamie Van Doren, Vivian Blaine, Kathryn Grayson, and Dorothy Lamour; before joining *Great Stars of the Silver Screen* with Gordon MacRae, Morey Amsterdam, Gloria DeHaven, and Forrest Tucker. Patty closed each show with a twenty-minute medley segment, which *Variety* reviewed: "She received strong mitting on the first few bars of each song, exiting to a standing ovation." While both sisters were in the midst of enjoying separate cabaret successes, Maxene suffered a massive heart attack after appearing in Illinois in 1982. She remained in intensive care for two weeks after undergoing quadruple bypass surgery, from which she successfully recovered. One of the nurses at the hospital tending the singer reported that Maxene received a visit from Patty during her stay. Maxene was performing in Denver just four weeks later, and soon after, Bainbridge Records released an album entitled *Maxene—An Andrews Sister.* A medley of the trio's greatest hits was recorded for the release, for which Maxene dubbed her own voice, singing all three parts. She said that Patty's lead and her soprano part were both easy enough, but that she had to "pray a lot" when it came to LaVerne's bass vocal.

Patty and Maxene did unite, albeit briefly, on October 1, 1987, when the Andrews Sisters received their own star on Hollywood's famous Walk of Fame, in commemoration of the sisters' fiftieth anniversary as recording artists. The reunion was probably more mandatory than desired, for both sisters were required to be present for the unveiling. They even joined forces to sing a few bars of "Beer Barrel Polka" for *Entertainment Tonight* camera crews that were covering the event. Ironically, an earthquake shook the area that very morning and the ceremony was nearly canceled. Jeff Hart of MCA Records, who compiled and coordinated volumes one and two of *The Andrews Sisters' Fiftieth Anniversary Collection,* jokingly remarked of the morning mayhem, "Do you think LaVerne was trying to tell us something?" The Lennon and Pointer Sisters received their own respective Walk of Fame stars not long after. Maxene received the Medal for Distinguished Public Service, the Pentagon's highest civilian honor, also during 1987.

Album, cassette, and compact disc compilations of the trio's

Decca, Capitol and Dot recordings have increasingly been imported from countries around the world, including England, Holland, Japan, and Denmark. Cassette packages of a handful of Patty's solos and the trio's gospel recordings were also released, as well as a few seasonal compilations featuring nearly all of the sisters' Christmas recordings. Even picture discs of the Andrews Sisters surfaced and have been displayed in record stores in major cities throughout the country, including New York, sharing wall space with picture discs of artists such as the Beatles, Elvis Presley, Marilyn Monroe, Michael Jackson, and Madonna.

Most of the trio's recordings on the Decca label (over four hundred titles total) remain unreleased in any form since their original releases some sixty years ago. This is truly unfortunate, as the sisters remain the top-selling girl group in popular music and show business history. MCA, which owns the trio's Decca and Dot catalogues, has not yet restored this material—a good percentage of which are charted hits—to release it in compact disc form. All of the recent releases that have come from MCA, with one or two exceptions, have been variously packaged discs that contain the same greatest hits selections. MCA has the golden opportunity to compile the sisters' work in new ways, as much of their recorded work is eclectic. Capitol has not taken advantage of their own Andrews Sisters masters; most of the trio's album work for the company still has not debuted on CD. Nor has any of Patty's solo work for the company—which could be compiled as a "Spotlight On" release—been reissued in over forty years.

Bear Family Records in Germany has tried unsuccessfully to obtain the rights to the trio's Decca catalogue from MCA in America. Bear is famous for their carefully restored and finely detailed compact disc boxed sets of many other famous artists of the sisters' era. They have restored and released *all* recorded material by such artists as Jim Reeves, Ernest Tubb, the Browns, Johnny Horton, and others, and they are in the process of making available everything on Doris Day (the Columbia label) and Connie Francis (the MGM label). Hopefully these hundreds of recordings, which range over a dozen or so musical categories, will be restored for compact disc release in the near future.

The current lack of attention to the trio transcends musical releases. Many books on the big band era and the artists that populated it fail to even acknowledge the trio, although they made significant contributions to the era. Even when Andrews Sisters recordings are used in motion pictures soundtracks, the sisters are sometimes not given a credit line at the end. For instance, the song "Mele Kalikimaka," used in both *National Lampoon's Christmas Vacation* and *L.A. Confidential,* is attributed only to Bing Crosby; there is no written mention of the sisters as the credits roll. Even though the trio has had major influence on many popular artists, they do not always receive the credit they deserve from these individuals. For instance, Bette Midler was quite vocal during the 1970s, especially during appearances on *The Tonight Show,* about what a fan she was of the sisters and how heavily they influenced her work; but in later years, she speaks highly of the Boswell Sisters with no mention of the Andrews Sisters. A member of the Manhattan Transfer was interviewed on radio in 1998 and he, too, mentioned how the Boswells had influenced the group. While both Midler and the Manhattan Transfer were undoubtedly influenced by the Boswells, it is obvious that their styles of vocalizing owe much more to the Andrews Sisters. This is evident in Midler's swinging "Miss Otis Regrets"—the Boswells just did not sing like that, the Andrews Sisters did. These puzzling slights have been happening for years in regard to the Andrews Sisters, and to some degree they have served as inspiration for this manuscript. The trio has not been given their due in recent years, although their popularity and achievements far outweigh other artists who have been extensively researched, written about, and generally acknowledged. Perhaps there is resentment of the trio's phenomenal success due to the fact that, technically, they were musically ignorant in the sense that they did not read music (except for LaVerne), they did not play any instruments as they recorded, and they did not write any of their own material. One must consider, however, that the sisters were from a time completely foreign to today's music market. Years ago, a performer did just that—he or she performed. There were big-name musicians to provide instrumentation, talented songwriters—individuals and teams—to pen melodies and lyrics, arrangers, choreographers, and such; but these circumstances certainly should not diminish the trio's talent or ability to achieve fame.

The music of the Andrews Sisters was brought into the limelight in the summer of 1991, thanks to celebrated choreographer Paul Taylor in his dance revue, *Company B*. The show premiered with the Houston Ballet before going on a national tour with Taylor's dance company. The show ran for a sold-out two-week engagement at New York's Manhattan City Center. Joseph H. Mazo, a freelance writer specializing in dance, wrote the following in a review: "'Company B' deserves an 'A.' Paul Taylor's new dance is irresistible. It's made to 1940s songs by the Andrews Sisters, and its finger-snapping swing dance steps recall the time when boy-met-girl and no one could even spell 'cholesterol.' To enjoy 'Company B,' you need only your eyes, your ears, and a willingness to look a few inches beyond the obvious." Anna Kisselgoff of the *New York Times* wrote, "'Company B' is as grand as it is because the work counters every expectation about its interpretation without doing harm to the original material."

Maxene greatly enjoyed the show, commenting, "I saw 'Company B' when the Houston Ballet performed it, and I liked it even more here in New York. The Taylor dancers seem to have more of a jazz style. They swing those songs. You know, last night they got called back for an encore. That doesn't happen every night at 'Swan Lake.'" Both Patty and Maxene were present at the performance by the Houston Ballet, and they appeared on stage as appreciative music fans obliged them to take nine curtain calls. Gossip columnist Cindy Adams wrote, "They still haven't spoken Word One. On stage, they were separated by six dancers. To make certain they never even glanced in one another's direction, let alone inadvertently accidentally faced one another, they backed up inch by inch on stage rather than turn their bodies around to actually see where they were walking."

Other tributes to the sisters have appeared on various sitcoms over the years, including *I Love Lucy*, *Three's Company*, *Mama's Family*, *Amen!*, *Spin City*, *The Statler Brothers Show*, *Veronica's Closet*, and a memorable episode of *Taxi*, wherein Alex, Tony, and Latka showed up at a costume party dressed as Maxene, Patty, and

LaVerne. The boys even sang the trio's "Bei Mir Bist Du Schon" at the end of the show. The trio's Decca, Capitol, and Dot recordings of their greatest hits have also served as musical backdrop, as well as forefront attractions, in such television and Hollywood productions as *War and Remembrance, The Summer of My German Soldier, Homefront, ER, The Brink's Job, 1941, National Lampoon's Christmas Vacation, Swing Shift, Raggedy Man, Summer of '42, Slaughterhouse Five, Maria's Lovers, Harlem Nights, Murder in the First,* and *L.A. Confidential.* Some of the trio's Decca recordings have been referenced in television's popular game show *Jeopardy!* in such categories as World War II, Bugle Calls, and Sisters. Not surprisingly, the famous board game Trivial Pursuit asks, "Which singing group consists of LaVerne, Maxene and Patty?"

Zebra Books released a hardcover book in 1993 entitled *Over Here, Over There: The Andrews Sisters and the USO Stars in World War II,* written by Maxene Andrews and Bill Gilbert. While not a biography of the sisters, the book contains a wealth of anecdotes and stories about the trio's involvement with the USO in America and Europe. The book also relates adventures of other popular stars of the day for the war effort, including Bing Crosby, Bob Hope, Judy Garland, Ann Miller, Mickey Rooney, Danny Kaye, and Glenn Miller. This, however, was not the book that fans of the trio were expecting. Maxene had said in several interviews that she had written an autobiography since the closing of *Over Here!,* but was having a bit of trouble finding a suitable publisher. She claimed that most publishers were looking for her to dish out the dirt—write more about the personal disagreement, the fights over boyfriends and husbands and such. She told interviewer Hugh Downs in 1979 that she had no interest in writing a tell-all book. If, in fact, the project was ever completed, it was never published.

In the fall of 1995, Maxene made her off-Broadway debut at the Blue Angel in New York City, in a show called *Swingtime Canteen.* She sang a medley of Andrews Sisters hits during each appearance of her month-long run before taking a hiatus, agreeing to return for the holiday season. While vacationing on Cape Cod, Maxene suffered a massive heart attack and died at Cape Cod Hospital on October 21, 1995. She was seventy-nine years old.

The suddenness of Maxene's death shocked the entertainment industry and made headlines around the world. She was survived by her two adopted children, one grandchild, and sister Patty. Bob Hope, who worked with the trio countless times and had remained friends with both Maxene and Patty over the years, said, "She was much more than part of the Andrews Sisters, much more than a singer. She was a warm and wonderful lady who shared her talent and wisdom with others." Not long before she passed away, Maxene told William Ruhlmann, "I have nothing to regret. We got on the carousel and we each got the ring and I was satisfied with that. There's nothing I would do to change things if I could—yes, I would. I would wish I had the ability and the power to bridge the gap between my relationship with my sister Patty. I haven't found the way yet, but I'm sure that the Lord will find the way."

When Maxene flew to Honolulu a month before her death for ceremonies marking the fiftieth anniversary of V-J Day, she participated in a motorcade parade, performed at the ceremonies, and joined Bob Hope and President Clinton in singing "America the Beautiful" before thousands of veterans. It was an extremely moving and fitting tribute, the apex to a long and illustrious career. Maxene once recalled, "In 1991 . . . I made a personal appearance in Clearwater, Florida, and sang many of the World War II songs. Minutes after I finished, a World War II veteran came up to me and said, 'I don't know if you think this is a compliment, but to me and my buddies, the Andrews Sisters are synonymous with World War II.' I told him it was one of the nicest compliments we ever had."

Patty rarely entertains today. With her husband acting as her conductor and pianist, Patty has performed on several different ships for various cruise lines, and her act featured most of the songs that catapulted the sisters to stardom. The trio became one of the first vocal groups inducted into the Vocal Group Hall of Fame in Sharon, Pennsylvania, in October 1998. Patty did not attend the ceremonies, but the award was forwarded to her by an attentive fan. More recently, Patty has become the spokesperson in a fund-raising campaign to erect an official World War II memorial on the National Mall in Washington, D.C., as a lasting tribute to the tens of thousands of servicemen and women she and her sisters devoted so much of their time to during the war.

Where did the good times go? Perhaps they have quietly faded into the wrinkled pages of America's musical history. Only Patty remains, and although the career of the Andrews Sisters is over, their music is alive and well. The sisters will never be remembered one without the other in the minds of their many fans, for they have become a legendary entity, frozen in time as a trio. Their incredible popularity has credited them with even more hits than they actually made famous, including "That's My Affair," "He's My Guy," "On Top of Old Smoky," "At Your Beck and Call," "Reuben's Goin' Cuban," "Old Paint," "Joe-See-Fus Jones," "Put that Kiss Back Where You Found It," "The Umbrella Man," "I've Got Those Peelin' Those Potatoes, Slicin' Those Tomatoes, Liftin' Up Those Garbage Can Blues," "Heartaches," "Between 18th and 19th on Chestnut Street," the McGuire Sisters' "Sugartime," and "Mr. Sandman," one of the Chordettes' biggest hits. Perhaps the Andrews Sisters sang these songs on radio or during stage shows, thus the association. Also, music publishers would often feature a picture of the trio on the cover of a sheet music copy of a song to boost its sales. Thus songs were attributed to the sisters that they had never actually recorded.

Aside from the erroneous musical connections, the cast of characters that the trio endowed to the world of popular music has become historical, providing memories for young and old alike: the boogie woogie bugle boy; that pistol packin' mama; the soldier boy who promised a wedding in apple blossom time; Queenie, the cutie of the burlesque show; Aurora, with her manners so Brazilian; bella, bella Marie, with love in her eyes divine; the three caballeros—always together; the blond sailor; the three little sisters, each one only in her teens; Miss Effy, who didn't know the gun was loaded; Billy boy, that charmin' Billy; the cockeyed mayor of Kaunakakai; Jimmy Brown, from the village hidden deep in the valley; the boogie-woogie washerwoman; sweet Molly Malone, cryin' cockles and mussels, alive, alive-o!; Lili Marlene, the sweetheart of the nation; Malagueña, whose gypsy eyes shamed the purple skies; Lilly Belle, with lips as fresh as autumn rain when summer is through; Clancy! Oh, that Clancy!; and many more.

The appeal of the group was all-consuming during the trio's heyday, and that appeal seems to have become timeless. The Andrews Sisters represent many different things to many different people. They are forever etched in the memory of that fighting soldier who felt as if they were singing to him only and for him only. Echoes of their popularizations of various ethnic melodies are still recalled by immigrants who appreciated any familiar sound of home in their newfound continent. Individuals mature enough to remember a pre-television era when radio ruled the airwaves can still recall the happy musical chirping of three sisters who literally immersed themselves in that medium. When television arrived on the scene, millions of viewers not yet old enough to know or remember the sisters were exposed to their nostalgic merriment and prime entertaining skills. Compact disc anthologies of their greatest hits are readily available from record stores and music clubs, at libraries and museums throughout the world. The sisters' singing and dancing can now be viewed through videotape and laser disc technologies in several of the best remembered Hollywood films of their era. The slick, time-transcending harmonies of the group are fresh and entertaining to many households where youngsters enjoy such Disney favorites as "Little Toot" and "Johnny Fedora and Alice Blue Bonnet." The sisters are also alive and well to the inquisitive Internet surfer, and a sample of their swinging musical stylings can be heard at the touch of a button. There are not many artists from the trio's era whose popularity remains so widespread.

Theirs was a sound that will most likely never be matched, let alone surpassed. Theirs was a career that has yet to be equaled by another girl group in terms of popularity, achievement, and endurance. Through the harmonious gems of the Andrews Sisters, the good times will never be forgotten—they will last for an eternity.

Appendix A

Top-Thirty Hits
(Compiled from *Billboard*)

Highest Chart Position (HCP)   Total Weeks Charted (TWC)

"Bei Mir Bist Du Schon (Means that You're Grand)." Charted: Jan. 1, 1938. HCP: #1 for 5 weeks. TWC: 10.

"Nice Work If You Can Get It." Charted: Jan. 8, 1938. HCP: #12. TWC: 12.

"Joseph! Joseph!" Charted: Mar. 19, 1938. HCP: #18. TWC: 1.

"Ti-Pi-Tin." Charted: Mar. 26, 1938. HCP: #12. TWC: 4.

"Shortenin' Bread." Charted: Mar. 26, 1938. HCP: #16. TWC: 2.

"Says My Heart." Charted: July 16, 1938. HCP: #10. TWC: 5.

"Tu-Li-Tulip Time." Charted: Sept. 10, 1938. HCP: #9. TWC: 4.

"Sha-Sha." Charted: Nov. 12, 1938. HCP: #17. TWC: 1.

"Lullaby to a Jitterbug." Charted: Dec. 10, 1938. HCP: #10. TWC: 3.

"Pros Tchai (Goodbye, Goodbye)." Charted: May 20, 1939. HCP: #15. TWC: 1.

"Hold Tight-Hold Tight (Want Some Sea Food, Mama?)" Charted: Jan. 14, 1939. HCP: #2. TWC: 11.

"You Don't Know How Much You Can Suffer." Charted: May 13, 1939. HCP: #14. TWC: 1.

"Beer Barrel Polka (Roll Out the Barrel)." Charted: May 27, 1939. HCP: #4. TWC: 7.

"Well, All Right! (Tonight's the Night)." Charted: June 17, 1939. HCP: #5. TWC: 15.

"Ciribiribin (They're So in Love)" (with Bing Crosby). Charted: Nov. 4, 1939. HCP: #13. TWC: 3.

"Yodelin' Jive" (with Bing Crosby). Charted: Nov. 18, 1939. HCP: #4. TWC: 12.

"Chico's Love Song." Charted: Nov. 25, 1939. HCP: #11. TWC: 5.

"Say Si Si (Para Vigo Me Voy)." Charted: Mar. 16, 1940. HCP: #4. TWC: 10.

"The Woodpecker Song." Charted: Apr. 6, 1940. HCP: #6. TWC: 12.

"Down by the O-Hi-O." Charted: Apr. 20, 1940. HCP: #21. TWC: 1.

"Rhumboogie." Charted: May 18, 1940. HCP: #11. TWC: 9.

"Ferryboat Serenade (La Piccinina)." Charted: Oct. 12, 1940. HCP: #1 for 3 weeks. TWC: 14.

"Hit the Road." Charted: Jan. 26, 1940. HCP: #27. TWC: 1.

"Beat Me Daddy, Eight to the Bar." Charted: Nov. 2, 1940. HCP: #2. TWC: 14.

"Scrub Me Mama with a Boogie Beat." Charted: Feb. 1, 1941. HCP: #10. TWC: 7.

"Boogie Woogie Bugle Boy." Charted: Mar. 1, 1941. HCP: #6. TWC: 8.

"I Yi, Yi, Yi, Yi (I Like You Very Much)." Charted: Apr. 12, 1941. HCP: #11. TWC: 6.

"I'll Be with You in Apple Blossom Time." Charted: Apr. 26, 1941. HCP: #5. TWC: 17.

"Aurora." Charted: May 31, 1941. HCP: #10. TWC: 11.

"Sonny Boy." Charted: Aug. 30, 1941. HCP: #22. TWC: 1.

"The Nickel Serenade." Charted: Sept. 27, 1941. HCP: #22. TWC: 1.

"Sleepy Serenade." Charted: Oct. 4, 1941. HCP: #22. TWC: 1.

"I Wish I Had a Dime (For Ev'rytime I Missed You)." Charted: Nov. 1, 1941. HCP: #20. TWC: 2.

"Jealous." Charted: Nov. 15, 1941. HCP: #12. TWC: 9.

"The Shrine of Saint Cecilia." Charted: Jan. 10, 1942. HCP: #3. TWC: 7.

"I'll Pray for You." Charted: Mar. 7, 1942. HCP: #22. TWC: 1.

"Three Little Sisters." Charted: May 23, 1942. HCP: #8. TWC: 17.

"Don't Sit under the Apple Tree (With Anyone Else but Me)." Charted: May 23, 1942. HCP: #16. TWC: 1.

"Pennsylvania Polka." Charted: Aug. 8, 1942. HCP: #17. TWC: 3.

"That's the Moon, My Son." Charted: Aug. 29, 1942. HCP: #18. TWC: 2.

"Mister Five by Five." Charted: Sept. 26, 1942. HCP: #14. TWC: 2.

"Strip Polka." Charted: Oct. 10, 1942. HCP: #6. TWC: 9.

"Here Comes the Navy." Charted: Oct. 24, 1942. HCP: #17. TWC: 2.

"East of the Rockies." Charted: June 5, 1943. HCP: #18. TWC: 1.

"Pistol Packin' Mama" (with Bing Crosby). Charted: Nov. 6, 1943. HCP: #2. TWC: 11.

"The Vict'ry Polka" (with Bing Crosby). Charted: Nov. 13, 1943. HCP: #5. TWC: 13.

"Jingle Bells" (with Bing Crosby). Charted: Dec. 25, 1943. HCP: #19. TWC: 1.

"Shoo Shoo Baby." Charted: Dec. 25, 1943. HCP: #1 for 9 weeks. TWC: 21.

"Down in the Valley (Hear That Train Blow)." Charted: Jan. 29, 1944. HCP: #20. TWC: 1.

"Straighten Up and Fly Right." Charted: June 17, 1944. HCP: #8. TWC: 13.

"Sing a Tropical Song." Charted: July 1, 1944. HCP: #24. TWC: 1.

"Tico-Tico." Charted: July 8, 1944. HCP: #24. TWC: 1.

"Is You Is or Is You Ain't (Ma' Baby?)" (with Bing Crosby). Charted: Sept. 9, 1944. HCP: #2. TWC: 12.

"There'll Be a Hot Time in the Town of Berlin (When the Yanks Go Marching In)" (with Bing Crosby). Charted: Sept. 23, 1944. HCP: #1 for 6 weeks. TWC: 14.

"Don't Fence Me In" (with Bing Crosby). Charted: Nov. 25, 1944. HCP: #1 for 8 weeks. TWC: 21.

"Rum and Coca Cola." Charted: Jan. 6, 1945. HCP: #1 for 10 weeks. TWC: 20.

"Corns for My Country." Charted: Jan. 13, 1945. HCP: #21. TWC: 1.

"Ac-cent-tchu-ate the Positive" (with Bing Crosby). Charted: Feb. 3, 1945. HCP: #2. TWC: 9.

"The Three Caballeros" (with Bing Crosby). Charted: Feb. 3, 1945. HCP: #8. TWC: 5.

"One Meat Ball." Charted: Feb. 17, 1945. HCP: #15. TWC: 1.

"Along the Navajo Trail" (with Bing Crosby). Charted: Sept. 15, 1945. HCP: #2. TWC: 11.

"The Blond Sailor." Charted: Sept. 29, 1945. HCP: #8. TWC: 8.

"Money Is the Root of All Evil (Take It Away, Take It Away, Take It Away)." Charted: Feb. 2, 1946. HCP: #9. TWC: 5.

"Patience and Fortitude." Charted: Mar. 16, 1946. HCP: #12. TWC: 1.

"Coax Me a Little Bit." Charted: June 1, 1946. HCP: #24. TWC: 1.

"South America, Take It Away" (with Bing Crosby). Charted: Aug. 3, 1946. HCP: #2. TWC: 19.

"Get Your Kicks on Route 66!" (with Bing Crosby). Charted: Aug. 10, 1946. HCP: #14. TWC: 2.

"I Don't Know Why (I Just Do)." Charted: Aug. 31, 1946. HCP: #17. TWC: 1.

"The House of Blue Lights." Charted: Sept. 28, 1946. HCP: #15. TWC: 5.

"Rumors Are Flying." Charted: Oct. 19, 1946. HCP: #4. TWC: 13.

"Winter Wonderland." Charted: Dec. 14, 1946. HCP: #22. TWC: 4.

"Christmas Island." Charted: Dec. 21, 1946. HCP: #7. TWC: 4.

"Tallahassee" (with Bing Crosby). Charted: July 5, 1947. HCP: #10. TWC: 10.

"There's No Business like Show Business" (with Bing Crosby and Dick Haymes). Charted: July 19, 1947. HCP: #25. TWC: 1.

"On the Avenue." Charted: Sept. 6, 1947. HCP: #21. TWC: 4.

"Near You." Charted: Sept. 27, 1947. HCP: #2. TWC: 17.

"The Lady from 29 Palms." Charted: Oct. 18, 1947. HCP: #7. TWC: 2.

"The Freedom Train" (with Bing Crosby). Charted: Oct. 25, 1947. HCP: #21. TWC: 1.

"Civilization (Bongo, Bongo, Bongo)" (with Danny Kaye). Charted: Nov. 22, 1947. HCP: #3. TWC: 8.

"Jingle Bells" (with Bing Crosby). Charted: Dec. 31, 1947. HCP: #21. TWC: 2.

"Christmas Island." Charted: Dec. 20, 1947. HCP: #20. TWC: 2.

"Your Red Wagon." Charted: Dec. 20, 1947. HCP: #24. TWC: 3.

"Santa Claus Is Coming to Town" (with Bing Crosby). Charted: Dec. 27, 1947. HCP: #22. TWC: 1.

"How Lucky You Are." Charted: Dec. 27, 1947. HCP: #22. TWC: 1.

"You Don't Have to Know the Language" (with Bing Crosby). Charted: Jan. 31, 1948. HCP: #21. TWC: 2.

"Teresa" (with Dick Haymes). Charted: Mar. 20, 1948. HCP: #21. TWC: 1.

"Toolie Oolie Doolie (The Yodel Polka)." Charted: Apr. 17, 1948. HCP: #3. TWC: 17.

"Heartbreaker." Charted: May 15, 1948. HCP: #21. TWC: 5.

"(Everytime They Play the) Sabre Dance." Charted: May 22, 1948. HCP: #20. TWC: 3.

"I Hate to Lose You." Charted: June 12, 1948. HCP: #14. TWC: 7.

"The Woody Woodpecker Song" (with Danny Kaye). Charted: July 19, 1948. HCP: #18. TWC: 6.

"The Blue Tail Fly" (with Burl Ives). Charted: July 31, 1948. HCP: #24. TWC: 1.

"Underneath the Arches." Charted: Sept. 4, 1948. HCP: #5. TWC: 12.

"You Call Everybody Darling." Charted: Sept. 4, 1948. HCP: #8. TWC: 12.

"Cuanto la Gusta" (with Carmen Miranda). Charted: Oct. 9, 1948. HCP: #12. TWC: 14.

"A Hundred and Sixty Acres" (with Bing Crosby). Charted: Nov. 6, 1948. HCP: #23. TWC: 2.

"Bella Bella Marie." Charted: Nov. 20, 1948. HCP: #23. TWC: 2.

"Christmas Island." Charted: Jan. 8, 1949. HCP: #26. TWC: 1.

"More Beer!" Charted: Jan. 29, 1949. HCP: #30. TWC: 3.

"I'm Bitin' My Fingernails and Thinking of You" (with Ernest Tubb). Charted: May 7, 1949. HCP: #30. TWC: 1.

"I Can Dream, Can't I?" Charted: Sept. 24, 1949. HCP: #1 for 5 weeks. TWC: 25.

"The Wedding of Lili Marlene." Charted: Oct. 1, 1949. HCP: #20. TWC: 2.

"She Wore a Yellow Ribbon" (with Russ Morgan). Charted: Dec. 10, 1949. HCP: #22. TWC: 2.

"Charley, My Boy" (with Russ Morgan). Charted: Dec. 17, 1949. HCP: #15. TWC: 4.

"Merry Christmas Polka." Charted: Jan. 7, 1950. HCP: #18. TWC: 1.

"Have I Told You Lately that I Love You?" (with Bing Crosby). Charted: Jan. 21, 1950. HCP: #24. TWC: 4.

"Quicksilver" (with Bing Crosby). Charted: Jan. 28, 1950. HCP: #6. TWC: 17.

"The Wedding Samba" (with Carmen Miranda). Charted: Jan. 28, 1950. HCP: #23. TWC: 3.

"I Wanna Be Loved." Charted: May 13, 1950. HCP: #1 for 2 weeks. TWC: 21.

"Can't We Talk It Over?" Charted: Sept. 27, 1950. HCP: #22. TWC: 1.

"A Bushel and a Peck." Charted: Dec. 9, 1950. HCP: #22. TWC: 4.

"A Penny a Kiss—A Penny a Hug." Charted: Mar. 3, 1951. HCP: #17. TWC: 7.

"Sparrow in the Treetop" (with Bing Crosby). Charted: Mar. 10, 1951. HCP: #8. TWC: 15.

Appendix B

Top-Ten Hits
(Compiled from *Variety*)

Highest Chart Position (HCP)   Total Weeks Charted (TWC)

"Bei Mir Bist Du Schon (Means that You're Grand)." Charted: Jan. 8, 1938. HCP: #1. TWC: 7.

"Ti-Pi-Tin." Charted: Mar. 19, 1938. HCP: #1. TWC: 3.

"Says My Heart." Charted: June 11, 1938. HCP: #1. TWC: 8.

"Tu-Li-Tulip Time." Charted: Oct. 15, 1938. HCP: #10. TWC: 1.

"Hold Tight-Hold Tight (Want Some Sea Food, Mama?)." Charted: Apr. 1, 1939. HCP: #4. TWC: 2.

"Beer Barrel Polka (Roll Out the Barrel)." Charted: June 24, 1939. HCP: #2. TWC: 10.

"Oh, Johnny! Oh, Johnny! Oh!" Charted: Dec. 9, 1939. HCP: #2. TWC: 9.

"The Woodpecker Song." Charted: Apr. 6, 1940. HCP: #1. TWC: 14.

"Ferryboat Serenade (La Piccinina)." Charted: Oct. 19, 1940. HCP: #1. TWC: 10.

"Daddy." Charted: June 21, 1941. HCP: #1. TWC: 14.

"Chattanooga Choo Choo." Charted: Nov. 22, 1941. HCP: #1. TWC: 12.

"Elmer's Tune." Charted: Nov. 29, 1941. HCP: #1. TWC: 11.

"The Shrine of Saint Cecilia." Charted: Jan. 24, 1942. HCP: #5. TWC: 8.

"Don't Sit under the Apple Tree (With Anyone Else but Me)." Charted: Apr. 25, 1942. HCP: #1. TWC: 11.

"Three Little Sisters." Charted: June 13, 1942. HCP: #6. TWC: 10.

"I've Got a Guy in Kalamazoo." Charted: Sept. 5, 1942. HCP: #1. TWC: 10.

"Mister Five by Five." Charted: Sept. 5, 1942. HCP: #2. TWC: 8.

"Pistol Packin' Mama" (with Bing Crosby). Charted: Oct. 2, 1943. HCP: #2. TWC: 13.

"Shoo Shoo Baby." Charted: Dec. 4, 1943. HCP: #1. TWC: 16.

"Is You Is or Is You Ain't (Ma' Baby?)" (with Bing Crosby). Charted: Aug. 12, 1944. HCP: #2. TWC: 11.

"Don't Fence Me In" (with Bing Crosby). Charted: Dec. 2, 1944. HCP: #1. TWC: 14.

"Ac-cent-tchu-ate the Positive" (with Bing Crosby). Charted: Jan. 20, 1945. HCP: #1. TWC: 11.

"Rum and Coca Cola." Charted: Feb. 17, 1945. HCP: #4. TWC: 10.

"Along the Navajo Trail" (with Bing Crosby). Charted: Sept. 22, 1945. HCP: #3. TWC: 9.

"Put That Ring on My Finger." Charted: Dec. 22, 1945. HCP: #6. TWC: 3.

"South America, Take It Away" (with Bing Crosby). Charted: Aug. 31, 1946. HCP: #2. TWC: 11.

"Rumors Are Flying." Charted: Oct. 5, 1946. HCP: #1. TWC: 6.

"Tallahassee" (with Bing Crosby). Charted: Aug. 16, 1947. HCP: #5. TWC: 5.

"Near You." Charted: Sept. 27, 1947. HCP: #1. TWC: 17.

"The Lady from 29 Palms." Charted: Sept. 27, 1947. HCP: #5. TWC: 8.

"Civilization (Bongo, Bongo, Bongo)" (with Danny Kaye). Charted: Nov. 15, 1947. HCP: #1. TWC: 13.

"The Too Fat Polka (She's Too Fat for Me)." Charted: Jan. 17, 1948. HCP: #7. TWC: 2.

"(Everytime They Play the) Sabre Dance." Charted: Apr. 3, 1948. HCP: #6. TWC: 10.

"Toolie Oolie Doolie (The Yodel Polka)." Charted: May 15, 1948. HCP: #2. TWC: 10.

"The Woody Woodpecker Song" (with Danny Kaye). Charted: June 26, 1948. HCP: #1. TWC: 10.

"You Call Everybody Darling." Charted: Aug. 7, 1948. HCP: #1. TWC: 16.

"Underneath the Arches." Charted: Oct. 2, 1948. HCP: #6. TWC: 6.

"Cuanto la Gusta" (with Carmen Miranda). Charted: Nov. 27, 1948. HCP: #7. TWC: 8.

"I Can Dream, Can't I?" Charted: Oct. 29, 1949. HCP: #1. TWC: 15.

"The Old Piano Roll Blues" (with Al Jolson). Charted: May 13, 1950. HCP: #4. TWC: 9.

"I Wanna Be Loved." Charted: June 17, 1950. HCP: #2. TWC: 14.

"A Bushel and a Peck." Charted: Nov. 11, 1950. HCP: #1. TWC: 14.

"A Penny a Kiss—A Penny a Hug." Charted: Feb. 17, 1951. HCP: #6. TWC: 6.

"Zing Zing, Zoom Zoom." Charted: Feb. 17, 1951. HCP: #7. TWC: 5.

"It Is No Secret (What God Can Do)" (with Red Foley). Charted: Mar. 31, 1951. HCP: #8. TWC: 5.

"Sparrow in the Treetop" (with Bing Crosby). Charted: Apr. 7, 1951. HCP: #4. TWC: 5.

Appendix C

Most Played Jukebox Records of World War II (Compiled from *Variety*)

Highest Chart Position (HCP)   Total Weeks Charted (TWC)

"Chattanooga Choo Choo." Charted: Dec. 17, 1941. HCP: #1. TWC: 10.

"Elmer's Tune." Charted: Dec. 17, 1941. HCP: #2. TWC: 6.

"Jealous." Charted: Dec. 17, 1941. HCP: #9. TWC: 1.

"The Shrine of Saint Cecilia." Charted: Jan. 28, 1942. HCP: #6. TWC: 1.

"Pistol Packin' Mama" (with Bing Crosby). Charted: Nov. 10, 1943. HCP: #1. TWC: 9.

"The Vict'ry Polka" (with Bing Crosby). Charted: Nov. 17, 1943. HCP: #4. TWC: 8.

"Shoo Shoo Baby." Charted: Jan. 19, 1944. HCP: #1. TWC: 10.

"Straighten Up and Fly Right." Charted: June 28, 1944. HCP: #7. TWC: 4.

"Is You Is or Is You Ain't (Ma' Baby?)" (with Bing Crosby). Charted: Sept. 13, 1944. HCP: #1. TWC: 7.

"There'll Be a Hot Time in the Town of Berlin (When the Yanks Go Marching In)" (with Bing Crosby). Charted: Nov. 1, 1944. HCP: #8. TWC: 2.

"Don't Fence Me In" (with Bing Crosby). Charted: Nov. 15, 1944. HCP: #1. TWC: 20.

"Rum and Coca Cola." Charted: Jan. 24, 1945. HCP: #1. TWC: 13.

"Ac-cent-tchu-ate the Positive" (with Bing Crosby). Charted: Feb. 7, 1945. HCP: #2. TWC: 9.

"Along the Navajo Trail" (with Bing Crosby). Charted: Oct. 3, 1945. HCP: #4. TWC: 8.

"The Blond Sailor." Charted: Oct. 31, 1945. HCP: #6. TWC: 7.

Other Andrews Sisters hits of the years before and after the war to be included in *Variety*'s Most Played Jukebox Records are: "I'll Be with You in Apple Blossom Time," "Daddy," "Aurora," "Music Makers," "South America, Take It Away" (with Bing Crosby), "Get Your Kicks on Route 66!" (with Bing Crosby), "Rumors Are Flying," "The House of Blue Lights," "Winter Wonderland," "On the Avenue," "Jack, Jack, Jack (Cu-Tu-Gu-Ru)," "The Lady from 29 Palms," and "Tallahassee" (with Bing Crosby).

Appendix D

Gold Records

"Nice Work If You Can Get It" and "Bei Mir Bist Du Schon (Means that You're Grand)," 1937. This coupling was the trio's second Decca release. "Bei Mir" was the B side of the platter and the reason the disc sold over one million copies, making the Andrews Sisters the first female vocal group in popular music history to achieve a gold record. By 1949, Decca Records estimated total sales of the disc to be fourteen million; the song grossed over three million dollars by 1961.

"Beer Barrel Polka (Roll Out the Barrel)" and "Well, All Right! (Tonight's the Night)," 1939. Jack Kapp, head of Decca, gave a Czechoslovakian polka to the trio, which he was eager to have them record. The sisters and arranger Vic Schoen disliked the melody, but the song was recorded at Kapp's insistence. Upon its release, the tune became a smash hit as the disc sold over eight hundred thousand copies and soon became a million seller. The polka became so popular that the trio used its melody and arrangement for their 1943 hit, "Here Comes the Navy," which sold over five hundred thousand copies.

"Pistol Packin' Mama" and "The Vict'ry Polka," 1943. This record was Decca's first release following the 1942 musicians' strike, and the sisters' first collaboration with Bing Crosby since their initial 1939 session, which had produced "Ciribiribin (They're So in Love)" and "Yodelin' Jive"—a platter that had sold over five hundred thousand copies upon its release. Fans made this second Crosby/Andrews effort a quick million seller and a top-ten *Billboard* hit. The sheet music copy of "Pistol Packin' Mama," featuring a picture of Crosby and the trio taken during the recording session, also sold over one million copies.

"Jingle Bells" and "Santa Claus Is Coming to Town," 1943. This seasonal disc was recorded just days after "Pistol Packin' Mama." It followed directly on the heels of Crosby's 1942 recording of Irving Berlin's "White Christmas." Sales of this disc shot well over the million mark following its fall release in 1943. Copies of "Jingle Bells" by Crosby and the sisters, in original and re-released forms, now total over ten million copies.

"Don't Fence Me In" and "The Three Caballeros," 1944. Bing Crosby arrived at Decca's Los Angeles studios completely unaware of what the trio intended to record with him, since he left the selection and arranging of all materials to the sisters. Patty taught him their arrangement of "Don't Fence Me In" in less than thirty minutes, and the end result was a million-selling record. The sheet music copy of this Cole Porter western satire also sold over one million copies.

"Rum and Coca Cola" and "One Meat Ball," 1944. Although "One Meat Ball" became a hit in its own right, it was "Rum and Coca Cola" that made the platter's sales skyrocket to platinum status. Recorded with just twenty minutes remaining in their studio session, the trio improvised a quick arrangement on the calypso number. "Rum and Coca Cola" gave the girls as much trouble as it did success. Radio stations refused to play the song because it mentioned an alcoholic beverage, as well as a popular soft drink. The song was even banned in certain cities throughout America due to the nature of the lyrics, which suggested that American servicemen on leave were soliciting Trinidad's women for nights of tropic lovemaking. Furthermore, the song became the center of a lawsuit, which claimed that the melody was plagiarized from an old calypso number written years earlier in Trinidad. The court's ruling declared that the melody was indeed copied from a 1906 composition, and the original composer, still living, was awarded a percentage of the royalties. Despite the opposition, the record sold a whopping seven million copies. Shellac, in short supply during the war, had to be borrowed from other record companies so that Decca could supply enough discs for public demand.

"South America, Take It Away" and "Get Your Kicks on Route 66!," 1946. The sisters joined Crosby once again, attempting to capitalize on the South American samba beat (Peggy Lee, Desi Arnaz, and others were soon to follow suit) by recording a new tune, "South America, Take It Away," which spoofed such dance crazes as the samba, the rhumba, and the conga. The quartet also recorded "Route 66!" and the platter became a million seller."Route 66!" was repopularized four decades later by the alternative rock group Depeche Mode.

"Christmas Island" and "Winter Wonderland," 1946. The trio's second collaboration with Guy Lombardo's Royal Canadians produced this seasonal coupling, which sold over a million copies, and both tunes became staples for the trio. The two recordings, in re-released forms, can still be found on jukebox panels during each holiday season. Collective sales of "Winter Wonderland," by such varied artists as the sisters, Perry Como, Steve Lawrence and Eydie Gorme, Johnny Mathis, and the Eurythmics, now total over forty million copies.

"I Can Dream, Can't I?" and "The Wedding of Lili Marlene," 1949. Backed by the lush strings and lilting chorus of Gordon Jenkins' impressive musical unit, the trio recorded these two lovely ballads in the summer of 1949. The timeless "I Can Dream, Can't I?" featured an extended solo by Patty, with her sisters providing harmony near the finale only. The record's success prompted other recordings by the trio with Jenkins, including "I Wanna Be Loved," "There Will Never Be Another You," "Can't We Talk It Over?," and the group's less popular but nevertheless classic performance of "The Three Bells." The disc's success also set the stage for Patty's solo records in the early 1950s.

Over Here!, 1974. This Columbia album is the soundtrack of the 1974 Broadway play in which Maxene and Patty starred for nine months at the Shubert Theater in New York City. It was certified and awarded to both sisters as a gold record.

If today's recording industry standard were applied to the Andrews Sisters, the current practice of awarding a gold record for sales over five hundred thousand copies (as opposed to the one million copies in sales required during the trio's heyday) would certify nearly one hundred of the trio's Decca platters as gold.

Appendix E

On the Air

The Paul Whiteman Show, 1938. The sisters sang "The Lonesome Road."

Just Entertainment starring Jack Fulton, March 21-Aug. 1, 1938. (See text pages 32-33.)

Honolulu Bound (also known as *The Phil Baker Show*), Jan. 14-Oct. 4, 1939. (See text page 37.)

The Moonlight Serenade (also known as *The Chesterfield Show*), Dec. 27, 1939-March 28, 1940. (See text pages 44-49.)

Millions for Defense, Mar. 11, 1941. Sponsored by the U.S. Treasury Department, the sisters sang "Boogie Woogie Bugle Boy" and "I'll Be with You in Apple Blossom Time."

Command Performance, Apr. 12, 1942. Hosted by Gene Tierney, the sisters appeared with Betty Hutton, Gary Cooper, Edgar Bergen and Charlie McCarthy, Ginny Simms, Bob Burns, and Ray Noble's orchestra.

Command Performance, Dec. 12, 1942. Host Cary Grant introduced the sisters, who sang "Here Comes the Navy."

The Texaco Star Theater (also known as *The Fred Allen Show*), Oct. 4, 1942. The sisters made a special guest appearance and sang "Pennsylvania Polka."

Command Performance, Dec. 24, 1942. A Christmas extravaganza hosted by Bob Hope, who introduced the trio opening the show with "Pennsylvania Polka." Also appearing were Red Skelton, Harriet Hilliard, Ginny Simms, Bing Crosby, Ethel Waters, Charles Laughton, Edgar Bergen and Charlie McCarthy, Dinah Shore, Jack Benny, Fred Allen, Kay Kyser's orchestra, and Spike Jones and the City Slickers.

The Roma Wines Show starring Mary Astor, Sept. 2-Nov. 4, 1943. (See text page 70.)

Command Performance, Sept. 11, 1943. Hosted by Ginny Simms, the guests included Roy Acuff and the Smokey Mountain Boys and the sisters, who sang "Send Me a Man, Amen!" and "Sing."

Command Performance, Jan. 1944. Host Bob Hope introduced Bing Crosby and the sisters, who sang "Ac-cent-tchu-ate the Positive."

Command Performance, June 24, 1944. Bob Hope hosted this all-western program. The sisters sang "Pistol Packin' Mama" and "Down in the Valley."

Command Performance, July 15, 1944. Hosted by Bing Crosby, who was joined by Judy Garland and the sisters. Crosby and the trio sang "Is You Is or Is You Ain't (Ma' Baby?)," and the foursome joined Garland for a spoof entitled "Your All-Time Flop Parade" (which lampooned "Your Hit Parade").

The Philco Radio Hall of Fame, Oct. 1944. The sisters sang "Is You Is or Is You Ain't (Ma' Baby?)."

The Philco Radio Hall of Fame, 1944. The sisters sang "Rhumboogie."

Mail Call, 1944. Host Herbert Marshall introduced the sisters, who sang "There'll Be a Jubilee" and "Straighten Up and Fly Right."

Mail Call, Nov. 22, 1944. Host Bing Crosby joined the trio for "Is You Is or Is You Ain't (Ma' Baby?)" and introduced them singing "Down in the Valley" and "Lullaby of Broadway."

Command Performance, Dec. 16, 1944. Host Bob Hope introduced the sisters, who sang "Rum and Coca Cola" and joined Bing Crosby for "Don't Fence Me In."

GI Journal, Dec. 22, 1944. Host Bob Hope introduced the sisters, who sang "Rum and Coca Cola."

The Andrews Sisters Show (also known as *The Eight-to-the-Bar Ranch*), Dec. 31, 1944-Sept. 23, 1945. (See text pages 78-81.) Songs sung by the sisters during the series' run: "The Trolley Song," "The Last Roundup," "I'm Beginning to See the Light," "Dream," "Saturday Night (Is the Loneliest Night of the Week)," "Ev'rytime," "Dance with a Dolly (With a Hole in Her Stocking)," "Together," "Home," "Blue Skies," "Come to Baby, Do," "Sentimental Journey," "I Don't Want to Love You (Like I Do)," "My Baby Said Yes," as well as solos by Patty, including "Sweet Molly Malone," "That Old Feeling," "Evalina," "Don't Blame Me," "Just A Prayer Away," "Katusha," and "If I Lost You."

The Eddie Cantor Show, Jan. 10, 1945. The sisters sang "Sonny Boy" with Cantor, and the foursome joined Harry Von Zell in a comedy sketch.

The Rudy Vallee Show, Jan. 18, 1945. The sisters sang "Bei Mir Bist Du Schon" and joined Vallee for "Blues in the Night" and "Vieni, Vieni."

The Kraft Music Hall starring Bing Crosby, Jan. 25, 1945. Crosby opened the show with the trio, singing "Don't Fence Me In." The sisters also sang "One Meat Ball" and an abbreviated version of "Ain't It a Shame about Mame."

Command Performance, Feb. 15, 1945. This episode, subtitled "Dick Tracy in B-flat" or "For Goodness Sake, Isn't He Ever Going to Marry Tess Trueheart?" spoofed the *Dick Tracy* comic strip characters. The all-star cast included Bing Crosby, Dinah Shore, Frank Sinatra, Bob Hope, Judy Garland, Jimmy Durante, the Andrews Sisters (who sang a parody of "Apple Blossom Time"), Frank Morgan, Jerry Colonna, and Cass Daley.

Command Performance, 1945. Host Frank Morgan introduced the trio, who sang "One Meat Ball."

Mail Call, Mar. 7, 1945. Host Jack Benny introduced the sisters, who sang "Good, Good, Good."

Mail Call, Mar. 14, 1945. Host Nelson Eddy chatted with the sisters, who sang "Saturday Night (Is the Loneliest Night of the Week)" and "Good, Good, Good." The trio also sang a snippet of "Frankie and Johnny" as part of a comedy sketch with Eddy and Cass Daley.

The Abbott and Costello Show, Apr. 26, 1945. The sisters sang "I'm Beginning to See the Light" and joined Costello for "Sonny Boy."

The Walgreen Birthday Party, June 10, 1945. Host Don Wilson introduced the sisters, who sang "Bei Mir Bist Du Schon" and joined Bing Crosby for "Don't Fence Me In."

Mail Call, June 20, 1945. Host Harry Von Zell clowned with Jimmy Durante and the sisters, who sang "Ev'rytime" and "Standin' in the Need of Prayer."

The Kraft Music Hall starring Edward Everett Horton, Sept. 6, 1945. The sisters sang "On the Atchison, Topeka, and the Santa Fe" and "The Blond Sailor."

GI Journal, 1945. Three songs from the Andrews Sisters' *Eight-to-the-Bar Ranch* radio series were inserted into this live show featuring Groucho Marx and Lucille Ball.

GI Journal, 1945. Host Bob Hope introduced the sisters, as well as Dorothy Lamour, Mel Blanc, and Connie Haines.

The Nash-Kelvinator Musical Showroom, Oct. 3, 1945-Mar. 27, 1946. Starring the Andrews Sisters. (See text pages 98-99.) Songs sung by the sisters during the series were: "If I Could Be with You (One Hour Tonight)," "Chickery Chick," "Californ-I-A," "The Talk of the Town," "My Blue Heaven," "On the Sunny Side of the Street," "Waitin' for the Train to Come In," "That Feeling in the Moonlight," "The Walter Winchell Rhumba," "Pennies from Heaven," "I Feel a Song Coming On," "Buckle Down, Winsocki," "Here Comes a Sailor," "Personality," "Baby, Won't You Please Come Home," as well as extravagant production numbers, including "Night and Day,"

"Symphony," "It's a Grand Night for Singing," "It Might as Well Be Spring," and "Look for the Silver Lining."

Songs by Sinatra (also known as *The Old Gold Show*), Nov. 14, 1945. The sisters sang "Begin the Beguine," and joined Frank for "Empty Saddles" and a comical song routine concerning the rugged schedule of shows at the Paramount Theater. Frank and Patty also sang a duet, "A Kiss Goodnight."

Command Performance, Dec. 13, 1945. The sisters hosted guests Garry Moore, Jimmy Durante, Celeste Holm, and the Delta Rhythm Boys. They sang "Ti-Pi-Tin" and "Money Is the Root of All Evil."

Command Performance, Jan. 10, 1946. Ken Carpenter hosted as the trio sang "Begin the Beguine" (dubbed from another episode and inserted into the broadcast).

Command Performance, Apr. 6, 1946. Bob Hope hosted "Army Day" with Bing Crosby, Frank Sinatra, Bette Davis, Spike Jones and his City Slickers, and Dinah Shore, who introduced the sisters singing "Chickery Chick."

Radio's Biggest Show starring Bob Hope, June 18, 1946. The trio sang "Atlanta, G.A." and joined Hope for "Sonny Boy" and a parody of "Thanks for the Memory."

Philco Radio Time starring Bing Crosby, Feb. 26, 1947. The sisters made a guest appearance and sang "South America, Take It Away" and "You Don't Have to Know the Language," both with Crosby.

Your Hit Parade, Mar. 22–Apr. 12, 1947. The sisters appeared as guest hosts for four consecutive Saturday nights and sang "Managua, Nicaragua," among others.

Guest Star, 1947. Winn Elliot introduced the sisters, who sang "Go West, Young Man" and "His Feet Too Big for de Bed."

Club 15. Sept. 2, 1947-Mar. 21, 1951. (See text pages 112-14.) Songs sung by the sisters during the series were: "At Sundown," "Spring in December," "For You," "Careless Hands," "Manana," "The Thousand Island Search," "Music, Music, Music," "Valentina," "Someone Like You," "The Hop Scotch Polka," "Down among the Sheltering Palms," "C'est Si Bon," "All My Love," "Cruising down the River," "The Chattanooga Shoe Shine Boy," "A Little Bird Told Me," "Make Believe You're Glad When You're Sorry," "That's a Plenty," "Baby Me," "Buttons and Bows," "Someday," "Need You," and "Wunderbar."

Command Performance, 1948. Host Beryl Davis welcomed Jerry Colonna, Ozzie and Harriet, Janet Blair, and the sisters, who sang "Near You."

Here's to Veterans, 1948. An episode of *Club 15* with the sisters and Bob Crosby, transcribed for the Veterans Administration.

The Wrigley Christmas Party, Dec. 25, 1948. Host Gene Autry joined Bing Crosby and the sisters for "Here Comes Santa Claus," and Crosby sang "Jingle Bells" with the trio.

Command Performance, 1948. Host Gordon MacRae welcomed Eve Arden and the sisters, who sang "Feudin' and Fightin'" and "You Call Everybody Darling." Patty sang a duet with MacRae, "The Pussy Cat Song."

Command Performance, 1949. Host Marie McDonald introduced Bob Crosby and the sisters, who sang "Cuanto la Gusta," "I've Got My Love to Keep Me Warm" (trio only), and "The Dum Dot Song" (Patty and Crosby).

The Kraft Music Hall starring Al Jolson, Feb. 24, 1949. Jolson opened the show singing "April Showers" and "'Way Down Yonder in New Orleans" with the sisters, who also sang a snippet of "Sabre Dance," as well as "Feudin' and Fightin'" (as part of a comedy sketch) and "Sonny Boy" (with Jolson).

Guest Star, June 19, 1949. The sisters sang "Sabre Dance," joined Bob Crosby for "Coca Roca," and Patty and Crosby teamed for "The Pussy Cat Song" during this transcribed episode of *Club 15* for the U.S. Treasury Department.

Guest Star, Jan. 8, 1950. Another *Club 15* syndicated show for the U.S. Treasury Department. Dick Haymes joined the trio for "Twenty-Four Hours of Sunshine" and "That Lucky Old Sun." The sisters also sang "I Can Dream, Can't I?"

The Bing Crosby Show, Feb. 22, 1950. The sisters sang three songs with Crosby: "The Wedding Samba," "Have I Told You Lately that I Love You?," and "I Can Dream, Can't I?"

The Bing Crosby Show, Mar. 29, 1950. The sisters sang "That's a Plenty" and joined Crosby for "Lock, Stock, and Barrel."

American Cancer Fund Benefit, May 13, 1950. Dick Haymes introduced the sisters, who sang "There's Something about a Hometown Band."

The Big Show. starring Tallulah Bankhead and Groucho Marx, Feb. 11, 1951. The sisters participated in a comedy sketch with Marx and sang a medley of their greatest hits, celebrating their fifteenth anniversary in show business.

The Bing Crosby Show, Feb. 28, 1951. The trio sang "Lullaby of Broadway," "The Tennessee Waltz" (with Crosby), and "May the Good Lord Bless and Keep You" (with Crosby and Nat King Cole).

Guest Star, June 16, 1957. Host Del Sharbutt welcomed the trio in a syndicated show for the U.S. Treasury Department. The trio's latest Capitol singles, "No, Baby" and "Rum and Coca Cola," were played during the broadcast.

Appendix F

The Small Screen

The Frank Sinatra Show, Oct. 9, 1951. The sisters opened the show with the comical "Peony Bush."

What's My Line?, Oct. 21, 1951.

Shower of Stars, 1956. Red Skelton introduced the newly reunited sisters, who sang a greatest hits medley.

The Perry Como Show, Feb. 23, 1957. The sisters sang a hits medley and joined Como for "Rum and Coca Cola." The trio also sang "Pennsylvania Polka" as puppets on strings operated by Como, Tony Bennett, and Ernie Kovacs.

The Julius LaRosa Show, July 6, 1957. The sisters sang two of their latest Capitol recordings, "Stars, Stars, Stars" and "Of Thee I Sing." They also joined LaRosa and Louis Nye in a comedy skit.

Washington Square starring Ray Bolger, 1957.

The Jimmie Rodgers Show, 1957.

Masquerade Party, 1957. The sisters appeared disguised as the Marx Brothers.

What's My Line?, 1957.

House Party starring Art Linkletter, Jan. 19, 1965. The sisters sang a greatest hits medley.

The Tonight Show starring Johnny Carson, Feb. 1, 1965. The sisters opened the show with "Got a Lot of Livin' to Do," "My Favorite Things," and "I Left My Heart in San Francisco" before performing a polka medley, which included a comical "striptease" by Patty. The trio also sang "Sonny Boy" with Carson.

The Tonight Show starring Johnny Carson, Mar. 12, 1965. The sisters opened the show with "Bei Mir Bist Du Schon" and also sang a ten-minute medley entitled "One More River."

The Tonight Show starring Johnny Carson, Oct. 1, 1965. The sisters sang "South America, Take It Away" and "I'll Be with You in Apple Blossom Time" before they joined Jerry Lewis on the couch to reminisce about past performances.

The Dean Martin Show, Dec. 9, 1965.

The Jimmy Dean Show, 1966. The sisters sang a hits medley and joined Jimmy Dean for "Don't Fence Me In."

The Joey Bishop Show, Feb. 1, 1966.

The Sammy Davis, Jr. Show, Mar. 4, 1966. The sisters sang a medley of songs from the Roaring Twenties, then joined Diana Ross and the Supremes for a medley of hits. The sisters sang "Stop! In the Name Of Love," "Baby Love," and "Where Did Our Love Go?," while the Supremes harmonized "Bei Mir Bist Du Schon," "I'll Be with You in Apple Blossom Time," and "Beer Barrel Polka." The groups joined forces for "Exactly like You" and "Birth of the Blues."

The Dean Martin Show, Sept. 29, 1966. The sisters opened the show with a rousing, hand-clapping "What Now, My Love?" followed by "That's How Young I Feel." They joined Dean for a hits medley, including "Memories Are Made of This" and "Rum and Coca Cola."

The Dean Martin Show, 1967. Patty and Maxene appeared with Joyce DeYoung (LaVerne's replacement) and sang a hits medley with Dean, including "Boogie Woogie Bugle Boy" and "Beat Me Daddy, Eight to the Bar." The foursome later joined Lena Horne in tramp costumes for "The Idle Rich."

Notes

vii   "We were such . . ." *Sing! Sing! Sing!* (Album liner notes).

Introduction

1   "They had so much energy . . ." *The Andrews Sisters Greatest Hits: Sixtieth Anniversary Collection* (CD liner notes).

11   "We did them all . . ." *The Andrews Sisters: Fiftieth Anniversary Collection* (CD liner notes).

12   "In 1940 . . ." *The Andrews Sisters: Sixtieth Anniversary Collection* (CD liner notes).

13   "If there was . . ." M. Andrews and B. Gilbert, *Over Here, Over There: The Andrews Sisters and the USO Stars in World War II,* 4.

14   "If, after half a century . . ." *The Andrews Sisters: Their All-Time Greatest Hits* (CD liner notes).

1. We'll Hit the Big Time

16   "The wonderful thing . ." *Goldmine,* Jan. 20, 1995.

18   "Musically, it was like . . ." Maxene Andrews (hereafter cited as MA) to Dick Cavett, PBS-TV interview, 1979.

19   "[He taught us] . . ." *The Andrews Sisters: Their All-Time Greatest Hits* (CD liner notes).

20   "People drove slower . . ." Andrews and Gilbert, *Over Here, Over There,* 8.

21   "An evening . . ." *Dallas News,* May 24, 1937.

2. "That's Us! That's Us!"

23   "Less than a year . . ." *The Andrews Sisters: Fiftieth Anniversary Collection, Volume 2* (CD liner notes).

23   "Mrs. Andrews, take . . ." *Film Fan Monthly,* 1974.

25   "The Edison . . ." *New Yorker,* Nov. 11, 1991.

25   "We only had . . ." *The Andrews Sisters: Their All-Time Greatest Hits* (CD liner notes).

26   "In the old days . . ." S. Cahn, *I Should Care: The Sammy Cahn Story,* 63-64.

27   "Lou Levy . . ." Ibid., 65-66.

29   "Nobody expected it . . ." *The Andrews Sisters: Sixtieth Anniversary Collection* (CD liner notes).

30   "Like shrimp trawlers." *Swank,* July 1946.

30   "Patty, Maxene, and LaVerne . . ." T. Palmer, *All You Need Is Love: The Story of Popular Music,* 147.

30   "You get with an orchestra . . ." *The Andrews Sisters: Their All-Time Greatest Hits* (CD liner notes).

30   "I was listening . . ." *The Andrews Sisters: Sixtieth Anniversary Collection* (CD liner notes).

30   "'Boogie Woogie Bugle Boy' . . ." *The Andrews Sisters: Their All-Time Greatest Hits* (CD liner notes).

31   "At one point . . ." V. Secunda, *Bei Mir Bist Du Schon: The Life of Sholom Secunda,* 150.

31   "The song was . . ." Ibid., 149.

32   "While one . . ." V. Greene, *A Passion for Polka: Old-Time Ethnic Music in America,* 130.

33   "When Fred Waring . . ." Andrews and Gilbert, *Over Here, Over There,* 84.

35   "A song with . . ." *The Andrews Sisters: Boogie Woogie Bugle Boy* (CD liner notes).

35   "Winchell . . ." *Goldmine,* Jan. 20, 1995.

36   "The dynamic Andrews . . ." *Swank,* July 1946.

36   "You did four . . ." *The Andrews Sisters: Sixtieth Anniversary Collection* (CD liner notes).

37   "Whatever became of . . ." MA to Joe Franklin, WWOR-AM Radio, Jan. 1979.

38   "Hated it . . ." G.T. Simon, *The Best of the Music Makers.*

38   "'Bei Mir' . . ." Greene, *A Passion for Polka,* 135.

38   "With Krupa . . ." *Variety,* July 5, 1939.

39   "A song . . ." Andrews and Gilbert, *Over Here, Over There,* 109

40   "When we came . . ." MA to Jim Harlan, WNEW-AM Radio, Feb. 1992.

40   "I was so nervous . . ." *Bing Crosby and the Andrews Sisters: Their Complete Recordings Together* (CD liner notes).

40   "Crosby was not . . ." Ibid.

40   "Bing loved . . ." MA to Jim Harlan, WNEW-AM Radio, Feb. 1992.

41   "He was open . . ." *Goldmine,* Jan. 20, 1995.

42   "Harry James . . ." *Tenderly: The Songs of Romance* (CD liner notes).

42   "The first thing . . ." MA to Jim Harlan, WNEW-AM Radio, Feb. 1992.

42   "A loner" MA to Joe Franklin, WWOR-AM Radio, Jan. 1979.

43   "Bing could be . . ." *Bing Crosby and the Andrews Sisters: Their Complete Recordings Together* (CD liner notes).

43   "I like singing . . ." Ibid.

43   "A happy marriage . . ." Ibid.

44   "The listener . . ." Andrews and Gilbert, *Over Here, Over There,* 14.

45   "Glenn Miller . . ." Ibid., 197-98.

46   "After a few weeks . . ." G.T. Simon, *Glenn Miller and His Orchestra,* 199-200.

46   "The Andrews Sisters . . ." Patty Andrews to Merv Griffin, 1985.

47   "I was the rebellious one . . ." *Goldmine,* Jan. 20, 1995.

47   "You mean . . ." Ibid.

48   "I went over . . ." Ibid.

49   "You know how . . ." Ibid.

49   "The Andrews Sisters' . . ." *Variety,* Mar. 6, 1940.

3. They Made the Company Jump

50   "Four years ago . . ." *Billboard,* Oct. 18, 1941.

50   "When we opened . . ." Andrews and Gilbert, *Over Here, Over There,* 19.

52   "The Andrews Sisters . . ." *Atlanta Constitution,* Nov. 21, 1940.

53   "The most frightening . . ." *Harvard Lampoon,* 1940.

53   "We don't hold . . ." *Disc,* Aug. 1946.

53   "We looked so ugly . . ." *Chicago Tribune,* Mar. 3, 1974.

54   "A definitely unusual platter . . ." *Billboard,* Nov. 23, 1940.

55   "With Abbott . . ." *New York Times,* Feb. 14, 1941.

56   "Don't record that . . ." MA to Joe Franklin, WWOR-AM Radio, Jan. 1979.

57   "Those song-sational . . ." Universal film trailer for *In the Navy,* 1941.

58   "We made two films . . ." S. Cox and J. Lofflin, *The Abbott and Costello Story: Sixty Years of "Who's on First?,"* 49.

59   "Bud, we didn't . . ." MA to Joe Franklin, WWOR-AM Radio, Jan. 1979.

59   "Universal was . . ." C. Costello and R. Strait, *Lou's on First,* 57.

59   "I used to watch . . ." Ibid., 59.

60   "Bud and Lou . . ." Cox and Lofflin, *The Abbott and Costello Story,* 49-51.

60   "The boys . . ." Ibid., 51.

60   "We were quite close . . ." Ibid., 49.

60   "Just a love-bug . . ." Ibid., 51

61   "Here's a man . . ." Ibid.

61 "We began . . ." C. Costello and R. Strait, *Lou's on First,* 110-11.

62 "Lou had . . ." Cox and Lofflin, *The Abbott and Costello Story,* 51.

62 "One of our constant . . ." Andrews and Gilbert, *Over Here, Over There,* 187.

63 "One of the effects . . ." Ibid., 20.

63 "This is a . . ." Ibid., 5.

4. Three of a Kind

65 "I wanted to be . . ." Andrews and Gilbert, *Over Here, Over There,* 191.

66 "Polkas fit . . ." Ibid., 11.

67 "While there have . . ." *Billboard,* Aug. 29, 1942.

68 "The first record . . ." Andrews and Gilbert, *Over Here, Over There,* 46-47.

68 "I used to . . ." *Goldmine,* Jan. 20, 1995.

5. Voices of an Era

71 "The Andrews Sisters have . . ." *Disc,* Aug. 1946.

72 "The farm animals . . ." Andrews and Gilbert, *Over Here, Over There,* 78-79.

72 "During our shows . . ." Ibid., 79-80.

75 "'Don't Fence Me In' . . ." C. Schwartz, *Cole Porter: A Biography,* 150.

75 "We had a . . ." Ibid.

76 "It was restricted . . ." Ibid.

76 "The rhythm . . ." MA to Jim Harlan, WNEW-AM Radio, Feb. 1992.

76 "Because the waitresses . . ." *Billboard,* Feb. 17, 1945.

78 "Hi-ya, Frankie . . ." *The Andrews Sisters Show,* ABC Radio, March 3, 1945.

79 "I like Bob Hope . . ." Ibid., March 25, 1945.

80 "I thought . . ." *Newsweek,* Sept. 18, 1944.

6. We've Got a Job to Do

82 "I remember how well . . ." Andrews and Gilbert, *Over Here, Over There,* 246-47.

82 "LaVerne, Patty, and I sang . . ." Ibid., 17.

83 "It was a tense . . ." Ibid., 54.

84 "The Andrews Sisters . . ." *Coronet,* Mar. 1943.

84 "One night . . ." Arthur Fleming to author, Jan. 1997.

85 "Every time . . ." Andrews and Gilbert, *Over Here, Over There,* 52.

86 "We went down . . ." Ibid., 34-35.

86 "A popular singer . . ." Ibid., 165.

87 "Everybody takes falls . . ." *Command Performance,* Feb. 1945.

88 "Not long after . . ." Andrews and Gilbert, *Over Here, Over There,* 223.

89 "[We were told] . . ." Ibid., 230.

89 "Call it sentimental . . ." Ibid., 232.

90 "As required . . ." Ibid., 238.

91 "Oh, they'll find . . ." Ibid., 243-45.

91 "The expressions . . ." *New York Times,* Aug. 1945.

91 "The national anthem . . ." Ibid.

91 "I really learned . . ." Andrews and Gilbert, *Over Here, Over There,* 92.

92 "Touring the camp . . ." T. Wilkerson and M. Borie, *The Hollywood Reporter: The Golden Years ,* 170-72.

92 "We were sent . . ." *New York Times,* Aug. 28, 1974.

93 "We always went . . ." Andrews and Gilbert, *Over Here, Over There,* 135-36.

7. Riding High

94 "The pictures were . . ." *Swank,* July 1946.

95 "The Andrews Sisters do . . ." *New York Times,* Feb. 14, 1941.

95 "The Andrews Sisters haven't . . ." Ibid., Aug. 28, 1942.

95 "The Andrews Sisters' harmony . . ." Ibid., June 25, 1942.

96 "Both personal . . ." *Disc,* Aug. 1946.

97 "The girls are . . ." UPI interview with James Bacon, 1952.

97 "Listen to those . . ." Newspaper article, n.p., n.d.

98 "We were partners . . ." *Goldmine,* Jan. 20, 1995.

99 "Watching his fingers . . ." M.A. Shaughnessy, *Les Paul: An American Original,* 132.

100 "Les is a genius . . ." Andrews and Gilbert, *Over Here, Over There,* 108.

100 "It was like . . ." M.A. Shaughnessy, *Les Paul: An American Original,* 134.

100 "When the hot . . ." Ibid.

100 "It was a cinch . . ." Ibid., 133.

101 "If Artie's guys . . ." Ibid., 132.

101 "Les' attitude . . ." Ibid., 132-33.

101 "It packs speed . . ." *Billboard,* Dec. 1946.

102 "Let's face it . . ." M. Bufwack and R. Oermann, *Finding Her Voice: The Saga of Women in Country Music,* 136.

103 "Andrews Sisters: #1 . . ." *Billboard,* Dec. 21, 1946.

103 "I found the . . ." Andrews and Gilbert, *Over Here, Over There,* 163.

103 "We never . . ." *The Andrews Sisters: Fiftieth Anniversary Collection* (CD liner notes).

104 "We used to . . ." *The Andrews Sisters: Sixtieth Anniversary Collection* (CD liner notes).

104 "I'm ignorant . . ." *Newsweek,* Sept. 18, 1944.

104 "Patty was . . ." Andrews and Gilbert, *Over Here, Over There,* 3.

105 "You couldn't . . ." Ibid., 243-45.

105 "The Andrews Sisters . . ." M. Torme, *My Singing Teachers,* 166-67.

106 "The girls . . ." AP interview with James Bacon, July 12, 1952.

106 "Their showmanship . . ." G.T. Simon, *The Best of the Music Makers,* 13-14.

107 "We were young . . ." M.A. Shaughnessy, *Les Paul: An American Original,* 133.

107 "Lou remained . . ." Ibid., 161-62.

107 "Levy owned nearly . . ." R. Sanjek, *American Popular Music and Its Business from 1900–1984,* 471.

109 "Even the croupiers . . ." *Billboard,* March 1947.

109 "He was one . . ." *New Yorker,* Nov. 11, 1991.

110 "I don't know . . ." MA to Dick Cavett, PBS-TV interview, Jan. 1979.

8. Success Abroad

112 "No matter how . . ." *Billboard,* Dec. 21, 1946.

113 "The only artist . . ." *Goldmine,* Jan. 20, 1995.

114 "Well, Patty . . ." *Club 15,* circa 1948.

116 "He seemed . . ." Andrews and Gilbert, *Over Here, Over There,* 241.

116 "It is by now . . ." *Variety,* June 1948.

117 "The girls are . . ." *Variety,* Aug. 1948.

117 "The audience gave . . ." *London Daily Express,* Aug. 1948.

117 "The fans were . . ." *London Daily Herald,* Aug. 1948.

117 "The Andrews Sisters gaily . . ." *London Times,* Aug. 1948.

119 "Many feel . . ." *Bing Crosby and the Andrews Sisters: Their Complete Recordings Together* (CD liner notes).

119 "What a bear . . ." *The Best of the Andrews Sisters,* volume 2 (double selection album liner notes).

120 "A bookkeeper . . ." *Goldmine,* Jan. 20, 1995.

121 "He sang . . ." *Goldmine,* Jan. 20, 1995.

9. A Love Song Is Born

122 "I will never . . ." *The Merv Griffin Show*, 1985.
123 "I don't want . . ." *Goldmine*, Jan. 20, 1995.
124 "But even if . . ." Ibid.
126 "At the time . . ." A.E. Hotchner, *Doris Day: Her Own Story*, 266-67.
126 "It has been said . . ." Ibid.
126 "What you've got . . ." Ibid.
127 "Patty was . . ." Ibid., 274-76.
128 "I always had . . ." Ibid., 236.
129 "Today, everybody . . ." *Bing Crosby and the Andrews Sisters: Their Complete Recordings Together* (CD liner notes).
129 "The Andrews Sisters . . ." *Variety*, June 1949.
130 "This is a magnificent . . ." *Billboard*, June 1950.
130 "Jolie was . . ." Andrews and Gilbert, *Over Here, Over There*, 207.
130 "About the Andrews . . ." *San Francisco Examiner*, 1950.
130 "The girls put . . ." Ibid.
131 "Easy to see . . ." *San Francisco News*, 1950.
131 "The Andrews Sisters are . . ." *San Francisco Chronicle*, 1950.
131 "A show the likes . . ." *This Is San Francisco*, 1950.
131 "The act has . . ." *The Ann Holden Hour*, 1950.
131 "It gives me . . ." Benjamin H. Swig to Lou Levy, *Billboard*, 1950.
131 "What were you . . ." *The Tonight Show*, NBC-TV, Oct. 1, 1965.
132 "To announce the . . ." *Birmingham Post*, Aug. 1951.
132 "The merry Andrews . . ." *Glasgow Evening News*, Aug. 1951.
133 "The Andrews Sisters have . . ." *Scottish Daily Mail*, Aug. 1951.
133 "A peculiar man" MA to Joe Franklin, WWOR-AM Radio, Jan. 1979.
133 "I guess they just . . ." MA to Jim Harlan, WNEW-AM Radio, Feb. 1992.
135 "The Andrews Sisters do . . ." *Billboard*, Nov. 1951.

10. Disharmony

136 "We've always had . . ." Newspaper clipping, n.p., n.d.
136 "It was very slow . . ." *Goldmine*, Jan. 20, 1995.
138 "There is nothing . . ." Decca album liner notes, 1952.
138 "The Groaner and . . ." *Billboard*, 1952.
138 "The biggest thrill . . ." *Bing Crosby and the Andrews Sisters, Their Complete Recordings Together* (MCA/Decca CD liner notes).
138 "A joyride for . . ." Ibid.
141 "I never could . . ." Simon, *The Best of the Music Makers*, 13-14.
141 "We were never . . ." MA to Jim Harlan, WNEW-AM Radio, Feb. 1992.
141 "The Andrews Sisters . . ." Ibid.

142 "We never, ever . . ." Ibid.
142 "Our husbands . . ." *Los Angeles Times*, Aug. 14, 1985.
143 "Patty was . . ." *Goldmine*, Jan. 20, 1995.

11. The Last Mile Home

146 "It's wonderful to . . ." *Detroit News*, 1959.
146 "It just wasn't . . ." *New York Times*, May 8, 1967.
147 "A strange thing . . ." *Detroit News*, Oct. 18, 1959.
147 "Nope, we can't . . ." UPI, 1956.
147 "We had advice . . ." Phyllis McGuire to Sally Jessy Raphael, 1990.
147 "There's no reason . . ." *Variety*, June 28, 1956.
148 "Fine piping from . . ." *Billboard*, Jan. 20, 1958.
149 "We had all . . ." *Goldmine*, Jan. 20, 1995.
150 "At the Talk . . ." *New York Times*, Apr. 28, 1974.
151 "I wish . . ." *Goldmine*, Jan. 20, 1995.
152 "Still the best . . ." *The Tonight Show*, NBC-TV, Feb. 1, 1965.
152 "You're the only . . ." Ibid.
152 "The Andrews were . . ." *In the Mood* (Famous Twinsets album liner notes).
153 "Actually, I'll tell . . ." *The Tonight Show*, NBC-TV, Feb. 1, 1965.
155 "Nothing but champagne!" Carroll Carroll, *None of Your Business*, 258.
155 "LaVerne was . . ." *Film Fan Monthly*, July-Aug. 1974.

12. The Love We Used to Know

156 "It would be . . ." *New York Daily News*, Jan. 5, 1975.
157 "Broadway finally has . . ." *New York Times*, theater advertisement, March 1974.
157 "Casting the two . . ." Simon, *The Best of the Music Makers*, 14.
158 "The minute Patty . . ." V. Secunda, *Bei Mir Bist Du Schon: The Life of Sholom Secunda*, 152.
159 "The Andrews Sisters . . ." *Harper's*, Apr. 1974.
159 "Patty created . . ." *Goldmine*, Jan 20, 1995.
159 "This is a breeze . . ." *New York Times*, Apr. 28, 1974.
159 "Patty and Maxene . . ." *Stereo Review*, Aug. 1974.
159 "Bette's record . . ." *New York Times*, Apr. 28, 1974.
160 "The Andrews Sisters . . ." Newsweek, Apr. 1974.
161 "I learned . . ." *New York Sunday News*, Jan. 5, 1974.
162 "This is the first . . ." Ibid.
162 "At Christmas . . ." M. Henner and J. Jerome, *By All Means Keep on Moving*, 94.

Notes

163   "Johnny's big show . . ." Ibid., 91.

164   "Andrews is . . ." *Variety,* Nov. 1979.

164   "One of the brightest . . ." *New York Daily News,* Jan. 1979.

164   "She seems to . . ." Marie Sforza to author, Jan. 1979.

165   "In her current . . ." *Variety,* Mar. 1980.

166   "She received strong . . ." *Variety,* Nov. 1982.

166   "Do you think . . ." Jeff Hart to the author, 1987.

169   "'Company B' deserves . . ." *New York Daily News,* Oct. 2, 1991.

169   "'Company B' is . . ." *New York Times,* Nov. 17, 1991.

169   "I saw . . ." *New Yorker,* Nov. 11, 1991.

169   "They still haven't . . ." *New York Post,* July 1, 1992.

170   "Which singing group . . ." Trivial Pursuit (board game).

171   "She was much more . . ." *People,* Nov. 1995.

171   "I have nothing . . ." *Goldmine,* Jan. 20, 1995.

171   "In 1991 . . ." Andrews and Gilbert, *Over Here, Over There,* 2.

Filmography

Argentine Nights (1940)

Universal; producer, Ken Goldsmith; director, Albert S. Rogell; screenplay, Arthur T. Horman, Ray Golden, and Sid Kuller, based on a story by J. Robert Bren and Gladys Atwater. 72 minutes; B&W.

Cast: The Ritz Brothers (Al, Harry, and Jimmy), The Andrews Sisters (Maxene, Patty, and LaVerne), Constance Moore (Bonnie Brooks), George Reeves (Eduardo), Peggy Moran (Peggy), Anne Nagel (Linda), Kathryn Adams (Carol), Ferike Boros (Mama Viejos), Paul Porcasi (Papa Viejos).

Songs: "Rhumboogie" (the Andrews Sisters), "Hit the Road" (the Andrews Sisters), "Oh, He Loves Me" (the Andrews Sisters), "The Brooklynonga" (the Andrews Sisters), "The Spirit Of 77B" (The Ritz Brothers), "The Brooklynonga" (The Ritz Brothers), "Amigo, We Go Riding Tonight" (male chorus).

Plot: Attempting to flee a group of angry creditors, three managers (the Ritz Brothers) stow away on a cruise ship bound for South America. The managers' clients (the Andrews Sisters and an all-girl orchestra led by Moore) supply most of the musical interludes.

Buck Privates (1941; working title *Rookies*)

Universal; producer, Alex Gottlieb; director, Arthur Lubin; screenplay, Arthur T. Horman. 82 minutes. B&W. Available on MCA/Universal Home Video and Laser Disc.

Cast: Bud Abbott (Slicker Smith), Lou Costello (Herbie Brown), Lee Bowman (Randolph Parker III), The Andrews Sisters (Maxene, Patty, and LaVerne), Jane Frazee (Judy Gray), Alan Curtis (Bob Martin), Nat Pendleton (Michael Collins), Samuel S. Hinds (Major Emerson), Nella Walker (Mrs. Parker), Douglas Wood (Mr. Parker), Don Raye (Dick Burnette), Shemp Howard (Cook).

Songs: "You're a Lucky Fellow, Mr. Smith" (the Andrews Sisters), "I'll Be with You in Apple Blossom Time" (the Andrews Sisters), "Boogie

Woogie Bugle Boy" (the Andrews Sisters), "Bounce Me Brother with a Solid Four" (the Andrews Sisters), "Wish You Were Here" (Jane Frazee), "When Private Brown Becomes a Captain" (Lou Costello).

Plot: Two street peddlers (Abbott and Costello), under the impression that they are signing themselves up for a raffle drawing at a local movie theater, unwittingly volunteer for the Draft and proceed to get themselves into some sticky situations with the U.S. Army. A number of USO entertainers (including the Andrews Sisters) provide the music and romance.

In the Navy (1941)

Universal; producer, Alex Gottlieb; director, Arthur Lubin; screenplay, Arthur T. Horman and John Grant. 85 minutes. B&W. Available on MCA/Universal Home Video and Laser Disc.

Cast: Bud Abbott (Smokey Adams), Lou Costello (Pomeroy Watson), Dick Powell (Tommy Halstead/Russ Raymond), The Andrews Sisters (Maxene, Patty, and LaVerne), Clair Dodd (Dorothy), Dick Foran (Dynamite Dugan), Shemp Howard (Dizzy), Robert Emmet Keane (Travers), Don Terry (Floor Manager), Butch and Buddy (Billy Lenhart and Kenneth Brown), The Condos Brothers (Dance Specialty).

Songs: "You're Off to See the World" (the Andrews Sisters), "Gimme Some Skin, My Friend" (the Andrews Sisters), "Hula Ba Luau" (the Andrews Sisters), "Starlight, Starbright" (the Andrews Sisters and Dick Powell), "We're in the Navy" (the Andrews Sisters, Dick Powell, and Dick Foran), "A Sailor's Life for Me" (Dick Foran), "We're in the Navy" (Dick Powell with male chorus).

Plot: A frustrated crooner named Russ Raymond (Powell) joins the U.S. Navy under the assumed name of Tommy Halstead in an attempt to flee a throng of adoring female fans. While enlisted, Raymond meets up with two bumbling fellow recruits (Abbott and Costello) and a group of singers (the Andrews Sisters), as well as with a very eager newspaper reporter (Dodd), hoping to reveal Halstead's true identity.

Hold That Ghost (1941, working title *Oh, Charlie!*)

Universal; producer, Alex Gottlieb; director, Arthur Lubin; screenplay, Robert Lees, Frederic T. Rinaldo, and John Grant. 85 minutes. B&W. Available on MCA/Universal Home Video and Laser Disc.

Cast: Bud Abbott (Chuck Murray), Lou Costello (Ferdinand "Ferdie" Jones), Evelyn Ankers (Norma Lind), Joan Davis (Camille Brewster),

Richard Carlson (Dr. Jackson), Marc Lawrence (Charley Smith), William Davidson (Moose Matson), Milton Parsons (Harry Hoskins), Shemp Howard (Soda Jerk), The Andrews Sisters (Maxene, Patty, and LaVerne), Ted Lewis and his Entertainers.

Songs: "Sleepy Serenade" (the Andrews Sisters), "Aurora" (the Andrews Sisters), "When My Baby Smiles at Me" (Ted Lewis), "Me and My Shadow" (Ted Lewis).

Plot: Two ex-nightclub waiters turned gas station attendants (Abbott and Costello) accidentally become heirs to a gangster's fortune, hidden somewhere in a supposedly haunted house. The Andrews Sisters and Ted Lewis supply music in nightclub scenes at the beginning and the end of the film.

What's Cookin'? (1942, working title *Wake Up and Dream*)

Universal; director, Edward F. Cline; screenplay, Jerry Cady, Stanley Roberts, and Haworth Bramley. 69 minutes. B&W.

Cast: The Andrews Sisters (Maxene, Patty, and LaVerne), Grace McDonald (Angela), Robert Paige (Bob), Jane Frazee (Anne), Peggy Ryan (Peggy), Donald O'Connor (Tommy), Gloria Jean (Sue), Susan Levine (Tagalong), Billie Burke (Agatha), Leo Carillo (Marvo), Charles Butterworth (J.P. Courtney), Franklin Pangborn (Professor Bistell), The Jivin' Jacks and Jills, Woody Herman and his orchestra.

Songs: "What to Do" (the Andrews Sisters), "I'll Pray for You" (the Andrews Sisters), "Amen (Yea-Man)" (the Andrews Sisters), "Il Bacio" (the Andrews Sisters and Gloria Jean), "Smile! Smile! Smile!" (the Andrews Sisters), "Blue Flame" (Woody Herman), "Woodchopper's Ball" (Woody Herman), "You Can't Hold a Memory in Your Arms" (Jane Frazee).

Plot: A group of youngsters are hoping to hit the show biz big-time, with the help of the Andrews Sisters and Woody Herman.

Private Buckaroo (1942)

Universal; director, Edward F. Cline; screenplay, Edmund Kelso and Edward James. 68 minutes. B&W. Available on video from Hollywood Classics Collectors Edition/Madacy Music Group Inc.

Cast: The Andrews Sisters (Maxene, Patty, and LaVerne), Dick Foran (Lon Prentice), Joe E. Lewis (Lancelot Pringle McBiff), Shemp Howard (Sgt. Muggsy Shavel), Mary Wickes (Bonnie-Belle Schlopkiss), Jennifer Holt (Joyce Mason), Richard Davies (Lt. Mason), Ernest Truex (Col. Weatherford), Peggy Ryan (Peggy), Donald O'Connor

(Donny), Huntz Hall (Cpl. Anemic), Susan Levine (Tagalong), The Jivin' Jacks and Jills, Harry James and his Music Makers.

Songs: "Three Little Sisters" (the Andrews Sisters), "Six Jerks in a Jeep" (the Andrews Sisters), "That's the Moon, My Son" (the Andrews Sisters), "Don't Sit under the Apple Tree (With Anyone Else but Me)" (the Andrews Sisters), "Johnny, Get Your Gun Again" (the Andrews Sisters), "We've Got a Job to Do" (the Andrews Sisters, voices only), "I Love the South" (Joe E. Lewis), "You Made Me Love You" (Helen Forrest with Harry James), "Private Buckaroo" (Dick Foran), "Nobody Knows the Trouble I've Seen" (Helen Forrest and Dick Foran with male chorus), "Nobody Knows the Trouble I've Seen" (Harry James), "Don't Sit under the Apple Tree (With Anyone Else but Me)" (Harry James), "The Flight of the Bumble Bee" (Harry James).

Plot: A bandleader (James) and his entourage, including the resident girl-trio (the Andrews Sisters), supply the music in this wartime film.

Give Out, Sisters (1942)

Universal; producer, Bernard W. Burton; director, Edward F. Cline; screenplay, Paul Gerard Smith and Warren Wilson. 65 minutes. B&W.

Cast: The Andrews Sisters (Maxene, Patty, and LaVerne), Grace McDonald (Grace Waverly), Dan Dailey (Bob Edwards), Charles Butterworth (Professor Woof), Walter Catlett (Gribble), William Frawley, Robert Emmet Keane (Peabody), Irving Bacon (Doctor), Edith Barrett (Agatha Waverly), Marie Blake (Blandina Waverly), Fay Helm (Susan Waverly), Peggy Ryan (Peggy), Donald O'Connor (Donny), The Jivin' Jacks and Jills.

Songs: "The New Generation" (the Andrews Sisters), "Who Do You Think You're Fooling?" (the Andrews Sisters), "You're Just a Flower from an Old Bouquet" (the Andrews Sisters), "Pennsylvania Polka" (the Andrews Sisters), "Jiggers, the Beat!"

Plot: A group of nightclub entertainers (the Andrews Sisters) try to help an heiress (McDonald) break into show business as a dancer.

How's About It? (1943)

Universal; producer, Ken Goldsmith; director, Erle C. Kenton; screenplay, Mel Ronson and John Grey. 60 minutes. B&W.

Cast: The Andrews Sisters (Maxene, Patty, and LaVerne), Grace McDonald (Marion Bliss), Robert Paige (George Shelby), Bobby Scheerer

(Bobby), Walter Catlett (Whipple), Mary Wickes (Mike Tracy), David Bruce (Oliver), Shemp Howard (Alf), Buddy Rich and his orchestra.

Songs: "Going Up" (the Andrews Sisters), "East of the Rockies" (the Andrews Sisters), "Don't Mind the Rain" (the Andrews Sisters), "Take It and Git" (the Andrews Sisters), "Here Comes the Navy" (the Andrews Sisters).

Plot: A music publishing building is the setting for an aggravated romance between a lyricist (McDonald) and a publishing agent (Paige), while a trio of elevator operators (the Andrews Sisters) supply the music.

Always a Bridesmaid (1943)

Universal; producer, Ken Goldsmith; director, Erle C. Kenton; screenplay, Mel Ronson. 61 minutes. B&W.

Cast: The Andrews Sisters (Maxene, Patty, and LaVerne), Patric Knowles (Tony Warren), Grace McDonald (Linda Marlowe), Charles Butterworth (Col. Winchester), Billy Gilbert (Nick), Edith Barrett (Mrs. Cavanaugh), Addison Richards (Martin Boland), O'Neill Nolan (Rigsy), Annie Rooney (Annie), Philip Van Zandt (Waiter).

Songs: "That's My Affair" (the Andrews Sisters), "Mister Five by Five" (the Andrews Sisters), "Thanks for the Buggy Ride" (the Andrews Sisters), "Ride On" (the Andrews Sisters), "Yoo-Hoo" (the Andrews Sisters), "As Long as I Have You."

Plot: Three operators of a lonely-hearts club (the Andrews Sisters) are investigated by two detectives (McDonald and Knowles).

Swingtime Johnny (1943)

Universal; producer, Warren Wilson; director, Edward F. Cline; screenplay, Clyde Bruckman. 60 minutes. B&W.

Cast: The Andrews Sisters (Maxene, Patty, and LaVerne), Harriet Hilliard (Linda Lane), Peter Cookson (Jonathan Chadwick), Tim Ryan (Mr. Sparks), Matt Willis (Monk), William Phillips (Steve), Ray Walker (Mike), John Hamilton (Caldwell), Jack Rice (Bill), Herbert Heywood (Pop), Alphonse Martell (Pierre).

Songs: "I May Be Wrong" (the Andrews Sisters), "When You and I Were Young, Maggie" (partial, the Andrews Sisters), "Boogie Woogie Choo Choo" (the Andrews Sisters), "You Better Give Me Lots of Lovin'" (the Andrews Sisters), "Boogie Woogie Bugle Boy" (partial, the Andrews Sisters), Medley—"Long, Long Ago"/"While Strolling through the Park One Day"/"Goodnight, Ladies"/"Merrily, We Roll Along" (the

Andrews Sisters), "Sweet and Low" (Harriet Hilliard), "Poor Nell" (Harriet Hilliard), "The Band Played On" (male quartet).

Plot: A young executive (Cookson) is faced with a dilemma when his pipe-organ manufacturing plant is converted into a wartime munitions factory. Assistance is provided by the executive's secretary (Hilliard) and a trio of nightclub entertainers (the Andrews Sisters).

Follow the Boys (1944, working title *Three Cheers for the Boys*)

Universal; producer, Charles K. Feldman; director, Edward Sutherland; screenplay, Lou Breslow and Gertrude Purcell. 122 minutes. B&W.

Cast: George Raft (Tony West), Vera Zorina (Gloria Vance), Charles Grapewin (Nick West), Grace McDonald (Kitty West), Charles Butterworth (Louie Fairweather), Ramsay Ames (Laura).

Guest Stars: Orson Welles, Marlene Dietrich, Dinah Shore, the Andrews Sisters, W.C. Fields, Peggy Ryan and Donald O'Connor, Jeanette MacDonald, Sophie Tucker, Arthur Rubenstein, Carmen Amaya, the Delta Rhythm Boys, Ted Lewis and his orchestra, Freddie Slack and his orchestra, Charlie Spivak and his orchestra, and Louis Jordan and his orchestra.

Songs: Medley—"Bei Mir Bist Du Schon"/"Well, All Right"/"Hold Tight-Hold Tight" (the Andrews Sisters), "Beer Barrel Polka"/"Boogie Woogie Bugle Boy"/"Apple Blossom Time" (the Andrews Sisters), "Pennsylvania Polka"/"Strip Polka"/"The Vict'ry Polka"/"Shoo Shoo Baby" (partial, the Andrews Sisters), "Beyond the Blue Horizon" (Jeanette MacDonald), "The House I Live In" (The Delta Rhythm Boys), "The Bigger the Army and the Navy . . ." (Sophie Tucker), "I'll Get By" (Dinah Shore), "Is You Is or Is You Ain't (Ma' Baby?)" (Louis Jordan and his orchestra).

Plot: Revolving around the marital problems of a dance team (Raft and Zorina), this film features an all-star cast providing wartime entertainment for the troops, as well as for the home front.

Hollywood Canteen (1944)

Warner Bros.; producer, Alex Gottlieb; director, Delmer Daves; screenplay, Delmer Daves. 124 minutes. B&W. Available on Warner Bros. Home Video.

Cast: Robert Hutton (Slim), Dane Clark (Sergeant), Janis Paige (Angela), Jonathan Hale (Mr. Brodel), Barbara Brown (Mrs. Brodel).

Guest Stars: Joan Leslie, the Andrews Sisters, Bette Davis, John Garfield, Jane Wyman, Jack Benny, Joan Crawford, Eddie Cantor, Roy Rogers and the Sons of the Pioneers, Peter Lorre and Sydney Greenstreet, Jack Carson, Ida Lupino, Eleanor Parker, Nora Martin, S.Z. "Cuddles" Sakall, Alan Hale, Paul Henreid, Kitty Carlisle, Jimmy Dorsey and his orchestra, Carmen Cavallaro and his orchestra.

Songs: "Hollywood Canteen" (the Andrews Sisters, voices only), "Corns for My Country" (the Andrews Sisters), "Don't Fence Me In" (the Andrews Sisters), "Don't Fence Me In" (Roy Rogers and the Sons of the Pioneers), "What Are You Doing the Rest of Your Life?" (Jane Wyman and Jack Carson), "We're Having a Baby" (Eddie Cantor and Nora Martin), "Once to Every Heart" (Kitty Carlisle), "Tumbling Tumbleweeds" (The Sons of the Pioneers), "King Porter Stomp" (Jimmy Dorsey and his orchestra).

Plot: Another all-star production for the war effort, this film concerns a soldier (Hutton) who wins a hotel suite, a car, and the girl of his dreams (Leslie) for a weekend of fun—all for being the one-millionth patron to enter the famous Hollywood Canteen.

Moonlight and Cactus (1944)

Universal; producer, Frank Gross; director, Edward F. Cline; screenplay, Eugene Conrad and Paul Gerard Smith. 60 minutes. B&W.

Cast: The Andrews Sisters (Maxene, Patty, and LaVerne), Elyse Knox (Louise Ferguson), Tom Seidel (Tom Garrison), Leo Carillo (Pasqualito), Eddie Quillan (Stubby), Tom Kennedy (Lucky), Murray Alper (Slugger), Minerva Urecal (Abigail), Shemp Howard (Punchy), Mitchell Ayres and his orchestra.

Songs: "Wa-hoo!" (the Andrews Sisters), "Down in the Valley" (the Andrews Sisters), "C'mere, Baby" (Patty Andrews), "Send Me a Man, Amen!" (the Andrews Sisters), "Home" (the Andrews Sisters), "Sing" (the Andrews Sisters), "The Hand-Clapping Song" (the Andrews Sisters).

Plot: A rancher (Seidel) returns home from active duty to find his ranch being operated by women, including a trio of entertainers (the Andrews Sisters).

Her Lucky Night (1945)

Universal; producer, Warren Wilson; director, Edward Lilley; screenplay, Clyde Bruckman. 60 minutes. B&W.

Cast: The Andrews Sisters (Maxene, Patty, and LaVerne), Martha O'Driscoll (Connie), Noah Beery, Jr. (Larry), George Barbier (J.L. Wentworth), Robert Emmet Keane (Lawson), Maurice Cass (Papa), Ida Moore (Mama), Olin Howlin (Prince de la Mour), Marie Harmon (Susie), Edgar Dearing (Casey), Rita Gould (Fannie), Grady Sutton (Joe).

Songs: "Straighten Up and Fly Right" (the Andrews Sisters), "Dance with the Dolly (With the Hole in Her Stocking)" (the Andrews Sisters), "Sing a Tropical Song" (the Andrews Sisters), "Is You Is or Is You Ain't (Ma' Baby?)" (the Andrews Sisters), "The Polka Polka" (the Andrews Sisters).

Plot: Three nightclub hostesses (the Andrews Sisters) lend some matchmaking assistance to a lovelorn friend (O'Driscoll).

Make Mine Music (1946)

Walt Disney/RKO; producer, Joe Grant; animation directors, Jack Kinney, Clyde Geronimi, Hamilton Luske, Rob Cormack, and Joshua Meador. 74 minutes. Color. Full-length, animated feature.

Cast (voices only): Nelson Eddy, the Andrews Sisters, Dinah Shore, Andy Russell, Jerry Colonna, Sterling Holloway, the Pied Pipers, the King's Men, the Ken Darby Chorus, Tatiana Riabouchinska, the Benny Goodman Quartet.

Songs: "Johnny Fedora and Alice Blue Bonnet" (the Andrews Sisters), "Shortenin' Bread" (Nelson Eddy), "Two Silhouettes" (Dinah Shore), "Without You" (Andy Russell), "Blue Bayou" (The Ken Darby Chorus), "All the Cats Join In" (The Pied Pipers with the Benny Goodman Quartet), "The Martins and the Coys" (The King's Men).

Road to Rio (1948)

Paramount; producer, Daniel Dare; director, Norman Z. McLeod; screenplay, Edmund Beloin and Jack Rose. 100 minutes. B&W. Available on Paramount Home Video.

Cast: Bing Crosby (Scat Sweeney), Bob Hope ("Hot Lips" Barton), Dorothy Lamour (Lucia Maria de Andrade), Jerry Colonna (Calvary Captain), Gale Sondergaard (Catherine Vail), Joseph Vitale (Tony), Frank Faylen (Trigger), Stanley Andrews (Captain Harmon), The Wiere Brothers (Musicians), The Andrews Sisters (Maxene, Patty, and LaVerne).

Songs: "You Don't Have to Know the Language" (the Andrews Sisters and Bing Crosby), "But Beautiful" (Bing Crosby), "Experience" (Dorothy

Lamour), "Apalachicola, FLA" (Bing Crosby and Bob Hope).

Plot: Two carnival entertainers (Crosby and Hope) stow away on a cruise ship bound for Rio; while on board, the jokesters meet an entranced beauty (Lamour), her evil aunt (Sondergaard), and the ship's musical entertainers (the Andrews Sisters).

Melody Time (1948)

Walt Disney/RKO; producer, Walt Disney and Ben Sharpsteen; animation directors, Jack Kinney, Clyde Geronimi, Hamilton Luske, and Wilfred Jackson. 75 minutes. Color. Full-length, animated feature. Available on Walt Disney Home Video.

Cast: Roy Rogers and the Sons of the Pioneers, Luana Patten, Bobby Driscoll, Ethel Smith. *Voices only:* Dennis Day, the Andrews Sisters, Buddy Clark, Jack Fina, Frances Langford, the Dinning Sisters, Freddy Martin and his orchestra, Fred Waring and his Pennsylvanians.

Songs: "Little Toot" (the Andrews Sisters), "The Flight of the Bumble Bee" (Freddy Martin and his orchestra with Jack Fina on piano), "Trees" (Fred Waring and his Pennsylvanians), "Once upon a Wintertime" (Frances Langord), "Pecos Bill" (Roy Rogers and the Sons of the Pioneers), "Blame It on the Samba" (Ethel Smith and the Dinning Sisters).

Discography

Note: All sessions are with Vic Schoen and his orchestra,
unless otherwise noted.

Decca Singles, 1937-1955

March 18, 1937, in New York with Leon Belasco's orchestra.

"There's a Lull in My Life" (Patty). From Twentieth Century-Fox picture
Wake Up and Live (1937). Matrix B20840. Brunswick 7872.

"Wake Up and Live." From Twentieth Century-Fox picture *Wake Up and
Live* (1937). Matrix B20841. Brunswick 7872.

"Jammin'." From Paramount picture *Turn Off the Moon* (1937). Matrix
B20743. Brunswick 7863. The flip side of Brunswick 7863, Matrix
B20842, featured Belasco vocalist Wes Vaughn singing "Turn Off the
Moon."

October 18, 1937, in New York.

"Why Talk about Love?" From Twentieth Century-Fox picture *Life Begins
in College* (1937). Matrix 62686. Decca 1496.

"Just a Simple Melody." Matrix 62687. Decca 1496.

November 24, 1937, in New York.

"Nice Work If You Can Get It." From RKO Radio picture *Damsel in
Distress* (1937). Featured in MGM picture *An American in Paris*
(1951). Matrix 62810. Decca 1562.

"Bei Mir Bist Du Schon (Means that You're Grand)." Original Yiddish
composition by Sholom Secunda; English lyrics by Sammy Cahn and
Saul Chaplin. From musical production *I Would If I Could.* Featured
in Warner Bros. picture *Love, Honor and Behave* (1938) and Universal picture *Follow the Boys* (1944). Matrix 62811. Decca 1562 (re-
released as Decca 11049 and Decca 23605).

February 21, 1938, in New York.

"Joseph! Joseph!" (Based on Yiddish melody "Yossele Yossele"). English
lyrics by Sammy Cahn and Saul Chaplin. Matrix 63300. Decca 1691
(re-released as Decca 23605).

"Ti-Pi-Tin." (Based on Chabrier's "Espana" and Lalo's "Symphonie Espagnole.") Adapted from Spanish melody "Ti-Pi-Tin" by Maria Grever. English lyrics by Raymond Leveen. Matrix 63301. Decca 1703 (re-released as Decca 25097).

February 22, 1938, in New York.

"Shortenin' Bread." (Traditional folk song.) Featured in Columbia picture *Louisiana Hayride* (1944) and Walt Disney's *Make Mine Music* (1946). Matrix 63314. Decca 1744.

"It's Easier Said than Done." Matrix 63315. Decca 1691.

"Where Have We Met Before?" Matrix 63316. Decca 1703.

"ooOO-Oh Boom!" (Based on "The Music Goes 'Round and 'Round.") Matrix 63317. Decca 1744.

June 4, 1938, in New York.

"Says My Heart." From Paramount picture *Cocoanut Grove* (1938). Matrix 63911. Decca 1875.

"Oh! Ma-Ma! (The Butcher Boy)." (Based on Italian melody "Luna Mezzo Mare.") Matrix 63912. Decca 1859

"Pagan Love Song." From MGM picture *The Pagan* (1929). Featured in Universal picture *Night Club Girl* (1944) and MGM picture *Pagan Love Song* (1950). Matrix 63913. Decca 1859.

"I Married an Angel." From musical production *I Married an Angel*. Featured in MGM picture *I Married an Angel* (1942). Matrix 63914. Decca 1912.

"Oh! Faithless Maid." Melody featured in Twentieth Century-Fox picture *A Letter to Three Wives* (1949). Matrix 63915. Decca 1875.

"From the Land of the Sky Blue Water." From *Four American Indian Songs*. Matrix 63916. Decca 1912.

"Ferdinand the Bull." From Walt Disney's *Ferdinand the Bull* (1938). Matrix 63917. (Rejected.)

July 27, 1938, in New York with Jimmy Dorsey's orchestra.

"Tu-Li-Tulip Time." Matrix 64350. Decca 1974. *Session Note:* Decca Matrix 64351 featured Dorsey vocalist June Richmond.

"Sha-Sha" Matrix 64352. Decca 1974. *Session Note:* Decca Matrix 64351 featured Dorsey vocalist June Richmond.

August 6, 1938, in New York.

"Love Is Where You Find It." From musical production *Singin' in the Rain*. Featured in First National picture *Garden of the Moon* (1938). Matrix

64423. Decca 2016 (re-released as Brunswick 02837 outside of the United States).

"When a Prince of a Fella Meets a Cinderella (A Modern Fairytale)." Matrix 64424. Decca 2016.

"A Jitterbug's Lullaby" (Part 1). Matrix 64425. (Rejected.)

"A Jitterbug's Lullaby" (Part 2). Matrix 64426. (Rejected.)

"One, Two, Three O'Leary." (Based on children's jump-rope rhyme.) Matrix 64427. Brunswick 02837 (released outside of the United States).

September 8, 1938, in New York.

"Lullaby to a Jitterbug." Matrix 64670. Decca 2082.

"Pross Tchai (Goodbye, Goodbye)." Matrix 64671. Decca 2082.

November 21, 1938, in New York with Jimmy Dorsey's orchestra.

"Hold Tight-Hold Tight (Want Some Sea Food, Mama?)." Featured in Universal picture *Follow the Boys* (1944). Matrix 64757. Decca 2214.

"Billy Boy" (with Ray McKinley). (Traditional folk song from England.) Matrix 64758. Decca 2214.

January 24, 1939, in New York with Woody Herman's orchestra.

"Begin the Beguine." Matrix 64942. (Rejected.)

"Long Time No See." Matrix 64943. (Rejected.)

February 6, 1939, in New York with Bob Crosby's Bobcats.

"Begin the Beguine." From musical production *Jubilee.* Featured in MGM picture *Broadway Melody of 1940* (1940) and Warner Bros. picture *Night and Day* (1946). Matrix 64988. Decca 2290 (re-released as Decca 25097). *Session Note:* Decca Matrix 64989 featured an instrumental by the Bobcats.

"Long Time No See." Matrix 64990. Decca 2290. *Session Note:* Decca Matrix 64989 featured an instrumental by the Bobcats.

March 31, 1939, in New York.

"You Don't Know How Much You Can Suffer." Matrix 65326. Decca 2414.

"Rock Rock Rock-a-Bye Baby." (Based on a nursery rhyme, circa 1765.) Adapted by Vic Schoen-Andrews Sisters; additional lyrics by Sid Robins and Patty Andrews. Original composition featured in MGM picture *Babes in Arms* (1939).

Discography

May 3, 1939, in New York.

"Beer Barrel Polka (Roll Out the Barrel)." (Based on Czechoslovakian melody "Skoda Lasky.") From musical production *Yokel Boy*. Featured in RKO Radio picture *Dance, Girl, Dance* (1940), Universal picture *Follow the Boys* (1944), Samuel Goldwyn's *The Best Years of Our Lives* (1946), and United Artists picture *A Night in Casablanca* (1946). Matrix 65531. Decca 2462 (re-released as Decca 23509).

"Well, All Right! (Tonight's the Night)." Featured in Universal picture *Follow the Boys* (1944). Matrix 65532. Decca 2462 (re-released as Decca 23606).

September 15, 1939, in New York with Decca's studio orchestra.

"The Jumpin' Jive (Jim Jam Jump)." Featured in Twentieth Century-Fox picture *Stormy Weather* (1943). Matrix 66591. Decca 2756.

"Chico's Love Song." Matrix 66592. Decca 2756.

September 20, 1939, in New York with Joe Venuti's orchestra.

"Ciribiribin (They're So in Love)" (with Bing Crosby). From Columbia picture *One Night of Love* (1934). Featured in Warner Bros. picture *So This Is Love* (1953) and MGM picture *Hit the Deck* (1955). Matrix 66632. Decca 2800.

"Yodelin' Jive" (with Bing Crosby). Matrix 66633. Decca 2800.

November 9, 1939, in New York.

"Oh, Johnny! Oh, Johnny! Oh!" Featured in Universal picture *Oh Johnny, How You Can Love! (1940). Matrix 66498. Decca 2840.*

"South American Way." From musical production *Streets of Paris*. Featured in Twentieth Century-Fox picture *Down Argentine Way* (1940). Matrix 66499. Decca 2840 (re-released as Decca 25095).

February 7, 1940, in New York.

"Say Si Si (Para Vigo Me Voy)." Featured in Twentieth Century-Fox picture *When My Baby Smiles at Me* (1948). Matrix 67180. Decca 3013 (re-released as Decca 25098).

"Let's Have Another One." Matrix 67181. Decca 3013.

"I Love You Much Too Much." Matrix 67182. (Rejected.)

February 21, 1940, in New York.

"The Woodpecker Song." (Based on Italian melody "Reginella Compagnola.") From Republic picture *Ride, Tenderfoot, Ride* (1940). Matrix 67225. Decca 3065.

"Down By the O-Hi-O." Matrix 67226. Decca 3065.

March 23, 1940, in New York.

"Rhumboogie." From Universal picture *Argentine Nights* (1940). Matrix 67383. Decca 3097 (re-released as Decca 23608).

"Tuxedo Junction." Featured in Universal picture *The Glenn Miller Story* (1954). Matrix 67384. Decca 3097.

April 23, 1940, in New York.

"The Cockeyed Mayor of Kaunakakai." Featured in Twentieth Century-Fox picture *Song of the Islands* (1942). Matrix 67613. Decca 3245.

"Let's Pack Our Things and Trek." Matrix 67614. Decca 3245.

July 7, 1940, in Los Angeles.

"Oh, He Loves Me." From Universal picture *Argentine Nights* (1940). Matrix DLA 2039. Decca 3310.

"Hit the Road." Matrix DLA 2040. (Rejected.)

"I Want My Mama (Mama Eu Quero)." From musical production *Earl Carroll's Vanities*. Featured in Twentieth Century-Fox picture *Down Argentine Way* (1940), MGM picture *Babes on Broadway* (1942), and Paramount picture *Ladies' Man* (1947). Matrix DLA 2041. Decca 3310.

July 15, 1940, in Los Angeles.

"Sweet Molly Malone." Matrix DLA 2054. (Rejected.)

"Ferryboat Serenade (La Piccinina)." (Based on Italian melody "La Piccinina.") Matrix DLA 2055. Decca 3328.

"Hit the Road." From Universal picture *Argentine Nights* (1940). Matrix DLA 2056. Decca 3328.

August 3, 1940, in New York.

"Johnny Peddler (I Got)." Matrix 67960. Decca 3553.

"Beat Me Daddy, Eight to the Bar." Matrix 67961. (Rejected.)

August 28, 1940, in New York.

"Pennsylvania 6–5000." Featured in Universal picture *The Glenn Miller Story* (1954). Matrix 68019. Decca 3375.

"Beat Me Daddy, Eight to the Bar." Matrix 68020. Decca 3375 (re-released as Decca 23607).

"My Love Went without Water (Three Days)." Matrix 68021. Decca 1873 (released in South Africa only).

Discography

September 5, 1940, in New York.

"Mean to Me." Featured in MGM picture *Love Me or Leave Me* (1955) and Paramount picture *Lady Sings the Blues* (1972). Matrix 68046. Decca 3440.

"Sweet Molly Malone." (Traditional Irish folk song.) Adapted by Hughie Prince and the Andrews Sisters. Matrix 68047. Decca 3440.

"I Love You Much Too Much." (Based on Yiddish melody "Ich Hob Dich Tzufil Lieb.") Matrix 68048. Decca 18536.

November 14, 1940, in New York.

"I'll Be with You in Apple Blossom Time." Featured in Universal pictures *Buck Privates* (1941) and *Follow the Boys* (1944). Matrix 68351. Decca 3622 (re-released as Decca 11049). An alternate take of "I'll Be with You in Apple Blossom Time" was later released as Decca 23608.

"Scrub Me Mama with a Boogie Beat." (Based on traditional Irish melody "Irish Washerwoman.") Matrix 68352. Decca 3553 (re-released as Decca 23607).

January 2, 1941, in Los Angeles.

"You're a Lucky Fellow, Mr. Smith." From Universal picture *Buck Privates* (1941). Matrix DLA 2324. Decca 3599.

"Bounce Me Brother with a Solid Four." From Universal picture *Buck Privates* (1941). Matrix DLA 2325. Decca 3598.

"Boogie Woogie Bugle Boy." Nominated for an Oscar for Best Song in a Motion Picture, 1941. From Universal picture *Buck Privates* (1941). Featured (excerpt only) in Universal pictures *Swingtime Johnny* (1943) and *Follow the Boys* (1944). Matrix DLA 2326. Decca 3598.

January 7, 1941, in Los Angeles.

"I Yi, Yi, Yi, Yi (I Like You Very Much)." From Twentieth Century-Fox picture *That Night in Rio* (1941). Matrix DLA 2356. Decca 3622.

"Yes, My Darling Daughter." Matrix DLA 2357. Decca 3599.

March 18, 1941, in Los Angeles.

"Aurora." From Universal picture *Hold That Ghost* (1941). Matrix 68827. Decca 3732 (re-released as Decca 25096).

"Music Makers." Matrix 68828. Decca 3732.

"Lonesome Mama." Matrix 68829. Brunswick 03416 (released outside of the United States).

Discography

May 21, 1941, in Los Angeles.

"Daddy." From Columbia picture *Two Latins from Manhattan* (1941). Featured in United Artists picture *Gentlemen Marry Brunettes* (1955). Matrix DLA 2395. Decca 3821 (re-released as Decca 27757).

"Sleepy Serenade." From Universal picture *Hold That Ghost* (1941). Matrix DLA 2396. Decca 3821.

"Sonny Boy." Matrix DLA 2397. (Rejected.)

May 29, 1941, in Los Angeles.

"Helena." (Based on "Helena Polka.") Matrix DLA 2425. Decca 18563.

"Sonny Boy." From Warner Bros. picture *The Singing Fool* (1928). Featured in Columbia picture *Jolson Sings Again* (1949) and Twentieth Century-Fox picture *The Best Things in Life Are Free* (1956). Matrix DLA 2426. Decca 3871.

"Gimme Some Skin, My Friend." From Universal picture *In the Navy* (1941). Matrix DLA 2427. Decca 3871.

"Hula Ba Luau." From Universal picture *In the Navy* (1941). Matrix DLA 2428. (Rejected.)

July 28, 1941, in New York.

"Jealous." Featured in Paramount picture *Somebody Loves Me* (1952). Matrix 69568. Decca 4019.

"For All We Know." Matrix 69569. Decca 4094.

July 30, 1941, in New York.

"Honey." Matrix 69578. Decca 4008.

"The Nickel Serenade." Matrix 69579. Decca 3960.

"Jack of All Trades." Matrix 69580. Decca 4097.

July 31, 1941, in New York.

"The Booglie Wooglie Piggy." (Based on "This Little Piggy Went to Market.") Matrix 69587. Decca 3960.

"I Wish I Had a Dime (For Ev'rytime I Missed You)." Matrix 69588. Decca 3966.

August 4, 1941, in New York.

"Why Don't We Do This More Often?" Matrix 69606. Decca 3966.

"Elmer's Tune." Featured in Universal picture *Strictly in the Groove* (9142). Matrix 69607. Decca 4008.

September 10, 1941, in New York.

"Rancho Pillow." Matrix 60738. Decca 4019.

"At Sonya's Café (Shikker, Ikker, Trinken, Mizzer)." (Based on Yiddish drinking song.) Matrix 69739. Decca 18312.

September 26, 1941, in New York.

"What to Do." Matrix 69770. (Rejected.)
"Elmer's Tune." Matrix 69771. (Rejected.)

October 18, 1941, in New York.

"Any Bonds Today?" Official song of the United States Treasury Department's Defense Savings Bond Campaign. Featured in Paramount picture *Blue Skies* (1946). Matrix 69831. Decca 4044. The flip side of Decca 4044 featured a recording of "Any Bonds Today?" by Jimmy Dorsey's orchestra, vocals by Bob Eberle and Helen O'Connell.

November 15, 1941, in New York.

"The Shrine of Saint Cecilia." Matrix 69946. Decca 4097. "The Shrine of Saint Cecilia" featured rhythm accompaniment—guitar and piano—and a male chorus under the direction of Vic Schoen.
"Chattanooga Choo Choo." From Twentieth Century-Fox picture *Sun Valley Serenade* (1941). Featured in Twentieth Century-Fox picture *Springtime in the Rockies* (1942) and Universal picture *The Glenn Miller Story* (1954). Matrix 69947. Decca 4094.
"Tica-Ti Tica-Ta." Matrix 69948. Brunswick 03337 (released outside of the United States).

December 27, 1941, in New York.

"I'll Pray for You." From Universal picture *What's Cookin'?* (1942). Matrix 70108. Decca 4153.
"What to Do." Matrix 70109. (Rejected.)
"He Said-She Said (The Story of the Newlyweds)." Matrix 70110. Decca 4253.

January 26, 1942, in Los Angeles.

"(Toy Balloon) Boolee Boolee Boon." Matrix DLA 2848. Decca 18319.
"A Zoot Suit (For My Sunday Gal)." Matrix DLA 2849. Decca 4182.
"What to Do." (Based on Jewish folk song.) From Universal picture *What's Cookin'?* (1942). Matrix DLA 2850. Decca 4182.

April 4, 1942, in Los Angeles.

"Three Little Sisters." From Universal picture *Private Buckaroo* (1942). Matrix DLA 2972. Decca 18319.

"Don't Sit under the Apple Tree (With Anyone Else but Me)." (Based on 1833 melody "Long, Long Ago"; originally titled "Anywhere the Bluebird Goes.") From Universal picture *Private Buckaroo* (1942). Featured in Twentieth Century-Fox picture *With a Song in My Heart* (1952). Featured in Twentieth Century-Fox picture *Kiss Them for Me* (1957). Matrix DLA 2973. Decca 18312 (also released as Brunswick 03337 outside of the United States).

April 23, 1942, in Los Angeles.

"That's the Moon, My Son." (Based on Yiddish folk melody.) From Universal picture *Private Buckaroo* (1942). Matrix DLA 2978. Decca 18398.

"When Johnny Comes Marching Home." (Civil War composition; originally titled "Johnny, Fill Up the Bowl," 1863.) Adapted by Vic Schoen and the Andrews Sisters. Featured in MGM picture *For Me and My Gal* (1942) and Universal picture *When Johnny Comes Marching Home* (1943). Matrix DLA 2979. Decca 18533.

"Six Jerks in a Jeep." From Universal picture *Private Buckaroo* (1942). Matrix DLA 2980. (Rejected.)

May 28, 1942, in Los Angeles.

"You're Just a Flower from an Old Bouquet." From Universal picture *Give Out, Sisters* (1942). Matrix DLA 3002. (Rejected.)

"Pennsylvania Polka." From Universal picture *Give Out, Sisters* (1942). Featured in Universal picture *Follow the Boys* (1944). Matrix DLA 3003. Decca 18398 (re-released as Decca 23609).

"I've Got a Gal in Kalamazoo." Matrix DLA 3004. (Rejected.)

July 17, 1942, in New York.

"I've Got a Gal in Kalamazoo." From Twentieth Century-Fox picture *Orchestra Wives* (1942). Featured in Twentieth Century-Fox picture *Kiss Them for Me* (1957). Matrix 71103. Decca 18464.

"The Humming Bird," Matrix 71104. Decca 18464.

"Strip Polka." Featured in Universal picture *Follow the Boys* (1944). Matrix 71105. Decca 18470.

July 22, 1942, in New York.

"East of the Rockies." From Universal picture *How's About It?* (1943). Matrix 71151. Decca 18533.

"Mister Five by Five." From Universal picture *Behind the Eight Ball* (1942). Featured in Universal picture *Who Done It?* (1942). Matrix 71152. Decca 18470.

"Massachusetts." Matrix 71153. Decca 18497.

"Here Comes the Navy." (Adapted to the melody of "Beer Barrel Polka."). New lyrics by Lt. Comdr. C.P. Oakes. From Universal picture *How's About It?* (1943). Matrix 71154. Decca 18497.

December 12, 1942, in Los Angeles.

"There Are Such Things." (Rejected.) On August 1, 1942, the American Federation of Musicians went on strike and a recording ban went into effect until September 18, 1943, when the strike was resolved. This was the only song the Andrews Sisters recorded for Decca Records during that time. The take has never been released.

September 27, 1943, in Los Angeles.

"Pistol Packin' Mama" (with Bing Crosby). Featured in Columbia picture *Beautiful but Broke* (1944). Matrix L3197. Decca 23277.

"The Vict'ry Polka" (with Bing Crosby). Featured in Columbia picture *Jam Session* (1944). Featured in Universal picture *Follow the Boys* (1944). Matrix L3198. Decca 23277.

September 29, 1943, in Los Angeles.

"Jingle Bells" (with Bing Crosby). (Originally titled "The One-Horse Open Sleigh"; original lyrics written by J.S. Pierpont in the 1850s.) Adapted and arranged by Vic Schoen and Patty Andrews. Matrix L3199. Decca 23281.

"Santa Claus Is Comin' to Town" (with Bing Crosby). Matrix L3200. Decca 23281.

October 5, 1943, in Los Angeles.

"Shoo Shoo Baby." From Universal picture *Follow the Boys* (1944). Featured in Republic picture *Trocadero* (1944). Matrix L3220. Decca 18572.

"Down in the Valley (Hear That Train Blow)" (with male chorus). (Traditional folk melody of the Kentucky mountains; based on "Birmingham Jail"/"Bird in a Cage"/"Down on the Level.") Adapted by Vic Schoen and the Andrews Sisters. Featured in Universal picture *Moonlight and Cactus* (1944). Featured in Republic picture *The Last Musketeer* (1952) and Columbia picture *Montana Territory* (1952). Matrix L3221. Decca 18572 (re-released as Decca 25149).

March 7, 1944, in New York.

"Tico-Tico." Featured in Walt Disney's *Saludos Amigos* (1943). Featured in MGM picture *Bathing Beauty* (1944), Columbia picture *Kansas City*

Kitty (1944), RKO picture *It's a Pleasure* (1945), Producers Releasing Association production *Club Havana* (1946), and United Artists picture *Copacabana* (1947). Matrix 71833. Decca 18606 (re-released as Decca 25098).

"There'll Be a Jubilee." Featured in Columbia picture *Swing in the Saddle* (1945). Matrix 71834. Decca 18581.

April 4, 1944, in New York.

"Sing a Tropical Song." From Paramount picture *Happy Go Lucky* (1943). Featured in Universal picture *Her Lucky Night* (1945). Matrix 71936. Decca 18581 (re-released as Decca 25095).

"Bei Mir Bist Du Schon (Means that You're Grand)." Matrix 71937. (Rejected; this was a re-recording of the original hit.)

"Rhumboogie." Matrix 71938. (Rejected; this was a re-recording of the original hit.)

May 2, 1944, in New York.

"Straighten Up and Fly Right." From Republic picture *Here Comes Elmer* (1943). Featured in Universal picture *Her Lucky Night* (1945). Matrix 72059. Decca 18606.

"Red River Valley" (with male chorus). (Based on James Kerrigan's "In the Bright Mohawk Valley.") Arranged by Lou Knox. Featured in Republic picture *King of the Cowboys* (1943). Matrix 72060. Decca 18780 (re-released as Decca 25149).

"I'll Be with You in Apple Blossom Time." Matrix 72061. (Rejected; this was a re-recording of the original hit.)

June 30, 1944, in Los Angeles.

"There'll Be a Hot Time in the Town of Berlin (When the Yanks Go Marching In)" (with Bing Crosby). Matrix L3449. Decca 23350.

"Is You Is or Is You Ain't (Ma' Baby?)" (with Bing Crosby). From Universal picture *Follow the Boys* (1944). Featured in Universal picture *Her Lucky Night* (1945). Matrix L3450. Decca 23350.

July 25, 1944, in Los Angeles.

"Don't Fence Me In" (with Bing Crosby). From Warner Bros. picture *Hollywood Canteen* (1944). Featured in Warner Bros. picture *Night and Day* (1946). Matrix L3475. Decca 23364. Cole Porter's 1933 composition of "Don't Fence Me In" was written as a satire of the West for an upcoming motion picture, *Adios, Argentina*. The film, however, was never made, and the song was not popularized until Roy Rogers and the Sons of the Pioneers introduced it in 1944's

Hollywood Canteen. The Andrews Sisters sang a reprise of the song in the same film, and achieved a million-selling record when they recorded the song with Bing Crosby shortly thereafter.

"The Three Caballeros" (with Bing Crosby). Featured in Walt Disney's *The Three Caballeros* (1945). Matrix L3476. Decca 23364.

August 24, 1944, in Los Angeles.

"Don't Blame Me." Featured in MGM picture *Dinner at Eight* (1933), Monogram picture *Freddie Steps Out* (1946), and MGM picture *Big City* (1948). Matrix L3546. Decca 23827 (re-released as Decca 24424).

"Corns for My Country." From Warner Bros. picture *Hollywood Canteen* (1944). Matrix L3547. Decca 18628.

"Lullaby of Broadway." (Based on a theme from a "Hungarian Dance" by Brahms and the "Barcarolle" from Offenbach's *Tales of Hoffman.*) Featured in Warner Bros. pictures *Gold Diggers of 1935* (1935) and *Lullaby of Broadway* (1951). Matrix L3548. Decca 23824 (re-released as Decca 27432).

August 31, 1944, in Los Angeles.

"(Pack Up Your Troubles in Your Old Kit Bag and) Smile! Smile! Smile!" (with Dick Haymes). (World War I composition.) Adapted by Vic Schoen and the Andrews Sisters. Featured in MGM picture *It's a Great Life* (1930), Universal picture *What's Cookin'?* (1942), MGM picture *For Me and My Gal* (1942), Warner Bros. pictures *On Moonlight Bay* (1951) and *Wait till the Sun Shines Nellie* (1952), and Twentieth Century-Fox picture *What Price Glory* (1952). Matrix L3570. Decca 23412.

"Great Day" (with Dick Haymes). Matrix L3571. Decca 23412.

October 18, 1944, in New York.

"I'm in a Jam (With Baby)." Matrix L72458. Decca 18628.

"One Meat Ball." (Based on "The Lone Fish Ball," 1855.) Matrix L72459. Decca 18636.

"Rum and Coca Cola." (Based on Lionel Belasco's calypso melody "L'Année Passée," 1906.) English lyrics by Morey Amsterdam; English adaption by Jeri Sullivan and Paul Baron. Arranged by Vic Schoen and the Andrews Sisters. Matrix L72460. Decca 18636 (re-released as Decca 25096).

Discography

December 8, 1944, in Los Angeles.

"There's a Fellow Waiting in Poughkeepsie" (with Bing Crosby). From Paramount picture *Here Come the Waves* (1944). Matrix L3684. Decca 23379.

"Ac-cent-tchu-ate the Positive" (with Bing Crosby). From Paramount picture *Here Come the Waves* (1944). Matrix L3685. Decca 23379.

June 26, 1945, in Los Angeles.

"The Blond Sailor." (Based on German melody "Fahr Mich in Die Ferne, Mein Blonder Matrose.") Matrix L3873. Decca 18700 (re-released as Decca 27878).

"Lilly Belle." Matrix L3875. Decca 18700.

June 29, 1945, in Los Angeles.

"Along the Navajo Trail" (with Bing Crosby). From Republic picture *Along the Navajo Trail* (1945). Featured in Republic picture *Don't Fence Me In* (1945) and Columbia picture *The Blazing Sun* (1950). Matrix L3876. Decca 23437.

"Good, Good, Good (That's You-That's You)" (with Bing Crosby). From Columbia picture *I Love a Bandleader* (1945). Matrix L3877. Decca 23437.

July 3, 1945, in Los Angeles.

"Happy, Happy, Happy Wedding Day" (with Bing Crosby). Matrix L3887. (Rejected.)

"Betsy" (with Bing Crosby). Matrix L3888. Decca 24718.

September 4, 1945, in New York.

"The Welcome Song." Matrix 73026. Decca 18726.

"Put That Ring on My Finger." Matrix 73027. Decca 18726.

November 15, 1945, in New York with Guy Lombardo's Royal Canadians.

"Money Is the Root of All Evil (Take It Away, Take It Away, Take It Away)." Matrix 73135. Decca 23474.

November 19, 1945, in New York with Guy Lombardo's Royal Canadians.

"Johnny Fedora." From Walt Disney's *Make Mine Music* (1946). Matrix 73142. Decca 23474.

December 26, 1945, in Los Angeles.

"Patience and Fortitude." Featured in Monogram picture *Freddie Steps Out* (1946). Matrix L4043. Decca 18780.

March 7, 1946 in Los Angeles.

"Coax Me a Little Bit." Matrix L4110. Decca 18833.
"Atlanta, G.A." Matrix L4111. Decca 18833.
"Her Bathing Suit Never Got Wet." Matrix L4112. Decca 18840.

March 18, 1946, in Los Angeles.

"Avocado." From Columbia picture *Talk about a Lady* (1946). Matrix L4124. Decca 18840.

March 25, 1946, in Los Angeles.

"Azusa." Matrix L4135. Decca 18899.

May 8, 1946, in Los Angeles.

"Three O'Clock in the Morning." Featured in MGM picture *Presenting Lili Mars* (1943), Twentieth Century-Fox pictures *Margie* (1946) and *Belles on Their Toes* (1952), and Columbia picture *The Eddy Duchin Story* (1956). Matrix L4174. Decca 27432.
"I Don't Know Why (I Just Do)." Featured in MGM picture *Faithful in My Fashion* (1946). Matrix L4175. Decca 18899.

May 11, 1946, in Los Angeles.

"Get Your Kicks on Route 66!" (with Bing Crosby). Featured in MGM picture *Three Daring Daughters* (1948). Matrix L4177. Decca 23569.
"South America, Take It Away" (with Bing Crosby). From musical revue *Call Me Mister* (1946). Featured in Twentieth Century-Fox picture *Call Me Mister* (1951). Matrix L4178. Decca 23569.

July 22, 1946, in Los Angeles with Les Paul (guitar) and Vic Schoen's orchestra.

"Rumors Are Flying." Matrix L4239. Decca 23656.

July 27, 1946, in Los Angeles with Eddie Heywood's orchestra.

"Them That Has—Gets." Matrix L4251. Decca 23656.
"The House of Blue Lights." Matrix L4252. Decca 23641.
"A Man Is a Brother to a Mule." From Columbia picture *Thrill of Brazil* (1946). Matrix L4253. Decca 23641.

September 30, 1946, in New York with Guy Lombardo's Royal Canadians.

"Christmas Island." Matrix 73694. Decca 23722.

"Winter Wonderland." From Republic picture *Lake Placid Serenade* (1944).
Matrix 73695. Decca 23722.

October 3, 1946, in New York.

"The Coffee Song (They've Got an Awful Lot of Coffee in Brazil)." From
musical production *Piccadilly Hayride*. Featured in Monte Proser's
Copacabana Revue. Matrix 73700. Decca 23740.

"A Rainy Night in Rio." From Warner Bros. picture *The Time, the Place,
and the Girl* (1946). Matrix 73701. Decca 23740.

"My Dearest Uncle Sam." (Based on a native song from the island of
Guam.) Matrix 73702. Decca 23824.

February 26, 1947, in Los Angeles.

"His Feet Too Big for de Bed." Matrix L4363. Decca 23860.

"Jack, Jack, Jack (Cu-Tu-Gu-Ru)." Matrix L4364. Decca 23860.

March 19, 1947, in Los Angeles.

"Anything You Can Do" (with Bing Crosby and Dick Haymes). From
musical production *Annie Get Your Gun*. Featured in MGM picture
Annie Get Your Gun (1950). Matrix L4377. Decca 40039. Matrix
L4377 was released on Decca's Premium Series label.

"There's No Business like Show Business" (with Bing Crosby and Dick
Haymes). From musical production *Annie Get Your Gun*. Featured in
MGM picture *Annie Get Your Gun* (1950). Matrix L4378. Decca
40039. Matrix L4378 was released on Decca's Premium Series label.

March 26, 1947, in Los Angeles.

"Go West, Young Man!" (with Bing Crosby). From Paramount picture *Go
West, Young Man* (1936). Matrix L4396. Decca 23885.

"Tallahassee" (with Bing Crosby). From Paramount picture *Variety Girl*
(1947). Matrix L4397. Decca 23885.

April 14, 1947, in Los Angeles.

"I'm So Right Tonight." Matrix L4409. (Rejected.)

"Red Silk Stockings and Green Perfume." Matrix L4410. (Rejected.)

May 26, 1947, in New York.

"The Turntable Song ('Round, an' 'Round, an' 'Round)." From Universal
picture *Something in the Wind* (1947). Matrix 73922. Decca 23976.

"The Lady from 29 Palms." Matrix 73923. Decca 23976.

May 29, 1947, in New York.

"The Freedom Train" (with Bing Crosby). Matrix 73927. Decca 23999.
Matrix L4265, the flip side of Decca 23999, was a recital of "The
Star-Spangled Banner" by Bing Crosby.

"Sweet Marie" (with Carmen Cavallaro at the piano). Featured in Warner
Bros. picture *Life with Father* (1947). Matrix 73931. Decca 24102.

"On the Avenue" (with Carmen Cavallaro at the piano). Matrix 73932.
Decca 24102.

August 4, 1947, in New York.

"Near You." Matrix 74021. Decca 24171.

"How Lucky You Are." Matrix 74022. Decca 24171.

September 27, 1947, in Los Angeles.

"Civilization (Bongo, Bongo, Bongo)" (with Danny Kaye). From musical
production *Angel in the Wings*. Matrix L4508. Decca 23940.

"Bread and Butter Woman" (with Danny Kaye). Matrix L4509. Decca
23940.

October 7, 1947, in Los Angeles.

"The Blue Tail Fly" (with Burl Ives). (Traditional; based on folk song
"Jimmy Crack Corn," 1846.) Matrix L4512. Decca 24463.

"I'm Goin' down the Road" (with Burl Ives). Matrix L4513. Decca 24463.

October 30, 1947, in Los Angeles.

"Your Red Wagon." From RKO picture *Your Red Wagon* (1947). Matrix
L4519. Decca 24268.

"Don't Worry 'bout Strangers." Matrix L4520. Decca 24533.

"Why Am I Always the Bridesmaid?" Matrix L4521. (Rejected.)

November 4, 1947, in Los Angeles.

"Carioca." From RKO picture *Flying Down to Rio* (1933). Matrix L4531.
Decca 27757. "Carioca" on Matrix L4531 was the flip side of a re-
release of the trio's 1941 recording of "Daddy."

"Too Fat Polka (She's Too Fat for Me.)" Matrix L4532. Decca 24268.

November 25, 1947, in Los Angeles.

"Apalachicola, FLA" (with Bing Crosby). From Paramount picture *Road to
Rio* (1948). Matrix L4576. Decca 24282.

Discography

"You Don't Have to Know the Language" (with Bing Crosby). From Paramount picture *Road to Rio* (1948). Matrix L4577. Decca 24282.

November 26, 1947, in Los Angeles.

"Some Sunny Day." Featured in Paramount picture *Blue Skies* (1946). Matrix L4578. Decca 24426.

"How Many Times." From Warner Bros. picture *The Time, the Place, and the Girl* (1946). Featured in Paramount picture *Blue Skies* (1946). Matrix L4579. Decca 24426.

November 29, 1947, in Los Angeles.

"Cuanto la Gusta" (with Carmen Miranda). From MGM picture *A Date with Judy* (1948). Matrix L4588. Decca 24479.

"The Matador" (with Carmen Miranda). Matrix L4589. Decca 24479.

December 3, 1947, in Los Angeles.

"When That Midnight Choo Choo Leaves for Alabam'." Featured in Twentieth Century-Fox picture *Alexander's Ragtime Band* (1938) and MGM picture *Easter Parade* (1948). Matrix L4609. Decca 24425.

"I Want to Go Back to Michigan (Down on the Farm)." Featured in MGM picture *Easter Parade* (1948). Matrix L4610. Decca 24424.

"Heat Wave." From musical production *As Thousands Cheer*. Featured in Twentieth Century-Fox picture *Alexander's Ragtime Band* (1938), MGM picture *Thousands Cheer* (1943), Paramount picture *Blue Skies* (1946), and Twentieth Century-Fox picture *There's No Business like Show Business* (1954). Matrix L4611. Decca 24425.

"Run, Run, Run." From Warner Bros. picture *Romance on the High Seas* (1948). Matrix L4612. Decca 23827.

December 10, 1947, in Los Angeles.

"Let a Smile Be Your Umbrella (On a Rainy Day)." From MGM picture *It's a Great Life* (1930). Featured in Twentieth Century-Fox picture *Give My Regards to Broadway* (1948). Matrix L4641. Decca 24548.

December 11, 1947, in Los Angeles.

"Whispering Hope." Matrix L4647. Decca 24717.

"Lovely Night." ("Barcarolle" from *The Tales of Hoffman*.) Matrix L4648. Decca 24717.

December 12, 1947, in Los Angeles.

"Beatin', Bangin', and Scratchin'" (with Danny Kaye). Matrix L4653. Decca 24536.

"Amelia Cordelia McHugh (McWho?)" (with Danny Kaye). Matrix L4654. Decca 24536.

December 13, 1947, in Los Angeles.

"Teresa" (with Dick Haymes). Matrix L4655. Decca 24320.

"My Sin" (with Dick Haymes). From First National picture *Showgirl in Hollywood* (1930). Featured in Twentieth Century-Fox picture *The Best Things in Life Are Free* (1956). Matrix L4656. Decca 24320.

December 17, 1947, in Los Angeles.

"A Hundred and Sixty Acres" (with Bing Crosby). Matrix L4676. Decca 24481.

"At the Flying 'W'" (with Bing Crosby). Matrix L4677. Decca 24481.

December 19, 1947, in Los Angeles.

"The Money Song." From musical production *That's the Ticket*. Matrix L4700. Decca 24494.

"The Bride and Groom Polka." Matrix L4701. Decca 24406.

"Toolie Oolie Doolie (The Yodel Polka)." Matrix L4702. Decca 24380.

December 20, 1947, in Los Angeles.

"Big Brass Band from Brazil" (with Danny Kaye). From musical production *Angel in the Wings*. Matrix L4705. Decca 24361.

"It's a Quiet Town (In Crossbone County)" (with Danny Kaye). Matrix L4706. Decca 24361.

December 27, 1947, in Los Angeles.

"Bella Bella Marie." (Based on German melody "Capri-Fischer.") Matrix L4747. Decca 24494.

"Alexander's Ragtime Band." From musical production *Hello, Ragtime*. Featured in Twentieth Century-Fox picture *Alexander's Ragtime Band* (1938). Matrix L4748. Decca 24424.

"We Just Couldn't Say Goodbye." Matrix L4749. Decca 24406.

December 31, 1947, in Los Angeles.

"I'd Love to Call You My Sweetheart" (with Dick Haymes). Matrix L4804. Decca 24504.

"What Did I Do?" (with Dick Haymes). From Twentieth Century-Fox picture *When My Baby Smiles at Me* (1948). Matrix L4805. Decca 24504.

"The Richest Man in the Cemetery." Matrix L4807. (Rejected.)

"I Hate to Lose You." From Universal picture *The Merry Monahans* (1947). Matrix L4808. Decca 24380.

March 23, 1948, in Los Angeles with the Harmonica Gentlemen.

"Heartbreaker." Matrix L4827. Decca 24427.

"(Everytime They Play the) Sabre Dance." (Based on Aram Khachaturian's "Sabre Dance" from *Gayne Ballet.*) Matrix L4828. Decca 24427.

June 4, 1948, in Los Angeles with the Harmonica Gentlemen.

"Put 'Em in a Box, Tie 'Em with a Ribbon (And Throw 'Em in the Deep Blue Sea)" (with Danny Kaye). From Warner Bros. picture *Romance on the High Seas* (1948). Matrix L4837. Decca 24462.

"The Woody Woodpecker Song" (with Danny Kaye). From the Walter Lantz cartoon "Wet Blanket Policy" (1948). Matrix L4838. Decca 24462.

July 26, 1948, in London with Billy Ternent's orchestra.

"You Call Everybody Darling." Matrix 74580. Decca 24490.

"Underneath the Arches." Matrix 74581. Decca 24490.

November 22, 1948, in Los Angeles.

"The Pussy Cat Song (Nyow! Nyot Nyow!)" (Patty Andrews and Bob Crosby). Matrix L4842. Decca 24533.

December 14, 1948, in Los Angeles.

"More Beer!" (Based on German melody "Der Kreuzfidele Kupferschmied"; known in the United States as "The Jolly Coppersmith.") Matrix L4847. Decca 24548.

"Underneath the Linden Tree." (Based on Swiss melody "Regenpfeiffer Sing Dein Lied.") Matrix L4848. Decca 24560.

January 15, 1949, in Los Angeles.

"You Was" (Patty Andrews and Bob Crosby). Matrix L4862. Decca 24560.

February 15, 1949, in Los Angeles with the Texas Troubadors, directed by Vic Schoen.

"Don't Rob Another Man's Castle" (with Ernest Tubb). Matrix L4897. Decca 24592.

"I'm Bitin' My Fingernails and Thinking of You" (with Ernest Tubb). Matrix L4898. Decca 24592.

February 28, 1949, in Los Angeles.

"Take Me Out to the Ballgame" (with Dan Dailey). From MGM picture *Take Me Out to the Ballgame* (1949). Matrix L4913. Decca 24605.

"In the Good Old Summertime" (with Dan Dailey). Featured in MGM picture *In the Good Old Summertime* (1949). Matrix L4914. Decca 24605.

March 11, 1949, in Los Angeles.

"I Had a Hat (When I Came In)" (with Dan Dailey). Matrix L4923. Decca 24610.

"Clancy Lowered the Boom!" (with Dan Dailey). Matrix L4924. Decca 24610.

March 17, 1949, in Los Angeles.

"Hurry! Hurry! Hurry! (Back to Me)." Matrix L4929. Decca 24613.

"I Didn't Know the Gun Was Loaded." Matrix L4930. Decca 24613.

April 4, 1949, in Los Angeles.

"Malagueña." (Based on Spanish composition by Ernesto Lecuona, 1930.) English lyrics by Mariam Banks. From the "Andalucia." Matrix L4958. Decca 24645.

"Good Times Are Comin'." Matrix L4959. (Rejected.)

April 14, 1949, in Los Angeles.

"Be-Bop Spoken Here" (Patty Andrews and Bing Crosby). Matrix L4973. Decca 24635.

"Weddin' Day" (with Bing Crosby). Matrix L4974. Decca 24635.

"Hohokus, N.J." Matrix L4975. Decca 24645.

May 10, 1949, in Los Angeles.

"The Twelve Days of Christmas" (with Bing Crosby). (Traditional Old English carol.) Adapted and arranged by Vic Schoen and the Andrews Sisters. Matrix L5004. Decca 24558.

"Here Comes Santa Claus (Right down Santa Claus Lane)" (with Bing Crosby). Matrix L5005. Decca 24658.

May 23, 1949, in Los Angeles.

"Only for Americans." From musical production *Miss Liberty*. Matrix L5002. Decca 24660.

"Homework." From musical production *Miss Liberty*. Matrix L5023. Decca 24660.

May 24, 1949, in Los Angeles with Russ Morgan's orchestra.

"Now! Now! Now! Is the Time" (with Russ Morgan). Featured in Warner Bros. picture *The Eddie Cantor Story* (1953). Matrix L5027. Decca 24664.

"Oh You Sweet One (The Schnitzelbank Song)" (with Russ Morgan). Matrix L5028. Decca 24664.

July 15, 1949, in New York with Gordon Jenkins' orchestra and chorus.

"I Can Dream, Can't I?" From musical production *Right This Way* (1937). Matrix 75074. Decca 24705.

"The Wedding of Lili Marlene." Matrix 75075. Decca 24705.

"The Windmill Song (The Windmill's Turning)." Matrix 75077. Columbia OB-50278 (released in India only).

July 19, 1949, in New York with Guy Lombardo's Royal Canadians.

"Christmas Candles." Matrix 75082. Decca 24748.

"Stars Are the Windows of Heaven." Matrix 75083. Decca 24965.

"Jolly Fella Tarantella (The Organ Grinder's Song)." (Based on Italian melody "Tarantella.") Matrix 75084. Decca 24965.

"Merry Christmas Polka." Matrix 75085. Decca 24748.

September 14, 1949, in Los Angeles.

"A Merry Christmas at Grandmother's (Over the River and through the Woods)" (with Danny Kaye). Matrix L5136. Decca 24769.

"All I Want for Christmas Is My Two Front Teeth" (Patty Andrews and Danny Kaye). Matrix L5137. Decca 24769.

October 24, 1949, in Los Angeles with Jerry Gray's orchestra.

"Why Won't Ya?" (Patty Andrews and Dick Haymes). Matrix L5158. Decca 24809.

"Wunderbar" (with Dick Haymes). From musical production *Kiss Me Kate*. Featured in MGM picture *Kiss Me Kate* (1953). Matrix L5159. Decca 24811.

October 26, 1949, in Los Angeles with Jerry Gray's orchestra.

"Time Has Come to Bid You Adieu" (with Dick Haymes). Matrix L5167. Decca 24811.

"He Rides the Range (For Republic)." From musical production *My L.A.* Matrix L5168. Decca 24809.

"Six Times a Week and Twice on Sunday." Matrix L5169. (Rejected.)

November 1, 1949, in Los Angeles.

"Open Door-Open Arms" (with the Lee Gordon Singers). (Based on
Swedish folk tune "En Dor Paa Klen.") Matrix L5176. Decca 24822.
"The Blossoms on the Bough" (with the Lee Gordon Singers). Matrix
L5177. Decca 24822.

November 3, 1949, in Los Angeles with Russ Morgan's orchestra.

"Charley, My Boy" (with Russ Morgan). Matrix L5183. Decca 24812.
"She Wore a Yellow Ribbon" (with Russ Morgan). (Based on traditional
folk song "All 'Round My Hat, I Wore a Yellow Ribbon," 1838.)
Featured in Argosy picture *She Wore a Yellow Ribbon* (released
through RKO Pictures, 1949). Matrix L5184. Decca 24812.

November 25, 1949, in Los Angeles.

"Quicksilver" (with Bing Crosby). Matrix L5215. Decca 24827.
"Have I Told You Lately that I Love You?" (with Bing Crosby). From
Republic picture *Calendar Girl* (1947). Matrix L5216. Decca 24827.

December 12, 1949, in Los Angeles.

"I See, I See (Asi Asi)" (with Carmen Miranda). Matrix L5256. Decca
24841.
"The Wedding Samba" (with Carmen Miranda). (Based on Yiddish melody
"Der Nayer Sher," 1940; originally titled "The Wedding Rhumba.")
From MGM picture *On an Island with You* (1948). Matrix L5257.
Decca 24841.

January 6, 1950, in Los Angeles with Bando Da Lua.

"Yip-Si-I-O" (with Carmen Miranda). From MGM picture *Nancy Goes to
Rio* (1950). Matrix L5312. Decca 24979.
"Ca-Room-Pa-Pa" (with Carmen Miranda). (Based on Spanish melody
"Baiao" by Luis Ganzaga and Humberto Teixeira.) From MGM
picture *Nancy Goes to Rio* (1950). Matrix L5213. Decca 24979.

**January 18, 1950, in Los Angeles with Gordon Jenkins' orchestra) and
chorus.**

"Can't We Talk It Over?" Featured in Warner Bros. picture *Illegal* (1955).
Matrix L5336. Decca 27115.
"There Will Never Be Another You." From Twentieth Century-Fox
pictures *Iceland* (1942). Featured in Twentieth Century-Fox picture
I'll Get By (1950). Matrix L5337. Decca 27115.

Discography

January 19, 1950, in Los Angeles.

"I Got No Talent" (Patty Andrews and Dick Haymes). Matrix L5340. (Rejected.)

"Can I Come in for a Second?" (Patty Andrews and Dick Haymes). Matrix L5341. Decca 24896.

"I Ought to Know More about You" (Patty Andrews and Dick Haymes). From musical production *A La Carte*. Matrix L5342. Decca 24896.

February 2, 1950, in Los Angeles with Victor Young's orchestra.

"In the Garden." (Gospel hymn.) Matrix L5369. Decca 14502. Matrix L5369 was released on Decca's Faith Series label.

"Count Your Blessings." (Gospel hymn.) Matrix L5370. Decca 14502. Matrix L5370 was released on Decca's Faith Series label.

"Softly and Tenderly (Jesus Is Calling)." (Gospel hymn.) Matrix L5371. Decca 14519. Matrix L5371 was released on Decca's Faith Series label.

"I Love to Tell the Story." (Gospel hymn.) Matrix L5372. Decca 14519. Matrix L5372 was released on Decca's Faith Series label.

February 15, 1950, in Los Angeles.

"Lock, Stock, and Barrel" (with Bing Crosby). Matrix L5390. Decca 24942.

"Ask Me No Questions (And I'll Tell You No Lies)" (with Bing Crosby). Matrix L5391. Decca 24942.

March 10, 1950, in Los Angeles.

"Muskrat Ramble." Featured in Universal picture *Walking My Baby Back Home* (1953). Matrix L5426. Decca 24991.

"Walk with a Wiggle." (Adapted to the melody of "American Patrol.") Matrix L5427. Decca 24991.

March 24, 1950, in Los Angeles.

"Life Is So Peculiar" (with Bing Crosby). From Paramount picture *Mr. Music* (1950). Matrix L5451. Decca 27173.

"High on the List" (with Bing Crosby). From Paramount picture *Mr. Music* (1950). Matrix L5452. Decca 27173.

March 28, 1950, in Los Angeles.

"I'm Gonna Paper All My Walls with Your Love Letters." Matrix L5459. Decca 24998.

"Choo'n Gum." From Twentieth Century-Fox picture *Mother Wore Tights* (1947). Matrix L5460. Decca 24998.

Discography

March 30, 1950, in Los Angeles with Gordon Jenkins' orchestra and chorus.

"I Wanna Be Loved." Matrix L5469. Decca 27007.

"I've Just Got to Get Out of the Habit." Matrix L5470. Decca 27007.

April 13, 1950, in Los Angeles with Victor Young's orchestra.

"Shall We Gather at the River?" (Gospel hymn.) Matrix L5527. Decca 14521. Matrix L5527 was released on Decca's Faith Series label.

"The Ninety and Nine." (Gospel hymn.) Matrix L5528. Decca 14521. Matrix L5528 was released on Decca's Faith Series label.

"Brighten the Corner." (Gospel hymn.) Matrix L5529. Decca 14522. Matrix L5529 was released on Decca's Faith Series label.

"Let the Lower Lights Be Burning." (Gospel hymn.) Matrix L5530. Decca 14522. Matrix L5530 was released on Decca's Faith Series label.

"Cleanse Me." (Gospel hymn.) Matrix L5531. (Rejected.)

"Blest Be the Tie that Binds." (Gospel hymn.) Matrix L5532. (Rejected.)

April 18, 1950, in Los Angeles.

"The Old Piano Roll Blues" (with Al Jolson). Featured in MGM picture *Rich, Young and Pretty* (1951). Matrix L554. Decca 27024.

"Way Down Yonder in New Orleans" (with Al Jolson). From musical production *Spices of 1922*. Featured in RKO picture *The Story of Vernon and Irene Castle* (1939), Columbia picture *Is Everybody Happy?* (1943), and Paramount picture *Somebody Loves Me* (1952). Matrix L5555. Decca 27024.

July 17, 1950, in New York.

"Sleigh Ride" (with chorus). Matrix 76646. Decca 27310.

July 18, 1950, in New York.

"The Telephone Song." Matrix 76660. Decca 27310.

"I Wish I Knew (You Really Loved Me)" (with male chorus). Matrix 76661. Decca 27421.

August 14, 1950, in New York with Guy Lombardo's Royal Canadians.

"A Rainy Day Refrain (Dadim Dadom Dadim Dadom)." Matrix 76699. Decca 27202.

"The Glory of Love." Matrix 76700. Decca 27202.

September 7, 1950, in Los Angeles.

"(The Toys Gave a Party for) Poppa Santa Claus" (with Bing Crosby). Matrix L5829. Decca 27228.

"Mele Kalikimaka (Merry Christmas)" (with Bing Crosby). Matrix L5830. Decca 27228.

"If I Were a Bell" (Patty Andrews and Bing Crosby). From musical production *Guys and Dolls*. Featured in Samuel Goldwyn picture *Guys and Dolls* (1955). Matrix L5831. Decca 27232.

September 15, 1950, in Los Angeles.

"Jing-a-Ling Jing-a-Ling." (Based on theme melody from Walt Disney's *Beaver Valley*, 1950.) Matrix L5841. Decca 27242.

"Parade of the Wooden Soldiers." (Based on German composition "Die Parade Der Holz Soldaten Zinnsoldaten," 1905.) Matrix L5842. Decca 27242.

"Guys and Dolls." From musical production *Guys and Dolls*. Featured in Samuel Goldwyn picture *Guys and Dolls* (1955). Matrix L5843. Decca 27252.

September 20, 1950, in Los Angeles.

"(Sweet Angie) The Christmas Tree Angel." Matrix L5846. Decca 27251.

"I'd Like to Hitch a Ride with Santa Claus." Matrix L5847. Decca 27251.

"A Bushel and a Peck." From musical production *Guys and Dolls*. Featured in Samuel Goldwyn picture *Guys and Dolls* (1955). Matrix L5848. Decca 27252.

September 28, 1950, in Los Angeles.

"Ching-Ara-Sa-Sa" (with Danny Kaye). Matrix L5858. Decca 27261.

"Orange Colored Sky" (Patty Andrews and Danny Kaye). Matrix L5859. Decca 27261.

December 14, 1950, in Los Angeles.

"Zing Zing-Zoom Zoom" (with male chorus). Matrix L5955. Decca 27414.

"A Penny a Kiss—A Penny a Hug" (with male chorus). Matrix L5956. Decca 27414.

December 19, 1950, in Los Angeles.

"Between Two Trees" (with male chorus). Matrix L5966. Decca 27421.

"All the World to Me (You Are)" (with male chorus). Matrix L5967. Decca 27878. "All the World to Me (You Are)" on Matrix L5967 was the flip side of a re-release of the trio's 1945 recording of "The Blond Sailor."

"Nobody's Darling but Mine." Matrix L5968. Decca 27834. "Nobody's Darling but Mine" featured guitar rhythm accompaniment.

Discography

January 4, 1951, in Los Angeles with Tommy Dorsey's orchestra.

"I Used to Love You (But It's All Over Now)." Matrix L5982. Decca 27700.

"Pass the Basket." Matrix L5983. (Rejected.)

January 19, 1951, in Los Angeles.

"I Remember Mama." Matrix L6009. Decca 27437.

"Love Sends a Little Gift of Roses." Matrix L6010. Decca 28929.

"My Mom." Matrix L6011. Decca 27537.

"This Little Piggie Went to Market." (Based on "This Little Piggy Went to Market.") Matrix L6012. Decca 28929.

February 1, 1951, in Los Angeles.

"Black Ball Ferry Line" (with Bing Crosby). Matrix L6030. Decca 27631.

"The Yodeling Ghost" (with Bing Crosby). Matrix L6031. Decca 27631.

February 8, 1951, in Los Angeles.

"Forsaking All Others" (with Bing Crosby). Matrix L6044. Decca 27477.

"Sparrow in the Tree Top" (with Bing Crosby). Matrix l6055. Decca 27477.

March 19, 1951, in Los Angeles.

"Goodbye Darling, Hello Friend (C'est Fini)." (Based on French melody "C'est Fini.") Matrix L6165. Decca 27834.

"Gotta Find Somebody to Love" (with male trio). Matrix L6166. Decca 27569.

March 20, 1951, in Los Angeles with Victor Young's orchestra.

"Too Young" (Patty). Matrix L6172. Decca 27569.

April 6, 1951, in Los Angeles with Sonny Burke's orchestra.

"The Mambo Man." Matrix L6210. Decca 28483.

April 7, 1951, in Los Angeles with Desi Arnaz's orchestra.

"Old Don Juan" (with Desi Arnaz). Matrix L6213. Decca 28483.

April 26, 1951, in Nashville.

"Satins and Lace" (with Red Foley). Matrix 80939. Decca 27609.

"Bury Me beneath the Willow" (with Red Foley). Matrix 80940. Decca 29222.

"Where Is Your Wandering Mother Tonight?" (with Red Foley). Matrix 80942. Decca 28163.

"I Want to Be with You Always" (with Red Foley). Matrix 80942. Decca 27609.

"Hang Your Head in Shame" (with Red Foley). Matrix 80943. Decca 28163.

"Unless You're Free" (Patty Andrews and Red Foley). Matrix 80944. Decca 28767.

April 27, 1951, in Nashville.

"He Bought My Soul at Calvary" (with Red Foley). (Gospel hymn.) Matrix 80945. Decca 14566. Matrix 80945, Decca 14566, was released on Decca's Faith Series label.

"It Is No Secret (What God Can Do)" (with Red Foley). (Gospel hymn.) Matrix 80946. Decca 14566. Matrix 80946, Decca 14566, was released on Decca's Faith Series label.

"Baby Blues" (Patty Andrews and Red Foley). Matrix 80947. Decca 28767.

"She'll Never Know" (with Red Foley). Matrix 80948. Decca 29222.

May 26, 1951, in Los Angeles with Gordon Jenkins' orchestra and chorus.

"I'm in Love Again" (Patty). Featured in musical productions *The Greenwich Village Follies* and *Up with the Lark*. Featured in Warner Bros. picture *Night and Day* (1946). Matrix L6290. Decca 27635. Decca Records was in error when it released Decca 27635—Matrix L6290 and Matrix L6291—listing the Andrews Sisters as vocalists; both recordings were solos by Patty Andrews.

"It Never Entered My Mind" (Patty). Matrix L6291. Decca 27635. Decca Records was in error when it released Decca 27635—Matrix L6290 and Matrix L6291—listing the Andrews Sisters as vocalists; both recordings were solos by Patty Andrews.

June 8, 1951, in New York with Guy Lombardo's Royal Canadians.

"There Was a Night on the Waters." Matrix 81144. Decca 27652.

"Dimples and Cherry Cheeks" (with Kenny Gardner). Matrix 81145. Decca 27652.

July 3, 1951, in Los Angeles with Victor Young's Singing Strings and Tommy Dorsey on trombone.

"How Many Times (Can I Fall in Love?)" (Patty). Matrix L6343. Decca 27700.

August 16, 1951, in London.

"Love Is Such a Cheat." Matrix 81420. Decca 27760.
"Lying in the Hay (Couches Dans Le Foin)." Matrix 81421. Decca 27760.

October 12, 1951, in New York with Paul Nealson's orchestra.

"Our Love Is Here to Stay" (Patty). From Samuel Goldwyn-United Artists
    picture *The Goldwyn Follies* (1938). Featured in MGM picture *An
    American in Paris* (1951). Matrix 81674. Decca 27845.
"It's All Over but the Memories" (Patty). Matrix 81675. Decca 27845.

October 22, 1951, in New York with Guy Lombardo's Royal Canadians.

"Play Me a Hurtin' Tune." Matrix 81747. Decca 27910.
"I'm on a Seesaw of Love." Matrix 81748. Decca 27910.

October 24, 1951, in New York with Sy Oliver's orchestra.

"Piccolo Pete." From Radio picture *The Vagabond Lover* (1929). Matrix
    81766. Decca 28481.
"East of the Sun." Matrix 81767. Decca 28482.
"Dreams Come Tumbling Down." Matrix 81768. Decca 28116.

**October 24, 1951, in New York with Gordon Jenkins' orchestra and
chorus.**

"The Three Bells (The Jimmy Brown Song)." (Based on French melody
    "Les Trois Cloches" by Jean Villard, 1945.) English adaption by Bert
    Reisfeld. Arranged by Gordon Jenkins and the Andrews Sisters.
    Matrix 81771. Decca 27853.
"The Windmill Song." Matrix 81772. Decca 27853.

**December 6, 1951, in Los Angeles with Gordon Jenkins' orchestra and
chorus.**

"If You Go" (Patty). (Based on French melody "Si Tu Partais.") Featured
    in RKO picture *Night without Stars* (1953). Matrix L6558. Decca
    27913.
"That's How a Love Song Is Born" (Patty). Matrix L6559. Decca 17913.

January 22, 1952, in Los Angeles with Richard Gail's orchestra.

"Wondering" (with the Mellomen). Matrix L6618. Decca 27979.
"Poor Whip-poor-will (Move Over, Move Over)" (with the Mellomen).
    Matrix L6619. Decca 27979.

Discography

February 4, 1952, in Los Angeles with George Cates' orchestra.

"That Everlovin' Rag." Matrix L6631. Decca 28042.

"Music Lessons." Matrix L6632. Decca 28116.

February 8, 1952, in Los Angeles with Russ Morgan's orchestra.

"Wabash Blues." Matrix L6633. Decca 28143.

"Linger Awhile." From Universal picture *King of Jazz* (1930). Featured in Twentieth Century-Fox pictures *Give My Regards to Broadway* (1948) and *Belles on Their Toes* (1952). Matrix L6634. Decca 28143.

February 11, 1952, in Los Angeles with Skip Martin's orchestra.

"Sing! Sing! Sing!" Featured in MGM picture *Strike Up the Band* (1940). Featured in Universal picture *The Benny Goodman Story* (1956). Matrix L6635. Decca 28480.

"Don't Be That Way." Featured in Universal picture *The Benny Goodman Story* (1956). Matrix L6636. Decca 28480.

February 15, 1952, in Los Angeles with Nelson Riddle's orchestra.

"I'll Walk Alone" (Patty). From Universal picture *Follow the Boys* (1944). Featured in Twentieth Century-Fox picture *With a Song in My Heart* (1952). Matrix L6645. Decca 28038.

"That's the Chance You Take" (Patty). Matrix L6646. Decca 28038.

February 15, 1952, in Los Angeles with George Cates' orchestra.

"Why Worry?" Matrix L6651. Decca 28042.

February 21, 1952, in Los Angeles with John Scott Trotter's orchestra.

"I'll Si-Si Ya in Bahia" (with Bing Crosby). From Paramount picture *Just for You* (1952). Matrix L6658. Decca 28256.

"The Live Oak Tree" (with Bing Crosby). From Paramount picture *Just for You* (1952). Matrix L6659. Decca 28256.

May 1, 1952, in Los Angeles with Nelson Riddle's orchestra.

"Here in My Heart" (with Dick Haymes). Matrix L6744. Decca 28213.

"I'm Sorry" (with Dick Haymes). Matrix L6744. Decca 28213.

May 20, 1952, in Los Angeles with Danny Stewart's Islanders.

"Goodnight, Aloha" (with Alfred Apaka). Matrix L6744. Decca 28297.

"My Isle of Golden Dreams" (with Alfred Apaka). Matrix L6745. Decca 28294.

"Nalani" (with Alfred Apaka). Matrix L6746. Decca 28294.

Discography

May 22, 1952, in Los Angeles with Danny Stewart's Islanders.

"The Cockeyed Mayor of Kaunakakai." Matrix L6782. Decca 28295.

"The King's Serenade (Imi Au Ia Oe)" (with Alfred Apaka). (Based on Hawaiian melody "Imi Au Ia Oe.") Matrix L6783. Decca 28295.

"Ke Kali Nei Au (Waiting for Thee)" (Patty Andrews and Alfred Apaka). (Also known as "The Hawaiian Wedding Song.") Matrix L6784. Decca 28296. The flip side of Matrix L6784, Decca 28296, was a recording of "Fair Hawaii," Matrix L6777, a solo by Alfred Apaka.

"Malahini Mele" (Patty Andrews and Alfred Apaka). Matrix L6785. Decca 28297.

May 26, 1952, in Los Angeles with Nelson Riddle's orchestra.

"One for the Wonder" (with the Mellomen). Matrix L6793. Decca 28276.

"Idle Chatter." (Based on "The Dance of the Hours" from *La Gioconda*.) Matrix L6794. Decca 28276.

July 5, 1952, in Los Angeles with Nelson Riddle's orchestra.

"Carmen's Boogie." (Based on "The Habanera" from *Carmen*.) Matrix L6836. Decca 28342.

July 5, 1952, in Los Angeles with Skip Martin's orchestra.

"In the Mood." Featured in Twentieth Century-Fox picture *Sun Valley Serenade* (1941) and Universal picture *The Glenn Miller Story* (1954). Matrix L6837. Decca 28482.

July 11, 1952, in Los Angeles with Skip Martin's orchestra.

"Adios." Featured in Universal picture *The Glenn Miller Story* (1954). Matrix L6838. Decca 28342.

"If I Had a Boy Like You." Matrix L6839. Decca 28482.

September 5, 1952, in Los Angeles with Matty Matlock's orchestra.

"South Rampart Street Parade" (with Bing Crosby). Featured in Universal picture *Walking My Baby Back Home* (1953). Matrix L6870. Decca 28419.

"Cool Water" (with Bing Crosby). Featured in Republic pictures *Hands across the Border* (1943) and *Along the Navajo Trail* (1945). Matrix L6871. Decca 28419.

October 22, 1952, in Los Angeles.

"No Deposit, No Return." Matrix L6913. Decca 28492.

"You Blew Me a Kiss" (Patty). Matrix L6914. Decca 28492.

Discography

March 23, 1953, in Los Angeles with Matty Matlock's orchestra.

"Fugue for Tinhorns." From musical production *Guys and Dolls*. Featured in Samuel Goldwyn picture *Guys and Dolls* (1955). Matrix L7102. Decca 28680.

"Now That I'm in Love." (Based on Gioacchino Rossini's "The William Tell Overture.") Matrix L7103. Decca 28680.

June 23, 1953, in Los Angeles.

"You Too, You Too." Matrix L7267. Decca 28773.

"Tegucigalpa." Matrix L7268. Decca 28773.

August 22, 1953, in Los Angeles with Jack Pleis's orchestra.

"I Forgot More than You'll Ever Know about Him" (Patty). Matrix L7314. Decca 28852.

"What Happened to You?" (Patty). Matrix L7315. Decca 28852.

November 11, 1953, in Los Angeles with Sonny Burke's orchestra.

"My Love, the Blues, and Me." Matrix L7463. Decca 29149.

"There's a Rainbow in the Valley." Matrix L7464. Decca 29149.

December 23, 1954, in Los Angeles with Joseph Lilley's orchestra.

"Dissertation on the State of Bliss (Love and Learn)" (Patty Andrews with Bing Crosby). Featured in Paramount picture *Take It Big* (1944). Matrix L8071. Decca 29409

April 21, 1955, in Los Angeles.

"It's Bigger than Both of Us" (Patty Andrews with Jimmy Durante). Matrix L8351. Decca 29537.

Victory Discs, 1943-1945

128–B: "Lullaby of Broadway" and "Is You Is or Is You Ain't (Ma' Baby?)" (with Mitchell Ayres' orchestra).

194: "Down in the Valley" and "Straighten Up and Fly Right" (with Vic Schoen's orchestra); "Sing a Tropical Song" and a hits medley ("Bei Mir Bist Du Schon"/"Well, All Right!"/"Hold Tight-Hold Tight"/"Beer Barrel Polka"/"Boogie Woogie Bugle Boy"/"Apple Blossom Time"/ "Pennsylvania Polka"/"Strip Polka"/"The Vict'ry Polka"—with Mitchell Ayres' orchestra).

196: "Don't Blame Me" and "Corns for My Country" (with Vic Schoen's orchestra).

259–B: "Twilight on the Trail" (Patty) and "Red River Valley" (with the Riders of the Purple Sage and Vic Schoen's orchestra).

452–A: "The Three Caballeros" and "The Vict'ry Polka" (with Vic Schoen's orchestra).

526–B: "Boogie Woogie Bugle Boy" (with Vic Schoen's orchestra) and "Home" (with Mitchell Ayres' orchestra).

570–B: "Put That Ring on My Finger," "The Blond Sailor," "Hollywood Canteen," and "Don't Blame Me" (with Vic Schoen's orchestra).

579: "Money Is the Root of All Evil" (with Vic Schoen's orchestra).

Decca 10" Albums, 1949-1953

The Andrews Sisters: Maxene, Patty, LaVerne (with Vic Schoen's orchestra). Released in November 1949. DL-5120.

The Andrews Sisters: Club 15 (with Dick Haymes and Jerry Gray's orchestra). Released in January 1950. DL-5055.

The Andrews Sisters: Tropical Songs (with Vic Schoen's orchestra and Bob Crosby's Bobcats). Released in February 1950. DL-5065.

The Andrews Sisters: Irving Berlin Songs (with Vic Schoen's orchestra). Released in November 1950. DL-5264.

The Andrews Sisters: Christmas Cheer (with Bing Crosby, Danny Kaye, Vic Schoen's orchestra, and Guy Lombardo's Royal Canadians). Released in November 1950. DL-5282.

The Andrews Sisters: Go West, Young Man (with Bing Crosby and Vic Schoen's orchestra). Released in January 1951. DL-5302.

The Andrews Sisters: Gospel Songs (with Victor Young's orchestra). Released in May 1951. DL-5360.

The Andrews Sisters: My Isle of Golden Dreams (with Alfred Apaka and Danny Stewart's Islanders). Released in August 1952. DL-5423.

The Andrews Sisters: Sing! Sing! Sing! (with Desi Arnaz and his orchestra, Sy Oliver's orchestra, Sonny Burke's orchestra, and Skip Martin's orchestra). Released in February 1953. DL-5438.

Capitol Singles, 1955-1959

"Without Love," Featured in MGM picture *Silk Stockings*, 1957, and "Where To, My Love?" (Patty Andrews with Nelson Riddle's orchestra). 1955. Capitol F-3159.

"Suddenly, There's a Valley" and "Boog-a-Da-Woog" (Patty Andrews with Harold Mooney's orchestra). 1955. Capitol F-3228.

"The Rains Came Down" and "I'll Forgive You" (Patty Andrews with Harold Mooney's orchestra). 1955. Capitol F-3268.

"I Never Will Marry" and "Daybreak Blues" (Patty Andrews with Harold Mooney's orchestra). 1956. Capitol F-3344.

"A Friendship Ring" and "Music Drives Me Crazy" (Patty Andrews with Frank DeVol's orchestra). 1956. Capitol F-3403.

"Too Old To Rock-n-Roll" and "Broken" (Patty Andrews with Frank DeVol's orchestra). 1956. Capitol F-3495.

"Crazy Arms" and "I Want to Linger" (with Vic Schoen's orchestra). 1956. Capitol F-3567.

"Silver Bells" and "A Child's Christmas Song" (with Lynn Murray's orchestra and Robert Mitchell's choir). 1957. Capitol F-3583.

"Rum and Coca Cola" (with Vic Schoen's orchestra) and "No, Baby!" (with Billy May's orchestra). 1957. Capitol F-3658.

"Stars, Stars, Stars" (with Gordon Jenkins' orchestra and chorus) and "Give Me Back My Heart" (with Billy May's orchestra). 1957. Capitol F-3707.

"I'm Going Home" (with Vic Schoen's orchestra) and "By His Word" (with Gordon Jenkins' orchestra and chorus). 1957. Capitol F-3784.

"One Mistake" and "Melancholy Moon" (with Bob Thompson's orchestra). 1958. Capitol F-3869.

"Torrero" and "Sunshine." 1958. Capitol F-3965.

"My Love Is a Kitten" and "I've Got an Invitation to a Dance" (with Jack Marshall's orchestra). 1959. Capitol F-4144.

Capitol Albums, 1957-1958

The Andrews Sisters in Hi-Fi (with Vic Schoen's orchestra). Released in 1957. Capitol W-790. "Bei Mir Bist Du Schon," "Beer Barrel Polka," "Rum and Coca Cola," "Rancho Pillow," "Tu-Li-Tulip Time," "Shoo Shoo Baby," "Beat Me Daddy, Eight to the Bar," "Don't Sit under the Apple Tree," "Apple Blossom Time," "Ti-Pi-Tin," "Hold Tight-Hold Tight," "Aurora," "Boogie Woogie Bugle Boy," "Begin the Beguine," "Well, All Right!," "Ferryboat Serenade."

The Andrews Sisters: Fresh and Fancy Free (with Billy May's orchestra). Released in 1957. Capitol T-860. "The Song Is You" (from musical production *Music in the Air*; featured in Twentieth Century-Fox picture *Music in the Air,* 1934), "You Do Something to Me" (from musical production *Fifty-Million Frenchmen;* featured in Warner Bros. pictures *Night and Day,* 1946, and *Starlift,* 1951; MGM picture *Because You're Mine,* 1952, Twentieth Century-Fox picture *Can Can,* 1960, and Universal picture *Evil under the Sun,* 1982), "Comes Love," "Nevertheless" (from MGM picture *Three Little Word,* 1950), "With Every Breath I Take," "Of Thee I Sing" (from musical production *Of Thee I Sing*), "Hooray for Love" (from RKO picture *Hooray for Love*, 1935), "My Romance," "Tea for Two" (from musical production *No No Nanette*; featured in First National picture *No No Nanette*, 1930, RKO picture *No No Nanette*, 1940, Warner Bros. picture *Tea for Two*, 1950, Twentieth Century-Fox picture *With a Song in My Heart*, 1952, and Warner Bros. picture *Sincerely Yours*, 1955), "I Could Write a Book" (from musical production *Pal Joey*; featured in Columbia picture *Pal Joey*, 1957), "Let There Be Love," "Younger than Springtime" (from musical production *South Pacific*; featured in Twentieth Century-Fox picture *South Pacific*, 1958).

The Andrews Sisters: The Dancing 20's (with Billy May's orchestra). Released in 1958. Capitol T-973. "Don't Bring Lulu," "Me Too," "That Naughty Waltz," "A Smile Will Go a Long, Long Way," "Barney Google," "Collegiate," "Last Night on the Back Porch," "When Francis Dances with Me," "Back in Your Own Backyard," "Keep Your Skirts Down, Maryann," "The Japanese Sandman," "Show Me the Way to Go Home."

More Singles, 1959-1961

"I've Got to Pass Your House" and "One, Two, Three, Four" (with Richard Wolf's orchestra). Recorded in 1959. Kapp Records 309X.

"Sailor" and "Goodnight and Good Dreaming" (with Bernard Ebbinghouse's orchestra). Recorded in 1961. Decca Records 11316.

Dot Albums, 1962-1967

The Greatest Hits of the Andrews Sisters, vol. 1 (with Billy Vaughn's orchestra). Released in 1962. Dot 25406. "Apple Blossom Time," "Beer Barrel Polka," "Beat Me Daddy, Eight to the Bar," "I Can Dream, Can't I?," "Pennsylvania Polka," "Hold Tight-Hold Tight," "Rum and Coca Cola," "Down in the Valley," "Bei Mir Bist Du Schon," "The Shrine of Saint Cecilia," "Rhumboogie," "Joseph! Joseph!"

Great Golden Hits of the Andrews Sisters (with Vic Schoen's orchestra). Released in 1962. Dot 25452. "Ti-Pi-Tin," "The Old Piano Roll Blues," "Near You," "Pistol Packin' Mama," "Don't Fence Me In,"" "Oh, Johnny! Oh, Johnny! Oh!," "Oh! Ma-Ma!," "I Wanna Be Loved," "Aurora," "The Irish Twist," "Daddy," "Boogie Woogie Bugle Boy."

The Andrews Sisters Present (with Don Trenner's orchestra). Released in 1963. Dot 25529. "Mr. Bass Man," "I Left My Heart in San Francisco," "Can't Get Used to Losing You," "Gravy Waltz," "Still,"

"Those Lazy, Hazy, Crazy Days of Summer," "Watermelon Man," "I Love You Because," "The End of the World," "The Doodle Song," "Puff! The Magic Dragon," "Sukiyaki (My First Lonely Night)."

The Greatest Hits of the Andrews Sisters, vol. 2 (with Allyn Furgeson's orchestra). Released in 1964. Dot 25543. "Don't Sit under the Apple Tree," "Nobody's Darling but Mine," "Cuanto la Gusta," "In the Mood," "Cool Water," "Three Little Fishies," "Get Your Kicks on Route 66!," "You Are My Sunshine," "Ciribiribin," "Sonny Boy," "Say Si Si," "Sabre Dance."

The Andrews Sisters: Great Country Hits. Released in 1964. Dot 25567. "Ragtime Cowboy Joe" (from Twentieth Century-Fox picture *Hello, Frisco, Hello,* 1943; featured in Paramount picture *Incendiary Blonde,* 1945), "The Tennessee Waltz," "Your Cheatin' Heart," "Sioux City Sue," "Mexicali Rose" (from Paramount picture *Rhythm on the Range,* 1936; featured in Republic picture *Mexicali Rose,* 1939, and Columbia picture *Barbed Wire,* 1952), "Jealous Heart," "Wabash Cannonball," "My Happiness," "Cold, Cold Heart," "Careless Hands," "Bouquet of Roses," "I'm Thinking Tonight of My Blue Eyes."

The Andrews Sisters Go Hawaiian. Released in 1965. Dot 25632. "My Little Grass Shack," "My Isle of Golden Dreams," "Song of the Islands," "Drifting and Dreaming," "Sweet Lelani," "Hawaii," "Cocoanut Grove," "To You, Sweetheart, Aloha," "Beyond the Reef," "The Hawaiian Wedding Song," "Hawaiian Sunset," "Blue Hawaii."

The Andrews Sisters: Favorite Hymns (with orchestra directed by Walter Weschler). Released in 1965. Hamilton (division of Dot) HL-12154. "Nearer My God to Thee," "Fling Out the Banner," "I Believe," "In the Garden," "Beautiful Isle of Somewhere," "Whispering Hope," "Just a Closer Walk with Thee," "Abide with Me," "Rock of Ages," "Jesus Calls Us," "It Is No Secret (What God Can Do)," "The Old Rugged Cross."

The Andrews Sisters: Great Performers. This album was released by Dot Records shortly after LaVerne's death. It contains the last known recordings of the original Andrews Sisters. Released in 1967. Dot 25807. "Theme from *A Man and a Woman,*" "Everybody Wants to Be Loved," "Theme from *Come September,*" "Is It Really Over?," "Dixie," "Satin Doll," "All the Colors of the Rainbow," "I Forgot More than You'll Ever Know about Him," "Rose's Theme," "Wild Is Love."

Discography

More Album Releases, 1974-1985

Over Here! Released in 1974. Columbia KS-32961. (Also available on cassette and compact disc.) "Overture: The Beat Begins" (The Big Band), "Since You're Not Around" (Jim Weston and company), "Over Here!" (the Andrews Sisters and company), "Buy a Victory Bond" (company), "Charlie's Place" (Maxene Andrews and company), "Hey, Yvette/The Grass Grows Greener" (Douglass Watson, William Griffis, and MacIntyre Dixon), "My Dream for Tomorrow" (April Shawhan and John Driver), "The Good Time Girl" (Patty Andrews and company), "Wait for Me, Marlena" (Janie Sell and company), "We Got It!" (the Andrews Sisters with Janie Sell and company), "Wartime Wedding" (the Andrews Sisters and company), "Don't Shoot the Hooey to Me, Louie" (Samuel E. Wright), "Where Did the Good Times Go?" (Patty Andrews), "Dream Drummin'/Soft Music" (John Travolta, Phyllis Somerville, the Big Band, and company), "The Big Beat" (the Andrews Sisters with Janie Sell), "No Goodbyes" (the Andrews Sisters and company).

The Andrews Sisters: Rarities. In 1980, MCA Records released this album of the Andrews Sisters' Decca recordings, all of which were previously unreleased takes of test recordings, alternate takes, and studio rejections. MCA-908. (Also available on cassette and compact disc.) "Beat Me Daddy, Eight to the Bar" (rejected), "Six Jerks in a Jeep" (rejected), "You're Just a Flower from an Old Bouquet" (rejected), "Long Time No See" (rejected), "I Love You Much Too Much" (rejected), "Boogie Woogie Bugle Boy" (alternate take), "Lullaby to a Jitterbug" (rejected), "Six Times a Week and Twice on Sunday" (rejected), "Hit the Road" (rejected), "Don't Fence Me In" (alternate take).

Maxene—An Andrews Sister. In 1985, Bainbridge Records released this album of solos by Maxene Andrews. BTC-6258. (Also available on cassette and compact disc.) "I Suppose," "Mama Llama," "Where Did the Good Times Go?," "Bei Mir Bist Du Schon"/"Don't Sit under the Apple Tree"/"Pennsylvania Polka"/"Beer Barrel Polka," "How Deep Is the Ocean?," "Show Me the Way to Go Home," "Apple Blossom Time," "You're My Everything," "Sweet and Slow," "Nature's Toys," "Remember," "Fascinating Rhythm."

Discography

Miscellaneous Album Releases, 1956-1990

The Andrews Sisters: At Their Very Best. Capitol/Pair PDL-21159. This
double selection is a collection of the trio's mid-1950s recordings for
Capitol of their greatest Decca hits, including "Begin the Beguine"
and "Apple Blossom Time." (Also available on cassette and compact
disc.)

The Andrews Sisters: At the Microphone. Take Two TT-305. This excellent
compilation features never-before-released radio material. Most of
the selections are taken from the trio's *Musical Showroom* broadcasts
for Nash-Kelvinator on CBS, 1945–1946. These include terrific
arrangements of "On the Atchison, Topeka, and the Santa Fe," "Blue
Skies," and "Personality." The remaining selections feature *Club 15*
transcriptions of "Malagueña," "Cruising Down the River," and "Let
a Smile Be Your Umbrella." Vocal assistance comes from Curt
Massey, the Ambassadors, and Bob Crosby. This has good audio.
Great package!

The Andrews Sisters: Beat Me Daddy, Eight to the Bar. MCA MFP-50556.
This Music for Pleasure compilation of the trio's hits includes many
Dot recordings, as opposed to the originals from Decca. The jacket is
attractive, but the audio is poor, especially on such takes as "Strip
Polka" and "South American Way."

The Andrews Sisters: Boogie Woogie Bugle Girls. MCA 27082. Originally
issued on Paramount Records (PAS-6075), this release offers much
of the same material found on the aforementioned MCA-27081, as
well as hits like "Daddy" and "Three Little Fishies." (Also available
on cassette.)

The Andrews Sisters by Popular Demand. Decca DL-8360. One of the first
twelve-inch compilations by Decca, this album features some of the
trio's best-selling hits, including "Boogie Woogie Bugle Boy" and
"Down in the Valley."

The Andrews Sisters: Christmas. MCA 20415. This 1987 release features ten
of the trio's Christmas recordings for Decca, including five hits with
Bing Crosby and one track with Danny Kaye. This issue is dedicated
to thirty-one-year-old Laird Forsmark, who died from heart failure
prior to the disc's release. Forsmark was a devoted fan of the
Andrews Sisters, and he supplied MCA with a rare 1942 photo of
the trio posing with Santa Claus, to which the company added color.
The photograph is included on the back cover of the album. (Also
available on cassette and compact disc.)

The Andrews Sisters: Golden Greats. MCA MCM-5015. This 1985 London
import contains sixteen of the trio's best-selling Decca hits, most of

them in pristine sound. Includes "The House of Blue Lights" and "Strip Polka."

The Andrews Sisters' Greatest Hits. Decca 74919. This album provides the listener with twelve of the trio's most identifiable Decca recordings, although "Boogie Woogie Bugle Boy" is surprisingly omitted.

The Andrews Sisters: In the Mood. Famous Twinsets PAS-21023. This double selection offers a varied sampling of the trio's recordings for Dot Records in the 1960s. Aside from re-recordings of their Decca hits, the album includes "The Tennessee Waltz," "Blue Hawaii," "Three Little Fishies," "Dixie," and "The Hawaiian Wedding Song."

The Andrews Sisters Live! Andros ANDS-4566. This release is currently one of two that contain television material: *The Sammy Davis, Jr. Show,* 1966, featuring the Andrews Sisters singing a hits medley with Diana Ross and the Supremes; *The Dean Martin Show,* 1967, featuring Maxene and Patty with Joyce DeYoung, LaVerne's replacement. The remaining selections are comprised of radio material, most of which is with Bing Crosby. Selections include "One Meat Ball," "Great Day," "Heartbreaker," and "May the Good Lord Bless and Keep You," featuring the trio with Bing Crosby and Nat Cole.

The Andrews Sisters: Near You. Vocalion VL-3622; MCA-739. This impressive release first surfaced on the Vocalion label, a division of Decca Records, and it was later re-released by MCA. This installment offers more of the trio's best-selling hits, without repeating the very obvious. Along with the title tune (a top-ten hit for the trio in 1947), there is lyrical material ("I Don't Know Why" and "How Lucky You Are"), boogie woogie ("Carmen's Boogie"), a wartime ballad ("The Blond Sailor"), calypso ("Sing a Tropical Song"), two numbers with Russ Morgan ("She Wore a Yellow Ribbon" and "Charley, My Boy"), sing-along ("One for the Wonder" with the Mellomen), and even a Broadway hit ("A Bushel and a Peck"). A nice sampling of the trio's musical range, this release also has excellent sound quality, despite the stereo-enhancing procedures. (Also available on cassette.)

The Andrews Sisters: On the Air. Pelican LP-123. This mid-1970s release features vocal selections from the trio's *Eight-to-the-Bar* radio series (1944–1945). Most of the selections on this release are live radio transcriptions, but some (including "Scrub Me Mama with a Boogie Beat" with Carmen Miranda) are rehearsal takes that were never aired. Nineteen songs in all, including "Come to Baby, Do," "June Is Busting Out All Over," "Ac-cent-tchu-ate the Positive," and "Sweet Molly Malone" (with Patty solo).

Discography

The Andrews Sisters: Pistol Packin' Mama. Sears SPS-451. This 1968 release offers a little bit of everything from the trio's Dot years (1962–1966). Selections range from novelty ("Three Little Fishies") to country-western ("Bouquet of Roses"), from ballads ("I Wanna Be Loved") to Hawaiian numbers ("Cocoanut Grove" and "My Little Grass Shack").

The Andrews Sisters: Rum and Coca Cola. Hep HN-4131. This Holland import is an exact reproduction of *The Andrews Sisters' Greatest Hits* (Decca 74919).

The Andrews Sisters Show/The Andrews Sisters on the Air. Radiola MR-1033. Side 1 of this release features the debut show, December 31, 1944, of the trio's Eight-to-the-Bar radio series, featuring guest Bing Crosby (the pilot of the show was aired one week earlier and featured Frank Sinatra). Side 2 features eleven songs taken from various radio shows (1945–1950), mostly from the girls' *Club 15* series with Bob Crosby and Dick Haymes. Included in this release are live performances of "The Trolley Song," "Saturday Night," "Sonny Boy" (with Bob Hope), a comical "Feudin' and Fightin'," and a brilliant performance of "Sabre Dance" from *Club 15.* (Also available on cassette and compact disc.)

The Andrews Sisters: Sing! Sing! Sing! MFP-5851. Music for Pleasure released this 1987 import, offering a nice jacket and sixteen original Decca hits. Although MCA ought to locate a better copy of "The Coffee Song," the remaining tracks are all of excellent sound quality. The title song is included, as well as "I've Got a Gal in Kalamazoo" and "Pennsylvania 6–5000." This is an exceptional package. (Also available on cassette and compact disc.)

The Andrews Sisters: Sing! Sing! Sing! Pickwick SPC-3382. This re-issue from Pickwick of the trio's 1952 Decca album of the same name offers eight enjoyable tunes. Among the selections are a swinging "In the Mood," a soft and mellow "East of the Sun," the title tune, and "Old Don Juan," with vocal assistance from Desi Arnaz.

The Andrews Sisters Sing W.W.II and Win! Official 12008. This second Denmark release concentrates on the trio's World War II hits (1941–1945), including "East of the Rockies," "Here Comes the Navy," "Put That Ring on My Finger," and "Any Bonds Today?" Dick Haymes assists on two tracks ("Great Day" and "Smile! Smile! Smile!"). Great material, less-than-great audio. (Also available on cassette.)

The Andrews Sisters: Sirens of Swing. Historia H-638. This German import traces the trio's early years at Decca, and it includes such rare items as "One, Two, Three O'Leary," but the sound quality is extremely poor on all takes.

Discography

The Andrews Sisters: Sixteen Great Performances. MCA 27081. Originally
available on ABC Records (ABDP-4003), this release was re-issued
by MCA, and it features the trio's early 1960s Dot re-recordings of
their greatest Decca hits, including "Pistol Packin' Mama" and "Don't
Sit under the Apple Tree." (Also available on cassette.)

The Andrews Sisters: Swinging Sweethearts. German MCA 52021. This
import provides a very nice selection of Andrews Sisters hits,
featuring some hard-to-find cuts, including "Carioca," "Muskrat
Ramble," and "Linger Awhile."

The Andrews Sisters: The Dancing 20's. Capitol ED-2604171. This album is
a re-issue of the trio's 1958 Capitol release of the same name,
saluting the zany and very danceable music of the 1920s.

The Andrews Sisters: The Early Years. Official 12005. The first of a three-
volume set of 1989 releases, this import from Denmark contains
sixteen of the trio's Decca recordings (1937–1942) never before
released in album form. Among the selections are the trio's very first
recordings for Decca ("Just a Simple Melody" and "Why Talk about
Love?"), as well as "Chico's Love Song," "I Want My Mama," "Music
Makers," "Honey," and an alternate take of "Let's Have Another
One." Although the choice of selections is inspired, no restoring or
filtering techniques were applied to the old, worn Decca discs, and
so the audio falls short of the mark. (Also available on cassette.)

The Andrews Sisters: The Early Years, vol. 2. Official 12011. The follow-up
to Official 12005 contains sixteen more of the trio's Decca recordings
(1938–1941), never before available in album form. Standouts
include "From the Land of the Sky Blue Water," "The Cockeyed
Mayor of Kaunakakai," "Mean to Me," and "Rock Rock Rock-a-Bye
Baby." A fourth and final Official release was planned, chronicling
the trio's post-war hits, but the record company claimed bankruptcy
before its completion. According to several prominent record dealers
in Manhattan, all three Andrews Sisters releases on the Official label
sold very well (selling out before replacement shipments arrived).
Perhaps this will prompt MCA to consider releasing this material,
restored to its original mono form, on a series of compact discs.
(Also available on cassette.)

The Andrews Sisters: The Fabulous Century. Joker 3240. This import from
Italy contains the same material as *The Andrews Sisters: Sirens of
Swing* (Historia H-638).

The Andrews Sisters: Their Greatest Hits. MSM-35117. Although this release
has some welcome selections (including "Rumors Are Flying" with
guitarist Les Paul and "Chattanooga Choo Choo"), some of the cuts
are greatest hits re-recordings that the trio made for Dot Records in

the late 1960s. The trio's seldom-heard Decca recording of "For All We Know" is also included, but the sound quality on this take is rather poor.

The Andrews Sisters: The Jumpin' Jive. England MCA MCL-1789. MCA provides the listener with more than just a few good selections with this release. Some of the standouts include the title tune, plus "Three Little Sisters," "Tu-Li-Tulip Time" (with Jimmy Dorsey's orchestra), a great vocalization of Glenn Miller's "Tuxedo Junction," "I'll Pray for You," and a solid "Massachusetts." Although the selections are prime, the sound quality is muffled. A fan with the original Decca discs in mint condition might be more pleased with those than with this release.

The Andrews Sisters: Twenty Greatest Hits. Scana GH-83001. Another release that does not include "Boogie Woogie Bugle Boy," this Holland import compensates for its somewhat muffled sound quality with solid song content, including "Bei Mir Bist Du Schon" and "Alexander's Ragtime Band." (Also available on compact disc.)

The Andrews Sisters: Worth Remembering. Magic AWE-4. This release offers a little bit of everything, including radio bits ("Club 15" with Bob Crosby and Dick Haymes), V-Disc sessions ("Put That Ring on My Finger" and a hits medley), and several Capitol recordings, including some promotional dialogue by the trio preceding the recordings.

The Best of the Andrews Sisters. Imperial House NU-9370. This 1978 release is yet another sampling of the trio's Dot years, including "Don't Fence Me In," "Near You," "Say Si Si," and "Boogie Woogie Bugle Boy."

The Best of the Andrews Sisters. MCA 2–4024. This double selection first surfaced on Decca in 1973, and it remains available on the MCA label. So far, this release (and its follow-up, volume two, also a double selection) is the closest that MCA has come, unfortunately, to doing any extensive work on the Andrews Sisters (excluding some recently released compact disc collections). Twenty-four of the trio's greatest Decca hits are featured herein, and all are original Decca gems. Surprisingly though, two selections ("South American Way" and "There Will Never Be Another You") are alternate takes and are not what was originally released in 78 rpm form. Both, however, are close in arrangement to the released takes and perhaps even better performance-wise. (Also available on cassette.)

The Best of the Andrews Sisters, vol. 2. MCA 2–4093. Twenty more of the trio's greatest hits make up this release. "Elmer's Tune" surfaces as an alternate take. Quite a few of the trio's slower numbers are included as well, such as "I Love You Much Too Much" and "I Remember

Mama." Also included is Patty's solo recording of "It Never Entered My Mind," with Gordon Jenkins' orchestra and chorus. When Decca originally released "It Never Entered My Mind," the label on the 78 rpm record gave vocal credits to the Andrews Sisters, rather than to Patty Andrews, who was the soloist on both sides. As a result, many think that the background voices toward the end of the recording (which is actually Patty re-recording herself) are Maxene and LaVerne. Some covered tunes show up here as well, including Nat Cole's "Straighten Up and Fly Right" and Arthur Godfrey's "Too Fat Polka," both dressed up in classic Andrews Sisters fashion. (Also available on cassette.)

The Best of Danny Kaye. MCA MCL-1704. This 1982 London import from MCA features fifteen of Kaye's best-sellers for Decca, including "Sweet Molly Malone" and "Oh, by Jingo." The Andrews Sisters are featured in the following four selections: "Civilization," "Bread and Butter Woman," "The Woody Woodpecker Song," and "Big Brass Band from Brazil." Excellent audio.

Bing and the Andrews Sisters: Twenty-Eight Hit Tracks. MCA CDMSP-804. This double selection British import is an excellent compilation and a nice alternative to the previously documented three-volume series. Twenty-eight great tracks comprise this release, including both recordings from the first session in 1939 ("Ciribiribin" and "Yodelin' Jive") and both recordings from the last session in 1952 ("South Rampart Street Parade" and "Cool Water"). Many of the group's country-western hits are included, as are two Irving Berlin compositions with Dick Haymes joining in ("There's No Business like Show Business" and "Anything You Can Do"). The million-sellers also appear in this release: "Pistol Packin' Mama," "Don't Fence Me In," "The Three Caballeros," and "South America, Take It Away." Excellent audio in original mono sound!

Bing Crosby and the Andrews Sisters, vol. 1. MCA CPS-80. This album is the first in a series of three British imports comprising just about every tune that the Andrews Sisters recorded with Bing Crosby between 1939 and 1952. This assortment of some of the quartet's best collaborations offers some mega hits ("Don't Fence Me In," "Pistol Packin' Mama"), some country-western hits ("Forsaking All Others," "Quicksilver") and eight other favorites. All three volumes in this series were released on the MCA-Coral label, but unfortunately, all tracks were stereo enhanced.

Bing Crosby and the Andrews Sisters, vol. 2. MCA CPS-91. After discovering that volume one of this series sold very well, MCA-Coral decided to follow up with a second volume. (Little did they know that they would soon be working on a third volume to satisfy public demand for this material in Europe.) This second volume features more of the group's country-western material, including "A Hundred and Sixty Acres" and "Lock, Stock, and Barrel," as well as more pop hits, including the quartet's first joint session that produced "Ciribiribin" and "Yodelin' Jive." An alternate take of the group's 1943 hit "The Vict'ry Polka" is also included.

Bing Crosby and the Andrews Sisters, vol. 3. MCA CPS-112. The third volume of this British series features most of the group's releases during the late 1940s and early 1950s, but earlier tunes, including "Ac-cent-tchu-ate the Positive," surface as well.

Bing Crosby's Greatest Hits. MCA 3031. This MCA re-issue of Decca DX-151 features the trio on "Don't Fence Me In," "Pistol Packin' Mama," and "Ac-cent-tchu-ate the Positive." (Also available on cassette and compact disc.)

Both Sides of Bing Crosby. Curtain Calls 100/2. This has the Andrews Sisters accompanying Crosby on an episode of *Command Performance* (1944) with Judy Garland, in which the group spoofs the popular radio show *Your Hit Parade.* The trio also is heard in a Decca out-take of "Jingle Bells," breaking up when Crosby fluffs his lines and starts swearing.

Club 15 with Dick Haymes and the Andrews Sisters. Sounds Rare 5004. This release features three *Club 15* shows hosted by Dick Haymes. Two of the shows feature the Andrews Sisters clowning with Haymes, Del Sharbutt, and orchestra leader Jerry Gray. They are singing "Never Too Busy to Say Hello," "Open Door, Open Arms," "Wunderbar," "Riders in the Sky," "Twenty-Four Hours of Sunshine," "I Can Dream, Can't I?," and "That Lucky Old Sun," among others. The remaining show features Evelyn Knight and the Modernaires joining Haymes in a salute to Walt Disney's *Cinderella.* Excellent sound quality as well.

Command Performance: Dick Tracy in B-flat. Radiola SH-2052. Radiola released this amusing one-hour episode of *Command Performance,* which spoofs the *Dick Tracy* comic strip characters. The all-star cast includes Bing Crosby as Tracy, Dinah Shore as Tess Trueheart, Bob Hope as Flat-Top, Judy Garland (who performs a shrilling operatic parody) as Snowflake, Frank Sinatra as Shaky, Jimmy Durante as the Mole, and Cass Daley as Gravel Gurtie, singing a booming rendition of "The Trolley Song." The Andrews Sisters portray the Summer Sisters—May, June, and July—and they sing a parody of "Apple Blossom Time." A very comical show from one of the most popular radio series of World War II. (Also available on cassette and compact disc.)

Film Tracks of Harry James. Joyce LP-3007. This mid-1970s release contains two motion picture soundtracks featuring Harry James and his band. The Andrews Sisters sing six songs from *Private Buckaroo* (Universal, 1942), their only film appearance with James. Other selections include vocalists Helen Forrest and Dick Haymes. The sound quality is rather muffled.

Glenn Miller and His Orchestra, 1940–1942. Soundcraft LP-1007. Although the Andrews Sisters appeared with Miller on more than three dozen episodes of CBS's *Moonlight Serenade* series, this compilation of live performances features the trio on only one number, "I've Got No Strings" from Walt Disney's *Pinocchio.*

The Greatest Hits of the Andrews Sisters, vols. 1 and 2. Telehouse SLB-6935. This 1974 double selection borrows from all three of the Andrews Sisters' Capitol albums from the late 1950s. Included with an assortment of the trio's best-sellers are "The Japanese Sandman," "Tea for Two," "A Smile Will Go a Long, Long Way," and "Comes Love." Great orchestra arrangements by Vic Schoen and Billy May.

Hits of the Andrews Sisters. Capitol T-1924. This album, first released in 1964, features Capitol re-recordings of the trio's Decca hits. Included in this collection are outstanding arrangements of "Shoo Shoo Baby" (featuring a classic solo by Patty) and "Begin the Beguine."

The Irving Berlin One Hundredth Anniversary Collection. MCA 39324. Commemorating Berlin's one hundredth birthday (May 11, 1988), MCA released a collection of some of the songwriter's best-known compositions, including Kate Smith's "God Bless America" and Bing Crosby's "White Christmas." The Andrews Sisters' 1947 recording of "Anything You Can Do" (with Bing Crosby and Dick Haymes) is also featured. (Also available on cassette and compact disc.)

The Jolson Story: Rainbow 'Round My Shoulder. MCA 2059. In 1980 MCA Records re-issued several Decca albums from a series of Al Jolson releases. This release features the Andrews Sisters assisting Jolson on their 1950 Decca record together, "'Way Down Yonder in New Orleans."

The Jolson Story: You Ain't Heard Nothin' Yet. MCA 27054. Another MCA re-issue in the Jolson series, this release features the flip side of the 1950 Decca record that Jolson recorded with the trio, "The Old Piano Roll Blues." Also joining Jolson are the Mills Brothers, in "Is It True What They Say about Dixie?"

More Hits of the Andrews Sisters. British MCA CDLM-8030. This album is a nice follow-up to any of the trio's greatest hits albums from Decca/

MCA. This installment includes many prime hits, including "Patience and Fortitude" and "Scrub Me Mama with a Boogie Beat." Original mono recordings, restored with great care.

Pop Singers on the Air. Radiola MR-1149. Perry Como, Vic Damone, Eddie Fisher, and Dick Haymes dominate this release. The Andrews Sisters are heard with Haymes in *Club 15,* singing "Jolly Fella Tarantella," "Let a Smile Be Your Umbrella," and "That Lucky Old Sun" (with Haymes). The show is given in its entirety; it includes the trio singing several commercial jingles for Campbell's soups and Franco-American products. (Also available on cassette and compact disc.)

Stagedoor Canteen/Hollywood Canteen. Curtain Calls 100/11–12. This double selection features quite an assortment of stars in original soundtrack recordings (part of the Silver Screen Soundtrack Series from Curtain Calls). The Andrews Sisters are heard on the soundtrack of the Warner Bros. film *Hollywood Canteen* (1944), singing "Hollywood Canteen," "Corns for My Country," and "Don't Fence Me In." Once again, the sound quality is rather poor.

Swingin' Sisters on the Air. Radiola 3–MR-3. This three-record boxed set from Radiola features radio transcriptions of many popular sister acts from the golden age of radio, including the Boswells, the Pickens, the Moylans, the De Marcos, the McGuires, the Fontanes, and so on (the Dinning Sisters are strangely omitted). The Andrews Sisters are heard in a complete half-hour show from their *Eight-to-the-Bar* series for ABC, singing "Great Day," "Dream," and "Happy Wedding Day," among others.

The Very Best of the Andrews Sisters. British MCA MCL-1635. This compilation is a good grouping of the trio's greatest hits, featuring nearly all of the usual, plus "Shoo Shoo Baby" and "Booglie Wooglie Piggy."

Compact Discs, 1985-1998

The Andrews Sisters: All-Time Favorites. Cema Special Markets CDL-57395. This 1991 budget CD release, part of a Ten Best series featuring Peggy Lee, the Kingston Trio, the Fleetwoods, and others, offers ten of the trio's greatest hits (re-recordings for Capitol), including "Beer Barrel Polka," "Rum and Coca Cola," "Hold Tight-Hold Tight," "Bei Mir Bist Du Schon," "Don't Sit under the Apple Tree," and "Boogie Woogie Bugle Boy." Excellent stereo audio.

The Andrews Sisters: At Their Very Best. Cema Special Markets CDL-9478. This 1990 release from Cema features thirteen re-recordings for Capitol of the trio's greatest Decca hits in excellent stereo sound quality, plus "Nevertheless" (from the trio's 1957 Capitol album

Fresh and Fancy Free) and "The Japanese Sandman" (from their 1958 Capitol album *The Dancing 20's*).

The Andrews Sisters: Beat Me Daddy, Eight to the Bar. MCA/EMI CDAX-701239. This 1990 Australian import contains many Decca hits, including "The Blue Tail Fly" with Burl Ives and "Cuanto la Gusta" with Carmen Miranda.

The Andrews Sisters: Boogie Woogie Bugle Boy. Pro-Arte Digital CDD 506. This 1990 release by Nichevo Productions features twenty-two early titles, including the rare "Wake Up and Live" (from the Brunswick label) and the trio's first Decca session ("Why Talk about Love?" and "Just a Simple Melody"). "Boogie Woogie Bugle Boy" and "In Apple Blossom Time" are taken directly from the *Buck Privates* soundtrack, as is "Bounce Me Brother with a Solid Four." "Sonny Boy" with Bob Hope is a live radio broadcast from 1946.

The Andrews Sisters: Boogie Woogie Bugle Boy: Forty Swing Era Memories. MSD2–35984. Available exclusively from Sound Exchange catalog (Time Warner Music) in conjunction with MCA Special Markets and Products, Inc., this two-CD set is an impressive issue. Forty Decca originals, including some fabulous material in pristine audio ("The Three Bells," "The Blond Sailor," "I Remember Mama," "I'm Bitin' My Fingernails and Thinking of You" with Ernest Tubb, "Tegucigalpa," "I'm Sorry" with Dick Haymes," "Rumors Are Flying" with Les Paul, "The House of Blue Lights," "Goodnight, Aloha" with Alfred Apaka, "The Too Fat Polka," "I'm Goin' down the Road" with Burl Ives, and a handful of tunes with Bing Crosby).

The Andrews Sisters: Boogie Woogie Bugle Boy in Sparkling Hi-Fi. Capitol/EMI CDAX 701114. This is another release containing some of the trio's mid-1950s stereo re-recordings of their greatest Decca hits, including "Begin the Beguine" and "Shoo Shoo Baby."

The Andrews Sisters: Capitol Collectors Series. Capitol CDP7–94078-s. This release is an excellent packaging of some of the trio's mid-1950s work for Capitol. It is only one in an impressive installment of Capitol Collectors Series, including releases by Frank Sinatra, Dean Martin, Sammy Davis Jr., Peggy Lee, Jo Stafford, Kay Starr, Johnny Mercer, the Pied Pipers, and many others. Crystal-clear stereo reproduction is featured on all twenty-five tracks, including "Crazy Arms" and "By His Word." The collection also contains some previously unreleased tracks, including "Alone Again," on which the girls really soar. Too many tracks, however, are previously released re-recordings of greatest hits rather than more of the trio's other Capitol sessions that haven't seen the light of day since their original releases over thirty-five years ago. Perhaps this material—the trio's single releases for Capitol, the trio's album releases for the company, and Patty's twelve solo recordings for the label—will soon find its way onto a "Spotlight On" compilation that Capitol packages for the same group of artists.

Andrews Sisters: Christmas. MCAD-20415. This is a nice package from MCA Special Products, featuring most of the trio's holiday recordings for Decca, ten selections in all. Great cover shot!

The Andrews Sisters: Fiftieth Anniversary Collection, vol. 1. MCAD-42044. This 1987 release marking the trio's fiftieth year as recording artists is beautifully packaged. Liner notes by Patty, Maxene, and Vic Schoen complement great photos. Great titles, including "Corns for My Country," "Bounce Me Brother with a Solid Four," and a pristine "Pagan Love Song."

The Andrews Sisters: Fiftieth Anniversary Collection, vol. 2. MCAD-10093. After nearly three years of planning, this release served as a nice follow-up to volume one, though more best-selling material (i.e., "The Blossoms on the Bough" and "Atlanta, G.A.") might have been a little more welcome than some of the obscure selections included herein ("Where Have We Met Before?" and "Sleepy Serenade"). Again, nicely packaged.

The Andrews Sisters: Greatest Hits. Curb D2–77400. This 1990 compilation of the trio's hits includes "I Can Dream, Can't I?" and "Don't Sit under the Apple Tree." Three of the tracks are Capitol re-recordings, as opposed to the Decca originals. (Also available on cassette.)

The Andrews Sisters' Greatest Hits. Reader's Digest RBD-105CDI. This 1987 package from *Reader's Digest* was offered as a free gift when purchasing a set of compact discs featuring live broadcasts by Glenn Miller and his orchestra. Three tracks are with Bing Crosby, and also featured is an alternate take (previously unreleased) of "I Can Dream, Can't I?"

The Andrews Sisters: In Apple Blossom Time. Classic Hits CDCD 1060. Made in the EEC and compiled and marketed by Charly Records, Ltd., this 1992 release contains twenty Decca hits, but half-a-dozen selections were lifted from the "Rarities" issue and are alternate takes.

The Andrews Sisters: Rarities. MCAD-31036/MCAD-22012. Re-issued in 1990, this 1984 package is a CD issue of the MCA album of the same name (MCA 908, released in 1980). All alternate takes and rejections, the selections include "Boogie Woogie Bugle Boy" (featuring a different trumpet solo).

The Andrews Sisters: Rum and Coca Cola. Eclipse 64002–2/Eclipse 64041– 2. An import from Canada, this budget CD has been released in two different forms (different covers, 1994 and 1995, but same material) and features twelve diverse selections, including "Alexander's Ragtime Band" and "Ti-Pi-Tin."

The Andrews Sisters: Rum and Coca Cola. Remember RMB 75018. This 1990 import from France features over sixty minutes of hits, including the title track, plus "Bei Mir Bist Du Schon," "Hold Tight-Hold Tight," and "Pennsylvania Polka." Poor audio on a few selections, while "Is You Is or Is You Ain't (Ma' Baby?)" and "Put That Ring on My Finger" surface as rare V-Disc sessions.

The Andrews Sisters: Sing! Sing! Sing! MFP/EMI CD-6044. Twenty prime selections make up this Music for Pleasure release from England. Great audio on "Don't Be That Way" and most other tracks.

The Andrews Sisters: Sixteen Original World Hits. MCA 8.62023LZ. The only original Decca hits herein are "Beer Barrel Polka" and "Yes, My Darling Daughter." The remaining fourteen hits are re-recordings for Dot Records.

The Andrews Sisters: Their All-Time Greatest Hits. MCA D2–11121. Compiled in honor of Decca's sixtieth anniversary, this 1994 two-CD set is unfortunately the closest MCA has come to releasing an extensive issue compiling the four hundred plus songs that the trio recorded for Decca Records. There are forty-six hits here (mostly top-tens) and most in pristine audio, especially "Strip Polka," "Shoo Shoo Baby," and "The Lady from 29 Palms." However, six tracks ("Ferryboat Serenade," "The Shrine of St. Cecilia," "The Blue Tail Fly" with Burl Ives, "I Can Dream, Can't I?" and two with Russ Morgan) are alternate takes previously unreleased and misplaced in a greatest hits collection. One can only wonder how many alternate takes, test recordings, rejected takes, and blow-ups are in the Decca vaults and remain unreleased.

The Andrews Sisters: Twenty Greatest Hits. Companion 6187172. An import from Denmark, this collection is comprised of all original Decca hits in excellent audio reproduction.

The Andrews Sisters: Twenty Greatest Hits. Scana CD-77019. Although this package offers twenty original Decca hits, including "Sonny Boy" and "The Woodpecker Song," most of the tracks have been electronically enhanced, resulting in a muffled effect.

The Andrews Sisters with the Glenn Miller Orchestra: The Chesterfield Broadcasts, volume 1. RCA Victor 09026–63113–2. This 1998 RCA Victor/BMG Entertainment release is an absolute find! Eleven vocal performances from the trio with Glenn Miller and the band, transcribed from the Chesterfield shows on CBS Radio. The audio is exceptionally good, and the excitement of the studio audience, comprised mostly of teenagers and young adults, can be heard at a feverous pitch. Actually, just before the girls swing into a hot arrangement of "I've Got No Strings," a fellow in the audience can be heard yelling out, "Let it go, Patty!" The overall disc serves as a great sound bite from an era full of musical fun and energy. Volume 2 is pending.

The Best of the Andrews Sisters. Blue Moon BMCD-3005. Twenty-seven Decca hits, good audio, and nice packaging comprise this 1994 import from Barcelona, Spain. Recommended.

The Best of the Andrews Sisters. CeDe International 66010. This EEC import contains sixteen Decca hits, including "Sing a Tropical Song." Also available under the same title on the World Star label (WSC 99010).

The Best of the Andrews Sisters. Music Club MCCD 199. A superb package! Eighteen Decca originals, including "Near You," "Rum and Coca Cola," "Boogie Woogie Bugle Boy," and plenty of guest appearances (Carmen Miranda in "Cuanto la Gusta," Russ Morgan in "Oh, You Sweet One," Danny Kaye in "Civilization," Dick Haymes in "Teresa," Al Jolson in "The Old Piano Roll Blues," and Bing Crosby in "Have I Told You Lately that I Love You?"). Great audio and terrific photos, including a color-added treat from *Give Out, Sisters* and a glamour shot on the back cover from *Road to Rio.* Highly recommended!

Bing Crosby and the Andrews Sisters: Their Complete Recordings Together. MCAD2–11503. This tremendous 1996 package from MCA features all forty-six songs that the trio recorded with Crosby from 1939 to 1952, nearly all in excellent audio thanks to digital transfers. As if this wasn't enough, MCA has also thrown in blow-ups of "Jingle Bells," "Don't Fence Me In," "The Three Caballeros," "Ac-cent-tchu-ate the Positive," and "The Freedom Train" (with much laughter going on as Crosby fluffs his lines), an alternate take of "There's a Fella Waitin' in Poughkeepsie" (a minute of pre-recording session dialogue can be heard between Crosby and the sisters as he sings them his own homespun verses of the tune), a funny parody of "A Hundred and Sixty Acres," and the extremely obscure, never before released recording of "Happy, Happy, Happy Wedding Day" from the *Dick Tracy* spoof on *Command Performance.* Inexplicably missing from the collection are the three Decca duets recorded by Patty and Crosby during these years. Great liner notes, good photos, and original Decca label art on each CD.

Christmas with the Andrews Sisters. Pickwick PWK-082. This is a substantial collection of the trio's seasonal hits, including twelve Decca

originals—three with Guy Lombardo, five with Bing Crosby, and one
with Danny Kaye. Excellent audio, especially on "Jing-a-Ling, Jing-a-
Ling," which is worth the price of the entire CD! The only draw-
back on this Great Britain import is the horrendous artwork on the
cover, but otherwise a great release.

An Evening with Frank Loesser. DRG 5169. This 1992 compilation of some
of Loesser's Broadway compositions (most of the tracks feature
vocals by Loesser himself) contains never before released material of
Maxene Andrews supplying solo vocals on selections from "The
Most Happy Fella," most notably the comical "Ohh! My Feet!" The
selections were apparently recorded by Maxene shortly after the trio's
separation in 1953.

The Immortal Hits of the Andrews Sisters. Lotus CD-0255. This import from
Italy boasts twenty-four original Decca hits, including the hard-to-
find "The Mambo Man."

Unforgettable! The Andrews Sisters: Sixteen Golden Classics. Castle UNCD-
25). The title of this import from France says it all. All Decca originals, including "She Wore a Yellow Ribbon" with Russ Morgan.
Excellent package!

The Very Best of the Andrews Sisters. Pickwick 064. This 1988 London
import features sixteen original Decca hits, including "In the Mood,"
"Chattanooga Choo Choo," and "Tico Tico." Recommended.

Bibliography

Andrews, Maxene, and Bill Gilbert. *Over Here, Over There: The Andrews Sisters and the USO Stars in World War II.* New York: Kensington, Zebra Books, 1993.

Bufwack, Mary A., and Robert K. Oermann. *Finding Her Voice: The Saga of Women in Country Music.* New York: Crown Press, 1993.

Cahn, Sammy. *I Should Care: The Sammy Cahn Story.* New York: Arbor House, 1974.

Carroll, Carroll, and J. Walter Thompson. *None of Your Business, or My Life With. . . .* New York: Cowles, 1970.

Clarke, Donald. *The Penguin Encyclopedia of Popular Music.* New York: Viking-Penguin, 1989.

Costello, Chris, and Raymond Strait. *Lou's on First.* New York: Cowles, 1981.

Dinning, John. *Tune in Yesterday: The Ultimate Encyclopedia of Old Time Radio, 1925–1976.* New Jersey: Prentice Hall, 1976.

Greene, Victor. *A Passion for Polka: Old Time Ethnic Music in America.* Berkeley and Los Angeles: Univ. of California Press, 1992.

Henner, Marilu, and Jim Jerome. *By All Means Keep on Moving.* New York: Pocket Books, 1994.

Hirschhorn, Clive. *The Hollywood Musical.* New York: Crown Press, 1981.

Hotchner, A.E. *Doris Day: Her Own Story.* Boston, Mass.: G.K. Hall, 1976.

Lennon, Dianne, Janet Lennon, Kathy Lennon, and Peggy Lennon. *Same Song—Separate Voices: The Collective Memoirs of the Lennon Sisters.* Santa Monica, Calif.: Roundtable, 1985.

Lofflin, John, and Stephen Cox. *The Abbott and Costello Story: Sixty Years of Who's on First.* Nashville, Tenn.: Cumberland House, 1997.

Maltin, Leonard. *The Disney Films.* New York: Popular Library, 1973.

McLelland, Doug. *The Golden Age of B Movies.* Tennessee: Charter House, 1978.

Mulholland, Jim. *The Abbott and Costello Book.* New York: Popular Library, 1975.

Murrells, Joseph. *Million Selling Records: From the 1900's to the 1980's.* New York: Arco, 1984.

Nash, Jay Robert, and Stanley Ralph Ross. *The Motion Picture Guide: 1927–1984.* Chicago: Cinebooks, 1987.

Bibliography

Palmer, Tony. *All You Need Is Love: The Story of Popular Music*. New York: Grossman, 1976.

Reed, Rex. "The Hassle Over—Over Here." *New York Daily News*, Jan. 5, 1975.

Ruhlmann, William. "The Andrews Sisters: Three Sides to Every Story." *Goldmine*, Jan. 20, 1995.

Sackett, Susan. *Hollywood Sings!* New York: Billboard, 1995.

Sanjek, Russell. *American Popular Music and Its Business: The First Four Hundred Years*. Vol. 3. New York: Oxford Univ. Press, 1988.

Schwartz, Charles. *Cole Porter: A Biography*. New York: Dial Press, 1977.

Secunda, Victoria. *Bei Mir Bist Du Schon: The Life of Sholom Secunda*. Weston, Conn.: Magic Circle Press, 1982.

Shapiro, Nat. *Popular Music: An Annotated Index of American Popular Songs*. Vols. 1, 2, and 4. New York: Adrian Press, 1964.

Shaughnessy, Mary Alice. *Les Paul: An American Original*. New York: William Morrow, 1993.

Simon, George T. *The Best of the Music Makers*. New York: Doubleday, 1979.

———. *The Big Bands*. New York: Macmillan, 1971.

———. *Glenn Miller and His Orchestra*. New York: Thomas Y. Crowell, 1974.

Thompson, Charles. *Bing*. New York: David McKay, 1975.

Torme, Mel. *My Singing Teachers*. New York and Oxford: Oxford Univ. Press, 1994.

Tyler, Don. *Hit Parade (1920–1955)*. New York: Quill, 1985.

Warner, Jay. *The Billboard Book of American Singing Groups: A History (1940–1990)*. New York: Billboard Books, 1992.

Wilkerson, Tichi, and Marcia Borie. *The Hollywood Reporter: The Golden Years*. New York: Coward-McCann, 1984.

Index

Abbott, Bud, 55, 59, 61, 207–8. *See also* Abbott and Costello

Abbott and Costello, 5, 8, 11, 41, 55, 57, 58, 59, 60, 62, 65, 78, 81, 88, 94, 98, 199, 200, 207–8, 267. *See also* Abbott, Bud; Costello, Lou

Abbott and Costello Show, The, 191. *See also* Abbott, Bud; Costello, Lou

Acuff, Roy, 189

Adams, Cindy, 169

Adams, Kathryn, 207

Allen, Fred, 20, 189

Allen, Steve, 138

Allyson, June, 65

Alper, Murray, 213

Always a Bridesmaid, 69–70, 210

Amaya Carmen, 212

Ambassadors, The, 98–99, 252

Ameche, Don, 83

Ames, Ramsay, 212

Ammons, Albert, 12

Amsterdam, Morey, 75, 166, 228

Andrews, LaVerne: birth of, 16; court case with Patty, 144–45; death of, 154–55; house fire, 150; marriage of, 118–19

Andrews, Maxene: birth of, 16; death of, 170–71; divorce of, 125; falling out with Patty, 160–65, 169, 171; marriage of, 62; suicide attempt, 145

Andrews, Olga (mother): 14, 17, 20, 23, 25, 48–49, 60, 71, 83, 89, 97, 117, 128–29, 136, 141, 144, 150

Andrews, Patty: birth of, 16–17; current activities, 171–72; divorce from Marty Melcher, 114–15; falling out with Maxene, 160–65, 169; marriage to Marty Melcher, 114–15; marriage to Walter

Weschler, 133; relationship with Vic Schoen, 46–49; separation from Maxene and LaVerne, 139–45

Andrews, Peter (father): 17, 18, 20, 23, 25, 28, 46–49, 60, 62, 63, 71, 83, 117, 119, 128–29, 136, 138, 141, 150

Andrews, Stanley, 214

Andrews Sisters, The: criticisms of, 95–97, 169–69; films, 207–15 (*see also individual titles*); friendship with Lou Costello, 59–62; impact on ethnic music, 11, 32, 38; musical versatility, 11–13, 35–36, 51–52, 66, 74–75, 103–4, 106; personal disagreements, 14–15, 45–49, 138–45, 160–65; sex appeal of act, 34–36, 75–76, 77, 152–53; USO activities, 13–14, 82–93; working relationship with Bing Crosy, 39–43, 68–69, 110–11, 129; working relationship with Glenn Miller, 44–46, 49; working relationship with Les Paul, 99–101; working relationship with Frank Sinatra, 78–80, 133

Andrews Sisters Show, The, 5, 78–81, 93, 190

Angie Bond Trio, The, 116

Ankers, Evelyn, 208

Apaka, Alfred, 121, 138, 245–46, 248, 262

Arden, Eve, 193

Argentine Nights, 52–54, 55, 207

Arnaz, Desi, 12, 134, 186, 242, 248, 255

Arnaz, Desi, Jr., 157

Arnaz, Lucie, 157

Arnold, Eddy, 120

Index

Astaire, Fred, 110
Astor, Mary, 70, 189
Atwater, Gladys, 207
Aubert, Lenore, 65
Autry, Gene, 83, 193
Ayres, Mitchell, 12, 70, 77, 213, 247–48

Bacon, Irving, 210
Bacon, James, 97, 105, 201, 202
Baker, Kenny, 83
Baker, Phil, 37, 189
Baker, "Wee" Bonnie, 34
Ball, Lucille, 1, 54, 156–57, 191
Ballard, Florence, 9
Bankhead, Tallulah, 193
Banks, Mariam, 236
Barbier, George, 214
Barbour, Dave, 28
Barnes, Clive, 157
Barnet, Charlie, 49
Baron, Maurice, 76
Baron, Paul, 228
Barrett, Edith, 210–11
Barry, Claire, 7
Barry, Merna, 7
Barry Sisters, The, 7
Basie, Count, 66
Beatles, The, 4, 5, 54, 108, 156, 167
Beery, Noah, Jr., 214
Belafonte, Harry, 74
Belasco, Leon, 21–22, 24, 114, 217
Belasco, Lionel, 75, 228
Bell Sisters, The, 11
Beloin, Edmund, 214
Bennett, Tony, 139, 195
Benny, Jack, 2, 51, 20, 189, 191, 213
Benny Goodman Quartet, The, 214
Bergen, Candice, 16
Bergen, Edgar, 1, 16, 189
Berigan, Bunny, 12, 18, 52
Berle, Milton, 11, 111
Berlin, Irving, 3, 118, 248, 258, 260
Berry, Chuck, 148
Bing Crosby Show, The, 193
Bing Crosby's Philco Radio Time, 1, 192. *See also* Crosby, Bing
Bishop, Joey, 196
Blaine, Vivian, 166
Blair, Janet, 192

Blake, Marie, 210
Blanc, Mel, 191
Block, Ray, 115
Bob Crosby's Bobcats, 36, 219, 248. *See also* Crosby, Bob
Bolger, Ray, 11, 149, 195
Boone, Pat, 139, 150
Boros, Ferike, 207
Boswell Sisters, The, 6–7, 18, 19, 21, 24, 29, 35, 40, 51, 168, 261
Bowman, Lee, 207
Bowron, Fletcher, 82
Bramley, Haworth, 209
Bren, J. Robert, 207
Breslow, Lou, 212
Brewer, Teresa, 139
Brown, Barbara, 212
Brown, Kenneth, 208
Brown, Les, 12, 125, 127–28
Brown, Lew, 37
Browns, The, 135, 167
Bruce, David, 211
Bruckman, Clyde, 211, 213
Bruff, Larry, 45–46
Buck Privates, 5, 55, 57, 58, 63, 95, 207–8
Burke, Billie, 209
Burke, Johnny, 110
Burke, Sonny, 242, 247, 248
Burns, Bob, 189
Burton, Bernard W., 210
Butterworth, Charles, 209, 210, 211, 212

Cady, Jerry, 209
Caen, Herb, 130
Cagney, Jimmy, 83
Cahn, Sammy, 25, 26–28, 31, 197, 217
Canova, Judy, 11
Cantor, Eddie, 11, 78, 190, 213
Carillo, Leo, 209, 213
Carlisle, Kitty, 213
Carlson, Richard, 209
Carmichael, Hoagy, 98, 108
Carpenter, Ken, 192
Carroll, Carroll, 154–55
Carson, Jack, 213
Carson, Johnny, 11, 131–32, 152–53, 195
Carter Family, The 10

Carter Sisters, The 10
Cash, Johnny, 10
Cass, Maurice, 214
Castle, Nick, 57
Cates, George, 138, 245
Catlett, Walter, 210, 211
Cavallaro, Carmen, 12, 213, 232
Cavett, Dick, 197, 202
Chaplin, Saul, 1, 26–29, 31, 217
Cherry Sisters, The, 11
Chordettes, The, 11, 147
Clark, Buddy, 123, 215
Clark, Dane, 212
Clawson Triplets, The, 11
Clinton, President William, 171
Clive, Edward F., 209, 210, 211, 213
Clooney, Rosemary, 3, 139
Club 15, 5, 112–14, 121, 129, 154,
    192, 193
Cole, Nat King, 11, 73, 108, 132,
    143, 186, 193, 254, 258
Colonna, Jerry, 191, 192, 214
Columbo, Russ, 35
Command Performance, 2, 87, 116,
    189–93, 201
Como, Perry, 8, 11, 69, 108, 149,
    187, 195, 261
Company B (dance revue), 169
Condos Brothers, The, 208
Conrad, Eugene, 213
Cookson, Peter, 211, 212
Cooper, Gary, 71, 189
Cormack, Rob, 214
Costello, Ann (Mrs. Lou Costello), 60
Costello, Lou, 55, 58–63, 191, 199,
    200, 207–8. See also Abbott and
    Costello
Costello, Lou, Jr., 61
Cox, Stephen, 60
Craig, Francis, 111
Cramer, Maria, 24
Crawford, Joan, 77, 213
Crosby, Bing, 3, 5, 7, 11, 18, 24, 39–
    44, 50–51, 67–69, 73, 74–75, 76,
    78, 79, 87, 88, 97, 98, 99, 101,
    108, 110–11, 112, 113, 114, 119,
    121, 125, 129, 133, 135, 138,
    143, 155, 157, 160, 168, 170,
    175–79, 181–82, 183–84, 185–86,
    198, 199, 202, 203, 214, 215,
    220, 226, 227, 228, 229, 230,
    231, 232, 233, 234, 236, 238,
    239, 240, 241, 242, 245, 246,
    247, 248, 253, 254, 255, 258,
    259, 260, 263, 264, 265, 266
Crosby, Bob, 11, 112, 113, 114, 121,
    138, 192, 219, 235, 253, 255, 257
Cugat, Xavier, 12, 99
Curtis, Alan, 207

Dailey, Dan, 11, 125, 210, 236
Daley, Cass, 11, 191, 259
Damone, Vic, 261
Dare, Daniel, 214
Daves, Delmer, 212
Davidson, William, 209
Davies, Richard, 209
Davis, Beryl, 192
Davis, Bette, 54, 77, 192, 213
Davis, Joan, 208
Davis, Rufus, 20
Davis, Sammy, Jr., 154, 196, 262
Day, Dennis, 51, 215
Day, Doris, 3, 105, 123, 125–28, 167
Dean, Jimmy, 196
Dearing, Edgar, 214
DeCastro Sisters, The, 148
DeHaven, Gloria, 166
de Havilland, Olivia, 82
DeJohn Sisters, The, 148
Delta Rhythm Boys, The, 40, 192, 212
DeMarco Sisters, 8
Devine, Andy, 51
DeVol, Frank, 249
Dexter, Al, 67, 68
DeYoung, Joyce (LaVerne's Replace-
    ment), 154, 196, 254
Dietrich, Marlene, 77, 84, 212
Dinning Sisters, The, 3, 7, 69, 102,
    108, 215, 261
Disney, Walt, 5, 7, 44, 74, 102, 116,
    214, 215, 218, 226, 229, 241,
    259, 260
Dixon, MacIntyre, 252
Dodd, Clair, 208
Dolly Sisters, The, 11
Dorsey, Jimmy, 3, 12, 34, 36, 40,
    213, 218, 219, 223, 257. See also
    Dorsey Brothers, The
Dorsey, Tommy, 3, 12, 25, 26–27, 30,

31, 49, 67, 84, 108, 134, 135, 242, 243. *See also* Dorsey Brothers, The
Dorsey Brothers, The, 18. *See also* Dorsey, Jimmy; Dorsey, Tommy
Dorso, Dick, 114, 126
Downey, Morton, 11, 98
Downs, Hugh, 170
Driscoll, Bobby, 215
Driver, John, 252
Duncan Sisters, The, 11
Durante, Jimmy, 9, 11, 87, 121, 143, 191, 192, 247, 259
Durbin, Deanna, 65, 71, 84, 96

Ebbinghouse, Bernard, 250
Eberle, Bob, 224
Eddie Cantor Show, The, 190. *See also* Cantor, Eddie
Eddy, Nelson, 71, 191, 214
Elliott, "Wild" Bill, 78

Fain, Sammy, 122
Faylen, Frank, 214
Feldman, Charles K., 212
Fields, W.C., 11, 212
films, 207–15. *See also individual titles*
Fina, Jack, 215
Fine, Sylvia (Mrs. Danny Kaye), 111
Fisher, Eddie, 139, 261
Fitzgerald, Ella, 3, 18, 28, 31, 108, 115, 122
Fleetwoods, The, 261
Flynn, Errol, 87
Foley, Red, 12, 134, 182, 242, 243
Follow the Boys, 5, 77, 152, 212
Fontaine, Joan, 150
Fontane Sisters, The, 3, 8, 69, 102, 108, 148, 150, 261
Foran, Dick, 65, 208, 209
Ford, Mary, 6, 99
Ford, Tennessee Ernie, 120
Forester Sisters, The, 10
Forrest, Helen, 3, 87, 260
Four Hits and a Miss, 108
Fox, Maxine, 157, 160–62
Francis, Connie, 124, 167
Franklin, Joe, 85, 198, 199, 203
Frawley, William, 210
Frazee, Jane, 207–8, 209

Frazee Sisters, The, 11
Friml, Rudolf, 44
Fulton, Jack, 32, 189
Furgeson, Allyn, 251

Gabor, Zsa Zsa, 150
Gail, Richard, 244
Gale, Bill, 38
Ganzaga, Luis, 238
Gardner, Kenny, 243
Garfield, John, 77, 213
Garland, Judy, 3, 11, 21, 24, 31, 70, 80, 84, 87, 91, 92, 96, 98, 105, 108, 110, 122, 143, 170, 191, 259. *See also* Gumm Sisters, The
Garrett, Betty, 99
Geronimi, Clyde, 214, 215
Gershwin, George, 26
Gershwin, Ira, 26
Gilbert, Bill, 170, 211
Gilbert, Ronnie, 108
Gilmore, Voyle, 148–149
Give Out, Sisters, 66, 95, 210
Glahe, Will, 37
Godfrey, Arthur, 8, 258
Golden, Ray, 207
Goldsmith, Ken, 207, 210, 211
Goldwyn, Samuel, 65, 220
Goodman, Benny, 3, 12, 30, 31, 214
Gorme, Eydie, 187
Gottlieb, Alex, 60, 207, 208, 212
Gould, Rita, 214
Grable, Betty, 96
Grant, Bert, 135
Grant, Cary, 189
Grant, Joe, 214
Grant, John, 208
Grapewin, Charles, 212
Gray, Glen, 38
Gray, Jerry, 12, 129, 237, 248, 259
Gray, John, 210
Grayson, Kathryn, 90, 166
Greene, Alice Craig, 36
Greene, Victor, 32, 38
Greenstreet, Sydney, 78, 213
Grever, Maria, 218
Griffin, Merv, 46, 122, 199, 203
Griffis, William, 252
Gross, Frank, 213

Index

Gumm, Frances Ethel, 20–21. *See also* Garland, Judy
Gumm Sisters, The, 20–21

Hackett, Bobby, 28
Haines, Connie, 191
Hale, Alan, 213
Haley, Bill, 148
Hall, Huntz, 210
Hamilton, John, 211
Harlan, Jim, 198, 200, 203
Harmon, Marie, 214
Harmonica Gentlemen, The, 115, 235
Harmonickings, The, 116
Harris, Emmylou, 10
Harris, Phil, 51
Hart, Jeff, 166, 205
Hawthorne, Alice, 124
Hayes, George "Gabby," 11, 78, 79, 81
Haymes, Dick, 3, 11, 87, 108, 112, 113, 114, 115, 121, 122, 123, 128, 129, 138, 178, 193, 228, 231, 234, 237, 239, 248, 255, 257, 258, 259, 260, 261, 262, 265
Heywood, Eddie, 101, 230
Heywood, Herbert, 211
Helm, Fay, 210
Hemming, Roy, 159
Henner, Marilu, 158, 162–63
Henreid, Paul, 213
Hepburn, Katharine, 77
Her Lucky Night, 94, 213–14
Herman, Woody, 12, 66, 111, 115, 209, 219
Hilliard, Harriet, 189, 211, 212
Hinds, Samuel S., 207
Hold That Ghost, 5, 58–59, 208–9
Hollingway, Sterling, 214
Hollywood Canteen, The, iv, 74, 84
Hollywood Canteen (film), 5, 77, 212–13, 261
Holm, Celeste, 192
Holt, Jennifer, 209
Holt, Will, 157
Honolulu Bound, 37, 189
Hope, Bob, 5, 11, 65, 78, 79, 87, 88, 91, 110–11, 128, 170, 171, 189–92, 214, 215, 255, 259, 262
Horman, Arthur T., 207, 208
Horne, Lena, 3, 196

Horton, Edward Everett, 191
Horton, Johnny, 167
Howard, Joe, 20
Howard, Shemp, 11, 65, 207, 208, 209, 211, 213
Howlin, Olin, 214
How's About It?, 69, 210–11
Hutton, Betty, 3, 105, 136, 189
Hutton, Ina Ray, 62
Hutton, Marion, 136
Hutton, Robert, 212

Ink Spots, The, 3, 56, 98, 108
In the Navy, 5, 57–59
Ives, Burl, 12, 111, 178, 232, 262, 264

Jackson, Michael, 167
Jackson, Wilfred, 215
Jacobs, Jacob, 27
James, Edward, 209
James, Harry, 3, 42, 65, 210, 260
Jean, Gloria, 66, 97, 209
Jenkins, Gordon, 122–23, 130, 133–34, 135, 148, 187, 237, 238, 240, 243, 244, 249, 258
Jessel, Georgie, 21
Jivin' Jacks and Jills, The, 209, 210
Johnson, Pete, 12
Jolson, Al, 3, 11, 24, 63, 105, 108, 130, 182, 193, 240, 260, 265
Jones, Spike, 189, 192
Jordan, Louis, 212
Judds, The, 10
Just Entertainment, 32, 189

Kahal, Irving, 122
Kapp, David, 24, 25, 27, 29, 39, 119–120, 122, 128, 136, 150
Kapp, Jack, 24, 25, 27, 29, 37, 39–40, 43, 56, 67, 119–20, 122–23, 124, 128, 136, 185
Karalis, James, 18
Kaye, Danny, 11, 108, 111, 117, 121, 170, 178, 182, 232, 233, 234, 235, 237, 241, 248, 253, 265, 266
Kaye, Sammy, 3, 38, 63
Kazan, Lainie, 166
Keane, Robert Emmet, 208, 210, 213
Kelso, Edward, 209
Ken Darby Chorus, The, 214

Index

Kennedy, Tom, 213
Kent, Larry, 34
Kenton, Erle C., 210, 211
Kerrigan, James, 227
Khachaturian, Aram, 115, 235
King, Stan, 28
King Sisters, The, 3, 7–8, 108
King's Men, The, 214
Kingston Trio, The, 261
Kinney, Jack, 214, 215
Kisselgoff, Anna, 169
Kitt, Ertha, 166
Knight, Evelyn, 112, 129, 259
Knowles, Patric, 211
Knox, Elyse, 213
Knox, Lou, 227
Kovacs, Ernie, 195
Krasner, Milton, 59
Kroll, Jack, 160
Krupa, Gene, 12, 38, 49, 163
Kuller, Sid, 207
Kurtz, M., 35
Kyser, Kay, 3, 189

Laine, Frankie, 123
Lamour, Dorothy, 5, 82, 88, 110–11, 166, 191, 214, 215
Lancaster, Burt, 150
Lane, Priscilla, 30
Langford, Frances, 84, 215
Laredo, Joseph, 40, 138
LaRosa, Julius, 11, 149, 195
Laughton, Charles, 83, 189
Laurie Sisters, The, 148
Lawrence, Jack, 42
Lawrence, Marc, 209
Lawrence, Steve, 187
Lecuona, Ernesto, 236
Lee, Peggy, 3, 122, 186, 261, 262
Lee Gordon Singers, The, 238
Lees, Robert, 208
Leiber, Jerry, 143
Lenhart, Billy, 208
Lennick, David, 35
Lennon Sisters, The, 6, 9, 150, 166
Les Compagnons de Chanson, 135
Leslie, Joan, 77, 213
Les Paul Trio, The, 99, 101. See also Paul, Les
Levant, Oscar, 116

Leveen, Raymond, 218
Levine, Susan, 209, 210
Levy, Al, 114
Levy, Aleda Ann (Maxene's adopted daughter), 102
Levy, Lou (manager and Maxene's husband), 24–25, 26, 27, 28, 32, 46–49, 56, 62, 64, 71, 72, 95, 98, 99, 102, 107–8, 125, 128, 131, 136, 137–38, 139–40, 142–43
Levy, Peter (Maxene's adopted son), 102
Lewin, David, 117
Lewis, Jerry, 131–32, 195. See also Martin and Lewis Show, The
Lewis, Joe E., 65, 209
Lewis, Meade Lux, 12
Lewis, Ted, 12, 209, 212
Lilley, Edward, 213
Lilley, Joseph, 246
Linkletter, Art, 195
Loesser, Frank, 266
Lofflin, John, 60
Lombard, Carole, 88
Lombardo, Guy, 12, 31, 35, 97, 101, 186, 229, 231, 237, 240, 243, 244, 248, 266
Long, Johnny, 62
Lorre, Peter, 78, 213
Lubin, Arthur, 56, 207, 208
Lum and Abner, 11, 78, 83
Lunceford, Jimmie, 31
Lupino, Ida, 213
Luske, Hamilton, 214, 215

MacDonald, Jeanette, 212
Mack, Ted, 5, 20
MacRae, Gordon, 116, 124, 125, 166, 193
MacRae, Sheila (Mrs. Gordon Mac Rae), 125
Mail Call, 87, 190, 191
Main, Marjorie, 11, 78
Make Mine Music, 5, 102, 214
Maltin, Leonard, 12
Mandrell Sisters, The, 10
Manhattan Transfer, 6, 168
Manilow, Barry, 6
Markham, Dewey "Alamo," 78
Marrow, Macklin, 116

Index

Marshall, Herbert, 190
Marshall, Jack, 249
Martell, Alphonse, 211
Martin, Dean, 11, 131–32, 143, 154, 196, 262. *See also Martin and Lewis Show, The*
Martin, Freddy, 111, 115, 215
Martin, Nora, 213
Martin, Skip, 138, 245, 248
Martin, Tony, 150
Martin and Lewis Show, The, 1, 11, 131–32, 156. *See also* Lewis, Jerry; Martin and Lewis; Martin, Dean
Martino, Al, 138
Marx, Groucho, 11, 78, 80, 191, 193. *See also* Marx Brothers, The
Marx Brothers, The, 88, 149, 195
Massey, Curt, 93, 98, 99, 253
Mathis, Johnny, 187
Matlock, Matty, 246, 247
May, Billy, 149, 249, 250, 260
Mazo, Joseph H., 169
McCarters, The, 10
McCarthy, Charlie, 1, 16, 189
McCary, Robert, 131
McDonald, Grace, 209, 210, 211, 212
McDonald, Marie, 193
McGuire Sisters, The, 8–9, 147, 148, 261
McGuirk, Pat, 131
McKinley, Ray, 40, 111, 219
McLeod, Norman Z., 214
Meador, Joshua, 214
Melcher, Marty (Patty's first husband), 114–15, 125–28
Mellomen, The, 246, 254
Melody Time, 5, 7, 116, 215
Mercer, Johnny, 3, 67, 123, 262
Merman, Ethel, 98
Merry Macs, The, 3, 108
Midler, Bette, 6, 152, 159, 163, 168
Miller, Ann, 170
Miller, Glenn, 3, 12, 44–45, 49, 63, 66, 95, 108, 136, 138, 170, 257, 260, 263, 264
Miller, Helen (Mrs. Glenn Miller), 45
Miller, Marvin, 78
Miller, Mitch, 143
Mills Brothers, The, 3, 18, 24, 55, 87, 98, 99, 108, 144, 150, 260

Mineo, Sal, 158
Miranda, Carmen, 11, 41, 78, 118, 125, 178–79, 182, 233, 238, 254, 262, 265
Modernaires, The, 3, 95, 108, 112, 128, 129, 259
Monroe, Marilyn, 167
Monroe, Vaughan, 3, 11, 69, 135
Moon Maids, The, 135
Mooney, Harold, 248, 249
Moonlight and Cactus, 78, 96, 213
Moonlight Serenade, The, 44–47, 49, 189
Moore, Constance, 207
Moore, Garry, 11, 192
Moore, Ida, 214
Moran, Peggy, 207
Moray, Ann, 86
Morgan, Frank, 11, 191
Morgan, Russ, 103, 125, 138, 179, 237, 238, 245, 254, 264, 265, 266
Morris, Mary, 103
Morrison, Patricia, 82
Morse, Ella Mae, 3
Moylan Sisters, The, 11, 261
Murray, Lynn, 249

Nagel, Anne, 207
Nash–Kelvinator Musical Showroom, The, 5, 98–99, 112, 191–92
Nealson, Paul, 244
Newman, Alfred, 12
1941, 170
Noble, Ray, 189
Nolan, O'Neill, 211
Norton Sisters, The, 11, 69, 108
Nye, Louis, 11, 195

Oakes, Lt. Comdr. C.P., 226
O'Connell, Helen, 3, 224
O'Connor, Donald, 66, 209, 210, 212
O'Driscoll, Martha, 214
Oliver, Sy, 138, 244, 248
Over Here! (Broadway play), 6, 13, 157–64, 170
Ozzie and Harriet, 192. *See also* Hilliard, Harriet

Page, Patti, 75, 108, 136, 139
Paige, Janis, 212

Index

Paige, Robert, 209, 210, 211
Palmer, Tony, 30
Pangborn, Franklin, 209
Parker, Eleanor, 213
Parsons, Milton, 209
Parton, Dolly, 10
Pastor, Tony, 12, 101, 102
Patten, Luana, 215
Patterson, Massie, 75
Paul, Ivan, 130
Paul, Les, 6, 12, 99–102, 230, 256, 262
Pendleton, Nat, 207
Pestalozza, A., 42
Philco Radio Hall of Fame, The, 190
Phillips, William, 211
Phynx, 156
Piaf, Edith, 135
Pickens Sisters, The, 7, 24, 29, 261
Pied Pipers, The, 3, 67, 108, 112, 214, 262
Pleis, Jack, 247
Pointer Sisters, The, 6, 10, 152, 166
Pollack, Bernie, 23
Porcasi, Paul, 207
Porter, Cole, 35, 36, 74–75, 186, 200, 227
Poston, Mike, 60
Powell, Dick, 208
Powell, Jane, 99
Power, Tyrone, 71, 72
Presley, Elvis, 5, 6, 36, 55, 143, 148, 167
Prima, Louis, 111, 150
Prince, Hughie, 222
Private Buckaroo, 65, 70, 95
Purcell, Gertrude, 212

Queen Elizabeth (cruise ship), 118
Quillan, Eddie, 213

Rackmil, Milton, 120
Raft, George, 77, 212
Raye, Don, 207
Reed, Rex, 156, 161–62, 164
Reese, Della, 166
Reeves, George, 207
Reeves, Jim, 167
Reinking, Ann, 158
Reisfeld, Bert, 135, 244
Rey, Alvino, 7

Riabonchinska, Tatiana, 214
Rice, Jack, 211
Rich, Buddy, 12, 211
Rich, Larry, 16, 17, 19–20
Richards, Addison, 211
Richmond, June, 218
Riddle, Nelson, 12, 138, 245, 246, 248
Riders of the Purple Sage, The, 78, 79, 93, 248
Rinaldo, Frederic T., 208
Ritz Brothers, 11, 51, 52, 207
Road to Rio, 5, 53, 110–11, 116, 214
Robbins, Sid, 219
Roberts, Stanley, 209
Robertson, Don, 148
Robinson, Edward G., 83
Rodgers, Jimmie, 149, 150
Rogell, Albert S., 207
Rogers, Lou (LaVerne's husband), 118–19, 128, 133, 150, 154
Rogers, Roy, 74, 77, 78, 213, 215, 227
Roma Wines Show, The, 70, 189
Romero, Cesar, 71
Ronson, Mel, 210, 211
Ronstadt, Linda, 10
Rooney, Anne, 211
Rooney, Mickey, 70, 170
Roos, Bo, 137
Roosevelt, Franklin D., 81, 83, 117
Rose, Jack, 214
Rosenbaum, Jack, 130
Ross, Diana, 9, 11, 118, 154, 196, 254
Royal Canadians, The, 101, 186, 229, 231, 240, 243, 244, 248
Rubenstein, Arthur, 212
Ruhlmann, William, 13, 30, 47, 48, 123, 136, 171
Rushing, Jimmy, 66
Russell, Andy, 214
Ryan, Peggy, 66, 209, 210, 212
Ryan, Tim, 211

Sakall, S.Z. "Cuddles," 213
Sammy Davis, Jr., Show, The, 154, 196, 254. See also Davis, Sammy, Jr.
Sanjek, Russell, 107
Schary, Dore, 147
Scheerer, Bobby, 210
Schoen, Vic, 21, 24, 27, 28, 29, 34,

37–38, 40–41, 43, 45–46, 48–49, 57, 67, 68, 69, 74, 78, 93, 98, 99, 100, 104, 108, 117, 118, 124, 128, 133, 136–37, 141, 148, 149, 185, 217, 219, 224, 225, 226, 228, 230, 235, 236, 247, 248, 249, 260
Schwartz, Charles, 75
Secunda, Sholom, 27, 31–33, 217
Secunda, Victoria, 31
Seidel, Tom, 213
Sell, Janie, 158, 252
Sharbutt, Del, 112, 113, 193, 259
Sharpsteen, Ben, 215
Shaughnessy, Mary Alice, 101
Shaw, Artie, 3, 12, 36, 101
Shawhan, April, 252
Sherman, Eddie, 59
Sherman, Maury, 21
Sherman, Richard, 157
Sherman, Robert, 157
Shore, Dinah, 3, 77, 80, 84, 87, 108, 123, 137, 189, 192, 212, 214, 259
Siegel, Benny "Bugsy," 109
Silvers, Phil, 133
Simms, Ginny, 189
Simon, George, T., 106, 157
Sinatra, Frank, 2, 3, 11, 36, 66, 67, 73, 74, 78–80, 87, 99, 108, 115, 122, 133, 135, 143, 191, 192, 259, 262
Skelton, Red, 91, 144, 147, 189, 195
Slack, Freddie, 212
Smith, Ethel, 215
Smith, Jack, 111
Smith, Kate, 3, 8, 260
Smith, Keely, 150
Smith, Paul Gerard, 210, 213
Somerville, Phyllis, 252
Sondergaard, Gale, 214, 215
Song Spinners, The, 3, 108, 115
Sons of the Pioneers, The, 77, 78, 213, 215, 227
Spivak, Charlie, 212
Squires, Dorothy, 144
Stabile, Dick, 49
Stafford, Jo, 3, 67, 112, 124, 143, 144, 262
Stage Door Canteen, The, 33–34, 84, 261

Stanwyck, Barbara, 84
Starr, Kay, 120, 123, 136, 137, 143, 262
Stewart, Danny, 138
Stoller, Mike, 143
Stordahl, Axel, 12
Storm, Gale, 150
Sullivan, Jeri, 228
Supremes, The, 9–10, 11, 118, 154, 196, 254
Susskind, David, 147
Sutherland, Edward, 212
Sutton, Grady, 214
Swanson, Billy, 24
Sweethearts of the Rodeo, The, 10
Swig, Benjamin H., 131, 203
Swingtime Canteen, 170
Swingtime Johnny, 70, 211–12

Taxi, 162, 169–70
Taylor, Elizabeth, 97
Taylor, Paul, 169
Teixeira, Humberto, 238
Temple, Shirley, 83
Ternent, Billy, 235
Terry, Don, 208
Thompson, Bob, 249
Thompson, J. Walter, 155
Tierney, Gene, 189
Timm, Vladimir, 37
Tonight Show, The, 131, 152–53, 168, 195
Torme, Mel, 3, 6, 19, 105–6
Travolta, John, 158, 163, 252
Treacher, Arthur, 116
Trenner, Don, 250
Trio, 10
Trotter, John Scott, 51, 245
Truex, Ernest, 209
Tubb, Ernest, 12, 120–21, 134, 167, 178, 235, 262
Tucker, Forrest, 166
Tucker, Orrin, 34
Tucker, Sophie, 77, 98, 212
Turner, Lana, 87

Urecal, Minerva, 213

Vallee, Rudy, 11, 34, 78, 99, 190
Van Doren, Mamie, 166

Index

Van Heusen, James, 35, 110
Van Zandt, Philip, 211
Vaughan, Sarah, 115
Vaughn, Billy, 150, 250
Vaughn, Wes, 217
Vejvoda, Jaromir, 37
Venuti, Joe, 12, 18, 41, 220
Victory Canteen, 157
Villard, Jean, 135
Vitale, Joseph, 214
Von Zell, Harry, 190, 191

Waissman, Kenneth, 157, 160–62
Wakely, Jimmy, 120
Walker, Nella, 207
Walker, Ray, 211
Wallace, Irving, 84
Waller, Fats, 34
Waring, Fred, 12, 33–34, 215
Waters, Ethel, 189
Watson, Douglass, 252
Wayne, John, 78, 125
Weavers, The, 108, 111, 122, 136
Weiss, Sam, 127
Welk, Lawrence, 9, 38, 150
Welles, Orson, 77, 83, 212
Weschler, Walter (Wally) (Patty's
  second husband), 123, 133, 137,
  139–40, 143, 151, 161, 164, 165,
  251

Weston, Jim, 252
What's Cookin'?, 66, 209
Whiteman, Paul, 12, 33, 40, 50, 189
Whiting, Margaret, 3, 91, 112, 120,
  123, 135
Wickes, Mary, 209, 211
Wiere Brothers, The, 214
Williams, Andy, 11, 149
Williams, Clarence, 107
Williams, Treat, 158
Willing, Foy, 78
Willis, Matt, 211
Wilson, Don, 191
Wilson, Mary, 9
Wilson, Warren, 210, 211, 213
Winchell, Walter, 34–35
Wolf, Richard, 250
Wood, Douglas, 207
Wright, Samuel E., 252
Wyman, Jane, 213

Young, Joe, 135
Young, Victor, 115, 134, 239, 240,
  242, 243, 248
Your Hit Parade, 111, 190, 192

Zorina, Vera, 212

278

Song Index

"Abide with Me," 86, 251

"Ac-cen-tchu-ate the Positive," 5, 74, 76, 177, 182, 183, 190, 229, 254, 259, 265

"Adios," 138, 246

"Again," 123

"Ain't It a Shame about Mame?," 190

"Alexander's Ragtime Band," 51, 104, 118, 234, 257, 264

"All I Want for Christmas Is My Two Front Teeth," 237

"All My Love," 192

"All the Colors of the Rainbow," 251

"All the World to Me (You Are)," 241

"Alone Again," 148, 262

"Along the Navajo Trail," 97, 177, 182, 183

"Amelia Cordelia McHugh," 111, 234

"Amen," 209

"Any Bonds Today?," 224, 255

"Anything You Can Do," 231, 258, 260

"Apalachicola, FLA," 43, 215, 232

"April Showers," 193

"Atlanta, G.A.," 192, 230, 263

"Ask Me No Questions (And I'll Tell You No Lies)," 239

"At Sonya's Café," 224

"At Sundown," 192

"At the Flying W," 234

"Aurora," 59, 172, 176, 184, 209, 222, 249, 250

"Ave Maria," 9, 86

"Avocado," 230

"A, You're Adorable," 8, 69

"Azusa," 230

"Baby Blues," 243

"Baby, It's Cold Outside," 123

"Baby Love," 9, 154, 196

"Baby Me," 192

"Baby, Won't You Please Come Home," 191

"Back in My Arms Again," 9

"Back in Your Own Backyard," 250

"Band Played On, The," 212

"Beatin', Bangin' and Scratchin'," 233

"Beat Me Daddy, Eight to the Bar," 5, 12, 51, 54, 176, 196, 221, 249, 250, 252, 253, 262

"Beautiful Isle of Somewhere," 251

"Be-Bop Spoken Here," 129, 236

"Beer Barrel Polka (Roll Out the Barrel)," 5, 37–39, 67, 147, 154, 166, 175, 181, 185, 196, 212, 220, 226, 247, 249, 250, 252, 261, 264

"Begin the Beguine," 12, 36, 99, 192, 219, 249, 253, 260, 262

"Bei Mir Bist Du Schon (Means that You're Grand)," 5, 26–33, 38–39, 51, 70, 109–10, 147, 153, 154, 158, 170, 175, 181, 185, 190, 196, 212, 217, 227, 247, 249, 250, 252, 257, 261, 264

"Bella Bella Marie," 118, 172, 178, 234

"Betsy," 229

"Between Two Trees," 241

"Beyond the Reef," 251

"Big Beat, The," 158, 252

"Big Brass Band from Brazil, The," 111, 234, 258

"Billy Boy," 40, 172, 219, 247

"Black Ball Ferry Line," 43, 242

"Blest Be the Tie that Binds," 240

"Blond Sailor, The," 66, 97, 172, 177, 183, 191, 229, 241, 248, 254, 262

"Blossoms on the Bough, The," 125, 238, 263

"Blue Hawaii," 251, 254
"Blues in the Night," 190
"Blue Skies," 190, 253
"Blue Tail Fly, The," 51, 111, 153, 178, 232, 262, 264
"Boog-a-da-Woog," 143, 248
"Boogie Woogie Bugle Boy," 5, 30, 51, 57, 58, 95, 97, 105, 159, 172, 176, 189, 196, 208, 212, 222, 247, 248, 249, 250, 252, 253, 254, 257, 261, 262, 263, 265
"Boogie Woogie Choo Choo," 70, 211
"Booglie Wooglie Piggy, The," 223, 261
"Born to Be with You," 147
"Bounce Me Brother with a Solid Four," 57, 208, 222, 262, 263
"Bouquet of Roses," 251, 255
"Bread and Butter Woman," 232, 258
"Bride and Groom Polka, The," 234
"Brighten the Corner (Where You Are)," 240
"Broken," 143, 249
"Brooklynonga, The," 207
"Buckle Down, Winsocki," 191
"Bury Me beneath the Willow," 134, 242
"Bushel and a Peck, A," 130, 179, 182, 241, 254
"Buttons and Bows," 7, 192
"By His Word," 148, 249, 262

"Californ-I-A," 191
"Can I Come in for a Second?," 239
"Can't Get Used to Losing You," 250
"Can't We Talk It Over?," 130, 179, 187, 238
"Careless Hands," 192, 251
"Carioca," 30, 232, 256
"Ca-Room-Pa-Pa," 238
"C'est Si Bon," 192
"Charley, My Boy," 125, 179, 238, 254
"Charlie's Place," 158, 252
"Chattanooga Choo Choo," 12, 63, 181, 183, 224, 256, 266
"Chattanoogie Shoe Shine Boy," 192
"Chickery Chick," 191, 192
"Chico's Love Song," 175, 220, 256

"Child's Christmas Song," A 249
"Ching-Ara-Sa-Sa," 241
"Chiquita Banana," 8
"Choo'n Gum," 239
"Christmas Candles," 237
"Christmas Island," 5, 101, 177, 178, 186, 231
"Ciribiribin," 41–42, 43, 49, 175, 220, 251, 258, 259
"Civilization," 111, 178, 182, 232, 258, 265
"Clancy Lowered the Boom!," 236
"Cleanse Me," 240
"C'mere, Baby," 213
"Coax Me a Little Bit," 177, 230
"Coca Roca," 193
"Cockeyed Mayor of Kaunakakai, The," 172, 221, 246, 256
"Cocoanut Grove," 251, 255
"Coffee Song, The," 231, 255
"Cold, Cold Heart," 251
"Collegiate," 250
"Come September," 151, 251
"Comes Love," 249, 260
"Come to Baby, Do," 190, 254
"Cool Water," 138, 246, 251, 258
"Corns for My Country," 74, 77, 177, 213, 228, 247, 261, 263
"Count Your Blessings," 239
"Crazy Arms," 148, 249, 262
"Crazy People," 6
"Cruising down the River," 192, 253
"Cry of the Wild Goose, The," 123
"Cuanto la Gusta," 118, 178, 182, 193, 233, 251, 262, 265

"Daddy," 30, 63, 181, 184, 223, 250, 253
"Dance with a Dolly with a Hole in Her Stocking," 190, 214
"Daybreak Blues," 249
"Der Kreuzfidele Kupferschmied," 235
"Dimples and Cherry Cheeks," 243
"Dinah," 18
"Dissertation on the State of Bliss," 143, 247
"Dixie," 251, 254
"Donkey Serenade, The," 44
"Don't Be That Way," 245, 264

"Don't Blame Me," 190, 228, 247, 248
"Don't Bring Lulu," 250
"Don't Fence Me In," 5, 13, 74–77, 87, 120, 177, 182, 183, 186, 190, 191, 196, 213, 227, 250, 252, 257, 258, 259, 261, 265
"Don't Mind the Rain," 211
"Don't Rob Another Man's Castle," 51, 235
"Don't Sit under the Apple Tree (With Anyone Else but Me)," 5, 65–66, 85–86, 96, 176, 181, 210, 225, 249, 250, 252, 256, 261, 263
"Don't Worry 'bout Strangers," 232
"Doodle Song, The," 151, 251
"Down among the Sheltering Palms," 192
"Down by the O-Hi-O," 176, 221
"Down in the Valley," 13, 36, 70, 77, 96, 120, 153, 177, 190, 213, 226, 247, 250, 253
"Dream," 190, 261
"Dreamer's Holiday, A," 8, 69
"Dream of Me," 33
"Dreams Come Tumbling Down," 244
"Drifting and Dreaming," 251
"Dum Dot Song, The," 193

"East of the Rockies," 97, 104, 176, 211, 225, 255
"East of the Sun," 244, 255
"Elmer's Tune," 181, 183, 223, 224, 257
"Empty Saddles," 79, 99, 192
"End of the World, The," 251
"Evalina," 190
"Everybody Loves My Baby," 6
"Everybody Wants to Be Loved," 251
"Ev'rytime," 190, 191

"Fairytale," 10
"Fascinating Rhythm," 252
"Ferdinand the Bull," 218
"Ferryboat Serenade," 54, 176, 181, 221, 249, 264
"Feudin' and Fightin'," 129, 193, 255
"Fling Out the Banner," 251
"For All We Know," 223, 257

"Forsaking All Others," 242, 258
"Forty-Second Street," 7
"For You," 192
"Freedom Train, The," 178, 232, 265
"Friendship Ring, A," 143, 249
"From the Land of the Sky Blue Water," 104, 218, 256
"Fugue for Tinhorns," 247

"Get Your Kicks on Route 66!," 177, 184, 186, 230, 251
"Gimme Some Skin, My Friend," 58, 208, 223
"Give Me Back My Heart," 148, 249
"Glory of Love, The," 240
"Going Up," 211
"Goodbye Darling, Hello Friend," 242
"Good, Good, Good (That's You-That's You)," 191, 229
"Goodnight, Aloha," 245, 262
"Goodnight and Good Dreaming," 250
"Goodnight, Ladies," 211
"Goodnight, Sweetheart, Goodnight," 8
"Good Time Girl, The," 158, 252
"Good Times Are Comin'," 236
"Got a Lot of Livin' to Do," 152, 195
"Gotta Find Somebody to Love," 242
"Go West, Young Man," 129, 192, 231, 248
"Grandpa, Tell Me 'bout the Good Old Days," 10
"Gravy Waltz," 250
"Great Day," 228, 254, 255, 261
"Greensleeves," 9
"Guys and Dolls," 241

"Hand-Clapping Song, The," 213
"Hang on the Bell, Nellie!," 113
"Hang Your Head in Shame," 243
"Happy, Happy, Happy Wedding Day," 229, 261, 265
"Have I Told You Lately that I Love You?," 125, 179, 193, 238, 265
"Hawaii," 117, 151, 251
"Hawaiian Sunset," 251
"Hawaiian Wedding Song, The," 151, 246, 251, 254

"Headless Horseman, The," 113
"Heartbreaker," 115, 178, 235, 254
"Hearts of Stone," 8
"Heatwave," 233
"He Bought My Soul at Calvary," 134, 243
"Heebie Jeebies," 7
"Helena," 223
"Her Bathing Suit Never Got Wet," 97, 230
"Here Comes a Sailor," 191
"Here Comes Santa Claus," 193, 236
"Here Comes the Navy," 66, 176, 189, 211, 226, 255
"Here in My Heart," 138, 245
"He Rides the Range," 129, 237
"He Said-She Said (The Story of the Newlyweds)," 224
"He's My Guy," 172
"His Feet Too Big for De Bed," 192, 231
"His Rocking Horse Ran Away," 2
"Hit the Road," 176, 207, 221, 252
"Hohokus, N.J.," 124–25, 129, 236
"Hold Tight-Hold Tight," 34–35, 51, 175, 181, 212, 219, 247, 249, 250, 261, 264
"Hollywood Canteen," 77, 213, 248, 261
"Home," 190, 213, 248
"Homework," 236
"Honey," 223, 256
"Hoop-Dee-Doo," 8
"Hooray for Love," 250
"Hop Scotch Polka, The," 192
"House of Blue Lights, The," 101, 177, 184, 230, 254, 262
"How Deep Is the Ocean?," 252
"How Lucky You Are," 111, 178, 232, 254
"How Many Times?," 233
"How Many Times (Can I Fall in Love?)," 134, 243
"Hula Ba Luau," 58, 208, 223
"Hummingbird, The," 225
"Hundred and Sixty Acres, A," 43, 69, 111, 178, 234, 259, 265
"Hurry, Hurry, Hurry (Back to Me)," 236
"Hut Sut Song, The," 8

"I Believe," 251
"I Can Dream, Can't I?," 5, 52, 122–24, 130, 139, 178, 182, 187, 193, 237, 250, 259, 263, 264
"I Could Write a Book," 250
"I Cross My Fingers," 8
"I Didn't Know the Gun Was Loaded," 13, 52, 108, 172, 236
"Idle Chatter," 246
"Idle Rich, The," 196
"I'd Like to Hitch a Ride with Santa Claus," 241
"I'd Love to Call You My Sweetheart," 234
"I Don't Know Why (I Just Do)," 177, 230, 254
"I Don't Want to Love You (Like I Do)," 190
"I Feel a Song Coming On," 191
"If I Could Be with You (One Hour Tonight)," 191
"If I Had a Boy Like You," 246
"If I Lost You," 190
"If I Were a Bell," 241
"I Forgot More than You'll Ever Know about Him," 151, 247, 251
"If You Go," 134, 244
"I Got No Talent," 239
"I Had a Hat," 108, 236
"I Hate to Lose You," 178, 235
"I Hear America Singing," 113
"I Hear a Symphony," 9
"Il Bacio," 97, 209
"I Left My Heart in San Francisco," 151, 152, 195, 250
"I'll Be with You in Apple Blossom Time," 5, 36, 55–56, 66, 154, 172, 176, 184, 189, 191, 195, 196, 207, 212, 222, 227, 247, 249, 250, 252, 253, 259, 262, 263
"I'll Forgive You," 248
"I'll Pray for You," 176, 192, 209, 224, 257
"I'll Si-Si Ya in Bahia," 43, 138, 245
"I'll Walk Alone," 138, 245
"I Love to Tell the Story," 239
"I Love You Because," 251
"I Love You Much Too Much," 35, 47, 220, 222, 252, 257
"I Married an Angel," 218

Song Index

"I May Be Wrong," 211

"I'm Beginning to See the Light," 190, 191

"I'm Bitin' My Fingernails and Thinking of You," 13, 120, 178, 235, 262

"I'm Goin' down the Road," 232, 262

"I'm Going Home," 249

"I'm Gonna Paper All My Walls with Your Love Letters," 239

"Imi Au Ia Oe," 246

"I'm in a Jam," 51, 75, 228

"I'm in Love Again," 134, 243

"I'm on a Seesaw of Love," 244

"I'm So Excited," 10

"I'm So Right Tonight," 231

"I'm Sorry," 245, 262

"I'm Thinking Tonight of My Blue Eyes," 251

"I Never Will Marry," 143, 249

"In the Garden," 51, 134, 239, 251

"In the Good Old Summertime," 125, 236

"In the Mood," 12, 159, 246, 251, 254, 255, 266

"Invitation to a Dance," 148, 249

"I Ought to Know More About You," 239

"I Remember Mama," 242, 258, 262

"Irish Twist, The," 150, 250

"Irish Washerwoman, The," 54, 222

"I See, I See (Asi Asi)," 238

"Is It Really Over?," 151, 251

"Is It True What They Say about Dixie?," 260

"I Suppose," 252

"Is You Is or Is You Ain't (Ma' Baby?)," 74, 77, 177, 181, 183, 190, 212, 214, 227, 247, 264

"It Is No Secret (What God Can Do)," 134, 182, 243, 251

"It Might As Well Be Spring," 192

"It Never Entered My Mind," 133, 243, 258

"It's a Grand Night for Singing," 99, 192

"It's All Over but the Memories," 244

"It's a Quiet Town," 111, 234

"It's Bigger than the Both of Us," 143, 247

"It's Easier Said than Done," 218

"I Used to Love You (But It's All Over Now)," 242

"I've Got a Guy in Kalamazoo," 12, 181, 225, 255

"I've Got My Love to Keep Me Warm," 193

"I've Got No Strings," 44, 260, 265

"I've Got to Pass Your House," 250

"I've Just Got to Get out of the Habit," 240

"I Wanna Be Loved," 5, 51, 130, 139, 179, 182, 187, 240, 250, 255

"I Want My Mama (Mama Eu Quero)," 221, 256

"I Want to Be with You Always," 134, 243

"I Want to Go Back to Michigan," 233

"I Want to Hold Your Hand," 108

"I Want to Linger," 249

"I Wish I Had a Dime (For Ev'rytime I Missed You)," 176, 223

"I Wish I Knew (You Really Loved Me)," 240

"I Yi, Yi, Yi, Yi (I Like You Very Much)," 176, 222

"Jack, Jack, Jack (Cu-Tu-Gu-Ru)," 184, 231

"Jack of All Trades," 223

"Jammin'," 51, 217

"Japanese Sandman, The," 250, 260, 262

"Jealous," 176, 183, 223

"Jealous Heart," 251

"Jesus Calls Us," 251

"Jing-a-ling Jing-a-ling," 241, 266

"Jingle Bells," 5, 51, 69, 176, 178, 185–86, 193, 226, 259, 265

"Jitterbug's Lullaby, A (Parts 1 and 2)," 219

"Johnny Fedora and Alice Blue Bonnet," 102, 173, 214, 229

"Johnny, Get Your Gun Again," 210

"Johnny Peddler (I Got)," 221

"Jolly Fella Tarantella (The Organ Grinder's Song)," 237, 261

"Joseph! Joseph!," 31, 175, 217, 250

"Jump," 10

Song Index

"Jumpin' Jive, The," 220, 257

"June Is Busting Out All Over," 254

"Just a Simple Melody," 25, 217, 256, 262

"Just a Closer Walk with Thee," 251

"Just a Prayer Away," 190

"Katusha," 190

"Keep Your Skirts Down, Mary Ann," 250

"Ke Kali Nei Au (Waiting for Thee)," 246

"King's Serenade, The," 246

"Kiss Goodnight, A," 99, 192

"Kneeling Drunkard's Plea, The," 10

"Lady Clown," 143

"Lady from 29 Palms, The," 178, 182, 184, 232, 264

"Last Night on the Back Porch," 250

"Last Roundup, The," 190

"Let a Smile Be Your Umbrella," 120, 233, 253, 261

"Let's Have Another One," 44, 220, 256

"Let's Pack Our Things and Trek," 221

"Let the Lower Lights Be Burning," 240

"Let There Be Love," 250

"Life Is So Peculiar," 239

"Lilly Belle," 172, 229

"Linger Awhile," 245, 256

"Little Bird Told Me, A," 192

"Little Toot," 116, 173, 215

"Live Oak Tree, The," 245

"Lock, Stock and Barrel," 193, 239, 259

"Lonesome Mama," 51, 222

"Lonesome Road, The," 33, 189

"Long, Long Ago," 211, 225

"Long Time No See," 219

"Look for the Silver Lining," 192

"Love Child," 9

"Love Is Such a Cheat," 244

"Love Is Where You Find It," 218

"Lovely Night," 51, 124, 233

"Love Sends a Little Gift of Roses," 242

"Lullaby of Broadway," 77, 159, 190, 193, 228, 247

"Lullaby to a Jitterbug," 175, 219, 252

"Lying in the Hay," 244

"Mairzy Doats," 8

"Make Believe You're Glad When You're Sorry," 192

"Malagueña," 124, 172, 236, 253

"Malihini Mele," 246

"Mama Llama," 252

"Mambo Man, The," 242, 266

"Mammy," 129

"Managua, Nicaragua," 111, 192

"Manana," 192

"Man and a Woman, A," 151, 251

"Man Is a Brother to a Mule, A," 230

"Massachusetts," 66, 226, 257

"Matador, The," 233

"May the Good Lord Bless and Keep You," 193, 254

"Me and My Shadow," 209

"Mean to Me," 35, 54, 222, 256

"Melancholy Moon," 249

"Mele Kalikimaka (Merry Christmas!)," 168, 241

"Memories Are Made of This," 154, 196

"Merrily, We Roll Along," 211

"Merry Christmas at Grandmother's House, A (Over the River and through the Woods)," 237

"Merry Christmas Polka," 179, 237

"Me Too," 250

"Mexicali Rose," 251

"Mister Five-By-Five," 66, 176, 181, 211, 225

"Money Is the Root of All Evil," 97, 177, 192, 229, 248

"Money Song, The," 118, 234

"More Beer!," 120, 178, 235

"Mr. Bass Man," 151, 250

"Mr. Sandman," 172

"Music by the Angels," 113

"Music Drives Me Crazy," 143, 249

"Music Goes 'Round and 'Round, The," 28

"Music Lessons," 245

"Music Makers," 184, 222, 256

"Music, Music, Music," 192

"Muskrat Ramble," 239, 256

"My Baby Said Yes," 190
"My Blue Heaven," 191
"My Dearest Uncle Sam," 231
"My Favorite Things," 152, 195
"My Happiness," 115, 251
"My Isle of Golden Dreams," 245, 248, 251
"My Little Grass Shack," 251, 255
"My Love Is a Kitten," 249
"My Love, the Blues and Me," 247
"My Love Went without Water (Three Days)," 221
"My Mom," 242
"My Romance," 80, 250
"My Sin," 234

"Nalani," 245
"Nature's Toys," 252
"Nearer My God to Thee," 251
"Near You," 5, 111, 153, 178, 182, 192, 232, 250, 254, 257, 265
"Need You," 192
"Nevertheless," 249, 261
"Never Too Busy to Say Hello," 259
"New Generation, The," 210
"Nice Work If You Can Get It," 25, 275, 185, 217
"Nickel Serenade, The," 176, 223
"Night and Day," 99, 191
"Ninety and Nine, The," 240
"No, Baby," 193, 249
"Nobody Knows the Trouble I've Seen," 210
"Nobody's Darlin' but Mine," 13, 93, 241, 251
"No Deposit, No Return," 246
"No Goodbyes," 158, 159, 252
"Now! Now! Now! Is the Time," 103, 236
"Now That I'm in Love," 247

"Oceana Roll, The," 58
"Oceans of Tears," 120
"Of Thee I Sing," 195, 249
"Oh! Faithless Maid," 218
"Oh, He Loves Me," 207, 221
"Ohh! My Feet!," 266
"Oh, Johnny! Oh, Johnny! Oh!," 30, 34, 181, 220, 250
"Oh, Ma-Ma!," 34, 218, 250

"Oh, You Sweet One," 237, 265
"Old Don Juan," 134, 242, 255
"Old Piano Roll Blues, The," 130, 182, 240, 250, 260, 265
"Old Rugged Cross, The," 251
"One for the Wonder," 246, 254
"One Meat Ball," 75, 177, 186, 190, 191, 228, 254
"One Mistake," 148, 249
"One More River," 153, 195
"One, Two, Three, Four," 250
"One, Two, Three O'Leary," 219, 255
"Only for Americans," 236
"On the Atchison, Topeka and the Santa Fe," 191, 253
"On the Avenue," 178, 184, 232
"On the Sunny Side of the Street," 16, 191
"ooOO-Oh Boom!," 218
"Open Door, Open Arms," 238
"Orange Colored Sky," 111, 241
"Our Love Is Here to Stay," 244
"Over Here!," 158, 187, 252

"Pack up Your Troubles in Your Old Kit Bag and Smile! Smile! Smile!," 209, 228, 255
"Pagan Love Song," 104, 218, 256
"Parade of the Wooden Soldiers," 241
"Pass the Basket," 242
"Patience and Fortitude," 97, 177, 230, 261
"Pennies from Heaven," 191
"Pennsylvania Polka," 39, 66, 95, 176, 189, 195, 210, 212, 225, 250, 252, 264
"Pennsylvania 6–5000," 12, 221, 255
"Penny a Kiss-Penny a Hug, A," 130, 179, 182, 241
"Peony Bush," 133, 195
"Personality," 191, 253
"Piccolo Pete," 244
"Pistol Packin' Mama," 5, 43, 67–68, 69, 70, 83, 120, 150, 172, 176, 181, 190, 226, 250, 255, 256, 258, 259
"Play Me a Hurtin' Tune," 244
"Polka Polka, The," 214
"Poor Whip-poor-will," 244

"Poppa Santa Claus," 240

"Private Buckaroo," 210

"Pross Tchai (Goodbye, Goodbye)," 175, 219

"P.S. I Love You," 108

"Puff! The Magic Dragon," 151, 251

"Pussy Cat Song, The," 121, 193, 235

"Put 'Em in a Box, Tie 'Em with a Ribbon (And Throw 'Em in the Deep Blue Sea)," 115, 235

"Put that Ring on My Finger," 97, 182, 229, 248, 255, 257, 264

"Quicksilver," 125, 179, 238, 258

"Ragtime Cowboy Joe," 251

"Rains Came Down, The," 143, 248

"Rainy Day Refrain, A," 240

"Rainy Night in Rio, A," 231

"Rancho Pillow," 223, 249

"Red River Valley," 227, 248

"Red Silk Stockings and Green Perfume," 231

"Remember," 252

"Rhumboogie," 53, 54, 176, 190, 207, 221, 227, 250

"Richest Man in the Cemetery, The," 234

"Ride On," 211

"Riders in the Sky," 129, 259

"Rockin' with the Rhythm of the Rain," 10

"Rock of Ages," 251

"Rock, Rock, Rock-a-Bye Baby," 219, 256

"Rose's Theme," 251

"Rum and Coca Cola," 5, 51, 69, 75–76, 87, 91, 118, 154, 177, 182, 183, 186, 190, 193, 195, 196, 228, 249, 250, 255, 261, 263, 264, 265

"Rumors are Flying," 99, 177, 182, 184, 230, 257, 262

"Run, Run, Run," 233

"Sabre Dance," 115–16, 178, 182, 193, 235, 251, 255

"Sailor," 250

"San Fernando Valley," 8

"Santa Claus Is Coming to Town," 69, 178, 185, 226

"Satin Doll," 151, 251

"Satins and Lace," 134, 242

"Saturday Night Is the Loneliest Night of the Week," 66, 190, 191, 255

"Say Si Si," 44, 49, 104, 176, 220, 251, 257

"Says My Heart," 51, 175, 181, 218

"Scarlet Ribbons," 9

"Scrub Me Mama with a Boogie Beat," 2, 54, 56, 151, 176, 222, 254, 261

"Send Me a Man, Amen!," 78, 189, 213

"Sentimental Journey," 190

"Seventeen," 8

"Shall We Gather at the River?," 240

"Sha-Sha," 175, 218

"She'll Never Know," 243

"She Wore a Yellow Ribbon," 125, 179, 238, 254, 266

"Shoo Shoo Baby," 70, 77, 83, 177, 181, 183, 212, 226, 249, 260, 261, 262, 264

"Shortenin' Bread," 175, 214, 218

"Shout, Sister, Shout," 7

"Show Me the Way to Go Home," 250, 252

"Shrine of Saint Cecilia, The," 63, 176, 181, 183, 224, 250, 264

"Shuffle Off to Buffalo," 7

"Silver Bells," 249

"Sincerely," 8, 148

"Sing," 189, 213

"Sing a Tropical Song," 74, 75, 177, 214, 227, 247, 254, 265

"Sing! Sing! Sing!," 245, 248, 255, 264

"Sioux City Sue," 251

"Six Jerks in a Jeep," 70, 95–96, 210, 225, 252

"Six Times a Week and Twice on Sunday," 237, 252

"Sleepy Serenade," 59, 176, 209, 223, 263

"Sleigh Ride," 240

"Smile Will Go a Long, Long Way, A," 250, 260

Song Index

"Softly and Tenderly (Jesus Is Calling)," 134, 239
"Someone Like You," 192
"Some Sunny Day," 233
"Song Is You, The," 249
"Song of the Islands," 251
"Sonny Boy," 63, 105, 129, 152, 176, 190, 191, 192, 193, 195, 223, 251, 255, 262, 264
"South American Way," 41, 104, 220, 253, 257
"South America, Take It Away," 5, 99, 177, 182, 184, 186, 192, 195, 230, 258
"South Rampart Street Parade," 51, 138, 246, 258
"Sparrow in the Treetop," 179, 182, 242
"Spring in December," 192
"Standin' in the Need of Prayer," 191
"Stardust," 98
"Starlight, Starbright," 208
"Stars Are the Windows of Heaven," 237
"Stars, Stars, Stars," 148, 195, 249
"Still," 151, 250
"Stop! In the Name of Love," 9, 154, 196
"Straighten Up and Fly Right," 177, 183, 190, 214, 227, 247, 258
"Strip Polka," 67, 152, 176, 212, 225, 247, 253, 254, 264
"Suddenly, There's a Valley," 144, 248
"Sugartime," 8, 172
"Sukiyaki (My First Lonely Night)," 151, 251
"Sunshine," 249
"Sweet and Slow," 252
"Sweet Angie, the Christmas Tree Angel," 241
"Sweet Lelani," 251
"Sweet Marie," 232
"Sweet Molly Malone," 54, 172, 190, 221, 222, 254, 258
"Symphony," 99, 192

"Take It and Git," 211
"Take Me Out to the Ballgame," 125, 236
"Talk of the Town, The," 191

"Tallahassee," 111, 177, 182, 184, 231
"Tea for Two," 250, 260
"Tegucigalpa," 247, 262
"Telephone Song, The," 240
"Tennessee Waltz," 75, 113, 151, 193, 251, 254
"Teresa," 178, 234, 265
"Thanks for the Buggy Ride," 211
"Thanks for the Memory," 192
"That Everlovin' Rag," 246
"That Feeling in the Moonlight," 191
"That Lucky Old Sun," 193, 259, 261
"That Naughty Waltz," 250
"That Old Feeling," 190
"That's a Plenty," 192, 193
"That's How a Love Song Is Born," 134, 244
"That's How Young I Feel," 154, 196
"That's My Affair," 172, 210
"That's the Chance You Take," 245
"That's the Moon, My Son," 176, 210, 225
"Them that Has-Gets," 230
"There Are Such Things," 67, 226
"There! I've Said It Again," 69
"There'll Be a Hot Time in the Town of Berlin (When the Yanks Go Marching In)," 2, 74, 77, 177, 183, 227
"There'll Be a Jubilee," 190, 227
"There's a Fella Waitin' in Poughkeepsie," 155, 229, 265
"There's a Lull in My Life," 217
"There's a Rainbow in the Valley," 247
"There's No Business Like Show Business," 113, 178, 231, 258
"There's Something about a Home-town Band," 193
"There Was a Night on the Waters," 243
"There Will Never Be Another You," 130, 187, 238, 257
"This Little Piggie Went to Market," 242
"Those Lazy, Hazy, Crazy Days of Summer," 251
"Thousand Island Search, The," 192

Song Index

"Three Bells, The (The Jimmy Brown Song)," 134–35, 187, 244, 262
"Three Caballeros, The," 74, 172, 177, 186, 228, 248, 258, 265
"Three Little Fishies," 150, 251, 253, 254, 255
"Three Little Sisters," 65, 96, 172, 176, 181, 210, 224, 257
"Three O'Clock in the Morning," 103, 108, 119, 230
"Tica-Ti Tica-Ta," 224
"Tico Tico," 74, 177, 226, 266
"Time Has Come to Bid You Adieu," 237
"Ti-Pi-Tin," 34, 150, 175, 181, 192, 217, 249, 250, 264
"Together," 190
"Tonight, You Belong to Me," 9
"Too Fat Polka (She's Too Fat for Me)," 182, 232, 258, 262
"Toolie Oolie Doolie," 111, 178, 182, 234
"Too Old to Rock and Roll," 143, 249
"Too Young," 132, 242
"Torero," 148, 249
"Toy Balloon (Boolee Boole Boon)," 224
"To You, Sweetheart, Aloha," 251
"Trolley Song, The," 2, 190, 255
"Tu-Li-Tulip Time," 175, 181, 218, 249, 257
"Turntable Song, The," 231
"Tuxedo Junction," 12, 221, 257
"Twelve Days of Christmas, The," 236
"Twenty-Four Hours of Sunshine," 193, 259
"Twilight on the Trail," 248

"Underneath the Arches," 118, 178, 182, 235
"Underneath the Linden Tree," 235
"Unless You're Free," 243

"Valentina," 192
"Vict'ry Polka, The," 3, 67, 176, 183, 185, 212, 226, 247, 248, 259
"Vieni, Vieni," 190

"Wabash Blues," 245

"Wabash Cannonball," 151, 251
"Wa-hoo!," 213
"Waitin' for the Train to Come In," 191
"Wake Up and Live," 217, 262
"Walk with a Wiggle," 239
"Wall to Wall Love," 10
"Walter Winchell Rhumba," 191
"Wartime Wedding," 158, 252
"Watermelon Man," 151, 251
"Way Down Yonder in New Orleans," 130, 193, 240, 260
"Weddin' Day," 236
"Wedding of Lili Marlene, The," 123, 172, 179, 187, 237
"Wedding Samba, The," 125, 179, 193, 238
"We Got It!," 158, 252
"Welcome Song, The," 229
"Well, All Right!," 37, 175, 185, 212, 220, 247, 249
"We're in the Navy," 208
"We've Got a Job to Do," 210
"What Did I Do?," 234
"What Happened to You?," 247
"What Now My Love?," 154, 196
"What to Do," 209, 224
"When a Prince of a Fella Meets a Cinderella," 35, 219
"When Francis Dances with Me," 250
"When Johnny Comes Marching Home," 66, 225
"When That Midnight Choo Choo Leaves for Alabam'," 233
"When You and I Were Young, Maggie," 211
"Where Did Our Love Go?," 154, 196
"Where Did the Good Times Go?," 158, 164, 252
"Where Have We Met Before?," 51, 218, 263
"Where Is Your Wandering Mother Tonight?," 13, 134, 243
"Where to, My Love?," 248
"While Strolling through the Park One Day," 211
"Whispering Hope," 51, 124, 151, 233, 251

Song Index

"White Silver Sands," 9

"Who Do You Think You're Fooling?," 210

"Why Am I Always the Bridesmaid?," 232

"Why Don't We Do This More Often," 223

"Why Do They Give the Solos to Patty When There's So Much of Us Going to Waste?," 133

"Why Talk about Love?," 25, 217, 256, 262

"Why Won't Ya?," 237

"Why Worry?," 245

"Wild Is Love," 251

"Windmill Song, The (The Wheel Kept Turning Around)," 244

"Windmill Song, The (The Windmill's Turning)," 237

"Winter Wonderland," 5, 101, 177, 184, 186–87, 231

"With Every Breath I Take," 249

"Without Love," 143, 248

"Wondering," 244

"Woodpecker Song, The," 104, 176, 181, 220, 264

"Woody Woodpecker Song, The," 115, 178, 182, 235, 258

"Wunderbar," 192, 237, 259

"Yes, My Darling Daughter," 222, 264

"Yip-Si-I-O," 238

"Yodeling Ghost, The," 242

"Yodelin' Jive," 41, 175, 220, 258, 259

"Yoo-Hoo," 211

"You Are My Sunshine," 150, 251

"You Better Give Me Lots of Lovin'," 211

"You Blew Me a Kiss," 138, 246

"You Call Everybody Darling," 118, 178, 182, 193, 235

"You Don't Have to Know the Language," 110, 111, 178, 192, 214, 233

"You Don't Know How Much You Can Suffer," 175, 219

"You Do Something to Me," 249

"Younger than Springtime," 250

"Your Cheatin' Heart," 251

"You're a Lucky Fellow, Mr. Smith," 55, 197, 222

"You're Just a Flower from an Old Bouquet," 210, 225, 252

"You're My Everything," 252

"You're Off to See the World," 208

"Your Red Wagon," 178, 232

"You Too, You Too," 247

"You Was," 235

"Zing Zing, Zoom Zoom," 182, 241

"Zoot Suit, A," 224